SHIVAJI AND HIS TIMES

SHIVAJI AND HIS TIMES

JADUNATH SARKAR. M.A., C.I.E.

THIRD EDITION

GYAN

Published by

GYAN

Gyan Publishing House
5, Ansari Road
Daryaganj, New Delhi-110002
Phone: 011-47034999, 9811692060
E-mail: books@gyanbooks.com

Distribution Network
gyanbooks.com
India, USA, Canada, UK, Australia, France

ISBN : 978-81-212-6757-1 (PB)
First Published, 1920

2nd Impression 2022

Printed at: Gyan Press, Delhi.

SHIVAJI AND HIS TIMES
Author: JADUNATH SARKAR

SHIVAJI AND HIS TIMES

JADUNATH SARKAR, M.A., C.I.E.,

Honorary Member, Royal Asiatic Society of Great Britain.

THIRD EDITION

THOROUGHLY REWRITTEN AND ENLARGED,

WITH FOUR PORTRAITS.

1929

WORKS BY PROF. JADUNATH SARKAR

History of Auiangzib, *based on original sources*

Vols ' & II Region of Shah Jahan, 2nd ed , Rs 5.

,, III. Northern India, 1658-1681, 3rd ed , Rs 3-8

,, IV. Southern India, 1645-1689, 2nd ed., Rs 3-8

,, V. Last Phase, 1689-1707, Rs 4

Studies in Mughal India, (*22 historical essays*), Rs 2.

Economics of British India, 5th edition, (*in prep*)

Anecdotes of Aurangzib, 2nd ed , Re 1-8

Ahkam-i-Alamgiri, (Persian text of the Anecdotes), 2nd ed , Re 1

Mughal Administiation, 2nd ed , Rs 3

Chaitanya's Life and Teachings, 2nd ed , Rs. 2.

India Thiough the Ages, a survey of the evolution of Indian life and thought, (6 lectures), Re. 1-8.

PREFACE TO THE THIRD EDITION

IN this edition more than half the narrative has been entirely re-written and expanded, and elsewhere, too, so many old statements and views have been modified as the result of a fresh study of the subject that in its present form the book has practically become a new one A larger format and type have been used Briefly speaking, the main points in which it differs from the two earlier editions are the following —

(*a*) The total rejection of 19th century fabrications, like the Chitnis *bakhar, Shiva-digvijaya,* the Vriha-dishwar inscription, etc

(*b*) A cautious and selective use of the middle 18th century sources, such as the *91-qalmi bakhar* in its different recensions

(*c*) The full use of contemporary French and Portuguese sources for the first time, and of the Marathi chronologies (*Shakavalis*)

(*d*) The addition of all the four portraits of Shivaji definitely known to be contemporary, and of a full chronology in which the dates make a closer approximation to exact precision An index has been now supplied for the first time

Besides adding the above features, I have made a fresh and detailed study of the old materials in the light of the newly acquired sources In the course of the eight years that have passed since the second edition was published, much new material has been collected, and a study of them as well as further reflection has naturally resulted in several minute corrections and changes in the details of the narrative and my opinion about certain persons and events

So far as the extant materials go, the present edition is definitive , but several dark corners still remain for future discovery of authentic records t illuminate This is especially the case with the boyhood and youth of Shivaji

When Captain J Grant Duff was writing his *History of the Mahrattas* (published in 3 vols in 1826), the veteran scholar-statesman Mountstuart Elphinstone, in a letter to him (20th April, 1822) exactly described the character of the materials then available for a life of Shivaji "Your difficulty was to get at facts and combine them with judgment, so as to make a consistent and rational history out of a mass of gossiping *bakhars* and gasconading *tawarikhs*" These two sources of admittedly dubious value were supplemented by the English factory records, which Grant Duff rightly declared to be "very important for fixing dates, and invaluable in corroborating facts admitted by native authorities"

Three classes of sources unknown to Grant Duff have now filled up many gaps in our knowledge and proved his narrative of Shivaji's career obsolete and erroneous in many places (*a*) The contemporary French and Portuguese MS sources are now available for the first time, thanks to the opening of the Paris archives (*sc* the *Memoires* of Francois Martin) and the scholarly and devoted work of Senhor P Pissurlencar among the Goa records The original history of Manucci has been made accessible in W Irvine's masterly translation The travellers' tales in the printed French and Dutch works to which Orme referred with justifiable disappointment, can be totally rejected now (*b*) The skeleton chronicles (*Shakavalis*) in Marathi supply many reliable dates and facts, after they have been tested with care and a knowledge of other sources The *91-qalmi bakhar* is a much earlier and less legendary work than the Chitnis *bakhar* (1810) on which Grant Duff so frequently depended, with the result of falsifying his narrative of Shivaji in many places (c) The same misfortune attended Grant Duff in connection with his Persian authorities He used the very late (1735) and traditional history of Khafi Khan, which must be now rejected equally with the Chitnis *bakhar* And he had no knowledge of the detailed and absolutely contemporary official histories of Aurangzib (*viz* *Alamgir-namah* and *Masir-i-Alamgiri*), the Court newsletters (*akhbarat*), the personal memoirs of Bhimsen, and the letters of Jai Singh,

—all of which are in Persian and have been fully utilized by me in this work

A synthesis of this vast and varied mass of new materials, made available during the century following the publication of Grant Duff's book, has naturally resulted in the supersession of Grant Duff's chapters on Shivaji on the one hand and of the Marathi *bakhars* (with the exception of the contemporary recollections of Sabhasad) on the other, both of which had so long held the field The same has been found to be the case in respect of the history of Shambhuji and Rajaram, which I have reconstructed in my *Aurangzib*, volumes 4 and 5

The critical bibliography at the end of this book discusses the character of the materials that have been rejected as well as that of the authorities followed by me

From the purely literary point of view, the book would have gained much by being made shorter But so many false legends about Shivaji are current in our country and the Shivaji myth is developing so fast (attended at times with the fabrication of documents), that I have considered it necessary in the interests of historical truth to give every fact, however small, about him that has been ascertained on unimpeachable evidence and to discuss the probabilities of the others.

The Marathas were only one among the many threads in the tangled web of Deccan history in the Seventeenth century. Therefore, to understand the true causes and full consequences of Shivaji's own acts and policy, it is necessary to have a detailed knowledge of the internal affairs of the Mughal empire, Bijapur and Golkonda also The present work is more than a mere biography of Shiva, it frequently deals with the contemporary history of these three Muslim States, though an exhaustive treatment of the subject finds its proper place in my *History of Aurangzib*, Vol. IV.

December, 1928 JADUNATH SARKAR

First edition, April 1919
Second edition, June 1920

CONTENTS.

SHIVAJI

B. (Orme, printed in England in 1782, really the British Museum portrait retouched by an English artist.)

SHIVAJI
C. (Paris, drawn by Mir Muhammad, before 1686.)

SHIVAJI
D. (Valentyn, before 1712.)

SHIVAJI AND HIS TIMES

CHAPTER I.

THE LAND AND THE PEOPLE

§1. *Extent, rainfall, soil and crops.*

To-day nearly eleven millions of men, forming about half the entire population of the Bombay Presidency (*minus* its unnatural adjunct, Sindh), speak Marathi, and another nine millions living in the Central Provinces, the Nizam's Dominions, and other parts, claim the same language as their mother-tongue.* This language has been steadily gaining ground since the days of the Peshwas, and its peaceful annexation of the children of ruder and less literary tongues has gone on unabated even during the British period.

But the Maratha country is not co-extensive with the land where the Marathi speech prevails to-day. Four centuries ago the name *Maha-rashtra* was confined to the western edge of the Deccan plateau, *i.e.*, to a tract bounded on the north by the Tapti, on the south by the upper courses of the Krishna (probably the Warna), and on the east by the Sina.† The cradle-land of Maharashtra was, therefore, formed by the Nasik, Puna and Satara

---

*The Census of 1911 showed a total of 19.8 millions as speaking Marathi (against 18.23 millions in 1901.) Of this total 10.74 millions live in Bombay and its States, 4.8 millions in the C. P., and 3.5 millions in the Haidarabad State. Marathi is spoken by above 86 p. c. of the population of the Konkan division, 85 p. c. of the Deccan division, and nearly 54 p. c. of Bombay city. In the C. P. 31 p. c. and in the Haidarabad State 26 p. c. of the population speak it.

† "The word Dekkan expresses the country watered by the upper Godavari and that lying between that river and the Krishna. The name

districts, parts of Ahmadnagar and Sholapur, and probably the western corner of Aurangabad,—a rough total of 28,000 square miles. The Maratha race was also settled in Konkan or the narrow land between the Western Ghats and the Indian Ocean. Here the districts of Thana, Kolaba and Ratnagiri and the State of Savant-vadi,—with a total area of over 10,000 square miles,—are now predominantly Marathi-speaking ; but in the 16th century a considerable portion of the population, probably one-half, belonged to other races and spoke other tongues

Four centuries ago the population of Maharashtra was very thin and forests covered much of the land The western edge of the Deccan plateau is subject to a low and uncertain rainfall, cultivation is poor and precarious, and it is only along the narrow margins of the few rivers that the peasant is assured of a good return for his labour. From nearly the whole of the Western Deccan the heavy clouds of the S. W. monsoon are either shut out by the Ghat range, or, if they surmount this barrier, they sail away to the east leaving the land unwatered and untilled, so that "the Deccan, generally speaking, yields to much labour a bare measure of subsistence."† (*Moral and Mat Prog.* 1911-12, p. 10.)

In such a soil rice cultivation is impossible, and wheat and barley grow in very small quantities. The

---

Maharashtra also seems at one time to have been restricted to this tract For that country is, in the Puranas and other works, distinguished on the one hand from Northern Konkan and from the regions on either side of the Narmada and the Tapti, as well as from Vidarbha" or Berar (*Bom Gaz* i pt ii pp 134, 587, xxiv 81)

† The rain is precipitated on the coast-line [i e , Konkan] at an average of 100 to 120 inches [in the year] Once the crest [of the Western Ghats] is passed, the precipitation decreases very rapidly, until a belt is reached only 35 miles from the hills where the rainfall is very

staple crop of most of this region is the hardy millet,—*jawari, bajra* and *ragi* or maize But even these cannot always be depended upon. One year the rain would fail, the sprouting plants would be scorched by the sun or the young heads of grain would shrink and wither before they can grow to fulness and ripen, and there would be famine throughout the length and breadth of the land. The soil, covered with bare rock at places and with only a thin layer of mould at others, would be baked to a brown dust, not a green blade would be seen anywhere, and in addition to the human victims the cattle would perish by tens of thousand.

§ 2 *Isolation of the People.*

The broken rocky nature of the country and its abundance of forests, while it kept the population down, also made travelling difficult and unprofitable. There were no rich courts, populous cities or thriving marts to attract merchants. Nor were there regular occasions for the march of large bodies of soldiers, as from one

---

precarious and averages only about 17 inches Further east again, the S W monsoon is nearly spent, but the influence of the N E monsoon begins to be felt and the rainfall improves South of Khandesh, we get the Deccan proper divided into three tracts [running parallel to the Ghats and called] the *Dang* or *Maval* to the west, the *Transition* in the centre, and the *Desh*, or black-soil plain to the east The soil, however, is not fertile, and there are ranges of bare rocky hills running east and west, spurs so to speak of the Ghats, which neither store water for cultivation nor attract the rainfall The Karnatak [i e, the Dharwar, Belgaum, and Bijapur districts] has a more certain and more copious rainfall and more fertile soil" (*Census of India*, 1911, vii pt I, pp 4-6) The western hilly belt is called *Dang* in the north (i e, Baglana), *Maval* in the centre (i e, the Nasik, Puna and Satara districts), and *Mallad* in the south (i e, Karnatak) The Konkan, on the other hand, is an area of certain and heavy rainfall, with rice for the predominant crop, "and along the sea-coast, wherever there is any soil a fringe of palms, mango-groves and plantain orchards add to the beauty of the landscape and the wealth of the inhabitants Thana and Kanara are forest-clad districts" (*Ibid*)

province of a compact and mighty empire to another. The country was cut up by Nature into small compartments in which the natives lived isolated self-contained lives, the world forgetting and by the world forgot

This was true in a special degree of the belt lying immediately east of the Ghats. The empires of the central and more level portion of the table-land, both in Hindu times and Muslim, had sent forth their conquering hosts westwards, but the flood of invasion had been broken at the foot of the hills or their numerous spurs, or, where a thin stream of it had poured through the passes, it had retired after a short and unprofitable stay. In their rugged and inhospitable nooks the natives had found safety and peace, while the richer plains had been the scenes of revolution and rapine.

This natural isolation of the western belt was no doubt occasionally broken by the pilgrim, the trader, and the soldier of fortune. Across this rugged tract lay all the routes from the ocean-ports of our western coast to the rich capitals and marts of Central Deccan. Through it alone could the stream of recruits from Persia, Arabia, Turkey, Abyssinia and even Central Asia reach the welcoming Muslim Courts of Kulbarga, Bidar, Ahmadnagar, Bijapur and Golkonda. Through Maharashtra alone could the cloth, metal-ware and spices of the upper Godavari and Krishna valleys reach their ports of embarkation for Europe.

Then, again, the sterile soil discouraged its sons from the thankless task of tilling it. Strong muscles and stout hearts found greater rewards and a higher position by serving in the armies of the mighty monarchies of the central plateau. An able partisan leader was sure of high pay, noble rank, and it might be the proud position of a king-maker, at any of these Courts, which were constantly at war with their neighbours, and prepared to bid high for the lances of useful *condottieri* from the Desh tract.

But such occasional visitors only brought a breath of the outer world to the sequestered vales of Maharashtra; they did not disturb the noiseless tenor of the life of the natives, for the natives themselves had hardly occasion to move. Even when they went abroad as soldiers, they usually settled there in the fiefs given to them and rarely returned to their barren ancestral homes.

The Maratha people's inborn love of independence and isolation was greatly helped by Nature, which provided them with many ready-made and easily defensible forts close at hand, where they could quickly flee for refuge and whence they could offer a tenacious resistance. Unlike the Gangetic plain, this country could not be conquered and annexed by one cavalry dash or even one year's campaigning. Here the natives had the chance of making a long struggle against superior numbers and, as often happened, of recovering their own when the invader was worn out. "The whole of the Ghats and neighbouring mountains often terminate towards the top in a wall of smooth rock, the highest points of which, as well as detached portions on insulated hills, form natural fortresses, where the only labour required is to get access to the level space, which generally lies on the summit. Various princes at different times have cut flights of steps or winding roads up the rocks, fortified the entrance with a succession of gateways, and erected towers to command the approaches; and thus studded the whole of the region about the Ghats and their branches with forts" "In many of them there are springs of the finest water, and in all a supply can be secured, in tanks or reservoirs, during the periodical rains from May to October." The soft trap dissolving has exposed the hard basalt in steep scarped precipices and smooth tops, which form natural forts.*

§ 3. *Poverty, simplicity and equality of society.*

In such a country no man can afford to lead a sheltered life. There was no parasite class in ancient Maharashtra. Even the village headmen, besides attending to their demesne fields, had to work as collectors of revenue, local judges and parochial policemen, to earn the fee on which they lived. There was hardly a rich man, except the trader who was also the only banker of this primitive society. Even the landlords were rich rather in grain-heaps and armed retainers than in gold and silver. Some temples, especially at the chief centres of pilgrimage, had accumulations of wealth, but their income was precarious, entirely dependent on voluntary gift, and incomparably smaller than the riches of the grand temples of Madras.

In a society so circumstanced, every man, and often every woman, has to work and work with the hand. Elegance and refinement cannot grow here. If culture can be rightly defined as the employment of the intellect in pleasure, then there is no room for culture among men who have to sacrifice pleasure to the bare necessaries of life. Where Nature enforces a Spartan simplicity, there can be no luxury, no learned leisure (except among

---

* Elphinstone's *History*, 6th ed 615 Duff i 7 *Bom Gaz*, xviii. pt 1, pp 9-10, xix. 16.

the priests), no æsthetic development, no polished manners even.

The Marathas, when they rose to political power, did not impress the subject population favourably. To the over-polished decadents of the Mughal capitals, the warriors from the South appeared as a race of upstarts, insolent in prosperity, and lacking in grace, refinement and even good manners. They had no taste for the fine arts, no elegance of address, no aptitude for the amenities of social life. Even their horsemanship was awkward and graceless, though eminently practical. The period of Maratha ascendency has not left India richer by a single grand building, or beautiful picture, or finely written manuscript. Even the palaces of the Peshwas are low, mean-looking, flimsy structures, with small rooms and narrow staircases—relieved from utter insignificance only by their richly carved wooden *facade*.

§ 4 *Maratha character.*

But such a country and climate have their compensating advantages, too. They develop self-reliance, courage, perseverance, a stern simplicity, a rough straightforwardness, a sense of social equality and consequently pride in the dignity of man as man. As early as the 7th century of the Christian era, a learned Chinese traveller thus noted the character of the Maratha people living in the more prosperous Central Deccan. "The inhabitants are proud-spirited and warlike, grateful for favours and revengeful for wrongs, self-sacrificing towards suppliants in distress and sanguinary to death with any who treated them insultingly." (Watters's *Yuan Chwang*, ii. 239.) "If they are going to seek revenge, they first give their enemy warning." (Beal, ii. 256).

This racial character was somewhat modified in the course of the next ten centuries. The disappearance of the protective influence of the large Hindu monarchies of the province, the growing rigour of the Muslim occupation of the country, and the ravages of constant warfare between rival States, forced the remnant of the Maratha population to be more cunning and less chivalrous. Shivaji did not "first give warning" to Afzal or Shaista Khan.*

But the basis of their character remained the same, —activity, courage, self-reliance, self-respect and love of equality With the loss of their own cities and capitals on the Godavari and the Krishna in the 14th century, they were pressed back to the sterile western edge of the plateau and became poorer and more isolated. In the lonely struggle with Nature and beasts, they developed greater cunning, without losing their valour and hardiness. Indeed, in their combination of courage, cleverness and power of endurance,—in their ability to plan and execute surprises and night-attacks, in the skill of their soldiers to extricate themselves from a tight corner or vary their tactics according to the changing phases of a battle, without waiting for guidance from a superior, —the Marathas resemble the Afghans most among all Asiatic races.

---

* In 1880 an English observer wrote of the Maratha peasantry (of the Kunbi caste), "They are hard-working, temperate, hospitable, fond of their children and kind to strangers At the same time they are cruel in revenge, and seldom scruple to cheat either Government or their creditors" (*Bom Gaz* xviii pt I, 288)

Social distinctions were fewer and much less sharp among the 16th century Marathas than among richer and more civilized communities. The rich man was not immeasurably above the poor in such a simple society, and even the poorest man had his value as a fighter or indispensable labourer; at least, he preserved his self-respect, because where few had anything to spare, none was tempted to lead the pampered life of the professional beggars and hangers-on of Agra or Delhi. Poverty and immemorial custom alike preserved the womankind of Maharashtra (except among those castes that aspired to be Kshatriyas) from seclusion in the harem, and thus the effective strength of society was doubled, while life gained in health and sweetness

§5. *Religious teachers.*

The same sense of equality was fostered by religion. The Brahmans, no doubt, tried to maintain their monopoly of the sacred lore and their aloofness from other castes as a sort of spiritual aristocracy. But strong religious movements arose and swept through the length and breadth of the land, teaching the sanctity of conduct rather than mere birth, the superiority of a living personal faith to mere ritual, and the oneness of all true believers before God. These popular movements were hostile to the haughty claims of the Brahman hierarchy, and their chief centre was Pandharpur, one of the most famous seats of pilgrimage in the land.

"Like the Protestant Reformation in Europe in the 16th century, there was a religious, social, and literary revival and Reformation in India, but notably in the Deccan in the 15th and 16th centuries. This religious revival was not Brahmanical in its orthodoxy, it was heterodox in its spirit of protest against forms and ceremonies and class distinctions based on birth, and ethical in its preference of a pure heart, and of the law of love, to all other acquired merits and good works This religious revival was the work also of the people, of the masses, and not of the classes. At its head were saints and prophets, poets and philosophers, who sprang chiefly from the lower orders of society,—tailors, carpenters, potters, gardeners, shop-keepers, barbers, and even *mahars* (scavengers)—more often than Brahmans. The names of Tukaram [born about 1568], of Ramdas [b. 1608], of Vaman Pandit [b. 1636], and of Eknath [b. 1528] still retain their ascendency over the minds of the people of Maharashtra." (Ranade, 10; also *Bom. Gaz.* xx. 473; Sardesai, i. 38-78.)

The fairs held at the chief places of pilgrimage on particular holy days tended to foster a sense of Hindu unity, like the national games of ancient Greece, though to a lesser extent, because caste has always remained with us a disintegrating force These shrines became distributing centres of cult and culture, and broke down tribal or parochial narrowness, though imperceptibly.

§6. *Literature and Language.*

Literature afforded another bond of union in Maharashtra. Its themes were taken from the ancient scriptures and epics which are the heritage of all the Hindus. The devotional songs and moral maxims of popular teachers like Tukaram and Ramdas, Vaman Pandit and Moro Pant, made their way to every home where Marathi letters could be read. "In every town and village in the Deccan and Konkan, especially during the rains, the pious Maratha will be found enjoying with his family and friends the recitation of the *Pothi* of Shridhar [b 1679], and enjoying it indeed Except an occasional gentle laugh, or a sigh, or a tear, not a sound disturbs the rapt silence of the audience, unless when one of those passages of supreme pathos is reached, which affects the whole of the listeners simultaneously with an outburst of emotion which drowns the voice of the reader" (Acworth's *Ballads,* xxvii)

The simplicity and uniformity of early Maratha society are also reflected in the language Their poetry consisted of short jingles and apopthegms or monotonous metrical couplets like the epics,—with no lyric outburst, no long-flowing sonorous verses, no delicate play on the whole gamut of sounds. Like the other daughters of Sanskrit, the Marathi vernacular had no literary prose till well into the 18th century The prose that was created by the official class in their letters and chronicles, was a barbarous jargon composed nearly three-fourths of Persian words and grotesque literal translations of Persian idioms. The highly Sanskritized, elegant and varied prose that is now used, is a creation of the British period. (Rajwade, viii Intro , fully discusses the Persian element.)

"On the whole it may be said that the written [Marathi] poetry, consisting as it does in such very large measure of moral disquisitions and reflections, and the praises of this deity or that, is little known to the ryots and the Mavalis of Maharashtra, and that it would not command their attention or admiration if it were known . In Maharashtra, where the immense majority of the peasantry can neither read nor write, it is a mere truism to say that the literature of their country is absolutely unknown to them.* It is not to be supposed, however, that they are without a poetry of their own. With the Marathas, the feelings of the commons have taken shape in the ballads, which are the genuine embodiment of national enthusiasm...Over the plains of the Deccan, and the deep valleys and bold ridges of the Sahyadris, from village to village, the humble *Gondhali* (minstrel) still travels, and still to rapt and excited audiences sings of the great days when the armed fathers of the men around him gave laws at the spear's point to all the princes of India, or retreated wounded and dismayed before the sword of the sea-dwelling stranger." (Acworth and Shaligram, *Powadas,* i and ii) But this national ballad literature was the creation of the age of Shivaji and his successors.

Not only was their literature poor, but their popular spoken tongue was a rough practical speech, incapable of expressing the ceremonious courtesy, indirectness, and delicate shades of meaning of the highly developed Urdu language. The democratic temper of the Maratha people is shown by their having no respectful mode of address like the *ap* ("your honour") of Northern India; all ranks are *theed* and *thoued.*

Thus, a remarkable community of language, creed, and life was attained in Maharashtra in the 17th century, even before political unity was conferred by Shivaji. What little was wanting to the solidarity of the people was supplied by his creation of a national State, the long struggle with the invader from Delhi under his sons, and the imperial expansion of the race under the Peshwas.

* But the entire mass of legends and traditions of the race was the common property of all classes of people throughout the land and gave them cultural homogeneity

Thus, in the end a tribe,—or rather a collection of tribes and castes,—was fused into a *nation*,* and by the end of the 18th century a Maratha *people* in the political and cultural senses of the term had been formed, though caste distinctions still remained. Thus history has moulded society.

§7. *Maratha soldiers and peasants of to-day.*

The backbone of Shivaji's army was composed of the peasantry, who belonged to two low castes, named *Maratha* and *Kunbi*. The Maratha caste,—a name which should not be applied to all Marathi-speaking people in general,—numbered five millions and the Kunbis (of the Bombay Presidency alone), two and a half millions, in 1911, and they bear the following character in our times

"As a class, Marathas (*i.e.*, the caste so called) are simple, frank, independent and liberal, courteous, and, when kindly treated, trusting. They are a manly and intelligent race, proud of their former greatness, fond of show, and careful to hide poverty. Stronger, more active, and better made than the Kunbis, many of the Marathas, even among the poorer classes, have an air of refinement. (They take animal food, including fowls, and drink toddy and other liquors, like the Kunbis.) No caste supplies the Bombay army with so many recruits as the Ratnagiri Marathas. Others go into the police or find employment as messengers Like the Kunbis, orderly, well-behaved, and good-tempered, the Marathas surpass them in courage and generosity. Very frugal,

* "The Marathas are a nation, and from the Brahman to the ryot they glory in the fact" (Acworth and Shaligram's *Powadas*, iii)

unassuming, respectable and temperate they are a very religious class."

"The Deccan Kunbis are [now] all cultivators, steady and hard-working.. A very quiet, easy-tempered and orderly class, singularly free from crime, they have much respect for the gods. In the Deccan they are strong, hardy, enduring and muscular, [but in Konkan, smaller, darker and more slightly made.] The Kunbi women, like their husbands, are strong and hardy, but the veiled Maratha women are generally weak Widows are generally allowed to marry." (*Bom. Gaz.*, xxiv. 70; x. 123, 121; xviii. pt. i, 285, 307.)

§ 8. *Defects of the Maratha character.*

We shall now turn to the other traits of the Maratha character. When a Government lives on plunder as a regular source of supply, its officers naturally see no immorality in taking bribes for themselves. The ethics of the servant easily slide into the ethics of the master. These Indian Spartans with their simplicity, hardiness and sense of equality, were no more proof against corruption than the Spartans of ancient Greece. Contemporary travellers have noticed how greedy of bribes the Brahman officers of the Maratha State were, even under the great Shivaji.

The chief defect of the Marathas, which has disastrously reacted on their political history, is their lack of business capacity. This race has produced no great banker, trader, captain of industry, or even commissariat organizer or contractor. Hence, on the economic side, in the broadest sense of the term, the Maratha administration was very weak. The Peshwas, in spite of the dazzling brilliancy of their political success, were bankrupts from the days of the great Baji Rao I. onwards. Even Shivaji had repeated money difficulties during his short reign,—though in his case it was due not so much to real insolvency, as to his aversion to touch his hoarded treasure for the normal expenses of his army.

But the Marathas have a historic advantage of unique importance in the India of to-day. Their near ancestors had faced death in a hundred battle-fields, had led armies and debated in the chamber of diplomacy, had managed the finances of kingdoms and grappled with the problems of empire, they had helped to make Indian history in the immediate and not yet forgotten past. The memory of these things is a priceless asset to their race. In the combination of intellectual keenness, patient industry, simplicity of life, devotion to the nobler ideals of man, in the courage necessary for translating thought into deed, in the spirit of sacrifice, grit of character, and a diffused sense of democratic equality, the vast middle class of modern Maharashtra have no superior and hardly any equal among the other races of India. Would that they also possessed the organizing skill, the power of co-operation, the tact in the management of instruments and colleagues, the foresight, and the saving common sense of the Anglo-Saxon race!

CHAPTER II.

BOYHOOD AND YOUTH, 1627-1656

§1. *Shivaji's ancestors.*

The Bhonslé clan of the Maratha caste was made up of many families, scattered over various places in Western India. Unlike a Rajput or Scottish clan, they had no union under a common and generally-recognized chieftain nor even mutual intercourse, but merely bore the same surname and married into other Maratha families. Agriculture was their original occupation, as with most Marathas. But the break up of the large monarchies of Western India, (namely, the Bahmani at the end of the 15th century and the Nizam Shahi at the beginning of the 17th) opened to the ablest men among them the chance of rising to military power and lordship over land. The history of Shivaji's family illustrates this transformation of the tiller of the soil by successive stages into the bandit, the captain of mercenaries, the feudal baron, and the sovereign ruler, which was so frequent during the troubled times that followed the downfall of central powers like the Bahmani or the Delhi empire and ended only with the establishment of British paramountcy and British peace.

In the middle of the 16th century, a Bhonslé named Babaji was living peacefully on the humble gains of agriculture and the dues of his office as headman (*patil*) of the villages of Hingani Beradi and Diwalgaon in the Puna district (Patas sub-division.) His two sons, Maloji and Vitoji, quarrelled with the other people of the place and migrated with their wives to the village of Verul (Ellora) at the foot of the Daulatabad hills. The prospects of agriculture here were unpromising, and the two brothers went in search of employment to Jadav Rao of Sindhkher, a Nizam Shahi noble, and entered his service as common soldiers (*bargirs.*) The tradition runs that at a festive gathering in his house, Jadav Rao praised the beauty of Maloji's little boy Shahji and his own daughter Jija Bai, drew them together on his knees, and cried out that they would form an excellent match, and that Maloji immediately stood up and called upon the other guests to witness that his master had betrothed his daughter to his son,—for which presumptuous claim he was forthwith dismissed by Jadav Rao.

So, the two brothers came back to their home at Ellora and lived there by agriculture for the next few years. One night Maloji, while watching his crops in the field, noticed a big snake coming out of a hole, and following the popular belief that snakes guard buried treasure he dug the place up and discovered seven pots full of gold coins underground. Here at last were the means of gratifying their ambition. Lodging the treasure with an honest banker at Chamargunda, they bought horses, saddles, arms and tents and equipped a force of one thousand troopers, at whose head they offered their swords to any master that would pay them. Joining a leader of banditti named Nimbalkar (of Phaltan), they soon gained so much importance and power that the decadent Nizam-Shahi Government was glad to enrol them among its captains. This happened at the beginning of the 17th century, when Akbar's conquest of the capital Ahmadnagar had thrown that monarchy into confusion and disruption, which raised the value of able mercenary bands and offered unlimited opportunities of

2

advancement to their captains. Jadav Rao had no objection now to giving his daughter in marriage to the son of the newly-exalted Bhonslé.

Maloji wisely spent a portion of his treasure trove in building temples, giving alms to Brahmans, and excavating a large tank on the Shambhu Mahadev hill, in the Satara district, which was a great boon to the tens of thousands of pilgrims who annually flocked to that shrine. These pious investments of his money brought him a good return by raising him immensely in social esteem. When he died, the family contingent of troops,—now greatly increased in number from the original thousand men,—was commanded in the Nizam-Shahi service by his younger brother Vitoji, and after Vitoji's death (probably in 1623), by Shahji, the eldest son of Maloji.*

§2. *The Rise of Shahji Bhonslé, 1625-36.*

Shahji's name first occurs in recorded history in 1628, two years after the death of Malik Ambar, when he was sent forth by Fath Khan, the son and successor of that Nizam Shahi *wazir*, to raid East Khandesh in the rear of a Mughal invading force. Soon afterwards, the plots of the Nizam Shah and his new wazir against each other, the imprisonment of Fath Khan by his king (*c.* April 1630), the murder of Lakhji Jadav Rao at Court (*c.* 1630),

---

*The accounts of the family given in the Persian histories of Delhi and Bijapur have been summarized in my paper on the "Rise of Shahji" published in the *Modern Review*, Sept 1917, (some of the dates of which require correction in the light of information from other sources) The Marathi accounts given in Malkaré (Persian version in *Tarikh-i-Shivaji*) and very briefly in Sabhasad, have been utilized here to some extent The exaggerations of Marathi Court-poets, in Sanskrit, have been rejected Of the eight sons of Vitoji (the younger brother of Maloji I) four are found in the Mughal service at the beginning of Shah Jahan's reign, *viz.*, Kheloji, Parsuji, Maloji II and Mambaji [Abdul Hamid, i A] the treacherous surrender of the Mughal portion of Ahmadnagar territory by the viceroy Khan-i-Jahan Lodi, (1627), a fresh Mughal invasion of the country (1628), and the Bijapuri efforts to seize as much of the wrecks of the Ahmadnagar kingdom as possible,—all combined to throw the Nizam Shahi Government into unspeakable weakness and confusion. This was a golden opportunity for an able enterprising and ambitious man like Shahji. After the murder of his father-in-law Jadav Rao, he left the Nizam Shah, got a band of men together, and tried to seize the country from Junnar to Ahmadnagar, creating a great disturbance at that ill-defined and ill-guarded meeting point of three kingdoms. Then he entered the Mughal service with his eldest son and younger brother (end of 1630), but deserted after a year and a half (June 1632) and went over to the service of Bijapur, where he completely fascinated Murari Jagadev, the right-hand man of the wazir Khawas Khan.

The murder of Burhan Nizam Shah (*c.* Feb. 1632) by his wazir and the Mughal capture of Daulatabad (the new capital) with his successor Husain Nizam Shah in it (17th June 1633), were followed by the final dismemberment of the once glorious Ahmadnagar kingdom. Its local governors declared their independence. Shahji now seized all the Nizam-Shahi territory from Puna and Chakan to the environs of Ahmadnagar and Nasik, and plundered right and left. With Bijapuri assistance he crowned a boy Nizam Shah in Premgarh (renamed Shahgarh) in August 1633, and carried on the government in the name of this puppet for three years,—seizing districts (including North Konkan), enlisting soldiers (especially 12,000 Nizam-Shahi troopers who had been disbanded after the fall of Daulatabad), and raiding the country as far as

Bidar and Daulatabād, to the great harassment of the Mughals.

But the imperialists launched huge forces against him in February 1636. The campaign, after much hard riding and fighting, ended next October in the completest defeat of Shahji, who was compelled to surrender to the victors his puppet Nizam Shah and seven of his forts, enter Bijapur service, and transfer his mischievous ambition and disturbing activity to regions far away from Maharashtra proper.

§3. *Difficulty of reconstructing Shivaji's early history.*

The true history of the first thirty years of Shivaji's life (1627—1657) presents a puzzling and almost insoluble problem. From the nature of the materials available, it is hopeless to reconstruct the narrative of his early career with any degree of certainty.* Here the widest differences of opinion are possible as to the details, but happily the broad outlines are clear and generally accepted.

My own conclusions,—often formed only by balancing probabilities against one another, and in a few cases adopted as "working hypotheses,"—will be given in detail in the rest of this chapter; but they may be briefly summarized as follows:—

(i) Shivaji was born on Monday, 10th April, 1627,

---

*It is impossible to come to any universal agreement on questions like,—Where did Shivaji spend the years 1637 and 1638, at Puna or at Bijapur? Was it Dadaji Kond-dev or Shivaji who subjugated the Mavals? When did Dadaji die? What was the first Bijapuri fort taken by Shivaji and in what year? In what year or years did he establish his own authority over those forts of his father, which had not been at first placed under him? What were the order and dates of his acquisition of the 40 forts of which he was admittedly in possession in 1659?

and lived in Shivner fort till 1637, when he was removed to Puna.

(ii) He first captured one or two obscure or out of repair forts in the western side of the Puna district, in the neglected and unsubdued new frontier of the Bijapur State, from 1646 to his father's arrest (25 July 1648); the arrest was due to a cause quite unconnected with the son's usurpations and was ended by other means than Shivaji's restoration of forts to Adil Shah.

(iii) From the release of Shahji (end of 1649) to the invasion of Javli (January 1656), Shivaji did nothing conspicuous or likely to give strong provocation to Bijapur; there were the usual small raids and (very doubtfully) conquests in the Kolaba district which did not then really own Bijapuri sovereignty. His military and financial resources* at this stage were very limited, and he could not have undertaken any extensive or distant conquest, though he was steadily and prudently increasing his power and placing it on a solid basis by building new and repairing old forts, increasing his army, and accumulating treasure by husbanding his revenue and gains from plunder. During these six years he took only a few forts (if any at all) subject to Bijapur, nor did he invade the Kalian district.

(iv) The forts in his father's Puna jagir were not taken by Shivaji immediately after Dadaji's death nor all

* His entire army consisted of 3,000 horsemen [besides a fluctuating number of Mavle infantry] But two thousand of these troopers were the owners of their horses and arms, and could have left Shivaji any day for a higher bidder He had remounts of his own for only 1,200 men [Sabh 8] The income of the *entire* Puna jagir of Shahji was only a lakh and a half of Rupees, and some portions of it were not yet in Shivaji's hands The building and repairing of forts consumed much of his small gains of treasure trove and booty

at the same time. The forcible expulsion of Shambhuji Mohite from Supa fits in better with the year 1656 than with 1647 or 1648.

(v) After the conquest of Javli (January 1656), came the rapid extension of his territory and forces. His striking power and material resources were at once more than doubled by this annexation, and soon afterwards he rounded off his possessions by completing the seizure of his father's entire western jagir and invaded Konkan. The four years 1656—1659 were for him crowded with conspicuous achievements, which made his ascent to an independent throne but a single and easy step.

§4. *Shivaji's birth and infancy.*

Shahji Bhonsle's first wife Jija Bai bore him two sons, Shambhuji and Shivaji. As the elder one died in early youth, history is not concerned with him. Shivaji, their second son, was born in the hill-fort of Shivner, which towers over the city of Junnar, in the extreme north of the Puna district. His mother had prayed to the local goddess, Shivā Bhavāni, for the good of her expected child, and she therefore named him after that deity.

Of the exact date of his birth there is no reliable contemporary record. Even his courtier, Krishnaji Anant Sabhasad, writing in 1694, is silent on the point.

Of the two different dates of his birth given by two different groups of writers, I am inclined to prefer Monday, 10th April 1627, which is recorded by the descendants of his secretaries.

The stories told in the later Marathi *bakhars* about the history of his parents during the year preceding his birth and the events of his own life up to the age of twenty, are in many points contrary to authentic history, and in others improbable, or at all events unsupported by any evidence We know from the contemporary Persian histories that during much of the period from 1630 to 1636 Shahji led a roving life, subject to frequent contests with diverse enemies and change of residence. Under these circumstances, he would naturally have left his wife and infant son for safety in a stronghold like Shivner But in reality they seem to have both fallen under his neglect It is a fair inference from the known facts that by the year 1630 or thereabout Jija Bai lost her husband's love, probably with the loss of her youth, and Shahji forsook her and her little son Shivaji and took a younger and more beautiful wife, Tukā Bai Mohité, on whom and whose son Vyankoji he henceforth lavished his society and all his gains.

It is expressly stated in the contemporary Persian history *Padishahnamah* (i. B. 150) that in March 1636 Shahji's family was living at Shivner As Shivner was one of the seven forts ceded by Shahji to the Mughals in the terms of the treaty of October 1636, Shivaji could not have continued to live in that fort much longer after the end of that year Shahji himself immediately after his defeat went to Bijapur and entering the Adil Shahi service was sent on campaign further south. He secured from that Government a grant of the Puna district from Chakan to Indapur and Shirwal as his jagir, and appointed Dadaji Kond-dev to administer the tract, telling him, "My wife Jija Bai is living in the fort of Shivner and has brought forth a son named Shivaji. Bring her and her son away and keep them in your charge [at Puna] and supply them with money for their necessary expenses"

Thus Shivaji took up his residence at Puna, probably

early in 1637. He was, therefore, practically a stranger to his father for several years after his birth (if we leave out of our account Shahji's visits to Shivner in the intervals of his campaigns), and he became totally so after this removal to Puna.*

Her husband's neglect drove the mind of Jija Bai inwards and deepened her natural religious spirit, which she imparted to her son. Shiva grew up in solitude, a mateless child, without brother sister or father. The isolation of their life drew mother and son very close together and intensified his love for her till it became almost an adoration for a deity. From a very early age, he was naturally thrown on his own resources, and learnt to carry out his own ideas unaided, and to take the initiative without any sense of subordination or responsibility to some higher authority. In the condition of the homes of their boyhood, their early life and training, and the development of their character,—even as in the steps by which they mounted to thrones,—the forsaken son of Shahji Bhonsle was the exact parallel of the forsaken son of Hasan Sur. Shivaji and Sher Shah were not only alike in character and genius, but also grew up amidst like circumstances.

§5. *Condition of the Puna jagir, 1637.*

Shahji's jagir of Puna and Supa, formerly held under Nizam Shah and henceforth under Adil Shah, included the Puna district from Chakan to Indapur, Supa, Shirwal, Wai (? Walti) and Jadgir, (*T. S.* 8*a*), or a tract bounded on the west by the Ghats, on the north by the

*In 1639 Jija Bai and Shivaji in the company of Dadaji paid a visit to Shahji at Bangalore, but were sent back to Puna with him (Sabh 7)

Ghod river, on the east by the Bhima and on the south by the Nira river.

The Puna district that Dadaji took over was in a sadly ruined condition Six years of warfare had desolated the land, and the work of the invading soldiery had been completed after their departure by robber chiefs who tried to profit by the anarchy. Indeed, the province had so recently passed from the Nizam-Shahi ownership to that of Bijapur that the authority of the new Government had not yet taken root there. It was only the rule of a strong jagirdar that could have given peace and prosperity to the district; but during 1630-1636 Shahji had been forced to lead a life of constant movement, danger and warfare. The Puna and Thana districts at the extreme north-western corner of the kingdom of Bijapur, therefore, formed a No man's Land, with none to administer and defend them.

In 1630 Shahji had plundered and seized the Nizam-Shahi country round Puna. Soon afterwards a Bijapuri army had looted and burnt Puna, Indapur and other villages of Shahji and "totally desolated them." (*B S.* 287.) Next he had recovered possession of them by force. Then had followed the famine of 1630-1631, the most terrible in the sad history of the Deccan (*Pad.* i. A. 362.) The Junnar or North Puna tract was the scene of repeated Mughal invasions in 1634-'36. Khan-i-Zaman in the course of his campaign against Shahji (July—October 1636) penetrated to Puna, but there was probably nothing left for him to plunder or burn there. During the dissolution of the Ahmadnagar sultanate, a revenue accountant (*deshpande*) named Moro Tandev Honap, "a proud rebel, well acquainted with the country round the Bhima, had raised a tumult and seized the neighbourhood of Puna. All these disorders had devastated the whole kingdom from Ahmadnagar to the boundary of Wai and Shirwal." (*T. S.* 8*a.*)

The desolation caused by man preying on his species favoured the growth of wild beasts. The Puna district, especially the Sahyadri hill-side forming its western border, was now infested by large numbers of wolves, which thinned the population and hindered cultivation. Dadaji Kond-dev offered rewards to the hillmen for killing the wolves and thus cleared the whole tract of these pests in a short time. He conciliated the hillmen and induced them to settle in the valleys and extend cultivation by offering very liberal terms. "Leases were granted to the effect that the new tenants should pay a rent of only Re. 1 per *bigha** in the first year, Rs. 3 in the second, Rs. 6 in the third, Rs. 9 in the fourth, Rs. 10 in the fifth, Rs. 20 in the sixth and the same rate as the older tenants in the 7th year, and at the rate of Malik Ambar's land settlement from the 8th year onwards. Thus the whole country was brought under tillage." (*T. S.* 9*a.*) When Dadaji took charge of the Puna jagir, its revenue on paper was only 40,000 *hun*, or Rs. 1,60,000, according to the current rate of exchange. (Sabh. 102) But only a fraction of this amount was actually collected.

The memory of his able and beneficent administration was long preserved, and a later chronicle tells us, "He did such strict justice that the very name of robbers and usurpers disappeared from the district" (*T. S.* 9*a.*) An anecdote illustrates his punctilious sense of justice:

---

* Does the Persian translator here use *bigha* in the sense of *chawar* (or 120 bighas)?

"He planted a garden of fruit trees, named it after Shahji, and gave strict orders that if any one plucked even a leaf from the trees, he would be punished. One day Dadaji with his own hand plucked a mango from a tree. For this offence he was about to cut off the hand when the other people prevented him To show his respect for the rules, however, he wore an iron chain round his neck" (*T S 9b*), or according to another account, "kept the offending arm confined in a long glove!" (Malkare, 20)

§6 *Shivaji's education*

On the subject of Shivaji's education, Sabhasad is silent. The *Tarikh-i-Shivaji* tells us that "Dadaji trained Shivaji and appointed an excellent teacher for him. In a short time Shiva became skilled in fighting, riding and other accomplishments." (*9a.*) The weight of evidence is in favour of the view that Shivaji was unlettered, like three other heroes of mediæval India,—Akbar, Haidar Ali, and Ranjit Singh. The many Europeans who visited him never saw him write anything; when they presented any petition to him the Rajah always passed it on to his ministers to be read to him. No piece of writing in his own hand is known to exist.*

But though he may not have been able to read books, he certainly mastered the contents of the two great Hindu epics by listening to recitations and story-tellings. The noble examples of doing and suffering, of action and sacrifice, of military skill and statecraft,

*At the conclusion of a letter to Ramdas there are a few words which have been taken by the editor of *Ramdasi Patravyavahar* (Mr Dev) as Shivaji s writing But the evidence is unconvincing, and the survival of only a single specimen after a long reign is unaccountable

which the stories of Rama and the Pandavas afford, the political lessons and moral maxims with which these epics are filled, deeply impressed his young mind. He loved to distraction religious readings and songs (*kirtan*) and sought the society of Hindu and Muslim saints wherever he went. The want of book-learning, therefore, did not leave his mind a dull and sterile soil, nor impair his efficiency as a man of action in a world that was mediæval.

§7. *The Mavals occupied.*

The western belt of the Puna district, running along the Western Ghats for a length of 90 miles and a breadth of 12 to 24 miles, is known as *Maval* or the Sunset Land. "It is extremely rugged, a series of table-lands cut on every side by deep winding valleys.... .From the valleys, hills of various heights and forms rise, terrace above terrace, with steep sides often strewn with black basalt boulders......Where the trees have been spared, they clothe the hill-sides with a dense growth mixed with almost impassable brushwood. Here and there are patches of ancient evergreen forests......The people in the northern valleys are Kolis and in the southern valleys Marathas. They have a strong strain of hill-blood and are dark, wiry and sallow .....The climate is dry and invigorating, the air is lighter, and the heat less oppressive than in most parts of Western or Southern India." (*Bom. Gaz.* xviii. pt. I, pp 2, 13, 15)

In popular speech, the valleys into which this western belt is divided are collectively known as the *twelve Mavals*, though their names end with the words *ner* and *khore* as well as *maval*, and their number exceeds twelve. A Marathi ballad speaks of 12 Mavals under Junnar and twelve others under Puna.

The Maval country is a purely agricultural region with no city and little trade. Its common people differed from the Marathas and Kunbis of the plains only by being stronger built, hardier, simpler, and less enervated by luxury or vice. Their social organization was neither tribal nor patriarchal (as with the hillmen of Scotland and Rajputana), but that of the ancient village community of the Deccan, in which each village formed a miniature self-complete republic of various castes and professions. Every sub-division of the province was under a *deshmukh,* who might be called a landed baron or, more correctly, the king's local agent. He took from the peasants through the headmen (*patils*) of the different villages the royal revenue and his own share of it, besides enjoying the produce of certain *de mesne* villages (or fields) which he owned free of rent.

These petty chieftains (*deshmukhs*) were mostly Marathas or members of the same caste as Shivaji. They entrusted the management of their affairs to Brahman stewards (*karbharis*) and the accounts and correspondence work to clerks of the Prabhu (Kayastha) caste, as elsewhere in Maharashtra. Each Maval *deshmukh* had to maintain an armed force, almost entirely recruited from his tenants, for the defence of his charge against the encroachments of his neighbours and the incursions of robber bands. In addition, he was often requested by his sovereign to raise troops for the royal service in times of need, and for this extra duty he was rewarded with cash bounties and grants of fresh villages.

Thus, the rise of Shivaji opened a wide field of employment all over the Deccan to the Mavle landlords and their sturdy tenantry as instruments of his raids and conquests, and brought them wealth, power and honour far beyond what the plough could have yielded them at home. Their ambition became inseparably linked with his, and the tie was strengthened by Shivaji's frequent tours through this tract and good comraderie with its people,—till the Mavles came to regard him almost as their Little Corporal, for whom they would do and dare to the point of death. The Maval country was the cradle of Shivaji's power and the Mavles formed the backbone of his army.

Dadaji established complete mastery over the *Mavals*. The local chiefs (*deshpandes*) were mostly won over by tactful handling and rewards. Those who defied his authority were attacked and forced to submit.* Thus peace and prosperity were established in that region and it became a source of wealth and strength to the owner of Puna, instead of being an unprofitable and even dangerous possession. (Sabh. 7.) From this region Shivaji drew his best soldiers, his earliest comrades, and his most devoted followers. Yesaji Kank and Baji Pasalkar were *Mavle* chieftains of his own age; they gathered round him very early and were enrolled as his first captains. So, also, were Tanaji Malusare and his brother Suryaji.

---

*Raj xv 316 and 393 records the story of one of his reverses · "Dadaji Kond-dev came to Shivapur Among the 12 Mavals, Krishnaji Nayak Bandal, the deshmukh of Hirdas Maval, had seized another man's lands and refused to give them up Dadaji marched against him, but was defeated and forced to retreat to Shivapur He then sent Kanhoji Nayak Jedhe to persuade Krishnaji and other Maval deshmukhs to come for an interview" The *Jedhe Karina* gives an inner view of the state of affairs in one part of this tract

§8. *Shivaji's choice of a career.*

In their company young Shivaji wandered over the hills and forests of the Sahyadri range, and along the mazes of the river valleys, thus hardening himself to a life of privation and strenuous exertion, as well as getting an intimate knowledge of the country and its people. During his residence at Puna his plastic mind was profoundly influenced by the readings from the Hindu epics and sacred books given by his guardian and other Brahmans, and still more by the teaching of his mother. The deeply religious, almost ascetic, life that Jija Bai led amidst neglect and solitude imparted by its example, even more than by her precepts, a stoical earnestness mingled with religious fervour to the character of Shiva. He began to love independence and loathe a life of servile luxury in the pay of some Muslim king. It is, however, extremely doubtful if at this time he conceived any general design of freeing his brother Hindus from the insults and outrages to which they were often subjected by the dominant Muslim sect.* An independent sovereignty for himself he certainly coveted; but he never posed as the liberator of the Hindus in general, at all events not till long afterwards.

The inconstancy, intrigue and bloodshed which stained the Court of Bijapur in those days foreboded for it a downfall like that of Ahmadnagar. Mughal service was a no better alternative to Shivaji. The imperialists had killed Kheloji Bhonslé, his grand-uncle, and their superior resources and organization made it unlikely for

*Basatin-i-Salatin, 350—355, frankly describes in detail how the Hindus were depressed as a deliberate policy of the State of Bijapur in the palmy days of Muhammad Adil Shah

the Hindus of the Deccan to enjoy greater toleration or power under them than under the weaker and smaller sultanates close at hand. Moreover, to the Deccanis, both Hindu and Muhammadan, Delhi was a far off city, with an alien speech and an alien ruling race, who would pitilessly discard their southern instruments after service had been taken from them. A career of independence was no doubt risky to Shivaji, but it had undreamt of advantages to compensate for the risks, if only he could succeed.

On the question of his future career he is held by one tradition to have come into conflict with his guardian. Dadaji Kond-dev was, no doubt, an able and honest land-steward, a man of methodical habits, leading a sober blameless and humdrum life, but quite incapable of lofty ideals, daring ambition or far off vision. Shivaji's love of adventure and independence appeared to his guardian as the sign of an untutored and wayward spirit, which would ruin his life's chances. He argued long with Shivaji, advised him to follow the footsteps of his ancestors and rise to wealth and position as an obedient vassal and captain of mercenaries under Adil Shah. The young lad's association with the hill brigands and his projects for robbery and the surprise of forts filled Dadaji with apprehensions about his future. He complained to Shahji, but without succeeding in effecting a reform. Worn out by anxiety and age, Dadaji died about the middle of 1647* and Shivaji became his own master at the age of twenty.

**Letters and Sanads*, 111, gives 1647 as the year of Dadaji's death. A *mahzar* issued by him on 31 May 1646 is extant (Raj. iv. 80 ; cf. xvi. 36.)

§9. *Shivaji's early conquest of forts.*

The death of Dadaji Kond-dev found Shiva ready for his task. He had already been trained in martial exercises and civil administration; he had familiarized himself with the troops of his father's western jagir and the people he would have to govern. Initiative and power of command had been freely developed in him without check or interference from his guardian. Administrative orders had in some cases been issued in his name, as his father's representative. Shivaji had also taken part, with his mother or his guardian, in some judicial investigations and public decisions of legal disputes (*mahzar.*)*

The band of officers already gathered round him were men of tried ability and devotion to him. Shyamraj Nilkanth Ranjhekar (the correct form of the name is *Rozekar*, according to some modern Maratha scholars) was the Chancellor (*peshwa*); Balkrishna Dikshit was Accountant-General (*majmuadar*); Sonaji Pant was secretary (*dabir*) and Raghunath Ballal Korde was paymaster (*sabnis.*) These four officers had been sent by Shahji about 1639. To them Shivaji now added Tukoji Chor Maratha as Master of the Horse (*sar-i-naubat*) and Narayan Pant as divisional paymaster. (Sabh. 7 and 8, *T. S.* 10*b*)

The year 1646 marks a crisis in the history of Bijapur The king fell seriously ill, and for some time his life was despaired of. Though he lingered on for ten years more, these years were by popular belief held to be a portion of the life of the saint Shah Hashim Uluvi,

* I have missed the reference, and cannot make the above statement with confidence. (Try Raj, xv-xviii)

given away by that holy man to the king. (*B. S.* 312.) During this time no serious business was attended to by Muhammad Adil Shah. The expansion of territory in the Karnatak went on under some of the nobles, but at the capital the king was inert, and the administration fell into the hands of the queen Bari Sahiba. The official history of Bijapur is significantly silent about Muhammad Adil Shah's doings from 1646 to his death in 1656.

This was Shivaji's opportunity. Even before the death of Dadaji, he had begun his annexations. About 1646 he had taken Torna fort from its Bijapuri commandant by some cunning device without fighting. Here he found Government treasure amounting to 2 *lakhs* of *hun*. The captured fort was newly named Prachandgarh, a name which it soon lost. Five miles east of it, on the crest of the same spur of hills, he built a new fort named Rajgarh, with three walled redoubts (*machi*) on the successive terraces of the hill-side. (*T. S.* 12*b*; Sabh. 9.)

These acts of aggression were reported to Bijapur. But Shivaji secured friends at Court by bribing the ministers, and they sided with him against the local jagirdars whom he had dispossessed. (K. K. ii. 114.)

After the death of Dadaji Kond-dev it was naturally the aim of Shivaji to bring all parts of Shahji's western jagir under his own control, so as to form a compact State ruled by one authority. But this was effected gradually and took years to complete, as it was not wise for him then to employ force on all sides.

The fort of Chakan, guarding the road to Puna from the north, had been entrusted by Dadaji Kond-dev to Firangji Narsala. This officer was induced to profess obedience to Shivaji and was confirmed in his post.

(*T. S.* 12*b.*) The petty officers of the *thanahs* of Baramati and Indapur on the eastern margin of the jagir, peacefully submitted to Shiva's authority. The fort of Kondana, 11 miles south-west of Puna, was next secured by bribing its Adil-Shahi governor.*

§10. *Adil Shah imprisons Shahji, 1648.*

Shivaji's first small beginnings of territorial expansion were suddenly checked about the middle of 1648 by alarming news from the Karnatak. There on 25th July his father was arrested and all his property and contingent attached by the Bijapuri commander-in-chief, Mustafa Khan, then investing Jinji in the South Arcot district. Later historians have misunderstood the cause of this act The contemporary Persian historian of Bijapur asserts that Shahji was imprisoned for displaying a spirit of insubordination and obstruction to the commander-in-chief.

Zahur, son of Zahuri, in his *Muhammad-namah* (pp. 371-372), written by order of Muhammad Adil Shah, gives the following earliest and most correct account of the incident :—"When the siege of Jinji was protracted and fighting continued long, the cunning Shahji sent an agent to Nawab Mustafa Khan begging leave to go to his own country and give repose to his troops. The Nawab replied that to retire then would be equivalent to disturbing [the work of the siege.] Then Shahji sent to say that grain was very dear in the camp, that his soldiers could not bear the privation and

*Sabh 9 The dates of the acquisition of Chakan and Kondana are not known The *Shivapur Deshpande Bahi* gives the year 1647 for the latter event, and names Bapuji Pant as the agent who effected the transfer to Shivaji, but the *Jedhe S*, from which most part of it is copied, is silent on this point

labour any longer, and that he would retire to his own country without waiting for permission [from the commander-in-chief.] The Nawab, being convinced that Shahji meant mischief and would show fight, had him arrested with such extreme cleverness and good arrangement that no part of his property was plundered, but the whole was confiscated to Government."

A later but very reliable Persian history of Bijapur, *viz.*, *Basatin-i-Salatin* (325-327), supplies some additional information:—"Shahji, withdrawing his head from obedience to the Nawab Mustafa Khan, began to oppose him, till at last the Nawab decided to arrest him. One day he made Baji Rao Ghorpade and Jaswant Rao Asad-Khani get their forces ready and sent them very early in the morning to Shahji's camp. Shahji, having passed the preceding night in mirth and revelry, was still sleeping in bed. As soon as the two Raos arrived and he learnt of their purpose, he in utter bewilderment took horse and galloped away from his house alone. Baji Ghorpade gave chase, caught him, and brought him before the Nawab, who threw him into confinement. His contingent of 3,000 cavalry was dispersed, and his camp was thoroughly looted.. Adil Shah on hearing of it......sent from his Court Afzal Khan to bring Shahji away and an eunuch to attach his property." Shahji was brought in chains to Bijapur and kept in prison along with his eldest son.

Shivaji was free but in a terrible dilemma. He could only resort to diplomacy for rescuing his father, and diplomacy pointed to only one path as open to a man in his position. The Mughal Emperor was the hereditary enemy of Adil Shah, and every rebel against Bijapur was sure to gain the Emperor's patronage if he could hold forth the chance of strengthening the imperial cause in the Deccan by the adhesion of his followers. The Mughal Emperor alone was strong enough to intimidate Adil Shah.

Shivaji first wrote to Prince Murad Bakhsh,* the Mughal viceroy of the Deccan, entreating him to secure the Emperor's pardon for Shahji's past conduct and protection for him and his sons in future, and offering to come and join the Mughal service if he was given a written assurance of safety (*qaul*) To this Murad replied on 14th March 1649, telling him to send a trusty agent first to report his demands. This was evidently done, and Murad after reporting the case to the Emperor and getting his assent, wrote to Shiva on 14th August asking him to come to Court with his father and kinsmen, that he might be created a 5-hazari, while Shahji would get back the rank he had once held in the Mughal peerage. Still later, on 31st October, Murad wrote directly to Shahji to inform him that he had received Shivaji's appeal for his father's release and that as he was soon going back to the imperial Court, he would there report the prayers of Shahji to the Emperor and take his orders. He asked the Maratha chief to send his agent to Court to receive the Emperor's *farman* and assurance of safety, and on his own behalf presented him with a robe of honour. In this letter Shambhuji and other sons of Shahji are spoken of as sharing his captivity.

Shivaji then sent Raghunath Pant Korde as his

---

*Shivaji neither wrote nor sent any envoy to Shah Jahan All his negotiations about his father were conducted with Murad, as the four original Persian letters of Murad in Parasnis's possession show Rajwade, viii 2-3, wrongly represents these letters as coming from Shah Jahan, but he is quite correct in ix, last section The Emperor never interfered for the release of Shahji

envoy to the Prince to ask for the *deshmukhi* of the Junnar and Ahmadnagar parganas. Murad, on 30th November, 1649, promised to try to secure these rights for him after reaching the Emperor's presence. Whether Shah Jahan really consented to put pressure on Adil Shah to release Shahji is very doubtful. No historian mentions it. Indeed, active Mughal intervention on behalf of Shahji seems to me very improbable. For one thing, Shah Jahan always treated Muhammad Adil Shah with marked courtesy and kindness, while Shahji was bitterly hated at the Mughal Court for the trouble he had given them in 1633-1636. Then, again, the Mughal Emperor had definitely promised in his treaties with Bijapur not to take into his service or extend his protection to any officer of Adil Shah. It is, therefore, historically true that the release of Shahji was due to the friendly mediation of Sharza Khan and the bail of Randaula Khan, two leading nobles of Bijapur. Shahji after his release is said to have lived for some time in the Tungabhadra region subduing the rebellious chieftains of his jagir in Northern Mysore. Here his eldest son Shambhuji fell in an attack on Kanakgiri, but he himself afterwards carried the fort by assault.* (*T. S.* 8*b*.)

---

* The *Jedhe Shakavali* gives 16th May 1649 as the date of this release, but it is inconsistent with Murad's letters cited above, except on the suppositions that Shivaji never replied to Murad's repeated letters [as Rajwade imagines, ix c 4-5] and that the Mughal viceroy of the Deccan did not hear of Shahji's release at Bijapur for six months after the event, though Shahji was then the foremost Hindu noble of Bijapur! Therefore, either these Persian letters (preserved at Satara) were forgeries, or Jedhe's early dates are unreliable. I am inclined to place the event at the very end of the year 1649. The *Jedhe S* says that the price of Shahji's freedom was the restoration of Kondana (*Shiva-bharat* adds, Bangalore also) to Adil Shah

The wildest stories are told by later Marathi writers about the attack on Kanakgiri, especially to connect Afzal Khan with Shambhuji's death.

§11. *Shivaji's doings from 1650 to 1655.*

Shivaji seems to have kept comparatively quiet during the six years from his father's release to his conquest of Javli , at all events he did not make many or extensive annexations, nor give any strong provocation to the Bijapur Government. I am inclined to place the acquisition of Purandar in this period

The strong fortress of Purandar, 18 miles s. s e. of Puna, was held under the nominal sway of Bijapur by a Brahman chief, Niloji surnamed Nilkanth Nayak, whose family had been in hereditary charge of it and its adjacent lands ever since the days of the Ahmadnagar dynasty. Niloji was a stern grasping man who denied his younger brothers, Pilaji and Shankaraji, any share of his power or of the income of the estate. They resented this exclusion from their birthright and appealed to Shivaji to arbitrate between them He was admitted into the fort at the Feast of Lamps (November) as a guest On the third day of his stay, the two younger brothers surprised and fettered Niloji and brought him before

---

Jedhe S has an entry stating that a son was born to Shambhuji on 25th Nov 1654

The *Shiva-bharat* gives the following account —During Shahji's captivity, the Bijapuri commander Mustafa Khan [then before Jinji and stricken by a mortal illness] sent an army under Farhad Khan to wrest Bangalore from Shahji's agent (and eldest son) Shambhuji, but it was defeated Another army was sent from Bijapur against Shivaji under Fath Khan It reached Belsar and encamped there A detachment from it, led by Balaji the son of Haibat Rao, advanced and laid siege to Shirwal, but was driven away by Shivaji's troops under Kavji Then Fath Khan marched against Purandar, where Shivaji was living, and delivered a rash assault on the fort, which ended in the rout of his army, with heavy loss *Chitnis* and the *Shedgaonkar Bakhar* tell two different tales about this attempt against Shivaji, and the *Jedhe Karina* merely supplies an embellishment to the *Shiva-bharat*, on its favourite subject of the bravery of the Jedhes and their devotion to Shivaji, but is silent about the rest of the campaign All these sources are unreliable

Shiva, who imprisoned all the three and took possession of the fort for himself! The Nayak's retainers were expelled and a Mavle garrison was placed there by Shivaji. After a few days the three captives were set free and granted the village of Chamli, in perpetuity for their maintenance. (Sabh. 9; *T. S.* 11*b*-12*a*.) From the traditions and papers of the present Nilkanth family of Chamli, V. L. Bhave has given the following account of their loss of Purandar:

Shankaraji, the second of the three brothers, was able and clever, and used at first to manage the affairs of the fort, all the brothers living together. But Niloji, the eldest, urged by his designing and imperious wife, who had secretly corrupted the garrison, one day attacked and severely wounded Shankaraji and gained control of the fort. Shivaji, who had been coveting Purandar, came to its foot with his mother and army to spend the rainy season. On the occasion of the *Dewali* he was admitted as a guest. In the night of the third day he surprised and chained all the three brothers when fast asleep and seized the fort and all the property in it. After a time, at the entreaty of that holy man the Dev of Chinchvad (whose son had married Niloji's sister), he released the brothers, gave the village of Chamli to Shankaraji, restored the *nayak*ship to Niloji, and employed their youngest brother Pilaji (alias Trimbakji) in his army. [*Sahavichar*.]

§12. *Conquest of Javli, 1656.*

At the extreme north-western corner of the Satara district lies the village of Javli, which was then the centre of a fairly large principality including nearly the whole of that district. The sub-division of Javli is "throughout hilly and thickly wooded with evergreen trees . . .The narrow rugged and steep crest of the Sahyadris, rising 4,000 feet or more above sea-level, forms its western wall; and in the valleys the tree growth is luxuriant, forming high forests." (*Bom. Gaz* xix, 3.) Within a length of 60 miles as many as 8 passes cross the range, two of them being fit for carts and now transporting a large traffic from the Deccan plateau to Mahad in Kolaba and Chiplun in Ratnagiri. There are, besides, countless gorges and foot-tracks leading from Javli to Konkan.

A Maratha family named Moré had received a grant of the State of Javli from the first Sultan of Bijapur early in the 16th century, and made the claim good by their sword. For eight generations they had conquered the petty chieftains around and amassed a vast treasure by raising forced contributions. They kept 12,000 infantry, mostly sturdy hillmen of the southern Mavals, and succeeded in getting possession of the entire district of Satara and parts of Konkan. The head of the family bore the hereditary title of Chandra Rao, conferred by a Bijapur king in recognition of the founder's personal strength and courage. The younger sons enjoyed appanages in the neighbouring villages.

The State of Javli, by its situation, barred the path of Shivaji's ambition in the south and south-west As he frankly said to Raghunath Ballal Korde, "Unless Chandra Rao is killed, the kingdom cannot be secured. None but you can do this deed I send you to him as envoy " The Brahman entered into the conspiracy, and went to Javli, attended by an escort of 125 picked men, on the pretence of making important diplomatic proposals from Shiva to Chandra Rao. (Sabh. 10.)

On the first day the envoy held the usual ceremonial

conversations. Finding out the ins and outs of the place and learning that Chandra Rao usually lived in a careless unguarded manner, Raghunath formed his plan of action. The second interview with Chandra Rao was held in a private chamber. Raghunath talked for some time, and then drew his dagger all of a sudden and stabbed Chandra Rao and his brother Surya Rao. The assassins promptly rushed out of the gate, cut their way through the alarmed and confused guards, beat back the small and hurriedly gathered band of pursuers and gained a chosen place of hiding in the forest.

Shivaji had kept himself ready to follow up his agent's crime. Immediately on hearing of the murder of the Mores, he arrived and assaulted Javli (15 Jan. 1656.) The leaderless garrison defended themselves for six hours and were then overcome. Chandra Rao's two sons and entire family were made prisoners. But his kinsman and manager, Hanumant Rao More, rallied the partisans of the house and held a neighbouring village in force, menacing Shivaji's new conquest. Shiva found that "unless he murdered Hanumant, the thorn would not be removed from Javli." (Sabh. 10.) So, he sent a Maratha officer of his household named Shambhuji Kavji with a pretended proposal of marriage to Hanumant Rao, who was then stabbed to death at a private interview. The whole kingdom of Javli now passed into Shivaji's possession and he was free to invade South Konkan with ease or extend his dominion southwards into the Kolhapur district.

§13. *The fate of the Mores critically discussed.*

Such is the account of the gaining of Javli written by Shivaji's courtier, Krishnaji Anant Sabhasad, for the eyes of that king's son Rajaram, only 14 years after Shivaji's death. There is no reason to disbelieve such an authority in a matter like this, though the writer's order of events may be rather mixed up (as it often is elsewhere in his book) Later writers tell the story somewhat differently as regards the details

T. S, *13b-14a* (also Malkaré, paras 28 and 29) says. "Shivaji sent Raghunath Ballal to Chandra Rao to ask for the hand of his fair daughter. On reaching the place, Raghunath first went to the diwan Hanumant Rao and stabbed him to death at the interview. He returned by a night-march to Shivaji (at Purandar), who was highly delighted and by quick marches arrived before Javli with a vast army and took it after six hours of fighting. The *sardars* Baji and Krishna Rao, aged 14 and 16 years respectively, were brought as prisoners to Puna and there beheaded The women and children were set free."

The *Jedhe Shakavali* (repeated by the *Karina*) merely states that Shivaji took Javli and three months later captured Raigarh, Chandra Rao (who was in it) was persuaded by two of Shivaji's Maval *deshmukhs* to evacuate the fort.

The *Shiva-bharat* (canto 18) is not more helpful. It says, "Shiva took Javli after slaying in battle Baji and Krishna Raj and their father Chandra Raj. Pratap Varma, a friend of Chandra Rao, fled to Bijapur. Coveting the position of C. R., he gratified Adil Shah by his [devoted] attendance, till that monarch promised to wrest Javli from Shiva and give it to him. Pratap helped Afzal during his campaign and brought him to Wai."

The most probable reconstruction of the history of the Javli affair, from a consideration of all the materials, seems to be this:—The then Chandra Rao, named Krishnaji and eight in succession from the founder, was a boy of sixteen and all his business was conducted by his kinsman, Hanumant Rao Moré, who was his *diwan*. Raghunath Ballal *Kordé* (and not *Atré*, as the latter was not *sabnis*), under Shivaji's orders visited Hanumant (the *diwan* or person who really ruled the estate) with a pretended offer of marriage between his master and the late Chandra Rao's daughter, and treacherously slew him at a private meeting. He escaped unscathed and quickly brought Shivaji to the scene with a vast army. Javli was captured after six hours' fighting, and several members of the More family were taken prisoner. But Chandra Rao himself was either absent from the place or had fled away before its fall. He took refuge in Raigarh (a fort belonging to him.) Shiva invested it and gained possession of it by negotiations. The two boys, Krishnaji Chandra Rao and his younger brother Baji Rao More, were carried away by Shivaji to Puna and there the elder one was beheaded. His offence is alleged by some modern theorists to have been the opening of correspondence with the Adil Shahi Government for recovering his heritage,—which would be a quite natural and legitimate desire.

The younger boy, Baji, escaped (on 28th August, according to the *Shivapur Daftar Yadi*), assumed the hereditary title of Chandra Rao, and in March 1665 joined Jai Singh for war against Shivaji. [*Haft Anjuman*, Paris MS. 113*a*, 123*a*.] With him came Ambaji Govind Rao More.

The acquisition of Javli was the result of deliberate murder and organized treachery on the part of Shivaji. His power was then in its infancy, and he could not afford to be scrupulous in the choice of the means of strengthening himself. In exactly similar circumstances, Sher Shah, his historic parallel, used similar treachery in gaining forts in South Bihar as the first step to a throne.

The only redeeming feature of this dark episode in his life is that the crime was not aggravated by hypocrisy. All his old Hindu biographers are agreed that it was an act of premeditated murder for personal gain and not a pardonable homicide done in self-defence or in the heated blood of an open fight Even Shivaji never pretended that the murder of the three Mores was prompted by a desire to found a "Hindu *swaraj*," or to remove from his path a treacherous enemy who had repeatedly abused his generous leniency

This last touch of infamy it has been left to the present generation to add. Unfortunately for the credibility of such theories, none of the genuine old historians of Shivaji in Marathi could anticipate that this line of defence would be adopted by the twentieth century admirers of the national hero; they have called the murder a murder.

Though all the three heads of the family were thus killed, some of the ordinary Mores remained at large and sought to be avenged on Shivaji, though in vain. In 1665, when Jai Singh opened a campaign against that Maratha chief, he invited these Mores to join him and carry on their blood-feud with the Bhonsles with greater hope of success.

§14. *Shivaji's further gains.*

The annexation of Javli not only opened to Shivaji a door for the conquest of the south and the west, but

* For the desperate and fantastic special pleading of Mr C V Vaidya, LL B, the reader is referred to the *Mahratta* (31 Aug 1924)

brought a very important accession to his strength, in the form of many thousands of Mavle infantrymen from among the subjects and former retainers of Chandra Rao. In short, his recruiting ground for these excellent fighters along the Sahyadri range was now doubled. The Mores had accumulated a vast treasure in eight generations of undisturbed and expanding rule, and the whole of it fell into Shivaji's hands.

Two miles west of Javli he built a new fort named Pratapgarh, and here he set up an image of his patron goddess Bhavani, as the more ancient Bhavani of Tulja-pur was beyond easy reach. On her he lavished his wealth in costly ornaments and trappings and to this shrine he made repeated pilgrimages. (Sabh. 26.)

Shivaji followed up his conquest of Javli (15th January 1656), by taking from Chandra Rao More in April his last refuge, the stupendous hill-fort of Raigarh, which was destined to be the capital of the Maratha king. On 24th September of the same year he acquired Supa about 35 miles s. e. of Puna, by one of his usual *coups d'etat*. Shambhuji Mohité, the brother of Shahji's second wife, had been left by that chief as his agent in the Supa sub-division, in independence of the administrator of Puna. But Shivaji paid him a friendly visit on a Hindu holy day of rejoicing, and overpowered his guards by a surprise attack and attached all his property. The dis-placed officer was packed off to Shahji with his personal effects, as he refused to serve under his nephew. Thus, the Supa sub-district was annexed. (Sabh. 8; *T. S.* 12.)

The possession of Supa, Baramati and Indapur rounded off the south-eastern corner of the Puna district, while the acquisition of Purandar, Rajgarh, Kondana and Torna secured Shivaji's territory by a strong chain of hill-forts on the south. Another fort in that quarter was Rohida, gained on some unknown date. North-west of Puna he acquired the forts of Tikona, Lohgarh, and Rajmachi,—the last of which stood on the Sahyadri crest (6 miles north of the Bhor pass) and overlooked the Konkan plain on the west

On 4th November 1656, Muhammad Adil Shah died, and a new scene opened in which Shivaji greatly profited, as will be described in the next chapter.

CHAPTER III.

RAPID EXTENSION OF TERRITORY AND FIRST WARS WITH MUGHALS AND BIJAPUR, 1657-1659

§1. *Relations with the Mughals up to 1657.*

For many years after his first assertion of independence, Shivaji carefully maintained peace with the Mughals. For one thing, his power was not yet secure, and it would have been the height of folly to provoke both Bijapur and Delhi at the same time. Secondly, from 1653 onwards Mughal Deccan was governed by Prince Aurangzib with singular efficiency and vigour, and his neighbours rightly dreaded giving him any offence. When Aurangzib was involved in war with Golkonda (January-March 1656), Shivaji was too busy organizing his conquests in Javli and the northern Ratnagiri district to raid Mughal territory during that Prince's absence from his charge.

On the death of Muhammad Adil Shah (4 Nov. 1656), Aurangzib began active preparations for the invasion of Bijapur, and tried to seduce as many Adil-Shahi nobles and vassals as he could. Shivaji then wrote a letter to Multafat Khan, the Mughal governor of Ahmadnagar, offering to join the imperialists if his desires were granted. To this a conciliatory reply was given, in accordance with Aurangzib's instructions to "keep the path of correspondence with him open." (*Adab.* 144*b*.)

12. *Shivaji's first raid into Mughal Deccan.*

Shivaji also wrote directly to Aurangzib. His envoy Sonaji reached the Prince's siege-camp before Bidar (in March 1657) and was assured that the Mughal Government would grant all the prayers of the Maratha chief, namely (*i*) a formal recognition of his right to all the Bijapuri forts and villages actually in his possession and (*ii*) the annexation of the port of Dabhol and the territory appertaining to it. A reply in these terms was also written to Shivaji by Aurangzib on 23rd April, 1657, when about to start for the siege of Kalianі, and Shivaji was urged to prove his devotion by rendering armed help to the Mughal cause. [Parasnis MS., letter No. 5; *Adab*. 146*a*.]

But long before this date, Shivaji had already decided on the different policy of fighting for his own hand. The vague promises of the Mughal Prince could not satisfy him. Even a less astute man than he must have known that such promises would amount to nothing in practice when the need of the imperialists would be over. He considered it more profitable to make a diversion in favour of Bijapur by raiding the south-western corner of Mughal Deccan while Aurangzib's forces were concentrated at the siege of Kaliani, beyond his south-eastern frontier. He had cunningly prepared for action by quietly recalling his envoy from Aurangzib's camp, on the pretext of consultation, (about the middle of April), and he launched on war immediately afterwards.

Two Maratha captains, Minaji Bhonslé at the head of 3,000 horse and Kashi, crossed the Bhima and plundered the Mughal villages in the Chamargunda and

Raisin sub-divisions respectively. They carried devastation and alarm to the very gates of Ahmadnagar, the chief city of Mughal Deccan. [Kambu, *3b; Adab.* 148*a*.]

A Maratha attempt to loot the city (*peth*) which nestled under shelter of the fort of Ahmadnagar was defeated, by a timely sortie of the garrison; but so great was the alarm it caused that Multafat Khan, the *qiladar* of the fort, removed the property of the inhabitants for greater safety within the fort. (*Adab.* 148*b*.)

While Minaji was raiding the Ahmadnagar district in the east, Shivaji was busy looting the Junnar sub-division in the north. In the dark night of 30th April, he silently scaled the walls of Junnar city with rope-ladders and after slaughtering the guards, carried off 300,000 *hun* in cash, 200 horses, and much costly clothing and jewellery. (Sabh. 8; *Adab.* 153*b*.) The success of the Maratha raiders was due to the negligence of the local Mughal officers (as the Delhi historian Kambu asserts) and probably also to their military weakness. Aurangzib, on hearing of these disturbances, censured the *thanahdars* and poured reinforcements into the Ahmadnagar district.

§3. *Aurangzib's defensive measures.*

Nasiri Khan, Iraj Khan and some other officers at the head of 3,000 cavalry were ordered there. Rao Karn, who was coming from Aurangabad to Bidar, was diverted from the way to the same place. Shaista Khan was ordered to detach 1,000 men from his contingent there. But Nasiri Khan's movements were provokingly slow. On 30th April he entered the pargana of Bir and four days later marched towards Ashti.[1] Thus, there was a great delay in his going to Ahmadnagar and Junnar, expelling the enemy, and ravaging Shivaji's territory, as ordered by Aurangzib. (Kambu, 3*b*; *Adab* 147*a*, 153*a*, 154*b*)

Meantime, Multafat Khan had issued from the fort of Ahmadnagar and relieved the beleaguered outpost at Chamargunda by defeating Minaji, (28th April.) But the Marathas continued to rove about the pargana for some time longer. However, the retainers of Multafat and Mirza Khan followed up their victory and at last cleared the Chamargunda sub-division (*Adab*. 110*b*, 153*b*, 154*a*)

Shivaji had stayed in the Junnar sub-division for some time, robbing the villages, as the Mughal reinforcements were late in arriving there and he found the field clear. But, at the approach of Rao Karn and Shaista Khan, he fled from the neighbourhood of Junnar city and wandered over the district for some time, as he could not be caught and crushed. (*Adab* 110*b*, 111*b*, 112*a*) But when the pressure became great, he slipped away to the Ahmadnagar district and began to plunder it. By this time (end of May), however, Nasiri Khan had reached the scene. By a forced march he surprised Shiva's army and nearly encircled it. Many of the Marathas were slain, many wounded, and the rest put to flight, (4 June.) But there was no pursuit, as the Mughal horses were too tired. (Kambu, 4*b*, *Adab* 154*a*, 156*a*.)

Aurangzib's letters to Nasiri Khan and other officers breathed fury and revenge; they must beat the raiders

---

[1] *Bir* (or Bid) is 68 m e and *Ashti* is 35 m s e of Ahmadnagar. Chamargunda (or Shrigunda) is 33 m s of Ahmadnagar (*Ind At* 39 N E) Raisin is 20 m s e of Chamargunda

back from the imperial dominions and make reprisals by entering Shiva's land from all sides, "wasting the villages, slaying the people without pity, and plundering them to the extreme"; Shivaji's possessions, Puna and Chakan, must be utterly ruined, and not the least remissness shown in slaying and enslaving the people; the village headmen and peasants of the imperial territory who had secretly abetted the enemy, must be slain without pity. (*Adab.* 147*a* and *b*, 148*a*.)

Aurangzib's new dispositions for guarding his south-western frontier showed excellent combination and judgment. Kar Talab Khan was posted near Junnar, Abdul Munim at Garh Namuna, and Nasiri Khan and Rao Karn at Panda "opposite Parenda fort," to guard the Chamargunda, Kara and Ashti parganas.* (*Adab.* 148*b*.) These officers stood facing the frontier and barring every path of the enemy's advance, so that the imperial ryots behind them might enjoy safety. The officers were further bidden to make a dash forward across the frontier, whenever they got an opportunity, ravage as much of the enemy's territory in front of them as they could, and then quickly return to the defence of their respective posts. (*Adab.* 147*b*.)

After Nasiri Khan's victory over Shiva in the Ahmadnagar district, he was ordered by Aurangzib to "pursue the Marathas and extirpate them." But this could not be done. The rains now set in with the full violence of the monsoons, and the campaign had to be

---

* *Panda* (in Pers text, *Pandeh*) is 16 m. n w of Parenda and 3 m s. of Karmala *Kara* is 9 m n w of Ashti I have followed Aurangzib's letters (in *Adab*) above, but Kambu omits Garh Namuna and says that Abdul Munim was posted at Chamargunda I have failed to trace *Garh Namuna*, unless it was a name given to the old and ruined outpost at *Pedgaon*, 8 m s of Chamargunda

closed. Shiva retreated to his own country and the Mughal officers fell back on their appointed stations, watching the frontier. "There was peace in the whole district." (*Adab.* 156*a*, 149*a*.)

June, July and August 1657 passed in enforced idleness for the imperial troops. In September the situation was complicated by the illness of Shah Jahan and the preparations for a War of Succession among his sons. Bijapur made peace with the Mughals But throughout the month of September Aurangzib continued to urge his officers not to relax their vigilance, but hold the s. w frontier in force, lest Shiva should renew his raids. About the middle of October he wrote to the governor of Ahmadnagar to take care of the city and keep his troops in readiness, lest when Nasiri Khan went back, Shiva finding the field clear should begin to plunder again (*Adab.* 149*b*, 157*b*.)

§4. *Shivaji makes peace with the Mughals.*

When in September his liege-lord, the king of Bijapur, made peace, Shivaji found it useless and even ruinous to himself to continue the war with the Mughal empire single-handed. He must try to save his patrimony. So, he wrote to Nasiri Khan offering submission, and the Khan replied in a conciliatory tone. Then Shiva, as requested, sent a trusty agent to the Khan to state his demands. These were reported to Aurangzib (*Adab.* 156*b*, 157*a*), but no definite agreement followed. Shivaji now sent Raghunath Pant to Aurangzib directly. The Prince was just then starting on his march to Northern India (25 Jan , 1658) and wrote to Shiva in reply, "Though your offences do not deserve pardon, I forgive you as you have repented. You propose that if you are granted all the villages belonging to your home [*i.e.*, Shahji's old jagir] together with the forts and territory of Konkan, after the imperialists have seized the old Nizam-Shahi territory now in the hands of Adil Shah,—you will send Sona Pandit as your envoy to my Court and a contingent of 500 horse under one of your officers to serve me, and you will protect the imperial frontiers. You are called upon to send Sonaji, and your prayers will be granted."*

But while Aurangzib received Shiva's submission with outward pleasure, his mind was not really composed about him. He omitted no precaution to maintain peace in that quarter by force, for he felt convinced that the young Maratha chief was a raider whose daring was only equalled by his cunning, and an ambitious adventurer who would place self-interest above fidelity to his plighted word or gratitude for favours received. He wrote to Mir Jumla (December, 1657), "At Nasiri Khan's departure that district has been left vacant. Attend to it, as the *son of a dog* is waiting for his opportunity." (*Adab*. 92*a*) Adil Shah was thus urged by the Prince: "Protect this country. Expel Shiva who has sneaked into the possession of some forts of the land. If you wish to entertain his services, give him jagirs in the Karnatak, far from the imperial dominions, so that he may not disturb them." (*Adab*. 163*a*.)

Aurangzib, therefore, left the Deccan without granting peace and pardon to Shivaji. The Mughals also repaired and garrisoned the old and ruined fort of Pedgaon, as a convenient outpost for operations against

* This letter, dated 24th February 1658, was not actually sent to Shivaji till after the battle of Dharmat (15 April), as a postscript reports Aurangzib's victory there (Parasnis MS, letter No 6)

Puna. (*Adab.* 157*b.*) But Shiva was freed from all fear of the Mughals by the War of Succession which kept Aurangzib busy for the next two years, 1658 and 1659.

§5. *Shivaji invades Konkan*

In the second half of the year 1657, the northward retreat of Prince Aurangzib, the likelihood of a civil war for the throne of Delhi, and the wrangles among the Bijapuri nobles about responsibility for their ill-success in the recent war with the Mughals (which culminated in the murder of the *wazir* Khan Muhammad),—all combined to remove the only checks on Shivaji's ambition, and he now launched forth on a fresh career of conquest and plunder unhampered by any fear or caution.

On 31st July he despatched Raghunath Pant to reinforce his attack on the Siddis of Janjira. And when the rains ceased and the dry season for campaigning began again (in October), he himself hastened to a new field Crossing the Western Ghats he burst into Konkan. The northern part of this coast-strip formed the Kalian (modern, Thana) district and was then held by an Arab named Mulla Ahmad of the Nawaiyat (emigrant) clan, one of the leading nobles of Bijapur. The protracted illness of Muhammad Adil Shah had detained this governor at Bijapur for a long time, and during his absence the defence of his jagir had grown slack and inefficient (*A. N.* 576). A considerable amount of disaffection and disorder seems to have prevailed among the petty chieftains of the district, which was a recent acquisition from the Nizam-Shahi State and where the authority of the new Government sat loose.

He easily seized the rich towns of Kalian* and Bhivandi (24 Oct. 1657), which were then without walls, and there took much wealth and costly merchandise. The fort of Mahuli, which had once been the last refuge of Shahji, was next captured (8 Jan. 1658.) The Kalian sub-division with some other parts of the Thana district, thus passed into Shiva's possession, and he got a firm footing in Northern Konkan, which he rapidly improved in the course of the year. His progress southwards into the Kolaba district seems to have been assisted by the petty local chiefs who were eager to throw off Muslim yoke and wrote inviting him to come. (*T. S.* 13*a.*) Surgarh (8 miles east), Birwadi (5 miles west), Tala (10 miles south), Ghosalgarh (5 m. s. w.), Bhurap or Sudhagarh (15 miles east of Roha town), Kangori (12 miles east of Mahad), and above all the impregnable fortress of Rairi (Raigarh) which was to be his future capital, all passed into his hands, and thus the Abyssinians of Janjira lost the eastern half of the Kolaba district to him. At Birwadi and Lingana (5 miles east of Raigarh) he built strong forts. From the base of Kalian, his troops plundered the neighbouring Portuguese territory (belonging to the province of Daman, called "the North" in the records), and established themselves in the fort of Aseri (midway between Mahim and Jawhar) as a permanent menace. The Portuguese are said to have bought his forbearance by promising an annual tribute, [according to the *Jedhe Karina,* but unsupported by the Portuguese records, *vide* Viceroy's letter to King of Portugal, dated Goa, 15 May 1658, in Pissurlencar, i. 4.] Kalian and

* Shivaji's chivalry to a Muhammadan girl (the daughter-in-law of Mulla Ahmad) captured in the Kalian campaign, *T S* 14*a* Tavernier (ii 205) reports the rumour that Shiva discovered buried treasure at Kalian *Jedhe S*, *T S* 13*a*—14*a*

Bhivandi were immediately turned into naval bases and dockyards by Shivaji. [*Ibid.*, letter of 16 Aug. 1659.]

But he did not occupy Mahad or the country south of that town in this campaign. Abaji Sondev was created viceroy of the province thus won in North Konkan, which included the eastern part of the Thana and Kolaba districts The history of the Maratha conflict with the Siddis of Janjira in this province will be narrated in Chapter 14.

We may conveniently pause here and take note of the exact size of the infant Maratha kingdom. At the cautious outset of his independent career (1647-48), Shivaji's territory embraced most parts of his father's western jagir and his own early annexations from Bijapur. These together covered the southern half of the Puna district, and their northern boundary was the old Mughal frontier,—a line running diagonally from the north-western to near the south-eastern corner of that district and avoiding the Mughal forts at Junnar, Visapur, and Parnir; *i e.*, for some distance the Ghod river divided the two dominions in the north; Junnar and Chamargunda belonged to the Mughals and Chakan to Shivaji. His southern boundary was marked by the outposts of Indapur and Baramati, and the forts of Rajgarh and Torna (and possibly also Kondana)

The above was his position in 1648. But by the year 1659 he had extended his dominions in the uplands or *Desh* to the southern limit of the Satara district, and in Konkan from Mahuli to near Mahad. Thus he now became master of the whole of North Konkan except the ports and adjacent lands on the west coast (which belonged to Bijapur, the Siddis, and the Portuguese) and the extreme north of the Thana district, while the country from Mahad southwards was yet to be won.

The greatly expanded Maratha kingdom was now organized on a stronger and more elaborate plan: Moro Trimbak Pingle was appointed Chancellor (*Peshwa*) in the place of the incompetent Shyamraj Nilkanth Ranjhekar, Nilo Sondev Accountant-General (*majmuadar*) *vice* Balkrishna Pant, and Netaji Palkar as Master of the Horse (*sar-i-naubat.*) Two new posts, those of *Surnis* (Superintendent of Correspondence) and *Waqnis* (News-writer) were created and given to Abaji Sondev and Gangaji Mangaji respectively.* The cavalry now mustered 10,000, out of whom 7,000 were mounted on Government horses and the rest on their own; the Mavle infantry numbered 10,000 and their commander was Yesaji Kank. (Sabh. 11.) The forts, old and newly acquired, held by Shivaji in 1659 numbered forty. (*A. N.* 576.) On 14 May, 1657 the newly-founded kingdom was blessed with the birth of an heir to the throne, the ill-fated Shambhuji.

§6. *Bijapur plans to subdue Shivaji.*

After the Mughal invasion of 1657 had rolled back and Aurangzib had marched away to Northern India, the Bijapur Government gained respite and some accession of vigour. True, the old prime-minister, Khan Muhammad, was murdered (11 Nov. 1657) on a false suspicion of collusion with Aurangzib during the late war; but his successor, Khawas Khan, was an able

* The reading of the Mahad MS of Sabh (11 *n*) has been accepted here *Jedhe S* says that Narahari Anand Rao was created *Peshwa* on 21 Aug 1661 (*T S* 13*b*), and Moro Pant *Majmuadar* on 2 Jan 1661 and *Peshwa* on 3 Apr 1662, when Nilo succeeded him as *Majmuadar*

administrator. The Queen Mother, Bari Sahiba, who virtually ruled the State till her fatal journey to Mecca (1660), was a woman of masterful spirit and experienced in the conduct of business Freed for the time being from the constant menace of the Mughals on the frontier, the Bijapur Government now began to call its refractory vassals to account Shahji was asked to punish Shivaji, but he frankly repudiated all responsibility for the conduct of his disobedient son and left the Government free to punish him without any consideration for his father's feelings Measures had, therefore, to be taken for crushing Shivaji by force.

This was, however, no easy task. Shiva's military strength was far from despicable; and the Bijapuri nobles shrank from the idea of a campaign among the hills and jungles of the Western Ghats. The command of the expedition against him went abegging at the Bijapur Court, till Afzal Khan accepted it. (Sabh. 12-13; *Jedhe S*, Malkare 30, *T. S.* 15)

§6. *Afzal Khan's expedition against Shiva.*

Abdullah Bhatari, surnamed Afzal Khan, was a noble of the first rank, who had risen to power and honour under the late Sultan of Bijapur As a general he was of the highest standing in the kingdom, being the peer of Bahlol Khan and Randaula Khan, and he had fought with conspicuous bravery and skill in the recent war with the Mughals. But the resources of Bijapur had been crippled by that war and the disorder and impoverishment natural in a regency under a veiled woman. Only 10,000 cavalry* could be spared to accompany Afzal, while

* This is the strength of Afzal's army as given by contemporaries, *viz*, *Tarikh-i-Ali II* 76 and the English letter quoted in the next note The

popular report had raised the strength of Shiva's Mavle infantry to 60,000 men as the result of his conquest of Javli, and he had also enlisted a regiment of valuable Pathan mercenaries from the disbanded soldiery of Bijapur. (*T. S. 13b.*) Afzal Khan, therefore, did not prefer an open contest of force with Shiva. Indeed, he was instructed by the Dowager Queen to effect the capture or murder of Shiva by "pretending friendship" with him and offering to secure his pardon from Adil Shah.*

The Bijapuri general had accepted the command in a spirit of bravado, and even boasted in open Court that he would bring Shiva back a captive without having once to dismount from his own horse. But his mind must have been oppressed by the heaviness of his task. He planned to effect his purpose if possible by diplomacy and raising the Maval chiefs against Shivaji. From Bijapur the expedition marched due north to Tuljapur, one of the holiest shrines in Maharashtra and the seat of Bhavani, the guardian goddess of the house of Bhonslé. Here, according to the story current among the Marathas, he ordered the stone image of Bhavani to be broken and pounded into dust in a hand-mill, and committed similar outrages at other Hindu shrines on his way.†

In a short time (probably in April), the Khan reached Wai (20 miles north of Satara), of which town and district

---

Maratha accounts, all very much later, put it at 12,000 cavalry besides infantry. (*T S* 15*b*, Sabh 13) In *A N* 577, *du hazar* is evidently a misprint for *dah hazar* The letter in *Shed* 25 is a fabrication

* "Against Shivaji the Queen this year sent Abdullah Khan with an army of 10,000 horse and foot, and because she knew with that strength he was not able to resist Shivaji, she counselled him *to pretend friendship* with his enemy, *which he did* And the other [*i e*, Shivaji], whether through intelligence or suspicion it is not known, dissembled his love toward him &c" (Revington at Rajapur to Company, 10 Dec 1659, *F R* Rajapur)

† Sabh 13 But V L Bhave gives good reasons for disbelieving these stories of atrocities, as later popular inventions (P 9 of his pamphlet)

he had been jagirdar and governor for the last ten or twelve years. At Wai he halted for several months, maturing his plan of campaign. As early as April, the Bijapur Government had sent a circular letter to all the *deshmukhs* of Maval to join Afzal Khan with their contingents and help him in subduing Shivaji As vassals of Adil Shah, they were bound in law to obey his orders, if they did not wish their hereditary land (*watan*) and office to be forfeited. The letter had some effect Khandoji Khopde, the *deshmukh* of Utroli and the rival of Kanhoji Jedhe (of Bhor) for the *deshmukhi* of Rohid-khore, waited on Afzal at Wai and gave him a written undertaking to arrest Shiva on condition of being granted the coveted *deshmukhi*. He was placed with his strong Mavle contingent in command of Afzal's vanguard. [Raj. xvii. 31, xv. 393 and 317; *Jedhe S*; *T. S. 16a*] The other Maval deshmukhs were frightened and perplexed as to what they should do. But Shivaji won seven of them over to his side with solemn promises of protection and reward.

friend his campaign was expected to open at the end of the rainy season, in October, and in the meantime Afzal halted at Wai, hatching his plots for getting Shiva seized. That chief had taken up his residence at Pratapgarh, some time before Afzal sent his land-steward Krishnaji Bhaskar to Shivaji with a very alluring message, saying, "Your father has long been a great friend of mine, and you are, therefore, no stranger to me. Come and see me, and I shall use my influence to make Adil Shah confirm your possession of Konkan and the forts you now hold I shall secure for you further distinctions and military equipment from our Government. If you wish to attend the Court, you will be welcomed. Or, if you want to be excused personal attendance there, you will be exempted." (Sabh. 13-14.)

§7. *Shivaji's danger and perplexity.*

Meantime, the news of Afzal's coming had caused great terror and perplexity among Shiva's followers. Hitherto they had surprised obscure forts, looted isolated convoys, or fought skirmishes with the small irregular forces of private jagirdars. Here was their first encounter with the regular forces of Bijapur, led by a famous general, and numbering 10,000 with artillery, transport, and all the other material of the best-equipped armies of that age. Moreover, Afzal's march from Bijapur to Wai had been an unbroken success; the Marathas had not ventured to oppose him in the open, and he had freely looted and laid waste the territory of Shiva that he had crossed. (*Tarikh-i-Ali II.* 76-77.) Tales of his irresistible strength and ruthlessness had reached the Maratha camp. Shivaji's officers naturally shrank from the idea of resistance. At the first council of war which he held, they urged him to make peace, as the enemy was strong and hostilities would only cause a great loss of life to their side. (Sabh. 14).

This was the most critical moment in the career of Shivaji. If he capitulated to Afzal Khan, all his hopes of independence and future greatness would be gone for ever, and he would have to end his days as a tame vassal of Bijapur, even if he escaped his sovereign's vengeance for his late rebellion. Yet, the open defiance of Bijapur authority now would for ever close the door to reconciliation with that State, and he must be prepared ever afterwards to defend his life and independence against the power of that kingdom and of the Mughals and other enemies, without a single friend or protector to turn to in the wide world. His ministers and generals advocated the more ignoble policy. Shiva himself was in a terrible dilemma. For a night he pondered on his life's choice and then chose the manlier part A legend, dating from his lifetime, tells us that the care-worn chieftain's sleep was broken by a vision of the goddess Bhavani who urged him to confront Afzal boldly and promised him victory and her full protection. (Sabh. 14)

His mind was made up. Next morning the council met again. Moved by Shiva's manly words, appeal to their sense of honour, and report of the goddess's blessings, they resolved on war. He now made his dispositions for the contest with the utmost forethought and skill. He took counsel of his mother, who blessed him and foretold his success, and then he left minute instructions for carrying on the government in the event of his being killed. The armies under Moro Trimbak Pingle and Netaji Palkar were summoned from Konkan and the Ghats respectively, and ordered to take post within easy reach of Pratapgarh. (Sabh. 15)

§8. *Plots and counter-plots.*

Then came Afzal's envoy, Krishnaji Bhaskar, with the invitation to a parley. Shiva treated him with respect, and at night met him in secrecy and solemnly appealed to him as a Hindu and a priest to tell him of the Khan's real intentions. Krishnaji yielded so far as to hint that the Khan seemed to harbour some plan of mischief. Shivaji then sent the envoy back with Gopinath Pant, his own agent, agreeing to Afzal's proposal of an interview, provided that the Khan gave him a solemn assurance of safety. Gopinath's real mission was to find out the strength of Afzal's army and other useful information about it and learn for himself what the Khan's real aim was. Through Gopinath Shiva vowed that no harm would be done to Afzal during the interview, and Afzal, on his part, gave similar assurances of his honesty of purpose. But Gopinath learnt by a liberal use of bribes that Afzal's officers were convinced that "he had so arranged matters that Shiva would be arrested at the interview, as he was too cunning to be caught by open fight." On his return, Gopinath told it all to Shiva and urged him to anticipate the treacherous attack on himself by murdering Afzal at a lonely meeting and then surprising his army. (Sabh. 16-18.)

Shiva, taking the hint from Gopinath, feigned terror and refused to visit Wai, unless the Khan met him nearer home and personally promised him safety and future protection. Afzal agreed to make this concession. By Shiva's orders a path was cut through the dense forest all the way from Wai to Pratapgarh and food and drink were kept ready for the Bijapur army at various points of it. By way of the Radtondi pass (below 'Bombay Point' of the Mahabaleshwar plateau), Afzal Khan marched to Par, a village lying one mile below Pratapgarh on the south, and his men encamped there in scattered groups, deep down in the valley near every pool of water at the source of the Koyna.

Gopinath was sent up the hill to report the Khan's arrival. The meeting was arranged to take place next day. The place chosen for the interview was the crest of an eminence, below the fort of Pratapgarh, and overlooking the valley of the Koyna. On both sides of the forest-path leading up the hill-side to the pavilion picked soldiers were posted in ambush at intervals by Shivaji.

Here he erected tents and set up a richly decorated canopy with gorgeous carpets and cushions worthy of a royal guest.

Then he prepared himself for the meeting. Under his tunic he wore a coat of chain armour and below his turban he placed a steel cap for the protection of the skull. What offensive arms he had, nobody could see; but concealed in his left hand was a set of steel claws (*baghnakh*) fastened to the fingers by a pair of rings, and up his right sleeve lay hidden a thin sharp dagger called the scorpion (*bichwa*) His companions were only two, but both men of extraordinary courage and agility,—Jiv Mahala, an expert swordsman, and Shambhuji Kavji, the murderer of Hanumant Rao More. Each of them carried two swords and a shield.

As the party was about to descend from the fort a saintly female figure appeared in their midst. It was Jija Bai. Shiva bowed to his mother She blessed him saying, "Victory be yours!" and solemnly charged his companions to keep him safe; they vowed obedience. Then they walked down to the foot of the fort and waited.

§9. *Interview between Shiva and Afzal.*

Meanwhile Afzal Khan had started from his camp at Par, with a strong escort of more than a thousand musketeers. Gopinath objected to it, saying that such a display of force would scare away Shiva from the interview, and that the Khan should, therefore, take with himself only two bodyguards exactly as Shiva had done. So, he left his troops some distance behind and made his way up the hill-path in a *palki* accompanied by two soldiers and a famous swordsman named Sayyid Banda, as well as the two Brahman envoys, Gopinath and

Krishnaji. Arrived in the tent, Afzal Khan angrily remarked on its princely furniture and decorations as far above the proper style of a jagirdar's son. But Gopinath soothed him by saying that all these rich things were meant to be soon sent to the Bijapur palace as the first fruits of Shiva's submission.

Messengers were sent to hurry up Shiva, who was waiting below the fort. He advanced slowly, then halted on seeing Sayyid Banda, and sent to demand that the man should be removed from the tent. This was done, and at last Shivaji entered the pavilion. On each side four men were present,—the principal, two armed retainers and an envoy. But Shiva was seemingly unarmed,* like a rebel who had come to surrender, while the Khan had his sword at his side.

The attendants stood below. Shiva mounted the raised platform and bowed to Afzal. The Khan rose from his seat, advanced a few steps, and opened his arms to receive Shiva in his embrace. The short slim Maratha's head only came up to the shoulders of his opponent. Suddenly Afzal tightened his clasp, and held Shiva's neck fast in his left arm with an iron grip, while with his right hand he drew his long straight-bladed dagger and struck at the side of Shiva. The hidden armour rendered the blow harmless. Shiva groaned in agony as he felt himself being strangled. But in a moment he recovered from the surprise, passed his left arm round the Khan's waist and tore his bowels open with a blow of the steel claws. Then with the right hand he drove the *bichwa* into Afzal's side.

---

* Khafi Khan, ii 116, states that both Afzal and Shivaji came to the interview unarmed But *kamar wa karda*, 'with no sword girt on the waist,' was the customary attitude of the defeated party, so often described in Persian histories, and Afzal was not in that humiliating position

The wounded man relaxed his hold, and Shivaji wrested himself free, jumped down from the platform, and ran towards his own men outside

The Khan cried out, "Treachery! Murder! Help! Help!" The attendants ran up from both sides. Sayyid Banda faced Shiva with his long straight sword and cut his turban in twain, making a deep dint in the steel cap beneath Shiva quickly took a rapier from Jiv Mahala and began to parry But Jiv Mahala came round with his other sword, hacked off the right arm of the Sayyid, and then killed him.

Meanwhile the bearers had placed the wounded Khan in his *palki*, and started for his camp. But Shambhuji Kavji slashed at their legs, made them drop the *palki*, and then cut off Afzal's head, which he carried in triumph to Shiva.*

§10. *Afzal's army routed and plundered*

Freed from danger, Shivaji and his two comrades then made their way to the summit of Pratapgarh, and fired a cannon This was the signal for which his troops were waiting in their ambush in the valleys below. At once the armies of Moro Trimbak and Netaji Palkar and the thousands of Mavles rushed on the Bijapuri camp from four sides. Afzal's officers and soldiers alike were panic-stricken at the news of their chief's death and this unexpected attack, in that unknown region, where every bush seemed to be alive with enemies. But the way of escape was closed and they had perforce to fight. For

* The head was buried beneath a tower (called *Abdullah burj*) in an outwork on the south-eastern side of the lower fort A short distance from it is the temple of Bhavani built by Shivaji (*Bom Gaz* xix, 546-547) For illustrations, see Parasnis's *Mahabaleshwar*, 143 and 144

three hours many of the entrapped soldiers made a desperate defence, evidently in isolated groups, without any common plan or superior guidance. The Marathas fought on their own ground, in the full flush of their initial triumph, confident of succour close behind, and led by eminent chiefs. The carnage in the Bijapuri army was terrible. "All who begged quarters holding grass between their teeth [as a mark of humility] were spared, the rest were put to the sword." 3,000 men were killed, according to the report that reached the English factory at Rajapur a few days later. The Mavle infantry hacked at the fleeing elephants, "severing the tails, breaking the tusks, or chopping off the legs." Even camels were cut down as they crossed the path of the assailants.

The booty taken was immense: all the artillery, waggons, ammunition, treasure, tents and equipage, transport-cattle and baggage of an entire army, fell into the victors' hands. Among them were 65 elephants, 4,000 horses, 1,200 camels, 2,000 bundles of clothing, and 10 *lakhs* of Rupees in cash and jewellery.

The prisoners included one sardar of high rank, two sons of Afzal, and two Maratha chiefs namely Lambaji Bhonslé and Jhujhar Rao Ghatgé. All the captured women and children, Brahmans and camp-followers were immediately released. One section of the beaten army, consisting of Afzal Khan's wives and eldest son, Fazl Khan, escaped round the source of the Koyna, under the guidance of Khandoji Khopde and his contingent of Mavle friendlies.*

---

* Meeting with Afzal Khan Sabh 19-21, *Jedhe S*, *T S* 16*a*—17*b*; *A N* 577, *Dilkasha* 19, K K ii 116-118, Rajapur Factory Records, Fryer, ii 61, *Powadas*, 12-18 Plunder of his army Sabh 23-24, *T S* 17*b*, *Powadas*, 19-20 Escape of Fazl Khan Sabh 24 *Tarikh-i-Ali Adil Shah*

A grand review was held by Shivaji below Pratapgarh The captured enemy, both officers and men, were set free and sent back to their homes with money, food and other gifts The Maratha soldiers who had fought so gallantly were rewarded, if the fallen warriors had grown-up sons, they were enlisted in their fathers' places; if otherwise, their widows were given pensions amounting to half their pay. The wounded received rewards from 25 to 200 *hun* according to the severity of their hurt. The officers were presented with elephants, horses, robes, jewellery and grants of land (Sabh. 25)

§11. *Legends about Afzal Khan.*

The tragic fate of Afzal Khan has most profoundly stirred the popular imagination in his own country and in that of his enemy. At his village of Afzalpura, close to Bijapur city, the gloomy legend sprang up that before starting on this fatal expedition, he had a premonition of his coming end, and killed and buried all his 63 wives, lest they should share another's bed after his death. The peasants still point to the height from which these hapless victims of man's jealousy were hurled into a deep pool of water, the channel through which their drowned bodies were dragged out with hooks, the place where they were shrouded, and the 63 tombs, of the same shape, size and age, standing close together in regular rows on the

---

II, 76-81, contains a maximum of mere words and rhetorical flourishes but few facts *B S* 370 is even more meagre in details, but concise *Jedhe S* and *T S* say that Khandoji Khopde was caught and beheaded by Shivaji, but *J Karina* (recent) alleges that he was only mutilated of one arm and one leg (by order of Shivaji) The *Akhbarat* proves that he was beheaded The Khan's artillery is said to have been left at Wai and captured the next day

same platform, where they were laid in rest. Utter desolation has settled on the spot. Where his mansion once stood with its teeming population, the traveller now beholds a lonely wilderness of tall grass, brambles and broken buildings, the fittest emblem of his ruined greatness. The only form of life visible is the solitary bird, startled by the unwonted presence of a human visitor.* Other traditions tell us that ill omens dogged his steps from the very outset of his campaign against Shivaji. (*Powadas*, 7, 11.)

§12. *Ballad of Afzal Khan.*

Among the Marathas the destruction of Afzal Khan caused the wildest exultation; it marked the dawn of their national independence. The defeat of Bijapur was complete: the chief had fallen, his army had ceased to exist, and the victory, both in respect of carnage and of booty, was the most complete possible. The incident caught hold of the public imagination of Maharashtra as the most glorious event in the history of the race. Ballads were composed by the wandering bards (*gondhalis*), in response to the popular demand, to celebrate the victory. The earliest and most valuable of them is lost (except for a single couplet) Another, but much later and quite untrustworthy, poem has been preserved, which expands the contest into a Homeric duel with all its details and supernatural adjuncts. Every class of Marathas, from

* This was the appearance of Afzalpura when I visited it in Oct, 1916 The French traveller Abbe Carre, who visited the place in 1673, states that he found a large number of workmen engaged in cutting the stones which were to be used in the mausoleum of Afzal Khan, and he was "surprised [to note] that in the epitaph were mentioned the [200] women of his harem whose throats he had caused to be cut" [*Voyage*, ii 16 and 11]

the officers of Shambhuji's Court to the soldiers in their camps and the peasants in their hamlets, welcomed the minstrel and crowded together to listen to this story of the first triumph of their national hero, set forth with graphic details which made the whole scene live before their eyes. The short ringing lines of the ballad (*powada*) almost reproduce the tramp of the soldiery, the journeys of the rival chiefs, their meeting, the exchange of abuse (quite in the style of the *Mahabharat* !), the death-grapple, the battle at Par, and the triumph of the Maratha army. As the bard's narrative passes rapidly from stage to stage of the whole contest, the audience follow him with breathless attention, their blood courses in unison with the verses, and they are wound up to a high pitch of excitement as the spirit of the actual march or fight catches them.

To the Marathas the fight with Afzal has always appeared as at once a war of national liberation and a crusade against the desecrator of temples. To them Afzal Khan typifies the bold bad man, who combines treachery with frightfulness, and defies God and man alike Their historians from the earliest times have seen no element of murder in the incident, but always described it as a glorious example of the sagacity, courage and agility with which their national hero averted a treacherous plot against his own life, made the treachery recoil on the plotter's head, and avenged the outraged shrines of their gods.

Flushed with their victory over Afzal Khan (10 November, 1659) and the destruction of his army, the Marathas poured into South Konkan and the Kolhapur district, capturing the fort of Panhala, defeating another Bijapuri army, and making extensive conquests (Dec

1659—Feb., 1660),* which will be described in Chapter 10. But in the following March Shivaji was called upon to meet a dangerous attack on his own dominions by a combination of the most powerful of his enemies.

APPENDIX I.

AFFAIR OF AFZAL KHAN

Was the slaying of Afzal Khan a treacherous murder or an act of self-defence on the part of Shivaji? No careful student of the sources can deny that Afzal Khan intended to arrest or kill Shivaji by treachery at the interview The absolutely contemporary and impartial English factory record (Rajapur letter, 10 Dec 1659) tells us that Afzal Khan was instructed by his Government to secure Shivaji by "pretending friendship with him" as he could not be resisted by armed strength, and that the latter, learning of the design, made the intended treachery recoil on the Khan's head This exactly supports the Marathi chronicles on the point that Shivaji's spies learnt, from Afzal's officers, about the Khan's plan to arrest him by treachery at the proposed interview, and that Afzal's envoy Krishnaji Bhaskar was also induced to divulge this secret of his master

Who struck the first blow at the interview? The old Maratha chroniclers (as distinct from the English-educated 20th century apologists of the national hero) all assert that it was Afzal These genuine old historians never shrink from charging Shivaji with murder or treachery whenever they know him to be really guilty They wrote long before Grant Duff's book had roused public indignation against Shivaji's alleged murder of an invited guest It is, therefore, impossible to contend that the story of Afzal having struck the first blow was an invention of the modern Marathas after English education had wakened their conscience to the wickedness of pre-meditated political murders Sabhasad (1694) and Malkare (? 1750) at least cannot be suspected of any design to whitewash their hero's character by falsifying history In saying that Afzal struck the first blow, they truly record a genuine old tradition and not a modern nationalist invention

Shivaji's elaborate protection of his person before going to the interview and his placing an ambush round Afzal's forces cannot be taken as proofs of a treacherous intention Secret assassination is the favourite weapon of decadent monarchies, and many such murders had taken place in the sultanates of the Deccan before this time, as I showed in detail in the *Modern Review*, (vol I 1907, p 441) Shivaji was fully convinced—and

---

* The *Shiva-bharat* gives a detailed and romantic description of these operations as well as the affray with Afzal Kh , which, from the character of this poem, I have been unable to accept as historical

with good reason, as we know,—that Afzal meant treachery. He would have been wanting in common prudence if he had not taken these precautions to save himself.

A friend (Prof. A. Rahman) has asked me, "If Afzal meant treachery why did he not keep his troops in readiness for delivering an assault or at least for defending themselves?" My answer is that Afzal believed that the death of Shivaji would lead to the immediate collapse of his upstart power and no attack on his leaderless troops would be necessary. He was, moreover, ignorant of the position and strength of the enemy's forces and did not know that two large Maratha armies had arrived by rapid marches in his neighbourhood, under Netaji and Moro Pant.

The weight of recorded evidence as well as the probabilities of the case supports the view that Afzal Khan struck the first blow and that Shivaji only committed what Burke calls, a 'preventive murder'. It was, as I wrote in the *Modern Review* in 1907, "a case of diamond cut diamond."

CHAPTER IV

Strenuous Warfare, 1660-1664

§1. *Shaista Khan sent against Shivaji.*

Among the administrative changes made by Aurangzib at his second coronation (July, 1659) was the posting of Shaista Khan to the viceroyalty of the Deccan, in the place of Prince Muazzam. This able and spirited general had already governed Malwa and the Deccan and had taken a distinguished part in Aurangzib's recent invasion of Golkonda. Chief among the tasks entrusted to him was the suppression of Shivaji. And in discharging this duty he was fortunate enough to secure the hearty co-operation of Bijapur, which forced the Maratha chief to divide his army into two and therefore to be defeated in both the theatres of war.

After Shivaji had followed up his victory over Afzal Khan's leaderless army by defeating the combined forces of Rustam-i-Zaman and Fazl Khan, and taking Panhala in the Kolhapur district and many places in Ratnagiri, Ali Adil Shah II. felt it necessary to march in person against the audacious rebel. But just at this time Siddi Jauhar, an Abyssinian slave who had usurped the fief of Karnul and defied the royal authority, wrote to Bijapur offering to make his submission if his position was recognized. The Sultan agreed, gave Jauhar the title of Salabat Khan, and sent him with an army to put down Shiva. Jauhar easily swept away the Maratha resistance in the open, and drove Shivaji into Panhala (2nd March), which he besieged with a force of 15,000 men.

§2. *Shivaji besieged in Panhala fort.*

The siege dragged on for over six months; all the paths of ingress and egress were closed to the garrison. Shivaji found himself in a fatal trap. So, he wrote a secret letter to Jauhar, deceitfully begging his protection and offering to make an alliance with him In order to negotiate for the terms he asked for a passport Jauhar, "who was both fool and traitor," swallowed the bait; he assured Shivaji of his protection, gave him a safe conduct, and flattered himself that with Shiva for an ally he would be able to create a kingdom of his own in independence of Adil Shah. Next day Shivaji with only two or three followers visited Jauhar at midnight, and was received in *darbar* After oaths of co-operation had been taken on both sides, Shivaji returned quickly to the fort, and the pretended siege was continued

But there was one determined enemy of Shivaji in the Bijapuri army. Fazl Khan, the son of Afzal, and his chief retainer Siddi Halal, pressed the siege in earnest. A huge fort like Panhala could not, however, be taken by 15,000 men, even if all of them put their heart in the work Shivaji had made some sorties and broken up the siege-trenches with heavy slaughter, forcing the Bijapuris to remove their camp to a safe distance from the fort. In these night-attacks Kartoji Gujar distinguished himself and won the title of *Pratap Rao* and the rank of a general (*sar-i-naubat*.) The Bijapuri army was terrified, and Fazl Khan henceforth avoided confronting Shivaji himself and transferred his operations against the neighbouring fort of Pavangarh. Seizing a hillock near it, he mounted guns and began to throw shells into the fort The Maratha commandant of Pavangarh found his position untenable and pressed Shivaji for relief.

Shivaji found that further delay would ruin him by making escape from that fatal trap impossible. With Pavangarh lost, Panhala could be easily starved into surrender. So, one dark night (13th July), leaving a part of his forces to hold Panhala as long as possible, he slipped out of it with the rest of his men, fell on the Bijapuri trenches below Pavangarh, and in the ensuing confusion took the road to Vishalgarh, 27 miles to the west.

His escape was soon detected and a strong Bijapuri force under Fazl Khan and Siddi Halal set out in pursuit. The day broke while the fugitives were still at Gajapur, eight miles short of their destination, and it was discovered that the pursuers had kept up with them by marching all night with the aid of Bengal lights (*mahtabs*.) Shivaji was hopelessly outnumbered and his escort was worn out. Happily, the road here led through a narrow ravine which a few desperate men could hold against odds. Baji Prabhu, the *deshpande* of Hirdas Maval, agreed to defend the mouth of the pass with half the troops till Shivaji should reach Vishalgarh with the other half and signal his safe arrival by gun-fire. The Bijapuris delivered three bloody assaults on the heroic rear-guard, all of which were beaten off. For five hours after dawn, the obstinate struggle was maintained, with a loss of 700 men. Then the signal gun was heard, announcing Shivaji's safe arrival in his asylum. But Baji Prabhu was lying down mortally wounded. The faithful servant had carried out his task, at the cost of his life, and the knowledge cheered his last moments. Karnataki musketeers are said to have at last cleared the pass with their fire, and the remnant of the defending Mavles fled to the hills with the body of their chief. The Bijapuris pushed on to

Vishalgarh, but wisely gave up the thought of undertaking a siege in that terrible region. They fell back on Panhala and thence on Bijapur.*

When the news of Jauhar's treacherous coquetting with Shivaji reached the ears of Ali Adil Shah, that king burst into anger, and left his capital (on 5th August) for the Panhala district in order "to punish both the rebels." He halted at Miraj and sent his vanguard towards Panhala. Jauhar now found that his master could not be befooled any longer. So, he made the Marathas at last give up Panhala to him (on 22nd September), and put an end to the long siege. The fort was soon afterwards handed over by Jauhar to the agents of Adil Shah.

A month after Shivaji had been forced to quit Panhala in the extreme south of his dominions, his arms met with another disaster in the extreme north. On 15th August, his fort of Chakan, 18 miles north of Puna, was captured by the Mughals. To explain how it happened, we shall have to trace the course of the war in that quarter from its commencement.

---

* Siege of Panhala, Foster, X 251, 370-387, *Tarikh-i-Ali II*, 82-93, *B S* 371-376, *T S* 19, Malkaré 37-38. *Jedhe* gives the dates thus: "2 March, Shivaji again comes to Panhala and is there besieged by Siddi Jauhar. 13 July Shivaji descends from Panhala and goes to Khelna, pursued by Jauhar's forces, Baji Prabhu being slain. 22 Sep., Shivaji cedes Panhala to Jauhar and makes peace with him."

accept the English factory numbers,—15,000 besiegers and five or six t[illegible]sand besieged,—as against the Marathi exaggeration of eighty thousa[illegible]d Bijapuris and sixty thousand Mavles. *Dilkasha*, i 37, says that Shiva[illegible] [illegible]ad only 3,000 cavalry and 5,000 infantry when besieged in Panhala. Jauhar established his head-quarters at Kolhapur. The English factor Revington tried to sell him some ordnance and ammunition and personally took a mortar and some shells to Jauhar's camp, early in April. He promised that these shells "would undoubtedly be the chiefest disturbers of the besieged." But the mortar had not the desired effect at trial, and Jauhar, refused to pay for the munitions, though the English traders continued, some at Panhala, others at Kolhapur as late as October 1660.

§ 3. *Shaista Khan occupies Puna.*

Early in 1660, Shaista Khan opened the campaign against Shivaji from the north, after arranging for an attack upon the Maratha dominions by the Bijapuris from the south at the same time. Leaving Ahmadnagar with a vast army on 25th February, the Khan marched southwards along the eastern side of the Puna district, methodically capturing and garrisoning all the strongholds that guarded the approaches to Puna on the east and south.

The Marathas at first retreated before him without risking a battle. By way of Sonwadi (close to the Dhond railway station) and Supa (16 miles s. w. of Dhond), he reached Baramati (18 miles s. e. of Supa) on 5th April. At the last two places were mud-forts which the enemy had evacuated. He next worked his way westwards up the valley of the Nira river, by way of Hol, reaching Shirwal, 26 miles south of Puna, on 18th April. Like a wise general, Shaista Khan left detachcments at all these outposts, to guard his line of communication and hold the forts. A flying column sent from Shirwal sacked the villages round Rajgarh (22 miles due west.)

From Shirwal the Mughal army moved along the Nira river 16 miles northwards to Shivapur (near Khed), and thence due eastwards through Garara, arriving at Saswad (13 miles east of Shivapur and 18 miles south-east of Puna) on 1st May.

Up to this point the Mughal advance had been unopposed, the Marathas only hovering at a distance to cut off supplies and skirmishing with the foraging parties. They made their first stand near the pass leading from Shivapur to Garara. On 30th April a body of 3,000 Maratha cavalry threatened the Mughal rear-guard under Rao Bhao Singh, but were attacked and routed after a long fight.

From Saswad a small Mughal detachment raided the villages at the foot of Purandar fort. They were attacked by 3,000 of the enemy, but held their ground by fighting desperately at close quarters, though they lost 50 in killed and wounded. Reinforcements arrived, routed the enemy, and pursued them to the pass which was commanded by the guns of Purandar. The Mughals, flushed with victory, cleared the pass at a gallop, in the teeth of a hot fire from the fort-walls, and dispersed the enemy assembled beyond it. The victors returned to their camp at Saswad in the evening. Thence, after a four days' halt at Rajwah, they entered Puna on 9th May.

§4. *Shaista Khan captures Chakan.*

Shaista Khan had decided to pass the rainy season with his army at Puna, then a small hamlet. But before his arrival there, the enemy had totally destroyed the grain and fodder in the country round Puna and Chakan and removed all traces of habitation. And now the many rivers between Puna and the Mughal frontier being in flood, no provision reached his camp, and his army had to undergo great hardship from scarcity. He, therefore, decided to remove his camp from Puna to Chakan, 18 miles northwards, as being nearer to Ahmadnagar and the Mughal dominion, whence supplies could more easily reach him. (*A. N.* 584-'5.)

Chakan is a place of great strategic importance. On the east it is separated from the imperial territory by the shallow upper courses of the Bhima and Ghod rivers only, with no difficult mountain pass to cross. Its possession would have greatly shortened Shaista Khan's line of communication with his base of supplies at Ahmadnagar and also secured his camp against any attack from the north. Moreover, Chakan is only 31 miles due east of the Bhorghat pass and commands the shortest route leading from Ahmadnagar to Konkan.

Leaving Puna on 19th June, the Khan arrived in the vicinity of Chakan on the 21st, reconnoitred the fort and distributed the lines of investment among his officers. The fort of Chakan is a square enclosure with bastioned fronts and towers at the four corners. The walls are high, with a ditch 30 ft. deep and 15 ft. wide all around. The only entrance is in the eastern face, and passes through five or six gateways. Beyond the walls there is an outwork of mud with a ditch, the remnant of a very old fortification. (*Bom. Gaz.* xviii. pt. iii., p. 121; *Ind. Antiq.* ii. 43, iv. 352.)

Shaista Khan, after throwing up defensive earthworks round the positions taken up by the four divisions of his army, began to run trenches towards the fort-walls, construct raised platforms at suitable points, and mount on them large pieces of artillery brought from the Mughal forts in the Deccan. Though the heavy showers of the rainy season hampered his work and the defenders kept up a galling fire, he pressed the siege vigorously. After 54 days of hard labour a mine was carried from his own position in the north to under the tower at the north-eastern corner, and it was exploded at 3 P.M. on 14th August, 1660. The work and its defenders were blown up; the Mughals rushed to the assault, but found to their surprise that behind the breach the enemy had thrown up a high embankment of earth which they held in force and from the shelter of which they assailed the Mughals with rockets, musket-shots, bombs and stones. The storming party was checked with heavy loss, but clung to the blood-stained ground for the night.

Next morning (15th August) they resumed the attack, scaled the wall, and captured the main fort, putting many of the garrison to the sword and driving the rest into the citadel. In a short time even the last-named work capitulated. But the imperialists had to purchase their victory at a heavy price, losing 268 killed and 600 wounded. [*A. N.* 585-588; Tavernier, i. 409 confused.]

Firangji Narsala, an old officer of the days of Shahji, had been left by Shiva in charge of Chakan, with orders to hold out as long as he could, but to surrender when driven to extremities, because it was impossible for Shiva, then battling with the Bijapuris near Panhala, to divert any force for the relief of Chakan, 140 miles away in the north. For nearly two months Firangji had defended his post with tireless energy, "incessantly showering shots, bullets and rockets at the besiegers." He had disputed every inch of the ground on the two days of assault. And now, hopeless of aid, he capitulated with honour. Shaista Khan greatly admired the gallant *qiladar* and pressed him to enter the imperial service on high pay. But Firangji refused to prove false to his salt, and was allowed to go back to his master with his troops.

§5. *The fighting in 1661-63 and conquest of Ratnagiri district.*

Shivaji's defeat at Chakan and Panhala was followed

by a lull in the war during the last three months of the year 1660, which he spent quietly at Rajgarh, in planning how to compensate himself for these losses in the Desh country by transferring the war to another part of Bijapuri territory, namely Konkan, or the country west of the Sahyadri range, where the government was very weakly exercised by countless petty vassal Rajahs and Bijapuri city-governors. There was in that province no single powerful viceroy with an army of his own, able to unite the local feudatories under one central authority, exact loyal service from them, and thus successfully oppose an invader like Shivaji, who was his own master and could direct all his resources with absolute unity of command and policy.

Shaista Khan, too, on his return to Puna (end of August 1660) after the capture of Chakan, spent the rainy season there in enforced inactivity. Nor was he eager to lay siege to any more Maratha forts, as even the small and comparatively weak castle of Chakan, situated in the plain, had cost him nearly nine hundred men to take it. He employed his time more usefully in inducing Ghalib, the Bijapuri commandant of Parenda, to surrender that fort to Aurangzib for a high price. The terms were approved by the Emperor, and large Mughal forces were detached from Puna to Parenda to take possession of it (20th November), overawe any opposition that might be made at the last moment, and occupy the district around it.

At the beginning of next year (1661), Shaista Khan turned his attention to the Kalian district or North Konkan. Here a small Mughal force, only 3,000 strong, under Ismail, had been operating since April last and had occupied a part of the country, though the important cities and forts (like Kalian) remained unconquered. These gains had been placed under a faujdar named Salabat Khan Deccani, with a contingent of friendly Marathas, among whom Babaji Bhonslé, Raghuji, Shambhuji Kavji and Babaji Ram (or Rana) Honap,—a former *deshpande* of Puna,—are named. [*A N.* 584; Malkaré, 42]

But local levies could effect little, and it was necessary to complete the Mughal conquest of Konkan and extinguish the last traces of Shivaji's power there by pouring into the country large reinforcements of imperial troops under a high commander. The general chosen for this purpose was Kar Talb Khan, an Uzbak, who had attained to the rank of a *4-hazari* as early as the battle of Dharmat (1657), and had recently commanded a division in the Parenda district. With him Shaista Khan sent many of his own Rajput and Muslim subordinates and local allies (such as Rai Baghini, the heroic widow of Udaji Ram, the jagirdar of Mahur in Berar.)

Marching from Puna by way of Lohgarh, Kar Talb Khan descended into Konkan by a pass a little to the south of the Bhorghat. While his soldiers, encumbered with artillery and baggage, struggled painfully and in alarm through the dense jungles, steep rocks and narrow broken roads on to Umbarkhind (about 15 miles due east of Pen), Shivaji by secret and rapid marches came up with them and cut off their lines of advance and retreat alike. Kar Talb had to offer battle under these adverse conditions and suffered heavy losses. His army seemed doomed to perish from thirst, without the power to move. In despair he gave up all the property in his camp and paid a large ransom to Shivaji and thus bought a safe retreat for his army (3rd February, 1661.)

The victorious Shivaji now divided his forces; and while one army under Netaji was detached to act against the Mughals, he himself with the other invaded Bijapuri territory in Konkan, "to avenge the loss of Panhala." The Kalian district having been thus freed from the new enemies, Shivaji left it alone, and marched southwards, easily capturing city after city, till all the coast-strip from Danda-Rajpuri to Kharepatan was commanded by him, and the country further south, as far as Goa, seemed to lie at his mercy, when he would renew the campaign next dry season. His movements were so rapid, the local authorities were so divided and unprepared for defence, that no resistance was offered, but the Rajahs and city-governors fled in consternation before the oncoming flood of Maratha invasion. The wiser among them recognized resistance to him as futile and expectation of support from Bijapur vain, and so made their peace with him by offering him obedience and tribute.

Nizampur (22 miles due east of Janjira) was raided, and then the port of Dabhol belonging to a chieftain surnamed Dalvé was captured and placed under an agent of Shivaji (Feb. 1661.) Jaswant Rao, the Rajah of Pallivana, who had loyally helped Jauhar during the Panhala campaign, took refuge with Surya Rao, the Rajah of Prabhavali, (its chief town being Shringarpur.)* The

---

* I take it that *Pallivana* is the Sanskritized form of *Palavna*, a town (giving its name to a district) situated 12 m n of Dapoli, while Mandangarh is 5 m n of Palavna The fort of *Palgarh* (built by Shivaji) is in the Khed sub-division, 6 m n of Khed *Sangameshwar* is a well-known holy city, 10 m n w of Devrukh *Shringarpur* is 8 m n e of Sangameshwar, and is overlooked by *Prachitgarh*, 2 m to its east, the Tivra pass being 4 m s of it [Degree sheet 47 G] *Prabhavali* or Pravanvalli is just below Vishal-

Muslim governor of Sangameshwar fled away, and so did all the inhabitants who had anything to lose. The town was thrown into the greatest disorder and alarm. Shivaji therefore sent Pilaji Nilkanth and Tanaji Malusaré with a small force to take possession of it, while he ordered Surya Rao to support this detachment. He himself pushed on to Devrukh by way of Chiplun (where he performed the pilgrimage at the shrine of Parashuram and made large gifts to the Brahmans.) His victorious march was continued to Rajapur, which he now sacked for the second time and finally occupied, on 3rd March, [Ch. 14],—and even further south to Kharepatan (on the Vaghotan river, 16 33 N) Most of the cities of the Ratnagiri district saved themselves from plunder by paying him *chauth*

Meantime, under pressure from his sovereign Adil Shah, the Rajah of Shringarpur had made a night-attack on Shivaji's detachment in Sangameshwar, but had been repulsed by the gallant Tanaji Malusaré. Shivaji now turned back northwards and conquered the Palli-vana State, conciliated and recalled the fugitive population, and restored cultivation and trade. For protecting this conquest, he fortified Chirdurg and named it Mandangarh, and built a second fort, Pálgarh.

He was now free to settle accounts with Surya Rao, the Rajah of Shringarpur, who had tried to save himself by promising homage to Shivaji ever since the fall of Javli (1656) and repeatedly broken his faith in fear of his Bijapuri master Punishment swiftly overtook the double-dealer Shivaji now invaded Shringarpur by such

---

garh to the s w In old records Dabhol and Prabhavali are coupled together, though the two towns are far apart

a rapid march from Palli-vana that Surya Rao was taken entirely by surprise, he had not anticipated the blow and made no preparation for defence; even his captains were enjoying leave home! The Rajah had barely time to escape with his life, while Shivaji entered his city in triumph (29th April.) The rest of the small State was easily occupied and placed under Trimbak Bhaskar as governor, while the neighbouring hill-fort of Pratitgarh (=Prachitgarh) was put in repairs to protect the city.*

The ferocity and greed of the Maratha troops, no less than their valour and rapidity of movement, had spread the wildest terror among the people of the invaded districts and all who could had fled away from the path of the invaders. Shivaji now very wisely won over Shirke, the minister and virtual ruler of Shringarpur, enlisted him in his own service, afterwards marrying into his family,—made large gifts to the local Brahmans and thus induced the population to return to their homes and usual occupations and submit to the new government.

But these successes were chequered by a great defeat. In May 1661 the Mughals wrested Kalian from the Marathas, and though Shivaji mustered an army in Mahad to attempt its recovery, his efforts did not bear fruit and this capital city remained in Mughal hands for nine years more. So, late in June, Shivaji retired to his fort of Wardhangarh, where he spent the entire summer in quiet. The fort of Deiri, in the Pen sub-division, was besieged by a Muslim general named Bulaki, but a Maratha relieving force under Kavji Kodhalkar drove him away after slaying 400 of his men (21 August 1661.)

---

* Several details of this campaign in the Ratnagiri district have been taken from the *Shiva-bharat* The dates are from *Jedhe S*

Maratha activities were resumed at the beginning of 1662 Shivaji attacked Namdar Khan, at Mira Dongar (6 miles south-east of Pen), and then raided the rich city of Pen. The Mughal defence was obstinate and Shivaji's forces suffered a heavy loss in killed and wounded

On the whole, throughout the year 1662 and the first quarter of 1663, some Mughal generals (especially Namdar Khan) showed great activity and success in attacking the Marathas, making reprisals into their territory, and spoiling their raids by close pursuit. In March 1663 we find two large and mobile divisions of Mughal horse,—12,000 and 7,000 strong,—posted at Upper Chaul and Rahamatpur respectively for these duties, while Kalian was held by a permanent garrison too large to be easily attacked.

The net result of the operations of these two years was that the Mughals kept their grip on the extreme north of Konkan, including the city and district of Kalian,—barring occasional raids into that debatable land the Pen sub-division,—while Shivaji remained master of the southern part, namely the south-eastern corner of the Kolaba district and nearly the whole of the Ratnagiri district, or roughly 18° to 16.30 North latitude

In March 1663, the Mughals gave a long and vigorous chase to Netaji, the Master of the Horse in Shiva's army. He had led his cavalry in a raid into the imperial territory, but a Mughal force of 7,000 horse pursued him so closely that "he was fain to travel 45 or 50 miles a day and yet [had] much ado to escape with a small [part of the] booty he had got. They left not the pursuit till they came within five leagues of Bijapur" But Rustam-i-Zaman met the Mughals and induced them to give up the pursuit, "by telling them that the country was dangerous for any strange army to march in and also promising to go himself and follow him, by which deceit Netaji got away, though not without loss of 300 horse and himself wounded." (*F. R.* Surat, vol. 103, Gyffard to Surat, 30 March, and 8 April 1663.)

But within a month of meeting with this reverse to him arms, Shivaji dealt a masterly blow at the Mughals,—a blow whose cleverness of design, neatness of execution and completeness of success created in the Mughal Court and camp as much terror of his prowess and belief in his possession of magical powers, as his *coup* against Afzal Khan had done among the Bijapuris He surprised and wounded the Mughal viceroy of the Deccan in the heart of his camp, in his very bed-chamber, within the inner ring of his body-guards and female slaves.*

§6. *Shivaji's night-attack on Shaista Khan.*

Shaista Khan had, as we have seen, occupied Puna in May 1660 and retired there after the capture of Chakan in the following August. He took up his residence in what was then the best house of the future Maratha capital, the unpretentious home of Shivaji's childhood. His harem was with him, and around his mansion lay the quarters of his guards and attendants, the band-room and offices. Further off, across the road leading southwards to Singh-garh lay the camp of his lieutenant,

---

* Night-attack on Shaista Khan the earliest records are Gyffard to Surat 12 April, 24 May, 1663 (*F R* Surat, vol 103) containing Shivaji's own version, Bernier, 187, *A N* 819 (only one sentence !), *Storia,* ii 104-106, Sabh 35-37, *Dil* 44-46 Khafi Khan (ii 172-'5) reports the narration of his father, a servant of Shaista Khan, but he wrote after 1730 *T S* 19*b*-20*a* *Jedhe*

Maharajah Jaswant Singh and his contingent of 10,000 men

The enterprise required no less agility and cunning than bravery and dash. Shivaji picked out a thousand of his bravest and most expert soldiers and took them with him, while two supporting divisions of one thousand each (including cavalry and Mavles) under Netaji Palkar and Moro Pant the *Peshwa*, were directed to take post on the two flanks of the vast Mughal encampment, at a mile's distance from its outer side. Babaji Bapuji and Chimnaji Bapuji, of Khed, accompanied Shiva as his body-guards and right-hand men in this enterprise.

The Maratha force, lightly equipped, set out from Singh-garh, covered the intervening eleven miles rapidly in the course of the day, and arrived at Puna after nightfall With 400 picked men Shivaji entered the limits of the camp, replying to the challenge of the Mughal guards that they were Deccani soldiers of the imperial army going to take up their appointed posts. After resting for a few hours in some obscure corner of the camp, the party arrived near the Khan's quarters at midnight. Shiva knew the ins and outs of the city and every nook and corner of the house where he had passed his boyhood and youth

It was the 6th day of Ramzan, the month of fasting for Muslims. The servants of the Nawab's household had mostly fallen asleep after their day's abstinence followed by the heavy meal at night. Some cooks who had risen from their beds to make a fire and prepare the meal which is taken a little before dawn in the month of Ramzan, were despatched by the Marathas without any noise. The wall dividing this outer kitchen from the body-servants' room within the harem once had a small door in it, but the opening had been closed with brick and mud to complete the seclusion of the harem. The Marathas began to take out the bricks and make an opening there. The noise of their pick-axes and the groans of the dying awoke some of the servants, who reported the suspicious noise to the Khan, but that general only rebuked them for disturbing his sleep for a trifle.

Soon the breach in the wall was large enough for a man to creep through. Shivaji, with his trusty lieutenant Chimnaji Bapuji, was the first to enter the harem, and was followed by 200 of his men. The place was a maze of canvas, screen-wall after screen-wall and enclosure within enclosure. Hacking a way through them with his sword, Shivaji reached the very bed-room of the Khan. The frightened women roused the Nawab, but before he could use his weapons Shivaji was upon him and severed his thumb with one stroke of his sword. It was evidently at this time that the lamps in the room were put out by some wise woman. In the darkness two of the Marathas tumbled into a cistern of water; and the confusion that followed was used by Shaista Khan's slave-girls to carry him away to a place of safety. The Marathas continued their work of slaughter in the darkness for some time, killing and wounding many of the Khan's women, without knowing their sex.

Meantime the other half of Shivaji's force, the 200 men, evidently under Babaji Bapuji, who had been left outside the harem, had rushed the main guard, slaying the sleepers and the awake and crying in derision, "Is it thus that you keep watch?" They next entered the band-room and ordered the bandsmen, as if from the Khan, to play. The loud noise of the kettle-drums drowned all voices, and the yells of the enemy swelled the confusion. The tumult in the harem, too, now grew so great that the Mughal troops became aware that their general was being attacked Shouting "The enemy have come," they began to take up their arms

Abul Fath, a son of Shaista Khan, had been the first to hasten to his father's rescue without waiting for others; but the brave youth was slain after he had struck down two or three Marathas Another Mughal captain who lodged just behind the harem enclosure, finding its gate closed from within by the wily Marathas, let himself down inside by means of a rope-ladder; but he was at once attacked and killed.

Shivaji, finding his enemies fully awakened and arming, delayed no longer, but promptly left the harem, called his men together, and withdrew from the camp by the direct route, while the Mughals, not knowing where their enemies were, fruitlessly searched all their camp

This night-attack was a complete success The retreat from the camp was unmolested and no pursuit was made. During the surprise the Marathas lost only six men killed and forty wounded, while they slew a son and a captain of Shaista Khan's, forty of his attendants and six of his wives and slave-girls, besides wounding two other sons, eight other women and Shaista Khan himself.*

* Gyffard at Rajapur wrote to Surat on 12th April 1663 "Yesterday arrived a letter from the Rajah written himself to Ravji [Pandit], giving him an account how that he himself with 400 choice men went to Shaista Khan's camp There, upon some pretence, he got into his tent to salam and presently slew all the watch, wounded Shaista Khan with his own hand, [one son was killed outright, two wounded, six women killed, eight more wounded, and 40 persons attending their general left dead in the place] After all this Shivaji returns, losing but six men [killed]

The daring and cunning of the Maratha hero were rewarded by an immense increase of his prestige. He was taken to be an incarnation of Satan; no place was believed to be proof against his entrance and no feat impossible for him. The whole country talked with astonishment and terror of the almost superhuman deed done by him; and there was bitter humiliation and sorrow in the Emperor's Court and family circle at this disaster to his maternal uncle and the "premier peer" (*amir-ul-umara*) of his empire.

This attack took place on 5th April, 1663. The morning following it, all the imperial officers came to Shaista Khan to condole with him in his loss. Among them was Maharajah Jaswant Singh, who had not raised a finger to defend his chief or to oppose the retreat of his assailant, though he had 10,000 horse under him and lay encamped across the road taken by Shivaji. Shaista Khan, with the polished sneer of a high-bred Mughal courtier, turned to Jaswant and merely remarked, "When the enemy fell upon me, I imagined that you had already died fighting against them!" Indeed, the public, both in the Mughal camp and throughout the Deccan, ascribed Shivaji's exploit to the connivance of Jaswant. Shivaji, however, asserted that this astonishing feat was performed by him under the inspiration of his God and not of any human counsellor. Immediately after his return from it, he wrote to Raoji Rao, his agent at Rajapur, boasting how he had been the chief actor

---

and forty wounded, 10,000 horse under Rajah Jaswant Singh standing still and never offered to pursue him, so it is generally believed it was done with his consent, though Shivaji tells his men his Permisera (*Parameshwār*, the great God) bid him do it" The figures for the loss suffered by Shaista Khan given in this letter have been replaced, within square brackets above, by the corrections made in Gyffard's letter of 24th May

in this business and had himself wounded Shaista Khan.

The Mughal viceroy, covered with shame and grief, retired to Aurangabad for greater safety. The Emperor heard of the disaster early in May, when on his way to Kashmir, and ascribed it to the viceroy's negligence and incapacity. As a mark of his displeasure, he transferred Shaista Khan to the government of Bengal (1 Dec. 1663), which was then regarded as a penal province, or in Aurangzib's own words, "a hell well stocked with bread," without permitting him even to visit the Emperor on his way to his new charge The Khan left the Deccan about the middle of January 1664, on being relieved by Prince Muazzam

§7. *Surat described.*

While this change of governors was going on at Aurangabad, Shivaji performed a feat of even greater audacity than he had ever displayed before From 6th to 10th January he looted the city of Surat, the richest port of the west coast and "the gateway to the holy places of Arabia" for Indian Muslims, who here embarked for the pilgrimage to Mecca

The *fort* of Surat stood on the south bank of the Tapti, 12 miles from the sea It was impregnable to a body of light raiders like Shiva's troopers. But the *city* close to the fort offered a rich and defenceless prize. It had, at that time, no wall to protect it Its wealth was boundless The imperial customs alone yielded a revenue of 12 *lakhs* of Rupees a year (in 1666, acc. to Thevenot, v. 81.)

The city of Surat covered nearly four square miles, including gardens and open spaces, and had a population of 200,000 souls. The streets were narrow and crooked; the houses of the rich were near the river-side and substantially built; but the town was mainly composed of poor men's huts built of wooden posts and bamboo walls and with floors plastered with mud. "In the greater part of the town scarcely two or three brick-houses were to be seen in a street, and in some parts... not one for many streets together. The whole town was unfortified either by art or nature and its situation was upon a large plain of many miles' extent. They had only made against the chief avenues of the town some weak and ill-built gates [more for show than for defence.] In some parts there was a dry ditch easily passable by a footman, with no wall on the inner side. The rest was left so open that scarcely any sign of a ditch was perceivable." (*Bom. Gaz.*, ii. 301, 90-91; Letter from the English chaplain Escaliot to Sir T. Browne, in *Ind Antiq.* viii. 256.)

Early in the morning of Tuesday, 5th January, 1664, Surat was suddenly alarmed by the news that Shivaji had arrived with an army at Gandavi, 28 miles southwards, and was advancing to plunder the town.* At once the people were seized with a panic, and began to flee away with their wives and children, mostly across the river, to save their lives. Rich men found shelter in the fort by bribing its commandant. Later in the day a courier brought the intelligence that Shivaji had

---

* First sack of Surat The most minute details and graphic accounts are found in the factory records Log of the *Loyal Merchant* (*Orme MSS* vol 263, pp 23-24), *F R* Surat 2 (Surat Consult 6 Jan, 1664), vol 86 (Surat to Persia, Surat to Co 18 and 28 Jan and 4 April), *Dutch Records*, vol 27, Nos 711 and 719 Letter of Escaliot very valuable Bernier, 188-190, *Storia*, ii 29, 112, 120, 132, iv 428 Ishwardas 52*a* (*A N*, K K. and Tavernier silent) For a good description of the city and fort, Kaeppelin, 52*n*, and Carré, i 16-49

come still nearer, and at night it was learnt that he had halted only five miles from Surat Inayet Khan, the governor of the town—who was quite distinct from the commandant of the fort,—had sent out an agent to treat with Shiva for terms of ransom But when he heard that the Maratha chief had detained the messenger and was approaching with all speed, he himself fled to the fort, leaving the town at the enemy's mercy He used to draw from the Treasury the pay of 500 soldiers, but had so long appropriated the money without maintaining a proper force His cowardice also prevented him from organizing a defence or even from standing at his post.

The townspeople were sheep worthy of such a shepherd A population composed mostly of money-loving traders, poor artisans, punctilious fire-worshippers and tender-souled Jains, cannot readily take to war even in self-defence The richest merchants, though owning millions of Rupees, had not the sense to hire guards for the protection of their wealth, though they might have done so at only a twentieth part of what they were soon to lose through pillage.

§8 *Heroic defence of the English at Surat.*

The shame of this cowardice in high and low alike was deepened by the contrast afforded by the manly spirit of a handful of foreigners. The English and Dutch merchants resolved to defend their own factories at all costs, though these were open houses, not built to stand an attack They might have sought safety by escaping to their ships at Swally on the coast, 10 miles west of Surat, but "it was thought more like Englishmen to make ourselves ready to defend our lives and goods to the uttermost than by a flight to leave money, goods, house to merciless people."

Sir George Oxenden, the English President, and his Council stood at their posts in Surat, and improvised a defence of the factory. They procured two small brass guns from a merchant in the town and four others from their own vessels. With the armed sailors promptly sent up from the English ships at Swally, they mustered in the factory 150 Englishmen and 60 *peons*, a total of 210 defenders. Four of the guns were mounted on the roof to scour two broad streets and command the large and lofty house of Haji Said Beg, adjacent to theirs. Two other guns were posted behind the front gate, in which port-holes were cut for firing into the passage leading to the factory. What provisions, water and powder could be got were hurriedly laid in. "Some were set to melt lead and make bullets, others with chisels to cut lead into slugs; no hand idle but all employed to strengthen every place. Captains were appointed and every man quartered and order taken for relieving one another upon necessity. To secure the approaches to the factory, the English went outside and took possession of a temple just under their house, and cleared it of its refugees, and also shut up a mosque on another side, whose windows looked into the outer courtyard of the factory. President Oxenden at the head of his 200 soldiers "drawn out in rank and file, with drum and trumpet," publicly marched through the town in the morning of the 6th, "declaring that he intended to withstand Shivaji with this handful of men."

The Dutch, too, defended their house, though its distance of a mile from the English factory made mutual aid between the two nations impossible. The example of the Europeans also heartened a body of Turkish and Armenian merchants to defend their property in their *serai*, close to the English factory.

§9. *First loot of Surat, 1664*

Shivaji had been heard of at Bassein, twenty-four miles north of Bombay, only nine days before. But he had made a forced march to Surat with 4,000 men mounted on choice horses with such speed and secrecy that he was at Surat a day after his approach had been detected His route lay by the forts of Nar-durg (probably *Naldurg*, s w. of Nana Ghat), Mahuli, and Kohaj and then across the zamindaris of Jawhar, Ramnagar and Lakdar(?), north of the Thana district. Two Rajahs had joined him on the way with their contingents in the hope of sharing the plunder, and his army now mustered 10,000

At 11 o'clock in the morning of Wednesday, 6th January, 1664, Shivaji arrived at Surat and pitched his tent in a garden a quarter of a mile outside the Burhanpur or eastern gate. The night before he had sent two messengers with a letter requiring the governor and the three most eminent merchants and richest men in the city, *viz.*, Haji Said Beg, Baharji Borah, and Haji Qasim, to come to him in person immediately and make terms, otherwise he threatened the whole town with fire and sword. No answer had been given to the demand, and the Maratha horsemen, immediately after their arrival on the 6th, entered the defenceless and almost deserted city, and after sacking the houses began to set fire to them. A body of Shivaji's musketeers was set "to play upon the castle, with no expectation to take it, but to keep in and frighten the governor and the rest that had got in, as also [to prevent] the soldiers of the castle from sallying out upon them whilst the others plundered and fired [the houses.]" The garrison kept up a constant fire, but the fort-guns inflicted more damage on the town than on the assailants. Throughout Wednesday, Thursday, Friday and Saturday, this work of devastation was continued, every day new fires being raised, so that thousands of houses were consumed to ashes and two-thirds of the town destroyed. As the English chaplain wrote, "Thursday and Friday nights were the most terrible nights for fire. The fire turned the night into day, as before the smoke in the day-time had turned day into night, rising so thick that it darkened the sun like a great cloud."

Near the Dutch factory stood the grand mansion of Baharji Borah, then "reputed the richest merchant in the world," his property having been estimated at 80 *lakhs* of Rupees. The Marathas plundered it at leisure day and night till Friday evening, when having ransacked it and dug up its floor, they set fire to it. From this house they took away 28 *seers* of large pearls, with many other jewels, rubies, emeralds and "an incredible amount of money."

Close to the English factory were the lofty residence and extensive warehouses of another very rich merchant, Haji Said Beg, who, too, had fled away to the fort, leaving his property without a defender. All the afternoon and night of Wednesday and till past the noon of Thursday, the Marathas continued to break open his doors and chests and carry off as much money as they could. Entering one of his warehouses they smashed some casks of quicksilver and spilt a great quantity of it on the floor. But in the afternoon of Thursday the brigands left it in a hurry, on being scared by a sortie which the English had made into the street to drive away a party of 25 Maratha horsemen who seemed intent on setting fire to another house in dangerous proximity to the English factory In this encounter one Maratha trooper was wounded with a bullet, and two Englishmen with arrow and sword, but slightly.

The English merchants next day put a guard of their own in the house of Said Beg and thus he suffered no further loss Shivaji was angry with the English at being balked of his prey, and in the afternoon of Friday he sent them a message calling upon them to pay him three *lakhs* of Rupees or else let his men freely loot the Haji's house, and threatening that in case they refused to do either he would come in person, kill every soul in the English factory, and raze their house to the ground. President Oxenden took time to consider the proposal till next morning (Saturday), when he rejected both the demands of Shivaji and boldly defied the Maratha chief to come and do his worst, saying, "We are ready for you and resolved not to go away. But come when you please; and [as] you have, as you say, resolved to come, I ask you to come one *prahar* sooner than you intend." To this challenge Shivaji gave no reply He was surfeited with booty and was too wise to run a needless risk by facing artillery concealed behind defences and served by resolute and disciplined men, for the sake of a few *lakhs* more.

§10　*How money was extorted.*

The plunder of Surat yielded him above a *kror* of Rupees, the city "not having been so rich [as then] in many years before." The looting was unresisted, and extended over fully four days and nights, and he "scorned to carry away anything but gold, silver, pearls, diamonds and such precious ware." (Log of the *Loyal Merchant.*)

On reaching Surat, Shivaji had publicly declared that he had not come to do any personal hurt to the English or other merchants, but only to revenge himself on Aurangzib for having invaded his country and killed some of his relations. But money was really his sole aim.* He had to make the most of his four days' free run at Surat and shrank from no cruelty to extort money as quickly as possible. As the English chaplain wrote, "His desire of money is so great that he spares no barbarous cruelty to extort confessions from his prisoners, whips them most cruelly, threatens death and often executes it if they do not produce so much as he thinks they may or desires they should;—at least cuts off one hand, sometimes both."

§11. *Attempt to murder Shivaji.*

The cowardly governor Inayet Khan, who had run into the fort in Tuesday night, formed an infamous plot from his safe refuge. On Thursday he sent a young follower of his to Shivaji with pretended terms of peace. These were so manifestly unreasonable that Shiva scorn-

* An old merchant who had brought 40 ox-loads of cloth from near Agra but sold none, tried to propitiate Shivaji by offering it to him. But on his answering that he had no ready money, his right hand was cut off by Shivaji's order, he was driven away, and his cloth burnt by the Marathas (Letter of Escaliot) Bernier, 190, for the narrow escape of a Jewish ruby-merchant from the death threatened by Shivaji to extort his wealth "Mr Smith was present when he cut off more than 26 hands in one day, and as many heads, whoever he was that was taken and brought before him that could not redeem himself, lost either his hand or his head, and his manner was first to plunder and then to cause the owner of the house to give him something over and above to redeem his house from being burnt, and yet that perfidious villain would fire it afterwards, though he had obliged himself to the contrary" (Surat to Co, 28 Jan)

fully asked the envoy, "Your master is now cooped up in his chamber like a woman. Does he think of me, too as a woman that he expects me to accept such terms as these?" The young man immediately replied, "We are not women, I have something more to say to you;" and whipping out a concealed dagger he ran full at Shivaji's breast. A Maratha body-guard that stood before the Rajah with a drawn sword, struck off the assassin's hand with one blow But so great was the force of the desperado's rush that he did not stop but drove the bloody stump of his arm on Shiva's person and the two rolled on the ground together. The blood being seen on Shiva's dress, his followers imagined that he had been murdered, and the cry ran through the camp to kill the prisoners. But the same guardsman clove the assassin's skull, Shiva rose up from the ground and forbade any massacre Then he ordered the prisoners to be brought before him and cut off the heads of four and the hands of 24 others from among them at his caprice, but spared the rest.*

At ten o'clock in the morning of Sunday the 10th, Shivaji suddenly departed from Surat with his army, on hearing that a Mughal force was coming to the relief of the town. That night he encamped twelve miles off and then retreated by rapid marches to Konkan.

---

* Mr Anthony Smith, a servant of the English E I Company, was seized on landing at the Dutch jetty and kept a prisoner in the Maratha camp for three days Along with other prisoners, his right hand was ordered to be cut off, at which he cried out to Shivaji in Hindusthani to cut off his head instead But on his hat being taken off, he was recognized as an Englishman and spared On Friday afternoon he was sent to the English factory with a message from Shiva, but President Oxenden detained him there The Log of the *Loyal Merchant* says that he was ransomed for Rs 350, (also the Eng President's letter)

For some days afterwards the fear of his return prevented the townspeople from coming back to their desolated homes. But the imperial army reached Surat on the 17th and then the cowardly governor ventured to return from the fort. The people hooted at him and flung dirt on him, for which his son in anger shot a poor innocent Hindu trader dead. Sir George Oxenden, the English President, won the people's praise and admiration for having made a gallant stand and saved not only the Company's property, but also the quarter of the town situated round the English factory.*

The Emperor showed his sympathy with the afflicted citizens by excusing the custom duties for one year in the case of all the merchants of Surat, and he rewarded the valour of the English and the Dutch traders by granting them a reduction of one-half per cent. from the normal import duties on their merchandise in future.

§12. *Shivaji's doings in 1664.*

The year 1664 that lay between the departure of Shaista Khan and the arrival of Jai Singh, was not marked by any Mughal success. The new viceroy, Prince

---

* As he wrote to the Company, 28th January, 1664, (*F R* Surat 86) "The townspeople cry out in thousands for a reward from the King to the English that had by their courage preserved them We were with the noblemen of the army that came to our relief, from whom we received great thanks for the good service we did the King and the country, whereupon your President, having a pistol in his hand, laid it before the chief, saying he now laid down his arms, leaving the future care and protection of the city to them, which was exceedingly well taken, [the general] telling the President [that] he accepted it, and he must give him a vest, a horse and gird a sword about him But your President told him they were things becoming a soldier, but we were merchants and expected favour from the King in our trade"

The reduction of import duty in favour of the English and the Dutch was withdrawn in Nov. 1679 [*Aurangzib*, v ch 60 §5]

Muazzam, lived at Aurangabad, caring only for pleasure and hunting. His favourite general, Maharajah Jaswant Singh, was posted at Puna. From this place he marched out and besieged Kondana (Nov. 1663.) The Rajputs are proverbially inefficient in sieges, and Jaswant, after wasting six months before the fort, delivered a rash and fruitless assault, in which he lost many hundreds of his soldiers, chiefly owing to a gunpowder explosion. Then he quarrelled with his brother-in-law Bhao Singh Hada, evidently on the question of responsibility for the failure, and the two officers abandoned the siege (28 May 1664) and with their armies retired to Aurangabad to pass the rainy season. The campaign ended in absolutely no gain. (*Dil.* 47; *A. N.* 867; *Jedhe.*)

The field being clear, Shivaji ranged at liberty in spite of the height of the rainy season, and plundered Ahmadnagar. (Karwar to Surat, 8th August, 1664. *F. R.* Surat, vol. 104.)

On 26th June the English factors write, "Shivaji is so famously infamous for his notorious thefts that Report hath made him an airy body, and added wings, or else it were impossible he could be at so many places as he is said to be at, all at one time...They ascribe to him to perform more than a Herculean labour that he is become the talk of all conditions of people...That he will lay siege to Goa we do hardly believe, in regard it is none of his business to lay siege to any place that is fortified against him, for it will not turn him to account. He is, and ever was, for a running banquet, and to plunder and burn those towns that have neither defence nor guard." (Surat to Karwar. *F.R.* Surat 86.)

And, again, on 26th November, "Deccan [*i.e.*, Bijapur] and all the South coast [*i.e.*, Kanara] are all embroiled in civil wars,...and Shivaji reigns victoriously and uncontrolled, that he is a terror to all the kings and princes round about, daily increasing in strength...He is very nimble and active, imposing strange labour upon himself that he may endure hardship. and also exercises his chiefest men that he flies to and fro with incredible dexterity." (Surat to Co., *F.R.* Surat 86) At the end of the monsoons, *i.e.*, in October, he burst into Kanara. (See Ch. 10.)

On 23rd January, 1664, Shahji died as the result of a hunting accident on the bank of the Tungabhadra, in the Basavapatan district. His younger son Vyankoji succeeded to all his personal effects and territories in Mysore and the Eastern Karnatak.

CHAPTER V

SHIVAJI AND JAI SINGH, 1665

§1. *Jai Singh sent against Shivaji.*

The failure of Shaista Khan and the sack of Surat caused bitter mortification to Aurangzib and his Court, and he decided to send his ablest Hindu and Muhammadan generals to the Deccan. Among the promotions and transfers on his birthday, 30th September, 1664, the Emperor appointed Mirza Rajah Jai Singh to put down Shivaji. Under him were deputed Dilir Khan, Daud Khan Qureshi, Rajah Rai Singh Sisodia, Ihtisham Khan Shaikhzada, Qubad Khan, Rajah Sujan Singh Bundela, Kirat Singh (a son of Jai Singh), Mulla Yahia Nawaiyat (a Bijapuri noble who had come over to the Mughals), and many other officers, with 14,000 troopers. (*A. N.* 868, *Storia,* ii. 120.)

After making the necessary preparations, and collecting his subordinates, Jai Singh left Upper India and crossed the Narmada at Handia on 9th January, 1665. He pushed rapidly on, never wasting a day by halting, except when strong necessity compelled him. On 10th February he arrived at Aurangabad, where Prince Muazzam was holding Court as viceroy of the Deccan. In three days Jai Singh finished the work of waiting on the Prince, receiving and returning the visits of the local officers and nobles, and settling some points connected with the expedition. Then, leaving Aurangabad on 13th February, he arrived at Puna on 3rd March and took over charge from Maharajah Jaswant Singh, who immediately afterwards (7th) started for Delhi, as commanded by the Emperor. (*H. A.* Paris MS. 110*b*, 112*a*, 114*b*, 116*a*.)

§2. *Character of Jai Singh.*

Jai Singh's career had been one of undimmed brilliancy from the day when he, an orphan of twelve, received his first appointment in the Mughal army (1617.) Since then he had fought under the imperial banner in every part of the empire,—from Balkh in Central Asia to Bijapur in the Deccan, and from Qandahar in the west to Mungir in the east. Hardly a year had passed during the long reign of Shah Jahan when this Rajput chieftain had not seen active service somewhere and received some promotion for conspicuous merit. His marked ability had found recognition in his being given the command of the Van or one of the wings in the Mughal armies led by princes of the blood in campaigns beyond India. Latterly he had commanded in chief. In diplomacy he had attained to a success surpassing even his victories in the field. Wherever there was a difficult or delicate work to be done, the Emperor had only to turn to Jai Singh. A man of infinite tact and patience, an adept in the ceremonious courtesy of the Muslims, a master of Turki and Persian, besides Urdu and the Rajput dialect, he was an ideal leader of the composite army of Afghans and Turks, Rajputs and Hindusthanis, that followed the crescent banner of the sovereign of Delhi.

Age and experience had cooled the impetuous ardour of his youth,—he had once led a forlorn hope, at the storming of Mau,—and he now employed stratagem in preference to force, and bribe in preference to war. His foresight and political cunning, his smoothness of tongue and cool calculating policy, were in striking contrast with the impulsive generosity, reckless daring, blunt straightforwardness, and impolitic chivalry which we are apt to associate with the Rajput character.

And now this veteran of a hundred fights donned his armour at the age of sixty to crush a petty chieftain, who in less than ten years had grown great enough to baffle all the resources of Bijapur and to challenge the prestige of the empire of Delhi.

§3. *Jai Singh's anxieties and far-sighted preparations.*

It was, however, with no light heart that Jai Singh* set himself to the task of subduing Shivaji, against whom Bijapuris and rival Maratha chiefs, Shaista Khan and Jaswant Singh, had toiled in vain. The Deccan had been the grave of many a reputation, and he had the failures of his predecessors before him. Shiva had already established a name for stratagem, and his Mavles had measured swords with the best regular troops on more than equal terms. Then, again, there was the likelihood that the arrival of a large Mughal force in the Deccan would alarm Bijapur and Golkonda and throw them into the arms of Shiva to make a common cause against the invader from the north. Jai Singh, therefore, could not

---

* My account of this war is based upon Jai Singh's copious letters (*Haft Anjuman*, Benares and Paris MSS., with a few extra letters in *Faiyyaz-ul-qawanin*), Aurangzib's letters (given in Paris MS. *Suppl.* 476, with two stray letters in a miscellaneous Delhi MS.) and certain other letters given in *Khatut-i-Shivaji* (R.A.S. MS.) Some of these have been translated by me in the *Modern Review*. *A. N.* 887-907, though contemporary and authentic, has no independent value after the use of the above materials. *Storia*, ii. 120-125, 132-137, gives Manucci's personal experience of the war. The Marathi chronicles, Sabh. 38-46, and Malkaré 49, contain later and partly legendary accounts.

give his undivided attention to the Marathas: he had to keep an eye on Bijapur too. The problem before him was no easy one. As he wrote to the Emperor, "Not for a moment, in day or night, do I seek rest or ease from being busy about the task on which I have been sent." We see from his letters how he employed every possible device for dealing with an enemy, how wide-awake and full of many-sided activity he was, how he looked far ahead, and how he handled his force so as to cause distraction to the enemy or deal a concentrated blow at a vital point.

In view of his two enemies, Jai Singh very wisely decided to take up a position between both, *i.e.*, in the eastern part of Shiva's dominion, whence he could also easily threaten Bijapur, instead of pushing the war into the Western Ghats or the Konkan plain further west. So convinced was he of the wisdom of this plan that when Aurangzib urged him to make a descent into Konkan, he strongly objected and succeeded in carrying his point. He knew that if he could strike a fatal blow at the heart of the Maratha kingdom, its distant limbs would drop down of themselves.

§4. *Coalition of all the enemies of Shivaji.*

Secondly, he played skilfully upon the hopes and fears of the Sultan of Bijapur, holding forth the chance of a reduction of his tribute and the removal of the Emperor's displeasure, if Adil Shah aided the Mughals and thus clearly proved his want of connection with Shivaji. Thirdly, he arranged to combine against Shivaji all his enemies and distract his attention by attacks from all possible quarters. As early as January he had sent two Portuguese captains in his service named

Francisco and Diogo de Mello,* to the western coast with letters to the chief of the Portuguese settlement at Goa, inviting him to co-operate with the imperialists in attacking Shiva, who had a fleet of his own plying on that sea. In May he wrote to the Emperor, "Now that Shiva is quite negligent and free from anxiety about the west coast, if our ships from Gujrat make a sudden descent on his maritime possessions much booty can be gained." He also wrote to the Siddis of Janjira seeking their friendship. (*H. A.* Paris 114*a;* Ben. 78*a*.)

In January he had sent his Brahman emissaries to various Deccani chieftains, to stir them up against Shiva. The zamindars of Karnatak were asked to help the Mughals by threatening Bijapur from the south; and agents from two such chiefs, namely Shivappa Nayak and the zamindar of Basavapatan, reached Jai Singh's camp in April with offers of service (Paris MS. 132*a*.)† Towards the end of January an envoy from the Rajah of Jawhar had met Jai Singh at Burhanpur with a proposal to join the Mughal side; he had been conciliated, promised a *mansab*, and asked to send his son or brother with a contingent of troops. Every one who bore a grudge to Shivaji or envied the sudden rise of the Bhonsles had been approached by the Mughal general's spies. Baji Chandra Rao and his kinsman Ambaji Govind Rao More,—the family from which Shivaji had wrested Javli,—in response to Jai Singh's invitation, sent

---

* Of the *Mello* family living in the Mughal country in banishment from Goa for having caused two murders there. Manucci (ii. 144.) Also Pissurlencar, i. app.; Biker, iv. •126.

† Shivappa Nayak, the Rajah of Bednur, had died in 1662, and his son Soma Shekhar was now on the throne, but the country was still called the realm of the great conqueror Shivappa.

to him a Brahman named Mudhá, asking for a safe conduct and money help, (middle of February.) These were given, and they reached his camp, along with Mankoji Dhangar, and were enlisted in the Mughal army (4th week of March) (Paris MS. 113*a*, 123*a*.) Similarly, Afzal Khan's son, Fazl Khan, solicited from Jai Singh a command and an opportunity of avenging his slaughtered father on Shivaji. (120*b*.) The adhesion of the petty Rajahs of the Koli country north of Kalian was secured through Niccolao Manucci, then chief of Jai Singh's European artillery. (*Storia*, ii. 132-133.)

Money and promises of high rank in the Mughal service were lavishly employed on Shivaji's officers to corrupt their loyalty (Ben. MS. 54*b*.), and with some success, as in February Atmaji and Kahar Koli and two other brothers of the former, who commanded 3,000 cavalry and were posted by Shiva at the foot of Purandar, in charge of his artillery, sent their agent to Jai Singh agreeing to desert to him. (Paris MS. 113*a* & *b*.) Rama and Hanumant, two captains descended from an ancient line of jagirdars of the Supa sub-division, were called away from the service of the Rajah of Chanda and employed under Jai Singh on account of their familiarity with the seat of war and local influence. (122*a*.)

Above all, Jai Singh concentrated all authority in his own hands, as an indispensable condition of success in war. The Emperor had at first given him the command of the field-operations only, while all administrative work, like the promotion, punishment and transfer of officers, the payment of the troops, and the regulation of jagirs, was left in the hands of the viceroy at Aurangábad. Jai Singh rightly insisted that in war there should be only one head, and that the 'man on the spot' should be given full authority, or else the work would suffer. The Emperor yielded to the argument and Jai Singh gained absolute civil and military authority alike. The commandants of the Mughal forts at Ahmadnagar and Parenda were also placed under his orders.

In Western Maharashtra with its heavy rainfall, campaigning is impossible during the monsoons. It was already 3rd March when Jai Singh reached Puna, and if he was to effect anything it must be done in the next three months. From his despatches we learn how he utilized every day, how he struck swiftly and hard, and how he followed up every success to the utmost. The mariner does not scan the sky for the storm-cloud with more anxiety than did this general for the herald of the monsoons which must interrupt his work in the middle and drive him into the forced inactivity of cantonments.

§5. *The theatre of war described.*

The Western Ghats form a long towering wall running north to south along the western side of the Deccan. They have thrown off a number of short spurs eastwards, every two of which enclose a valley, the bed of some stream rolling east to join its sisters and form the mighty rivers of the south, the Godavari and the Krishna. Towards the east the spurs end, the valleys widen out and merge in the vast plains of the kingdom of Bijapur. This land, almost locked among the hills, is the cradle of the Maratha kingdom. Open, and therefore vulnerable, on the east, it is almost impenetrable from the west on account of hills and jungles. And it is in the west that the historic forts of Shivaji are situated, almost every peak being crowned with the Maratha eagle's eyrie.

Going southwards from Junnar (which is 55 miles west of Ahmadnagar) and crossing the old Mughal frontier, we have first the valley of the Indrayani, overlooked by the hill-forts of Lohgarh and Tikona in the west and Chakan in the centre. Next comes the valley of the Bhima, in which Puna stands. Further south, across a long range, lies the valley of the slender brook Karha, with the cities of Saswad and Supa in the plain and the forts of Singh-garh on the western hills and Purandar on its southern rocky barrier. Beyond these hills lies the valley of the Nira, with the town of Shirwal on its bank and the forts of Rajgarh and Torna in the west and Rohira in the south-west.

Puna is roughly the same distance (about 28 miles) from Lohgarh in the north-west and Rajgarh in the south. Saswad was admirably situated for attacking Purandar (6 miles south-west of it), Singh-garh and Rajgarh (18 and 24 miles in the west), and Puna (18 miles north-west of it),—while the widening plain east of it enabled cavalry to make an easy and rapid dash into Bijapur territory, or bar the path of reinforcements coming from that side. Even now five main roads meet at Saswad.

§6. *Mughals set up outposts.*

Jai Singh, therefore, with a true general's eye for the ground, made Saswad his base. Puna was strongly garrisoned. An outpost was established opposite Lohgarh to observe and blockade it and guard the road leading north to the Mughal frontier near Junnar. A flying column was organized to ravage the Maratha villages embosomed among the hills to the west and south-west of Saswad. On his eastern side he was quite secure from attack, from the nature of the ground, the position of Saswad close to the boundary line between Shiva's dominion and Bijapur, and the existence of a Mughal advanced post at Supa.

After arriving at Puna (3rd March), Jai Singh spent some days in settling the country and establishing outposts, which he regarded as the "first of the pillars supporting the work of this expedition." Qutb-ud-din Khan was sent with 7,000 cavalry with orders to guard the country from Junnar in the north to the foot of the hills (*painghat*) of Konkan opposite Lohgarh, to set up one permanent outpost facing Lohgarh (to be garrisoned by 3,000 men), another facing fort Nar-durg with a strong force, and other outposts to bar the paths usually followed by the enemy, and to be constantly touring through his jurisdiction and inspecting his outposts. Ihtisham Khan with 4,000 cavalry was left to guard Puna and its surrounding district. Between Puna and Lohgarh, a distance of some 28 miles, is a difficult pass, where a guard of 2,000 cavalry was posted. Sayyid Abdul Aziz was appointed with 3,000 horse to hold the *thanah* of Shirwal and prevent aid from reaching Purandar from the south With him went Baji Chandra Rao, Ambaji Govind Rao (zamindars of Javli), and Mankoji Dhangar who had joined the Mughals

There was already another *thanah* at Supa, in charge of Sayyid Munawwar Khan of Barha, and some other Muslim and Hindu officers.

§7. *Jai Singh opens the campaign.*

Deciding, for the reasons given above, to take up his position at Saswad and besiege Purandar, Jai Singh marched out of Puna on 14th March.

But he had immediately afterwards to make a long halt in its environs, as news came to him that Qutb-ud-din had gone to Junnar to escort treasure and Shiva had come to Lohgarh to make a dash into the imperial territory as soon as Jai Singh's back would be turned on Puna. Jai Singh quickly recalled Qutb-ud-din to his post opposite Lohgarh to watch Shiva's movements and resumed his march on the 23rd. Loni, some 12 miles east of Puna, was next reached ; here a block-house or enclosure for sheltering the troops was built in 3 days, and a *thanah* established under Rama and Hanumant, with 300 cavalry and 300 foot-musketeers, to guard the line of communication with Puna and the two roads which led to the imperial territory.

Arriving on 29th March at a place one day's march short of Saswad, he sent on Dilir Khan with the van-guard and the artillery to cross the pass lying in the way, advance four miles, and then halt.

Next day the Rajah crossed the hill and pushed on to Dilir Khan's camp, leaving Daud Khan below the pass to see to the safe transit of the army up to noon. The rear-guard were to bring up the stragglers.

On this very morning (30th March) Dilir Khan went with the Van to Saswad in order to select a place for encampment. In this reconnaissance he approached fort Purandar. A large body of Maratha musketeers, who occupied an enclosed village in the waist of the hill—called *machi* in the local language,—now came down and attacked the imperialists, who, however, routed them and captured the *machi*. The houses there were burnt and the Mughal Van very boldly improved their victory by at once pushing on as near Purandar as they could and entrenching just beyond the fire of the fort-guns.

Jai Singh on hearing of it, at once sent up 3,000 of the troops of his command under Rai Singh, Kirat Singh, Qubad Khan, Mitrasen, Indraman Bundela and other officers at a gallop. He also despatched an urgent order to Daud Khan to come to him, take charge of the camp, and enable the Rajah to go to supervise the siege. But Daud Khan, on hearing the news, had hastened to join Dilir Khan, without coming to Jai Singh

The day was far spent, there was no high officer left to guard the camp, and so Jai Singh had to stay there perforce He had already sent forward a party of pioneers and water-carriers, shot, powder, gun munitions, and entrenching tools for the use of Dilir Khan.

Next morning (31st March), Jai Singh carefully escorted the baggage to a permanent camp serving as a base, between Saswad and Purandar, only 4 miles from the latter. Then he reconnoitred the fort from the position of Daud Khan and Kirat Singh. It was not a single fort, but a fortified mass of hills; hence to surround and closely blockade it was impossible. (Paris MS. 125*b*.)

§8. *Purandar described.*

Six miles south-west of Saswad rises the stupendous mountain mass of Purandar, the highest point of which towers 4,564 feet above sea-level and more than 2,500 feet above the plain at its foot. It is really a double fort, with an independent and very strong sister enclosure, named Vajragarh, on a ridge running out east of it. Purandar consists of an upper fort or citadel with precipitous sides all around and a lower fort or *machi*, 300 feet or more below it. The latter is a ledge running round the waist of the hill with many a winding, the entire circuit being four miles. On the north side the ledge widens out into a broad terrace, containing the barracks and offices of the garrison. This terrace is bounded on the east by the high spur named Bhairav Khind, which starts from the base of the steep overhanging north-eastern tower (called *Khad-kala* or the Sky-scraper)* of the upper fort, and runs for about a mile eastwards in a narrow ridge, ending in a small table-land (3,618 feet above sea-level), crowned with the fort of Rudramal, (now called Vajragarh.)

This Vajragarh commands the *machi* or lower fort of Purandar on its northern and most important face, as the garrison has to live here. It was by seizing Vajragarh that Jai Singh in 1665 and the English in 1817 made Purandar untenable for the Marathas. Jai Singh, like a true general, decided to attack Vajragarh first. (*Bom. Gaz.* xvii. pt. iii, pp. 428-435.)

§9. *Mughals open the siege.*

Dilir Khan with his nephews and Afghan troops, Hari Bhan and Udai Bhan Gaur, entrenched between Purandar and Rudramal. In front of him were the chief of the artillery, Turktaz Khan, and the party sent by Jai Singh. Kirat Singh with the 3,000 troopers of the Rajah and a few other *mansabdars* made a stockade opposite the north gate of Purandar. On the right were the trenches of Rajah Narsingh Gaur, Karn Rathor, Jagat Singh of Narwar, and Sayyid Maqbul Alam. Behind Purandar and facing its postern gate (*khirki*) was the position of Daud Khan, Rajah Rai Singh, Md. Salih Tarkhan, Ram Singh [Hada?], Sher Singh Rathor, Raj Singh Gaur and others. To the right of this position

* Molesworth, 2nd ed., 192, explains *Khadkal* as 'a rocky plateau'

were posted Rasul Beg Rozbhani and his Rozbhani followers. Opposite Rudramal, Chaturbhuj Chauhan with a party of Dilir Khan's followers entrenched, and behind them Mitrasen, Indraman Bundela and some other officers.

Jai Singh removed his quarters from the camp to the foot of the hill to be nearer the besieged fort, while the soldiers pitched their tents along the hill-side. He visited the trenches every day, encouraged his men, and supervised the progress of the siege. At first all his efforts were directed to dragging guns to the top of the steep and difficult hill. It took three days to raise a gun, named *Abdullah Khan*, and mount it opposite Rudramal. In 3½ days more a second gun, named *Fath Lashkar*, was taken there. A third, named *Haheli*, was painfully approaching the summit The incessant bombardment of the Mughals demolished the bases of the tower in front, and pioneers were sent to its foot to dig a hole underneath.

§10. *Capture of Vajragarh.*

At midday, 13th April, Dilir Khan's division stormed the tower and drove the enemy into an enclosure behind it, leaving on the field seven slain and four wounded. Jai Singh reinforced Dilir Khan with a party of his own Rajputs. Next day, the victorious Mughals pushed on to the inner enclosure and tried to capture it by escalade. The garrison, oppressed by their fire, capitulated in the evening (14th April), left the fort, and were disarmed. But Jai Singh very wisely allowed them to return home in order to tempt the garrison of Purandar, by this example of leniency, to surrender instead of fighting to the last. The heroic leaders of the defence were chivalrously given robes of honour by Dilir Khan and Jai Singh alike. The imperialists lost 80 killed and 109 wounded, as the price of this success. (Paris MS. 126*b*.)

§11. *Flying columns ravage Shivaji's villages.*

The possession of Vajragarh was the stepping-stone to the capture of Purandar, or in Jai Singh's own language, "the key that would unlock Purandar." Dilir Khan now turned to the latter fort, while Jai Singh organized raids into the Maratha country, in order, as he wrote to the Emperor, to convince Shiva and the Sultan of Bijapur that the Mughal army was large enough to be able to spare troops from the siege, and also to prevent any concentration of forces under Shivaji by creating constant terror and disturbance in various parts of his kingdom. (Paris MS. 133*a*.)

There was also a secret reason for thus sending away certain generals from the siege-camp. He had some disloyal officers under him, whose presence was worse than useless. Daud Khan Qureshi was posted to watch the postern gate (*khirki*) of the fort ; but after a few days it became known that a party of Marathas had entered the fort by that gate, without being opposed by him. Dilir Khan severely rebuked Daud Khan for his failure, and a bitter quarrel broke out between the two. Jai Singh then transferred Daud Khan to his own division and posted Purdil Khan and Subh-Karn Bundela opposite the postern. But matters did not improve: "Subh-Karn did not at all give his heart to the work, but preferred above everything else to favour Shiva!" Daud Khan, too, was a source of mischief in his new station. He constantly declared that the capture of Purandar was beyond the range of possibility, and that the siege was a waste of men and money. His intention in talking in this way was, as Jai Singh detected, to discourage the commander-in-chief from heartily supporting the siege-operations, so that Dilir Khan would be left to bear the burden of the fight unaided and would have to retire with failure and disgrace. Jai Singh removed the mischief-maker from the camp by creating an independent flying column and sending him at its head, to make raids daily, or on alternate days, on different places in the district. (Ben. MS. 191*b*, *Faiyyaz*. 592.)

On 25th April, the flying column, six thousand strong under Daud Khan, accompanied by Rajah Rai Singh, Sharza Khan (a Bijapuri general), Amar Singh Chandawat, Achal Singh Kachhwa (the principal officer of Jai Singh's household troops), and 400 of Jai Singh's own troopers, marched out with orders to enter the region of Rajgarh, Singh-garh and Rohira from two sides and "not to leave any vestige of cultivation or habitation, but make an utter desolation." (Paris MS. 133*b*.) At the same time Qutb-ud-din Khan and Ludi Khan were ordered to harry the district from the north and thus distract and wear out Shivaji

Daud Khan's party arrived near fort Rohira on the 27th and burnt and totally ruined about 50 villages. A body of Mughal skirmishers entered four populous villages hidden among the hills, which had never before been visited by an enemy; the invaders soon received reinforcements, overcame the opposition, occupied the villages, razed them to the ground, and brought away many of the peasants and their cattle and other property as spoils of war. After a day's halt here, the Mughals marched towards Rajgarh on the 30th, burning the villages on the way. Without stopping to besiege the fort (for which they were not prepared), they sacked the villages around it,—the garrison watching the work of ruin from the shelter of the fort-guns, without venturing to make a sally.

The ground in the neighbourhood was hilly and uneven. So, the column retreated four miles to a level place, near the pass of Gunjankhora, where they encamped for the night, and next day (1st May), reached Shivapur. Thence Daud Khan marched towards Singhgarh and harried its environs, returning to Puna on 3rd May, by order of Jai Singh.

Meantime Qutb-ud-din Khan, in the midst of his raids into the passes of Pur-khora and Tasi-khora, near fort Kumari, was urgently recalled to Puna, where he joined Daud Khan. The cause of this new order was that Jai Singh had learnt that Shivaji had mustered a large force near Lohgarh, which required to be immediately broken up.

The two Mughal columns were, therefore, diverted to that side (the north-west.) Leaving Puna they halted at Chinchwad (10 or 12 miles north) on the 4th and reached Lohgarh on the 5th. When the Mughal skirmishers arrived near the fort, 500 Maratha horse and 1,000 infantry sallied forth and attacked them. But the imperialists held their ground, were soon reinforced, and routed the enemy with heavy loss after a severe fight. Then they burnt the houses on the skirt of the hill, taking many prisoners and cattle. The villages enclosed by the four forts,—Lohgarh, Visapur, Tikona, and Tangai,—were devastated, and much of Balaghat (highlands) and Painghat (lowlands) harried. Thereafter they returned, Qutb-ud-din Khan and his party taking up an outpost near Puna, and Daud Khan and his comrades rejoining the main army on 19th May.

§12. *Maratha efforts to raise the siege.*

Meantime the Maratha captains had not been idle, but tried hard to harass the Mughals and raise the seige. Early in April, Netaji Palkar, Shiva's kinsman and cavalry leader, made a dash on Parenda, but a Mughal detachment from Supa hastened in pursuit, and the Maratha host melted away at the news and offered no fight About the middle of May, Qutb-ud-din Khan had to advance up to fort Urouda,* to break up a gathering of the enemy of which he had got news. The villages on the way were plundered, and the enemy dispersed wherever they assembled round any of their forts The hill of Lohgarh was scaled, and a body of Marathas on the top slain or routed, Daud Khan returning with 300 captives and nearly 3,000 cattle. Then, again, a body of 300 Maratha cavalry, who were sheltering at Narkot, were dislodged by a detachment sent by Qubad Khan, the new *thanahdar* of Puna (*vice* Ihtisham Khan deceased), the victors returning with the captured peasants and cattle. (*A. N.* 897-99)

But the Marathas did not invariably fail. As Jai Singh admits, "sometimes we have failed to prevent the enemy from accomplishing their hostile designs." (136*b*) Khafi Khan is more explicit: "The surprises of the enemy, their gallant successes, attacks on dark nights, blocking of roads and difficult passes, and burning of jungles, made it very hard for the imperialists to

* The *Alamgir-namah* (897) gives *Ur-drug* I suggest *Urouda*, 11 miles west of Puna It may also have been *Udai-durg*

move about. The Mughals lost many men and beasts." (ii. 180.)

After the capture of Vajragarh in the middle of April, Dilir Khan advanced along the connecting ridge and laid siege to the *machi* or lower fort of Purandar. His trenches approached the tower of Khad-kala at the north-eastern angle of the fort. At first, the garrison made sorties to drive away the besiegers. One night they attacked Kirat Singh, who was quite prepared and repulsed them with slaughter. Another attack was made in a dark night on the trenches of Rasul Beg Rozbhani: he was caught napping, the guns in his trenches were spiked, and 15 of his soldiers wounded. But reinforcements, attracted by the din of battle, poured in from the neighbouring trenches, and the enemy were repulsed with loss. Next day there was a sharp skirmish over the removal of the corpses, in which the Mughals lost 8 men.

But Dilir Khan sat down before Purandar like grim Death, his men "doing in a day what could not be achieved elsewhere in a month."

§13. *Outworks of Purandar stormed.*

When, in the course of May, the Mughal trenches reached the foot of the two White Towers, which had been dismantled by bombardment, the garrison began to throw down lighted naphtha oil, leather bags full of gunpowder, bombs and heavy stones, which effectually stopped the further advance of the Mughals. Jai Singh ordered a high wooden platform of logs and planks to be made, on which guns were to be mounted and parties of gunners and musketeers placed, to command the enemy's position. His first two attempts were frustrated:

on the first occasion the upright posts had been just set up, on the second the cross-pieces had been joined, when the enemy burnt them down. On 30th May, however, the parts of the third tower were joined together in the rear and sent to the appointed place in front of the White Tower, in charge of Rup Singh Rathor and Giridhar Purohit, with orders to set up a defensive wall in front first of all, and then plant the two rows of posts Next some Rajput marksmen were to climb to the top and keep the enemy down with their bows and matchlocks while the tower was being completed This was done two hours before sunset

Then the general's hands were forced by the impetuosity of his men. Before artillery could be mounted on the wooden tower and the enemy opposite crushed, with only two hours of daylight remaining, some Rohila soldiers, without informing Dilir Khan, tried to storm the White Tower. The enemy crowded the wall in large numbers and checked them. But reinforcements rapidly arrived the men of the trenches on both hands scaled the wall with ladders, and ran towards the enemy. Jai Singh's officer Bhupat Singh Puar, a commander of 500, was slain on the right side of the smaller White Tower, with several other Rajputs On the left side Balkrishna Sakhawat and some Afghans of Dilir Khan carried on the fight Just then the line of supports, under Achal Singh and Kirat Singh, arrived on the scene of battle from their shelter behind the wooden structure. After an obstinate struggle at close quarters, the Marathas lost heavily, vacated the White Tower, retreated to behind the Black Tower (formerly known as Shah Burj or Royal Tower), and began to gall the Mughals by hurling down bombs, kettles full of gunpowder, rockets, stones, etc. Finding further advance impossible, Jai Singh was contented with the capture of the three bastions made that day and ordered his men to dig trenches exactly where they had reached and to hold the White Tower, without attempting to push on to the Black Tower.

In the course of the next two days the wooden structure was completed and two small pieces of cannon were mounted on it. The enemy, unable to reply to this fire from a superior height, evacuated the Black Tower and another bastion near it and took refuge in a stockade adjoining the wall of the tower. But they could not show their heads. The stockade was untenable, and they retired to the trenches behind it. (Ben. MS. 187*b*—189*a*.) Thus five towers and one stockade of the lower fort fell into the hands of the Mughals.

Purandar now seemed doomed. And, as if to complete its destruction, the Emperor had at Jai Singh's request despatched a train of very heavy artillery which were now on the way to the fort. The garrison had suffered heavy casualties during two months of incessant fighting.* Early in the siege they had lost their gallant commandant Murar Baji Prabhu.

§14. *Death of Murar Baji Prabhu.*

Taking seven hundred select men with himself, Murar Baji made a sortie on Dilir Khan, who was trying to climb the hill with 5,000 Afghans and some more troops of other races. The Marathas dashed forward, mingled with the enemy on all sides, and there was severe

* *Alamgir-namah,* 903, says that the fort had 4,000 combatants left in it at capitulation. Therefore Sabhasad's figure of 2,000 for the original garrison is wrong

fighting at close quarters. Murar Baji with his Mavles slew 500 Pathans besides many *Bahlia* infantrymen, and at the head of sixty desperate followers cut his way to Dilir's camp.

His comrades were slain by the overwhelming body of the Mughals, but Murar Baji rushed straight on towards Dilir. The Khan, in admiration of his matchless courage, called upon him to yield and promised him his life and a high post under him. Murar indignantly refused, and was going to strike at Dilir when the latter shot him down with an arrow Three hundred Mavles fell with him, and the rest retreated to the fort But the garrison, with a courage worthy of the mother of Brasidas the Spartan, continued the struggle, undismayed by their leader's fall and saying, "What though one man Murar Baji is dead? We are as brave as he, and we shall fight with the same courage!" (Sabh. 43-44; *T. S.*)

§ 15. *Shivaji negotiates for submission.*

But at last the steady pressure of Jai Singh bore fruit. Purandar was closely invested, the garrison had been thinned by two months of fighting, and now the capture of five bastions of the lower fort made the stronghold untenable. Its fall was only a question of time. Shiva found it futile to prolong the resistance. The families of the Maratha officers were sheltered in Purandar, and its capture would mean their captivity and dishonour. He had also failed to prevent the Mughal flying columns from ravaging his country. Defeat and ruin stared him in the face wherever he looked.

With his usual foresight, he had for some time past been sending envoys to Jai Singh to beg for terms, but the astute Rajput did not take him seriously.* Then, as the Mughal success became more and more evident, Shiva began to rise in his offer of tribute and forts as the price of peace; but his terms were not proportionate to the military advantage gained by Jai Singh, and were therefore uniformly rejected.

The Mughal victory of 2nd June, and the impending fall of the lower fort decided Shivaji. He resolved to interview Jai Singh and offer fresh terms for peace with the imperialists, and if these were rejected he would make an alliance with Adil Shah by restoring Konkan and continue the war against the Mughals with renewed vigour. He had about 20th May sent his Chief Justice Raghunath Ballal (Pandit Rao) on a secret mission to learn Jai Singh's terms, which were that Shiva must come in person and make an unconditional surrender, after which imperial mercy would be shown to him.†

Shivaji next demanded and secured from Jai Singh an assurance, confirmed with solemn oaths, that he would be allowed to visit Jai Singh and return home in safety, whether his terms were accepted or not. This visit was to be made in strict secrecy, as "the Emperor had forbidden Jai Singh to hold any negotiations whatever with Shiva."

---

* "After the arrival of the imperial army near Pabal, Shiva's agents began to visit me, and by the time of my arrival at Puna they had brought two letters from him But I gave no answer and sent them back in disappointment Then he sent a long Hindi letter with a trusted servant named Karmaji, who repeatedly entreated me to read the contents only once In it Shiva offered to be loyal and to help us in a war with Bijapur as more likely to succeed than a war in his hilly and intricate country In reply I asked him to enter the Emperor's service if he desired his life and safety" (Ben MS 54*a*)

† Shiva's next move was to send the Pandit Rao back with an offer to send his *son* to make the submission Jai Singh declined (Ben MS 55*a*)

§16. *Shivaji interviews Jai Singh.*

Raghunath Ballal returned to his master on 9th June On the 10th he sent word to Jai Singh that Shivaji would come next day. On the 11th at 9 o'clock in the morning, while Jai Singh was holding Court in his tent at the foot of Purandar, Raghunath came in and reported that Shivaji had arrived at hand in a *palki* accompanied by six Brahmans only Jai Singh immediately sent his secretary Udairaj and Ugrasen Kachhwa to meet him on the way and tell him that if he agreed to surrender all his forts he might come, otherwise he should turn back from the place. Shiva agreed to the terms in general and proceeded forward with the two officers. At the door of the tent he was welcomed by Jai Singh's Paymaster and ushered in. The Rajah advanced a few steps, embraced Shiva, and seated him by his side, while armed Rajputs stood around to guard against any treacherous movement on the part of the slayer of Afzal Khan !

Jai Singh had got up a little scene to conquer any lingering reluctance that Shiva might still have had. In anticipation of the Maratha chief's arrival he had sent word to Dilir Khan and Kirat Singh, whose trenches were the most advanced, to be ready to deliver an assault on Purandar After Shiva had entered, Jai Singh gave the signal, the Mughals attacked and captured the remaining part of the Khad-kala defences The garrison made a sortie to check them, but were driven back with the loss of 80 killed and many wounded. The fighting could be distinctly seen from the interior of the Rajah's tent. Shiva then offered to surrender the fort in order to prevent the useless slaughter of his men Jai Singh, therefore, sent his Mir Tuzuk, Ghazi Beg, to Dilir

Khan and Kirat Singh with an order to stop the fight and allow the garrison to depart unmolested. An officer of Shiva was sent with Ghazi Beg to order the garrison to capitulate. They begged respite for the night. (*A. N.* 903.)

§17. *Terms of the Treaty of Purandar, 1665.*

Shiva had travelled without any baggage or retinue, and therefore Jai Singh lodged him in his office-tent as his guest. Up to midnight the two sides higgled for the terms of a permanent peace.* But Jai Singh knew the strength of his position. As he wrote in his despatches to the Emperor, "I declined to abate a single fort. Gradually, after much discussion, we came to this agreement: (*a*) That 23 of his forts, the lands of which yield 4 *lakhs* of *hun* as annual revenue, should be annexed to the empire; and (*b*) that 12 of his forts, including Rajgarh, with an annual revenue of 1 *lakh* of *hun*, should be left to Shiva, on condition of service and loyalty to the imperial throne."

Shivaji, however, begged to be excused from attending the Emperor's Court like other nobles and Rajahs, and proposed to send his son, as his representative, with a contingent of 5,000 horse, (to be paid by means of a jagir), for regular attendance and service under the Emperor or the Mughal governor of the Deccan. This was exactly the favour shown to the Maharana of Udaipur. As he pleaded with Jai Singh, "By reason of my late unwise and disloyal acts, I have not the face to wait on the Emperor. I shall depute my son to be His Majesty's servant and slave, and he will be created a

---

* *H A.* Ben. MS 56*a*, 66*b*

Commander of Five Thousand with a suitable jagir . As for me sinner, exempt me from holding any *mansab* or serving in the Mughal army. But whenever in your wars *in the Deccan,* I am given any military duty, I shall promptly perform it."

In addition to the above terms, Shivaji made another and a conditional engagement with the Mughals: "If lands yielding 4 *lakhs* of *hun* a year in the lowlands of Konkan and 5 *lakhs* of *hun* a year in the uplands (Balaghat Bijapuri), are granted to me by the Emperor and I am assured by an imperial *farman* that the possession of these lands will be confirmed in me after the expected Mughal conquest of Bijapur, then I agree to pay to the Emperor 40 *lakhs* of *hun* in 13 yearly instalments." He was expected to wrest these lands from the Bijapuri officers by means of his own troops.

Here we detect the shrewdness of Jai Singh's policy in throwing a bone of perpetual contention between Shivaji and the Sultan of Bijapur. As he wrote to the Emperor, "This policy will result in a threefold gain · *first,* we get 40 *lakhs* of *hun* or 2 *krores* of Rupees, *secondly,* Shivaji will be alienated from Bijapur, *thirdly,* the imperial army will be relieved from the arduous task of campaigning in these two broken and jungly regions, as Shivaji will himself undertake the task of expelling the Bijapuri garrisons from them." In return for it, Shiva also agreed to assist the Mughals in the invasion of Bijapur with 2,000 cavalry of his son Shambhuji's *mansab* and 7,000 expert infantry under his own command. (Ben MS. 70.)

§18. *Shivaji receives Mughal favours.*

Dilir Khan was greatly offended at this pacific end

of the siege, which robbed him of the chance of military glory, and at Shiva's not having made him the intermediary of the Emperor's pardon. So he refused to move from his trenches or consent to an armistice. The politic Jai Singh now turned to soothe him. On the 12th, as the public did not yet know of Shiva's arrival, he was mounted on an elephant and sent with Rajah Rai Singh to wait on Dilir Khan, who, mollified by this attention, presented him with two horses, a sword, a jewelled dagger, and two pieces of precious cloth. Then Dilir Khan conducted Shiva back to Jai Singh, took his hand, and entrusted him to the Rajah. The Rajah now presented Shiva with a robe of honour, a horse, an elephant, and an aigrette (*jigha*) for the turban. Shiva, who had come unarmed, with cunning policy girt on the sword for a short time and then put it off saying, "I shall serve the Emperor as one of his devoted but unarmed servants."

That day (12th June) according to the agreement, 7,000 men and women, (of whom 4,000 were combatants), left Purandar, and the Mughals entered into possession of it; all the stores, weapons, artillery, and other property found within were attached by the Government. Mughal officers were sent with Shivaji's men to take charge of five other forts to be surrendered by the Marathas.

Some time before this, while Shiva had been sending Brahman envoys to Jai Singh, the latter with his usual foresight had written to the Emperor begging him to send to him a gracious imperial *farman* (letter) addressed to Shiva. This was to be delivered to Shiva in the event of his making submission. By a happy coincidence the *farman* and a robe of honour sent by the Emperor arrived on the day following Shiva's surrender. By the Rajah's advice he followed the Court etiquette, advanced six miles on foot to welcome the *farman* on the way, and put on the robe of honour (*A N* 904)

On the 14th Shiva was presented by Jai Singh with an elephant and two horses, and sent away to Rajgarh with Kirat Singh, after paying a ceremonious visit to Daud Khan.

Reaching Kondana at noon of the 14th, Shivaji delivered the fort to Kirat Singh and left for Rajgarh, where he arrived on the 15th On the 17th he sent away Shambhuji from Rajgarh, in charge of Ugrasen Kachhwa and they arrived in Jai Singh's camp on the 18th. (Ben MS 57*a*.)

The Maratha forts surrendered to the Emperor by the treaty of Purandar (*A N* 905) were:—*in the Deccan*: (1) Rudramal or Vajragarh, (2) Purandar, (3) Kondana, (4) Rohira, (5) Lohgarh, (6) Isagarh, (7) Tanki, (8) Tikona, *in Konkan* (9) Mahuli, (10) Muranjan, (11) Khirdurg, (12) Bhandardurg, (13) Tulsi-khul, (14) Nardurg, (15) Khaigarh or Ankola, (16) Marg-garh or Atra, (17) Kohaj, (18) Basant, (19) Nang, (20) Karnala, (21) Songarh, (22) Mangarh, (23) Khad-kala near Kondana.

These terms were reported to the Emperor for ratification, together with a letter of submission and prayer for pardon from Shiva (but really drafted by Jai Singh's secretary Udairaj) and a despatch from Jai Singh recommending the acceptance of the terms and the granting of a robe of honour to Shiva They reached Aurangzib at Delhi on 23rd June and he was pleased to accede to them all [*H. A* Ben MS. 207*a*, *A. N.* 907; Parasnis MS. No 8]

Thus, in less than three months from the date when

he opened the campaign, Jai Singh had succeeded in bringing Shiva down on his knees; he had made this haughty chief cede a large part of his dominions and consent to serve as a dependent vassal of the Emperor. It was a splendid victory. Shiva loyally carried out his promises: in the war with Bijapur he with his contingent rendered distinguished service under the Mughal banner and was mentioned in the despatches.

§19. *Shivaji assists the Mughals in the invasion of Bijapur.*

The war with Shiva having been thus happily ended and the terms of the Treaty of Purandar faithfully carried out, Jai Singh now began to make preparations for the invasion of Bijapur, in order to prevent his large army from eating its bread in idleness after its recent victorious campaign in Maharashtra. In September he received the Emperor's despatch accepting all his recommendations about Shiva together with a gracious *farman* (stamped with the impression of his palm) and a robe of honour for the latter. Jai Singh invited Shiva to come and receive these marks of imperial favour with befitting solemnity. "Shivaji, then in Adil-Shahi Konkan, immediately on hearing of it, travelled quickly and reached my camp on 27th September, 1665. On the 30th, I sent him, with my son Kirat Singh and my Paymaster Jani Khan, to advance and welcome the imperial letter on the way."

A little mummery was acted on this occasion, to satisfy the etiquette of the Mughal Court: "As Shiva had worn no weapon on his person from the day when he had come like a penitent offender to wait on the Rajah up to this date, Jai Singh now gave him a jewelled sword and dagger and pressed him to put them on." (*A. N.* 907.) The ceremony completed his restoration to the good grace of the Emperor.

Jai Singh then dismissed Shivaji to enable him to gather his contingent of 9,000 men and make the necessary preparations for the coming campaign, offering him two *lakhs* of Rupees from the imperial treasury for the purpose Shiva promised to join Jai Singh the day before he started.

At last, on 20th November, 1665, Jai Singh set out on the invasion of Bijapur,* from the fort of Purandar. The Maratha contingent, 9,000 strong, under Shiva and his kinsman (*khwesh*) Netaji Palkar,—"whom the Deccanis regard as a second Shivaji,"—formed the Left Centre of the Mughal army.

During the first month of the campaign, Jai Singh's march was an uninterrupted triumph. From Purandar to Mangalbirah (Mangalvedhe), a fort 52 miles north of Bijapur, the invaders advanced without meeting with any opposition, the Bijapuri forts on the way were either evacuated in terror or surrendered at call to Shiva's troops, who had been sent ahead by Jai Singh to capture them. Phaltan, about forty miles south-east of Purandar, was entered on 7th December, Thathora, 14 miles south-west of Phaltan, on the 8th; Khatav (25 miles s of Phaltan) about a week later; and Mangalbirah itself

---

* The invasion of Bijapur by Jai Singh and Shivaji *Haft Anjuman*, (Ben MS) *78a—94a*, *138b*, *172b—173b*, *190b*, *192a—193b*, *201b—202a*, *214a—215a*, *231a—233b*, *Storia*, ii 141—142, *A N* 988—1021, *B S* 406—427, the narrative in *Tarikh-i-Ali II* is useless, the sense being completely buried under the flowers of rhetoric. The Maratha writers are totally silent For details about the war, see my *History of Aurangzib*, vol iv ch xli In Nov 1665, Prince Muazzam left for the Court after handing over the viceroyalty of the Deccan to Jai Singh (*A N* 924)

on the 18th. For these services Shivaji received a letter of praise, a robe of honour, and a jewelled dagger from the Emperor. (Parasnis MS. letter No. 9.)

The invaders marched on, and then, on 24th December, they came into touch with the enemy for the first time. Next day, a Mughal detachment under Dilir Khan and Shivaji marched 10 miles from their camp and fought a Bijapuri army of 12,000 under the famous generals Sharza Khan and Khawas Khan and their Maratha auxiliaries under Jadav Rao [Ghorpare?] of Kaliani and Vyankoji, the half-brother of Shivaji. The Deccanis evaded the charge of the cavaliers of Delhi, but harassed them by their "cossack tactics," dividing themselves into four bodies and fighting loosely with the Mughal divisions opposite. After a long contest, Dilir Khan's tireless energy and courage broke the enemy force by repeated charges, and they retired in the afternoon, leaving one general (Yaqut the Abyssinian) and 15 captains dead on the field and many flags, horses and weapons in the Mughal hands. But as soon as the victors began their return march to camp, the elusive enemy reappeared and galled them severely with rockets from the two wings and rear. The Maratha rear-guard under Netaji bore the brunt of the attack, but stood its ground well. When the Deccanis hemmed Neta round and pressed him hard, he called for reinforcements from Kirat Singh and Fath Jang Khan, and with their aid repulsed the enemy. Jadav Rao of Kaliani received a musket-shot, of which he died in five or six days. Shivaji and his brother Vyankoji fought on opposite sides!

After a two days' halt, Jai Singh resumed his march on the 27th. The next day, after reaching the camping-ground in the evening, he detached a force to attack and expel the Bijapuri army from the neighbourhood The fight soon became general, and Jai Singh himself had to charge the enemy's largest division. Shivaji and Kumar Kirat Singh, seated on the same elephant, led his Van and dashed into the Deccani ranks. After a hard fight, the enemy were put to flight leaving more than a hundred dead and many more wounded

On 29th December, 1665, Jai Singh arrived at Makhnapur,* ten miles north of Bijapur fort Here his advance was stopped, and after waiting for a week, he was forced to begin his retreat on 5th January, 1666, as he found his fondly hoped-for chance of taking Bijapur by a *coup de main* gone. He was not prepared for a regular siege, because, in his eagerness "to grasp the golden opportunity" of attacking Bijapur while undefended and torn by domestic factions, he had not brought any big artillery and siege-materials with himself. On the other hand, Adil Shah had put the fort of Bijapur in a strong posture of defence, its walls had been repaired, large quantities of provisions and material laid in, its regular garrison augmented by 30,000 Karnatak infantry, and the country round for a radius of seven miles laid waste, drained of its water-supply, and denuded of its trees At the same time he had sent a picked force under Sharza Khan and Siddi Masaud to invade the Mughal dominions and make a diversion in Jai Singh's rear.

On 27th January, the retreating Mughal army reached a place 16 miles from Parenda,. and there halted for 24 days Here we shall leave it, as the historian of Shivaji is not concerned with its operations any further.

---

* In the Persian MS the name may be read either as *Makhanah* or as *Nagthana* The latter is a village 8 miles n n e of Bijapur

§20. *Shivaji fails at Panhala. 1666.*

On receiving the unexpected check before Bijapur, Jai Singh looked round, to create a diversion. As he writes in a despatch to the Court, "At my request the Emperor had [on 25th Dec.] sent a robe of honour and a jewelled dagger for Shiva, who was ready to co-operate at the siege of Bijapur, but......I did not deem it expedient. Shiva said to me,—'If you detach me, I can go and capture for the Emperor Panhala, of which I know all the exits and entrances, while the garrison are off their guard. I shall raise so much disturbance in that district that the enemy will be compelled to divert a large force from their army to oppose me.' As his words bore promise of action, I sent him away on his promised errand." (*H. A.*, Ben. MS. 84*b*.)

But there was a deeper reason for this step, as we learn from Jai Singh's secret correspondence. The unexpected failure before the fort of Bijapur gave rise to dissensions in the Mughal camp. The party hostile to Jai Singh, which was led by Dilir Khan,* ascribed his ill-success to the lukewarmness or treachery of Shivaji, and demanded that he should be imprisoned as a punishment. Jai Singh saw the danger in which Shiva stood among the defeated and sullen Mughal soldiery. To safeguard the liberty of the Maratha chief, and send him

---

* Manucci attests that Dilir Khan several times urged Jai Singh "to take Shivaji's life, or at least to give him (Dilir Khan) leave to do so He would assume all responsibility, and see that the Rajah was held blameless" (*Storia*, ii 137.) The English factory records state, "In a battle between the Mughals and this country people, Shivaji ran away, being afraid that Dilir Khan would put him to death, he having told the said wazir [Dilir] that he would take Bijapur in 10 days' time, upon which persuasion he set forwards with 20,000 horse, but to his cost he found the contrary, being forced quickly to retire" (Deccan News in *F R*. Surat, vol. 104)

out of the reach of his enemies, he gladly accepted the proposal that the Maratha contingent should make a diversion in the western provinces of Bijapur. (*H A*, 195*a*, 84*b*, 192*a*; hints only.)

Shiva left Jai Singh about 11th January, 1666. Five days later he reached the environs of Panhala, and delivered an assault on it three hours before sunrise. But the garrison were on the alert and offered a stubborn defence A thousand of Shiva's followers fell, killed and wounded. When the rising sun lit up the scene, Shiva at last recognized that it was madness to continue the struggle, and drew back sullenly to his own fort of Khelna [Vishalgarh], about 27 miles westwards. But his troops continued to ravage that quarter and succeeded in drawing and detaining there a force of 6,000 Bijapuris under Siddi Masaud and Randaula Khan. (*H. A.* 84*b*—85*a*; *A. N.* 1002.)

The news of Shivaji's failure at Panhala reached Jai Singh on 20th January. The evil was aggravated by the desertion of Netaji. Taking offence with Shiva for some reason or other,—probably because he deemed his valuable services and gallant feats of arms inadequately rewarded,—Neta accepted the Bijapuri bait of 4 *lakhs* of *hun* and, deserting to Adil Shah, raided the Mughal territory with great vigour and effect. Jai Singh could not afford to lose such a man; and so he lured Netaji back (20th March) with many persuasive letters and the granting of all his high demands, *viz.*, the *mansab* of a Commander of Five Thousand in the Mughal peerage, a jagir in the settled and lucrative old territory of the empire (as distinct from the ill-conquered, unsettled, ever-ravaged recent annexations in the Deccan), and Rs. 38,000 in cash. (*H. A.* 193).

Netaji's defection at the end of January, 1666, coming so soon after the recent reverses, greatly alarmed Jai Singh. If Shiva were to do the same, the entire Maratha army would join the enemy's ranks and the Mughal invaders would be crushed between the two. As he wrote to the Emperor, "Now that Adil Shah and Qutb Shah have united in mischief, it is necessary to win Shiva's heart by all means and to send him to Northern India to have audience of Your Majesty." (94*a*) The Emperor having consented to this proposal, Jai Singh set himself to induce Shiva to visit the imperial Court.

CHAPTER VI

Visit to Aurangzib, 1666

§ 1. *Shivaji's fears and hopes from a journey to the Mughal Court.*

Jai Singh had undertaken to send Shivaji to the imperial Court But it was no easy task. In the Treaty of Purandar, Shivaji had expressly stipulated that he was not to be called upon to enter the Mughal military service (*mansab*), nor to attend the imperial Court There were strong reasons for it. For one thing, he and his countrymen had no faith in Aurangzib's word and believed the Emperor to be capable of any act of treachery and cruelty Then, again, the Maratha chief had an inborn repugnance to bending his head before a Muslim; he had been brought up in the freedom and solitude of hill and woodland, away from cities and Courts; he had imbibed the orthodox Hindu spirit from his mother and his tutor, from the comrades of his boyhood and the saints whom he adored; and he had risen to independent sovereignty without ever filling any subordinate post as the servant of a higher authority. He was therefore at first averse to visit the imperial Court.

But Jai Singh plied him with hopes of high reward and "used a thousand devices" (as he repeatedly wrote in his letters), to induce him to go to Agra. The Maratha chronicles assert that Jai Singh gave Shiva hopes that after his visit to the Emperor he was likely to be sent back as Viceroy of Mughal Deccan, with sufficient men and money for the conquest of Bijapur and Golkonda.

The Emperor never committed himself to any such promise, and the Persian histories and Jai Singh's correspondence are silent about it. But it is very probable that among the vague hopes which the wily Rajput general held out to Shiva, was that of being appointed Viceroy of the Deccan, where all the preceding imperial representatives, including Jai Singh himself, had failed, and only a born general and renowned conqueror like Shiva could be expected to succeed. The Deccan charge was so heavy and mere generals had so often wasted imperial resources there, that in 1656 and 1666 the Emperor had talked of going there in person and conducting the war against the local Sultans. Shiva's past achievements promised success for such an enterprise, if the vast resources of Delhi were placed under a tried military genius like him. What could be more reasonable (Jai Singh may have argued) than that the Emperor, after seeing Shiva and personally learning of his merits, would appoint him Viceroy of the Deccan* to achieve its conquest and save himself the trouble?

Besides the problematical viceroyalty of the Deccan, Shiva had some humbler but more necessary objects which could be gained only by a personal interview with the Emperor. He had requested that the Emperor should order the Siddi, now an imperial servant, to cede Janjira island to him. On this point the reply from Delhi had been evasive; but much better result could be expected from an interview and personal representation.

In spite of these temptations, Shiva hesitated long.

---

* Sabhasad, 46 and 50, says that Shiva himself made the offer of conquering Bijapur and Golkonda for the Emperor, if he were appointed Mughal commander-in-chief in the Deccan and permitted to annex the former Nizam-Shahi dominions, and that Jai Singh merely agreed to the proposal.

Both he and his friends were as much alarmed at the idea of his going to the Mughal Court as they had been at the prospect of his interview with Afzal Khan six years ago They feared that a visit to Aurangzib would be only rushing into the jaws of an ogre (Ravan) But the soothsayers whom he consulted assured him of a safe return home (Sabh. 47, *T S. 22b*)

Jai Singh took the most solemn oaths possible for a Hindu that Shiva would not be harmed during his visit, while the Rajput Rajah's son and agent at Court, Kumar Ram Singh, similarly pledged his word for the safety of Shiva during his stay at the capital. In the Maratha council of ministers the majority favoured the journey.

§2. *His arrangements for his absence.*

Shivaji's arrangements for the administration of his kingdom during his expected absence in Northern India, were a masterpiece of forethought and organization. His plan was to make his local representatives absolutely independent of any need for his orders or guidance during his absence. The administration of his territories and forts would go on as efficiently as before, even if he were imprisoned or killed at Agra. His mother Jija Bai was left as Regent, with Moro Pant the *Peshwa*, Niloji Sondev the *majmuadar*, and Netaji Palkar the commander-in-chief under her orders. (Sabh. 47). The commandants of his forts were strictly ordered to be watchful day and night and to follow his rules implicitly, so as to guard against surprise or fraud. The civil officers were to follow his current regulations and practice in all matters.

After making a tour of inspection throughout his small kingdom, and even paying surprise visits to some of his forts, and repeating, as his final instructions to his officers, "Act as I had previously laid down," Shivaji took leave of his family at Rajgarh, and began his journey to Northern India, about the third week of March, 1666, with his eldest son Shambhuji, seven trusty chief officers, and 4,000 troops.* A *lakh* of Rupees from the Deccan treasury was advanced to him by order of the Emperor for his expenses, and Ghazi Beg, an officer of Jai Singh's army, was deputed to act as his guide.

§ 3. *Shivaji's journey to Agra.*

On the way, he received an imperial letter, written from Agra on 5th April, saying, "Received your letter stating that you have started for my Court. Come quickly with composure of mind, and after receiving my favours you will be permitted to return home. I send you a robe of honour [with this.]" (Parasnis MS., Letter No. 10).

When he reached Aurangabad, his fame and splendidly dressed escort drew all the people out of the city to gaze on him. But Saf Shikan Khan, the governor of the place, despising Shiva as a mere zamindar and a Maratha, remained with his officers in the audience-hall, and merely sent his nephew to receive Shiva on the way and ask him to come and see him there. Shivaji was highly offended at this intended slight of the governor and asserted his dignity by riding straight to his appointed quarters in the city, entirely ignoring the governor's existence. Saf Shikan Kan then climbed down and visited Shiva at his residence with all the Mughal officers! Next day, Shiva returned the visit, showing great

---

*Sabh 47 *Dil* 57 says 1,000 soldiers, which I consider as more probable

politeness and cordiality to all. After a halt of some days, he resumed his march, receiving rations and presents from the local officers along his route, as ordered by the Emperor. (*Dil.* 57-58.) On 9th May he arrived in the outskirts of Agra, in which city the Emperor was then holding Court.

§ 4. *Shivaji's interview with Aurangzib.*

The 12th of the month was appointed as the day of his audience.* It was the 50th lunar birthday of the Emperor. The Hall of Public Audience in Agra Fort was splendidly decorated for the occasion. The courtiers appeared in their most gorgeous robes. All things were ready for weighing the Emperor against gold and silver, which would then be given away in charity. The nobles of the empire and their retainers in thousands stood in marshalled ranks filling that vast hall of pillars and the ground beyond on three sides of it, which was covered with costly canopies.

Into this *Diwan-i-am*, Kumar Ram Singh ushered Shivaji with his son Shambhuji and ten of his officers. On behalf of the Maratha chief, 1,500 gold pieces were laid before the Emperor as present (*nazar*) and Rs. 6,000 as benedictory offering (*nisar*). Aurangzib graciously cried out, "Come up, Shivaji Rajah!" Shivaji was led to the foot of the throne and made three *salams*. Then, at a sign from the Emperor, he was conducted back to the place reserved for him among the third-grade nobles, the work of the *darbar* proceeded, and Shivaji seemed to have been forgotten.

* Shivaji's audience with Aurangzib: *A. N.* 963, 968—970; *H. A.* 238*a*; Surat to Karwar, 8 June, 1666, in *F. R.* Surat, vol. 86; (all contemporary.) Sabh. 49; *Storia*, ii. 138; K. K. ii. 189—190; *Dil.* 58—59; (all reliable.)

This was not the kind of reception he had so long been picturing to himself and expecting* as almost a certainty from his many conversations with Jai Singh. Ever since coming to Agra his mind had been ill at ease. First, he had been welcomed on behalf of the Emperor in the environs of the city by Ram Singh and Mukhlis Khan, two petty officers holding the nominal ranks of 2,500 and 1,500 respectively. No costly present, no high title, no kind word even, had followed his bow to the throne. He found himself standing behind several rows of nobles who almost shut him from the Emperor's view. He learnt from Ram Singh that he was standing among the commanders of 5,000. "What!" he exclaimed, "my little son of seven years was created a 5-hazari without having had to come to the Emperor's presence. My servant Netaji is a 5-hazari. And am I, after rendering all these services and coming all the way to the Court, to get the same low rank?" Then he asked, who the noble standing in front of him was. Ram Singh replied that it was Maharajah Jaswant Singh. At this Shiva cried out, "Jaswant, whose back my soldiers have seen! I to stand behind him! What does it mean?"†

* This view is supported by the Persian and English accounts "Shiva cherished some absurd fancies and hopes So, after standing for a while, he created a scene, retired to a corner and told Kumar Ram Singh that he was disappointed, making unreasonable and foolish complaints" (*A N* 969) "His spirit could not bear such humiliation as the other Umarahs to wait at a distance with their hands before them, like mutes The thought thereof put him into a fever, which the king hearing (it is said) sent to comfort him with promises of great preferment" (Surat to Karwar, 8 June) Also K K

† Here I follow Sabhasad *Dilkasha*, 58, says that it was Rai Singh Sisodia (a subordinate of Jai Singh and the son of Maharana Bhim Singh), who was created a 5-hazari for his services at Purandar (*M U* ii 300; *A N* 868, 989)

Stung to fury by what he considered a public humiliation, Shivaji expostulated with Ram Singh in a high tone, and even wanted to commit suicide* rather than outlive such a shame. Ram Singh, alarmed at this unexpected development and the breach of Court etiquette caused by Shiva's loud voice and violent gestures, tried his best to pacify him, but in vain Swelling with suppressed anger and fretting within himself in bitterness of mortification, Shivaji fell down in a swoon. (*Dil.* 59; K. K. ii. 190, Surat to Karwar.) There was a stir among the courtiers The Emperor asked what the matter was. Ram Singh diplomatically replied, "The tiger is a wild beast of the forest. He feels oppressed by heat in a place like this and has been taken ill." He also apologized for the Rajah's rude conduct by saying that he was a Deccani unfamiliar with Courts and polished manners. Aurangzib graciously ordered the sick Rajah to be removed to an ante-room and sprinkled with rose-water, and, on his restoration to his senses, gave him leave to go to his quarters without waiting for the close of the *darbar*.

§5. *Shivaji placed under guard by order of Aurangzib.*

On returning from the Court, Shivaji openly taxed

* Here I follow K K ii 190 and *Storia,* ii 138 But Sabhasad, 49, says that he begged for Ram Singh s dagger in order to kill Jaswant! The prolific imagination of the Hindi poet Bhushan has distorted the incident into the following absurd shape "On the day of the Court festivity [birthday], Aurangzib sat on the throne like Indra, with his subjects around him But the sight of all this splendour could not make Shiva tremble He made no *salam,* he despised the pomp and force of the Padishah They made him stand in the ranks of the 5-hazari *mansabdars,* as if he were not distinct from them Bhushan says that Aurangzib's ministers had no sense of propriety He (Shivaji) could not get the sword from the belt [of Ram Singh] and the Muslim (Aurangzib) saved himself [by running] into the ghushalkhana" (Bhushan, *Granthavali,* pp 66, 70, also 68)

the Emperor with breach of faith towards him, and asked to be put to death as a lesser evil. There were men about him who reported his angry words and complaints here and in the darbar hall to Aurangzib, and it only increased the Emperor's dislike and distrust of the Maratha chief. Ram Singh was ordered to lodge him in the Jaipur House outside the city-walls, and be responsible for his custody. Shiva was forbidden the Court, though Shambhuji was asked to come now and then. Thus, Shivaji's high hopes were finally dashed to pieces and he found himself a prisoner instead. (*Dil.* 59; *A. N.* 969)

He took counsel with his devoted followers and with Raghunath Pant Korde, his agent at the imperial Court, as to how he could effect his release. They advised him to play on the Emperor's greed of territory and to promise the conquest of Bijapur and Golkonda* as the price of his restoration to liberty. A petition to this effect was presented by the hand of Raghunath Korde, but the Emperor only answered, "Wait a little and I shall do what you ask for." Shiva knew the answer was evasive. He had begged for a private interview with the Emperor in which he promised to make a secret communication very much to the benefit of the latter. The Maratha chronicles say that the prime-minister Jafar Khan, warned by a letter from Shaista Khan, dissuaded the Emperor from risking his person in a private interview with a magician like Shiva. But Aurangzib hardly needed other people's advice in such a matter. He was too wise to meet in a small room with a few guards the man who had slain Afzal Khan almost within sight of his 10,000

---

* Or Qandahar, according to *Dil* 69

soldiers, and wounded Shaista Khan in the very bosom of his harem amidst a ring of 20,000 Mughal troops, and escaped unscathed Popular report credited Shiva with being a wizard with "an airy body," able to jump across 40 or 50 yards of space upon the person of his victim. The private audience was refused.

Shivaji next tried to win over the prime-minister, and paid him a visit, begging him to use his influence with the Emperor to send him back to the Deccan with adequate resources for extending the Mughal empire there. Jafar Khan, warned by his wife (a sister of Shaista Khan) not to trust himself too long in the company of Shiva, hurriedly ended the interview, saying "All right; I shall speak to the Emperor and make the arrangements" Shiva knew that he meant to do nothing. (Sabh 50-51.)

He was now thrown entirely upon his own resources. At the same time his position became worse than before. Fulad Khan, the police chief of Agra, was ordered to place a guard with artillery round the house of Shiva, who now became a prisoner in appearance as well as reality. "This made the Rajah lose heart; he felt sad and lamented long, clasping Shambhuji to his breast." In this state he passed three months.

§ 6. *Mughal policy during Shivaji's confinement at Agra.*

We now turn to the policy of the imperial Government and the action of Jai Singh during this interval. Aurangzib had intended to present Shiva with an elephant, a robe of honour, and some jewels at the end of his first audience. But Shiva's violation of Court etiquette made him change his mind, and as a mark of displeasure he withheld these gifts, at least for a time. (*H. A.* 238*a.*) The Maratha chief, on his part, complained that the promises made to him on behalf of the Mughal Government had not been kept. Aurangzib, therefore, wrote to Jai Singh asking him to report fully and exactly what promises he had made. The Rajah replied by repeating and explaining the clauses of the Treaty of Purandar, and solemnly asserting that nothing beyond them had been promised. (*A. N.* 970. But *H. A.* does not contain Jai Singh's reply.)

Jai Singh was placed in a dilemma by this unexpected result of Shiva's visit to the Court. True, he had sent Shiva away to Northern India "by a thousand devices" in order to get him out of the Deccan when the military situation there turned against the Mughals; but he had also pledged his honour for the safe return of his ally. He, therefore, tried to persuade the Emperor that he would gain nothing by imprisoning or killing Shiva, as the Maratha chief's wise arrangements had made his Government independent of his personality; on the contrary the imperial interests in that quarter would be best promoted by turning Shiva into a friend, at the same time that such a course would convince the public of the sacredness of the imperial officers' words. All the while Jai Singh continued to write to his Court agent, Ram Singh, to see to it that Shiva's life was safe and the solemn assurances of Jai Singh and his son remained inviolate. (*H. A.* 234*a.*)

This, however, was no easy matter. It was impossible for Jai Singh to change Aurangzib's crooked policy, or, at times, even to divine it. The Emperor seemed at first to have played a waiting game—to keep

Shiva under surveillance in order to prevent his escape, and to decide after the conclusion of the Deccan campaign if and when he would be released. At first Ram Singh was ordered to stand bail and security for the good conduct and presence of Shiva at Agra. Jai Singh protested against this responsibility being thrown on his son, and urged the latter to try his best to be relieved of it. After a short time, Aurangzib changed his mind, evidently because he distrusted a Hindu prince as the keeper of another Hindu prince, and for a few days talked of taking Shiva out of his bail and sending him to Afghanistan, where he would be beyond the possibility of escape, as was actually done in the case of Netaji Palkar afterwards But the idea was soon dropped. (*H. A.* 196*b*; *Dil.* 69, Surat to Karwar) Then the Emperor proposed to set out for the Deccan to conduct the war in person, while Shiva would be left a State-prisoner at Agra in charge of Ram Singh, who would be appointed *qiladar* of the capital for the purpose Jai Singh vehemently urged his son to avoid this disagreeable duty, but advised the Emperor to leave Shiva at Agra. "When I prayed that Shiva might be permitted to return home, affairs [in the Deccan] were in a different condition. Now that they have changed altogether [against us,] it is not at all politic to send him to this side Please detain him in such a way that his officers may not despair [about his return], go over to Adil Shah and raise disturbances [against us.]. .... It would be expedient to leave Shiva at Agra. He ought to be conciliated and assured that he would be summoned to the Court after it had arrived in the Deccan. His son should, as a matter of policy, be kept with the Emperor, in order that his followers may not be thrown into despair, but may loyally serve us." [*H. A.* 194*a*, 197*a*.] But the war in the Deccan steadily went against the Mughals, and Shiva's hope of an early release grew dimmer and dimmer.

§7. *Shivaji's escape from Agra.*

He, therefore, turned to his own inner resources to effect his liberation.* After a few days of captivity, he made a loud profession of submission and fear and entreated courtier after courtier to intercede with the Emperor for his pardon, but with no success. (*Akhbarat*, 9-32.) He, however, succeeded in getting permission for his Maratha escort to return to the Deccan. The Emperor felt that he would then have fewer enemies to watch and Shiva would be utterly friendless at Agra.

The Maratha civil officers, too, at a hint from their chief, returned home in small parties. Being thus freed from anxiety about his followers, Shivaji set about devising plans for his own escape. He feigned illness and began to send out of his house every evening sweetmeats for Brahmans, religious mendicants and courtiers. These were carried in huge baskets slung from a pole which was borne by two men on their shoulders. The guards searched the baskets for some days and then began to let them pass out unchallenged. This was the opportunity for which Shivaji had been waiting. In the afternoon of 19th August, he sent word to his guards that he was very ill and had taken to his bed and that they should not disturb him. His half-brother Hiraji Farzand, who looked somewhat like him, lay down on his cot,

---

*Shivaji's escape from Agra *A N* 971 (one sentence only !), Bernier, 190, (same), *Storia*, ii 139-140, Sabh 52-55 and K K ii 198-201, 217-220, (most detailed), *Dil* 59-61, Malkaré, 52-56, *T S* 23*a*-25*a*; Fryer, ii 65.

with a quilt covering all his body except the outstretched right arm adorned with Shiva's gold wristlet,—while Shiva and his son crouched down in two baskets, which were safely sent out shortly after sunset through the lines of unsuspecting guards, being preceded and followed by baskets of real sweets.

The baskets were deposited at a lonely spot outside the city; the porters were dismissed; and then Shiva and his son issued forth and made their way to a village six miles from Agra, where the trusty Niraji Raoji (his Chief Justice) was waiting for them with horses. After a hurried consultation in a jungle the party divided; Shiva with his son and three officers, Niraji Raoji, Datta Trimbak and Raghumitra, smeared themselves with ashes like Hindu ascetics, and hastened towards Mathura, while the others took their own way homewards.

§8. *His escape discovered by the police.*

Meanwhile, at Agra, Hiraji lay in Shivaji's bed all that night and well into the afternoon of the next day. The guards who peeped in in the morning were satisfied when they saw Shiva's gold bracelet on the sleeper's wrist, and a servant sitting on the floor massaging the royal patient's feet. About 3 P.M. Hiraji quietly walked out of the house with the servant, warning the sentries at the gate, "Make less noise; Shivaji is ill and under treatment." Gradually the guards' suspicion was aroused; the house seemed strangely deserted, no crowd of visitors came to see Shiva as usual; and there was no sound, no stir in the house They entered his room and found that the bird had flown away! They at once ran with the astounding news to their chief Fulad Khan, who reported it to the Emperor, ascribing Shiva's flight to witchcraft and saving himself from all blame. "The Rajah," so he said, "was in his own room. We visited it regularly. But he vanished all of a sudden from our sight. Whether he flew into the sky or disappeared into the earth, is not known, nor what magical trick he has played."

Aurangzib was not the man to be taken in by such a tale. A hue and cry was immediately raised, and fast couriers and sergeants-at-arms were sent off to watch the road to the Deccan through Berar and Khandesh, and to warn the local officers to look out for the fugitives. The Maratha Brahmans and other followers of Shivaji were arrested wherever found, at Agra or near it. But by this time Shiva had had twenty-four hours' clear start over his pursuers.

The vigorous inquiry made at the capital gradually brought to light the details of the romantic flight. Suspicion naturally fell on Ram Singh, as he had so often tried to avoid accepting responsibility for Shiva's presence at Agra, and it was his interest to effect the Maratha chief's safe return home, for which he and his father had pledged their honour. Some of the Maratha Brahmans who were caught admitted, probably under torture, that their master had fled with the connivance of Ram Singh. (*H. A.* 201*a.*) The Rajput prince was punished, first by being forbidden the Court and then being deprived of his rank and pay.*

---

*Trimbak Pant (*Dabir*) and Raghunath Pant Korde were arrested on 20th August, and escaped from Agra on 3rd April next year (*J S*) The three leading Brahmans of Shiva's service under arrest were probably tortured by Fúlad Khan They alleged that the flight of Shivaji was due to the advice of Ram Singh and resulted from the latter's neglect to watch him well (*H A* 200*a*, 201*a*) Eleven months later, on the death of his

§9. *Route of Shivaji's flight.*

With consummate cunning Shiva threw his pursuers off the scent, by following a route exactly opposite to that which leads to Maharashtra. Instead of moving due south-west from Agra, through Malwa and Khandesh or Gujrat, he travelled *northwards* to Mathura, then *eastwards* to Allahabad, Benares and Gaya, and finally south-westwards through Gondwana and Golkonda, describing a vast loop round India before returning to Rajgarh.

Arrived at Mathura, he found the boy Shambhu worn out by fatigue and unable to proceed further. Three Deccani Brahmans,—Krishnaji, Kashi, and Visaji, brothers-in-law of Moro Trimbak (the Peshwa), were living at this holy city. Niraji knew them and confided to them the story of Shiva's escape and his present plight. They nobly responded to the appeal in the name of their country and faith, and braving all risks of imperial vengeance in the event of detection, they agreed to keep Shambhuji* till Shiva should reach home and write for him. One of the brothers, Krishnaji, even undertook to guide the fugitives as far as Benares

Shivaji had crammed the hollow core of a *sannyasi's* staff with gems and gold coins. Some more money was concealed in his shoes, and a diamond of great value and several rubies coated with wax were sewn in the dresses of his servants or carried in their mouths.

At Mathura, which was reached within six hours of leaving Agra, he shaved off his beard and moustaches,

---

father, Ram Singh was taken back into favour and created a 4-hazari, but was soon afterwards sent to join the army fighting in Assam, to die of pestilence there (*A N* 1051)

* According to the Maratha chroniclers, also *Dil* 61, Shambhuji was left at Mathura in charge of Kashi Pant and his brothers But K K (ii 201 & 218) incorrectly says that he was entrusted to Kavi Kulesh at Allahabad

smeared himself with ashes, and put on the disguise of *sannyasis*. "Travelling in the darkness of the night with swift Deccani couriers, who were practised in the art of moving in various disguises and assumed characters," he rapidly left the capital behind him. Forty or fifty of his servants accompanied him divided into three parties and dressed as monks of the three Hindu orders, Bairagis, Gosains, and Udasis. (K. K. ii. 200 and 217.)

§10. *Adventures of Shivaji during his flight.*

The fugitives pursued their way, constantly changing their disguise, sometimes passing for religious mendicants, sometimes as petty traders, and escaped detection because no one dreamt of their going to the eastern provinces of India while their destination was the west. They, however, had some hairbreadth escapes.

In one town they were arrested on suspicion by the *faujdar* Ali Quli, who had learnt of Shivaji's flight from a letter of his Court agent before he received the official intimation of it. A close examination of the prisoners was begun. But at midnight Shivaji met the *faujdar* in private, boldly disclosed his identity and offered him a diamond and a ruby worth a *lakh* of Rupees as the price of his liberation. The *faujdar* preferred the bribe to his duty. (K. K. ii. 218.)

After performing his bath at the junction of the Ganges and Jamuna at Allahabad, Shivaji proceeded to Benares. Here he hurriedly went through all the rites of a pilgrim in the dim morning twilight and slipped out of the town just as a courier arrived from Agra with the proclamation for his arrest and a hue and cry was started.*

Still moving eastwards, he visited the famous Hindu shrine of Gaya and was joined by two of his men whom he had sent there beforehand. Then they turned south-westwards and returned home by way of Gondwana, Haidarabad and Bijapur territories "Through travelling long distances on foot every day, he felt a desire for riding At the time of buying a pony he had not a sufficient number of Rupees with him. So, opening his purse of gold coins, he gave a few of them to the horse-dealer The flight of Shivaji had already been noised abroad, and the man cried out, 'You must be Shiva, as you are paying so much for a little pony!' At this Shivaji gave him the whole purse [as hush money] and fled from the place " (*Dil.* 61)

We have a characteristic anecdote about an incident during this journey The story runs (Malkaré 54), that the pretended *sannyasis* one evening took refuge in the house of a peasant in a village on the Godavari The old mother of the host apologized to the holy men for

---

* In this connection Khafi Khan (ii 219-220) writes —"When I was at the port of Surat, a Brahman physician named Nabha [or Babha] used to tell the following tale "I had been serving one of the Benares Brahmans as his pupil but he stinted me in food At last, one morning when it was still dark, I went to the river-side as usual , a man seized my hand, thrust into it a quantity of jewels, *ashrafis* and *huns*, and said, 'Don t open your fist, but quickly finish the bathing rites for me ' I immediately hastened to shave and bathe him, but had not done ministering to him, when a hue and cry was raised and the news spread that sergeants at the mace had arrived [from the Court] in search of Shiva When I became attentive I found that the man to whom I had been ministering had slipped away I [then] knew that it was Shivaji He had given me 9 gems, 9 *ashrafis* and 9 *huns* Then without going to my preceptor I returned to my country and reached Surat The grand house that I have here was bought with that money "

the poor fare placed before them, saying that the troopers of the brigand Shivaji had recently robbed the village. She cursed them and their master to her heart's content. Shivaji noted the names of the peasant and the village carefully, and on his return home, summoned the family of his host and gave them more than what they had lost in the raid.

A late tradition gives a charming picture of the scene of Shivaji's home-coming. "He went to the gate of Raigarh (*sic*), where his mother resided, and requested admittance to the presence of Jija Bai. The guards informed her that some strange Bairagis or religious medicants were at the gate of the fort and requested to see her. She desired that they should be admitted. When they came into her presence, Niraji Pant blessed her after the manner of the Bairagis; but Shiva advanced towards her and threw himself at her feet. She did not recognize him and was surprised......that a Bairagi should place his head on her feet......Shivaji then placed his head in Jija Bai's lap and took off his cap. She immediately perceived, by a mark on his head, that he was her son and embraced him." (Malkaré 54; Forrest, i. 17.)

His return to Rajgarh (20th November 1666) was followed by widespread rejoicings among his family, officers and subjects. It was a national deliverance, as providential as it was romantic.

He spread a false report that Shambhuji had died, and even went into mourning for him. Then, when the suspicion of the Mughal officers along the Deccan road had been thus lulled asleep, and some months had elapsed, he wrote to Mathura for his son, and the three of thers with their whole family migrated to Maharashtra, bringing Shambhuji disguised as a Brahman kinsman, with them.

At a certain outpost on the road, the Mughal officer suspected that Shambhuji was not of their family or caste, but his Brahman protectors dined with him to prove their kinship, and the danger was passed. (*T. S* 25*a*, *Dil* 61 gives a variant.) Shiva royally rewarded the faithful three—Krishnaji, Kashi Rao and Visaji,—gave them the title of *Vishwas Rao* (Lords Fidelity) and a *lakh* of gold pieces, and settled on them an annual revenue of 10,000 *hun* The devoted companions of his own escape were similarly rewarded. (Sabh. 57.)

Shivaji's escape from captivity caused lifelong regret to Aurangzib As the Emperor wrote in his last will and testament · "The greatest pillar of a Government is the keeping of information about everything that happens in the kingdom,—while even a minute's negligence results in shame for long years. See, how the flight of the wretch Shiva, which was due to carelessness, has involved me in all these distracting campaigns to the end of my days." (*Anec.* §10)

§11. *Jai Singh's anxieties and plans about Shivaji.*

We now turn to Jai Singh's anxieties, plans, and measures during Shivaji's absence from the Deccan. His correspondence with the Emperor and with Kumar Ram Singh during the three months of Shiva's captivity has been given before.

His position was rendered infinitely worse by Shiva's escape from Agra (19th August) He had been disgraced in the eyes of the Emperor by the failure of his invasion of Bijapur. And now his son Ram Singh was openly suspected of having connived at Shiva's flight.

As he writes in bitterness, "All the plans and devices that I had employed in sending Shiva to Court have been spoiled, and measureless distraction has fallen to my lot. But there is no remedy against Fate and what is written on a man's forehead. I learn from the letters of some Court agents that there is a proposal to dismiss Ram Singh from his rank (*mansab*) and jagir, because Shiva's Brahman followers, at the instigation of selfish men [my enemies at Court], have alleged that the flight of Shiva was due to the advice of Ram Singh, and resulted from the latter's omission to watch him well. May God give death to the man who cherishes the very thought of such an act of faithlessness in his heart! Why should Shiva's men's words be believed against mine, when I had reduced him to such an extremity [in war]?" [*H. A.* 201*a.*]

The anticipated return of Shivaji to the Deccan, greatly added to Jai Singh's fears. As he wrote on 5th November, 1666:—"The times are bad for me. My anxieties are ceaseless. The lying Bijapuris are wasting time [by delusive negotiations.] There is no trace or news of the fugitive Shiva. My days are passing in distraction and anxiety. I have sent trusty spies, in various disguises, to get news of Shiva." [*H. A.* 199*b*—200*a.*]

About this time the officers left by Shiva in the Deccan when starting for Agra began to display ominous activity. Sayyid Masaud, the Mughal *qiladar* of Rohira, wrote to Jai Singh's Paymaster complaining of the lack of provisions, etc. in the fort, and the collection of lead, gunpowder, rockets and infantry in the neighbourhood by some men who gave themselves out to be Shiva's followers and pretended that they intended to invade

Bijapuri territory. At this alarming news Jai Singh sent orders to provision the fort as a precaution and to hold it strongly, pending the arrival of Udai-bhan [the permanent *qiladar*?] A reinforcement of 500 infantry under Sukh-man Chauhan was also ordered to be thrown into the fort if necessary. [*H A*. 234.]

At last in December, 1666, definite news was received of Shiva's arrival at Rajgarh. As Jai Singh's secretary wrote, "Trusty spies have now brought the news that Shiva himself has arrived but is very anxious about his son who has not returned with him. He professes a determination [to submit] to the imperial Government. But who knows what is in his heart? For some time past Mahadji Nimbalkar, the son of Bajaji, the zamindar of Phaltan and son-in-law of the infernal Shiva, has been causing disturbances in the region of Puna and other places. My master [i e , Jai Singh] has appointed the jagirdars of that tract, such as, Tanaji [or Babaji?] Bhonslé and others to Supa, Halal Khan to Indapur, Ghalib Khan to Chamargunda, Hasan Khan, Abdur Rasul and other Deccanis also to that side, and Trimbakji Bhonslé and others to Raisin. Before the others could arrive at their posts, Tanaji Bhonslé went to his jagir and getting an opportunity attacked Mahadji, sent many of his followers to hell, captured his flag, *torah*, 150 horses, arrows, etc., and returning lived in peace of mind As the Deccanis have some [unknown] need for the flag and *torah*, Mahadji trod the path of submission and humility; but Tanaji declined [to restore them] At last, four days afterwards, that wretch got help from the Bijapuris and attacked Tanaji by surprise. That loyal and martial officer fought valiantly on foot, till he fell in the Emperor's service. And Anaji (or

Dataji) Deshmukh went to hell in the neighbourhood of Pandharpur. It is reported that Mahadji also was wounded .....Jai Singh at first wanted to march there in person [and retrieve the disaster], but was persuaded to give up the idea, lest the Bijapuris should take advantage of his absence. So, he has decided to send Abdul Hamid with 5,000 men to that quarter." [*H. A.* 211*b*.]

Then, in a letter to the prime-minister Jafar Khan we have this astounding proposal from Jai Singh to entrap Shiva by the false proposal of a marriage between his daughter and Jai Singh's son, and get him murdered during his journey to the Rajput general's camp :—

"I have not failed, nor will I do so in future, to exert myself against Bijapur, Golkonda and Shiva in every possible way.. ..... I am trying to arrange matters in such a way that the wicked wretch Shiva will come to see me once, and that in the course of his journey or return [our] clever men may get a favourable opportunity [of disposing of] that luckless fellow in his unguarded moment at that place. This slave of the Court himself, for furthering the Emperor's affairs, is prepared to go so far, regardless of the praise or blame of his act by other people,—that if the Emperor sanctions it, I shall set on foot a proposal for a match with his family and settle the marriage of my son with his daughter,—though the pedigree and caste of Shiva are notoriously low and men like me do not eat food touched by his hand (not to speak of entering into a matrimonial connection with him), and in case this wretch's daughter is captured I shall not condescend to keep her in my harem.' As he is of low caste, he will very likely be caught by this bait. But great care should be taken to keep this plan secret. Send me quickly a reply to enable me to act accordingly." [*H. A.* 139*a*]

This letter throws a lurid light on the political morals of the 17th century. When people argue that Afzal Khan could not have possibly intended to stab Shivaji during an interview, they should remember that the sanctimonious Jai Singh was prepared to prove his loyalty by lowering his family honour and laying a fatal snare for Shivaji, a brother Hindu.

CHAPTER VII

1667—1670

§1. *State of Mughal Deccan, 1667.*

On returning home from Agra in November 1666, Shivaji found the political situation in the Deccan entirely changed. The Mughal viceroy, Jai Singh, was no longer in a position to repeat his former success over the Marathas. Worn out by age, toil, disappointment and domestic anxieties, discredited in his master's eyes by the failure of his invasion of Bijapur, and expecting every day to be removed from his post, Mirza Rajah was visibly hastening to his grave. In May 1667 Prince Muazzam, the newly appointed governor, reached Aurangabad and relieved Jai Singh of his charge. The Rajput veteran set out on his homeward journey in extreme misery of mind and sense of public humiliation, and died on the way at Burhanpur on 2nd July.

The return of the weak and indolent Muazzam and the friendly Jaswant to power in the Deccan (May 1667) relieved Shivaji of all fear from the Mughal side. It is true that soon afterwards an able and active general, bearing implacable hatred to the Marathas, joined the Mughal camp. Dilir Khan returned from the Gond country to the side of Prince Muazzam in October 1667, but the coming of this famous warrior brought no accession of strength to the imperialists. The Prince was jealous of Dilir's influence and prestige at his father's Court, resented his insubordinate spirit, and regarded him as a spy on behalf of the Emperor. The proud Rohila general, on his part, publicly slighted Maharajah Jaswant

Singh, the right-hand man and trusted confidant of the Prince. Nor was this the only source of discord in the Mughal army in the Deccan. Rao Karn Rathor, the chief of Bikanir, was an officer in Dilir's contingent. His Rajputs practised gang-robbery in the camp at night. Dilir Khan, to save his credit with the Emperor, reported the matter to Court, and the Emperor in reply ordered him to arrest the Rao. Dilir was sent towards Bidar to punish the enemy, but Rao Karn remained behind at Aurangabad by order of the Prince. (*Dil.* 66-68.) The Prince used to help the Rao with money in his distress and enforced idleness. Thus, Dilir's enemies found a ready shelter with Muazzam.

But even if the viceroy of the Deccan had been a man of greater spirit and enterprise, it would have been impossible for him for some years from this time to get the men and money necessary for crushing Shivaji. The resources of the empire had to be concentrated elsewhere, to meet more pressing dangers. Within a fortnight of Shivaji's escape from Agra, a large army had to be sent to the Panjab to meet the threat of a Persian invasion, and the anxiety on this point was not removed before December. But immediately afterwards, in March 1667, the Yusufzai rising in Peshawar took place, which taxed all the strength of the empire for more than a year afterwards.

It was, therefore, the Emperor's interest not to molest Shivaji at such a time.

§2. *Shivaji makes peace with the Mughals, 1668.*

The Maratha chief, on his part, was not eager for a war with the imperialists. For three years after his return from Agra, he lived very quietly at home, and avoided giving any fresh provocation to the Mughals. He wanted peace for a time to organize his Government, make a revenue settlement of his lands, repair and provision his forts, and consolidate and extend his power on the western coast at the expense of Bijapur and the Siddis of Janjira. As early as April 1667 he had sent a letter to the Emperor professing terror of the imperial army which was reported to have been despatched against him, and offering to make his submission again and send a contingent of 400 men under his son to fight under the Mughal banners.*

Aurangzib had taken no notice of this letter. But Shivaji made another attempt. He entreated Jaswant Singh to be his intermediary in making peace with the empire. He wrote to the Maharajah, "The Emperor has cast me off. Otherwise I intended to have begged the task of recovering Qandahar with my unaided resources. I fled (from Agra) in fear of my life. Mirza Rajah, my patron, is dead. If through your intercession I am pardoned, I shall send Shambhu to wait on the Prince and serve as a *mansabdar* at the head of my followers wherever ordered." (*Dil.* 69-70.)

Jaswant Singh and Prince Muazzam jumped at the offer and recommended Shiva to the Emperor, who accepted the proposal,† and recognized Shiva's title of Rajah, but so far as we can judge did not restore to him any of his forts. Thus a peace was made which lasted nearly two years.

**Akhbarat*, 10-9 Shivaji's three years' peace with the Mughals 1667-1669 and the causes of rupture · Sabh 59-62, *Jedhe S*, *Dil* 69-71. The terms of this treaty are nowhere given in detail *F R* Surat, 105.

† Muazzam's letter to Shivaji, dated 9th March 1668, informs him of the granting of the title of Rajah, and states that his other demands were under consideration (Parasnis MS, Letter No 11)

In terms of the agreement with the Mughals, Shambhuji was sent to the viceroy's Court at Aurangabad. He interviewed the Prince on 4th November 1667 and was next day permitted to return home. On 5th August next year a Maratha contingent was sent to Aurangabad under Pratap Rao and Niraji Raoji. [*Jedhe.*] Shambhuji was created a Commander of Five Thousand again and presented with an elephant and a jewelled sword. Jagirs were assigned to him in Berar Half his contingent attended at Aurangabad, while the other half was sent to the new jagir to help in collecting the revenue. (*Dil* 70) For a year and a half the Maratha contingent lived in the jagir, "feeding themselves at the expense of the Mughal dominion," as Sabhasad frankly puts it.

During 1667, 1668 and 1669, Shivaji lived at peace with the Mughal Government The English factory letters at the close of 1668 and in 1669 describe him as "very quiet" and as "Aurangzib's vassal, (bound) to do whatsoever is commanded by the Prince " His relations with Bijapur also were pacific. "The country all about [Karwar] at present is in great tranquillity Shivaji keeps still at Rajgarh, and though as yet there is no peace made between this king [Adil Shah] and him, yet both refrain from committing any acts of hostility against one another " [*F. R.* Surat Vol 105, Karwar to Surat, 16 Sep , 1668.] Still later, on 17th July, 1669, the English traders at Hubli speak of "Shivaji being very quiet, not offering to molest the king's country." (*Ibid*)

In fact, during these three years (1667-69), he was busy framing a set of very wise regulations, which laid the foundations of his Government broad and deep, and have remained an object of admiration to after ages. (Sabh. 27-33, 58.)

But the peace was essentially a hollow truce on both sides. Shivaji's sole aim in making it was to save himself from the possibility of a combined attack by three great Powers and to recover his strength during this respite from war. Aurangzib, ever suspicious of his sons, looked upon Muazzam's friendship with Shiva as a possible menace to his throne, and he secretly planned to entrap Shivaji a second time, or at least to seize his son and general as hostages. (Sabh. 62)

Sabhasad tells us that Aurangzib wrote to his son to arrest Pratap Rao and Niraji Pant, the Maratha agents at Aurangabad, and attach the horses of their troops, and that the Prince, who had learnt of the order beforehand from his Court agent, revealed it to Niraji and instigated the Marathas to escape, while the imperial order arrived a week afterwards, when it was too late to carry it out. (Sabh. 61-62.)

The rupture, inevitable in any case, was precipitated by financial causes. Retrenchment of expenditure had now become a pressing necessity to Aurangzib, and he ordered the Mughal army in the Deccan to be greatly reduced. The disbanded soldiery took service with Shiva, who had to find employment for them. Another ill-judged measure of imperial parsimony was to attach a part of Shiva's new jagir in Berar in order to recover the *lakh* of Rupees advanced to him in 1666 for his journey to the Court. The news of it reached Shivaji when he had completed his military preparations.* He

* There is no evidence for holding that Shivaji broke the peace with Aurangzib (Jan 1670) as a protest against the latter's general order for

sent a secret message to Pratap Rao to slip away from Aurangabad with his men. The other half of the contingent fled from Berar at the same time, plundering the villages on the way! (*Dil.* 71.)

§3. *War with the Mughals renewed, 1670.*

This breach with the Mughals occurred early in January 1670, or a fortnight earlier. On 11th Dec. 1669, the Emperor received a despatch from the Deccan reporting the desertion of four Maratha captains of Shiva's clan (*biradari*) from the imperial service. Aurangzib soon set to strengthening his forces in the Deccan. On 26th January 1670 an order was sent to Dilir to leave Deogarh in the Gond country and hasten to Aurangabad. Daud Khan was ordered to arrange for the defence of his province of Khandesh and then go to Prince Muazzam's assistance. Many other officers were transferred from North India to the Deccan. (*Akhbarat*, year 12.)

Shivaji opened his offensive with great vigour and immediate success.* His roving bands looted Mughal territory, and he attacked several of the forts which he had ceded to Aurangzib by the Treaty of Purandar. "The imperial officers in command of most of these forts fell after fighting heroically. Every day the Emperor got news of such loss of forts. But some of these places defied capture by reason of the strength of

---

temple destruction (9 April 1669), though the two events are placed immediately after one another in an English Factory letter (Foster, xiii. 256) and *Jedhe*.

*Sabhasad, 59, says, "In four months he recovered the 27 forts he had ceded to the Mughals." But it is an exaggeration. There is a most spirited but legendary ballad on the capture of Singh-garh (*Powadas*). The *Akhbarat* and *Dilkasha* have been of invaluable help in the history of the campaigns of 1671 as reconstructed here, with a few dates from *Jedhe*.

their fortifications and abundant supply of war material." (*Dil.* 64.)

His most conspicuous success was the capture of Kondana from Udai-bhan, its Rajput *qiladar*, (4th Feb. 1670). Assisted by some Koli guides who knew the place well, one dark night Tanaji Malusare, with 300 picked Mavle infantry men, scaled the less abrupt hill-side near the Kalian gate by means of rope-ladders and advanced into the fort, slaying the sentinels. The alarm was given; the Rajputs, stupefied with opium, took some time to arm and come out; but in the meantime the Marathas had made their footing secure. The garrison fought desperately, but the Mavles with their war cry of *Hara! Hara! Mahadev!* carried havoc into their ranks. The two chiefs challenged each other and both fell down dead, after a single combat. The Marathas, disheartened by the fall of their leader, were rallied by his brother Suryaji Malusare, opened the Kalian gate to their supporting columns, and took complete possession of the fort. The rest was butchery. Twelve hundred Rajputs were slain, and many others perished in trying to escape down the hill-side. The victors set fire to the thatched huts of the cavalry lines and the signal blaze informed Shivaji at Rajgarh, nine miles southwards, that the fort had been taken. He mourned the death of Tanaji as too high a price for the fort, and named it *Singh-garh* after the lion-heart that had won it.

On 8th March, Nilo Pant recovered Purandar, capturing its *qiladar* Razi-ud-din Khan. (*M. A.* 99.) A few days later the Marathas looted the village of Chandor, seizing an elephant, 12 horses and Rs. 40,000 belonging to the imperial treasury, then entered the town and plundered it, while the imperial *qiladar* was shut up in the fort. At one place, however, he met with repulse. The fort of Mahuli (in North Konkan, 50 miles n. e. of Bombay) was held for the Emperor by a gallant and able Rajput named Manohar Das Gaur, the nephew of Rajah Bithal Das of Shah Jahan's time. Shiva invested it in February 1670 and attempted a surprise at night. He sent up 500 of his men to the ramparts by means of rope-ladders. But Manohar Das, who "used to be on the alert day and night," fell on the party, slew most of the men and hurled the rest down the precipice. Shivaji then raised the siege, turned to Kalian-Bhivandi and recovered it after slaying its *thanahdar* Uzbak Khan and driving out the Mughal outpost there (*Dil.* 65, *O. C.* 3415, Surat to Co., 30 March 1670.) Ludi Khan, the *faujdar* of Konkan, was wounded in a battle with the Maratha forces, defeated in a second encounter, and expelled from his district. The Mughal *faujdar* of Nander (?) fled away, deserting his post.

The only officer who made an attempt to uphold the imperial prestige in the Deccan was Daud Khan Qureshi, who had been second only to Dilir Khan during Jai Singh's Maratha campaign of 1665. Leaving the province of Khandesh in charge of his son, Daud Khan arrived at Ahmadnagar on 28th March 1670 Six days afterwards he set out with 7,000 cavalry to expel Shiva's men who were roving near Parnir, Junnar, and Mahuli. They evacuated Parnir and Junnar and retired before him, while he occupied these two posts Meantime, Shivaji had invested three Mughal forts in that region, and Daud Khan left Junnar to relieve them. But at the approach of his Van (under his gallant son Hamid and Ludi Khan) the Marathas raised the siege and fled away, and the Mughal advanced division fell back on their main body.

Soon afterwards, these two officers went with a detachment and destroyed an old fort which the Marathas were repairing on the frontier, 20 miles from Mahuli. Towards the end of April, Daud Khan himself marched to Mahuli, and after throwing provisions into the fort, returned to Junnar. The Emperor in open Court highly praised Daud Khan for his spirit in invading the enemy's country, regardless of the smallness of his own force, and thereby creating a useful diversion of Shivaji's attention. (*Akhbarat,* year 13.)

On 16th June Mahuli too was lost to the Emperor. Manohar Das, conscious of the inadequacy of the garrison and provisions in the fort to repel another attack of the superior Maratha forces, resigned his post in despair of getting reinforcements. Shivaji seized the opportunity, and captured Mahuli, slaying its new commandant Alawardi Beg and his garrison of 200 men. (*Dil.* 65.) By the end of April 1670* he had looted 51 villages near Ahmadnagar, Junnar and Parenda.

§4. *Quarrel between Muazzam and Dilir.*

But the Mughal administration of the Deccan was in no condition to make a stand against Shivaji. For half of the year 1670 it was passing through a civil war of its own. In obedience to the Emperor's anxious and repeated orders, Dilir Khan† had left the Gond country,

*The text of *Akhbarat* here is doubtful *Jedhe* says that in August Shivaji raided the Mughal dominions and laid siege to Junnar , captured Lohgarh (13 May), Hindola (15 June), Karnala (22 June), Rohida (24 June)

† Quarrel between Muazzam and Dilir Khan in 1670. *Dil* 73-75, 80-82 (main source) , Ishwardas (important) 59*a*—60*a* , *Storia,* ii 161-166 ;

where he had been profitably employed in squeezing the local chieftains, and set off for the Deccan. Starting from Nagpur on 29th March 1670, he expected to reach Aurangabad and to wait on the Prince on 12th April. But at his near approach the old quarrel between the viceroy and his general broke out afresh We have seen how they had disagreed in 1667. So, now too, when Dilir, after pursuing some enemy raiders, reached Pathri, 26 miles w of Aurangabad (about 8th April) and received an order from the Prince to wait on him, he feared to go to the interview lest he should be treacherously imprisoned or killed by the Prince. "Twice or thrice he took horse for the purpose of visiting the Prince, but returned from the way, and spent some days on the plea of illness."

At this act of insubordination, Muazzam and Jaswant wrote to the Emperor accusing Dilir Khan of rebellion. The Khan had already denounced the Prince to the Emperor, saying that he was in collusion with Shivaji and had done nothing to defend the imperial dominions, and offering to crush the Maratha chief if the command of the army in the Deccan were left in his (Dilir's) hands for two years with an adequate supply of artillery and siege-material.

So, at the end of March 1670 the Emperor had sent his Chamberlain (*Khan-i-saman*), Iftikhar Khan, to Aurangabad to investigate how matters really stood,—whether Muazzam was really bent on rebellion and what his relations with Shivaji were. This officer was now

---

while *M A* 102, *Akhbarat*, year 13, and English records give dates and a few details *O C* 3415, *F R* Surat Vol 3, Vol 105 (Bombay to Surat, 5 Sep) &c *Mirat-i-Ahmadi*, 290, merely copies Ishwardas

instructed to inquire into the Prince's charges against Dilir Khan.

Iftikhar, no doubt moved by kindly intentions, became guilty of double-dealing. As an English gunner in Muazzam's service wrote, "He played the Jack on both sides, and told the Prince that Dilir Khan was his enemy, and went to Dilir Khan and told him that the Prince would seize on him if he came to Aurangabad." (John Trotter to President of Surat, 20 Dec. 1670, in *F. R.* Surat, Vol. 105.) His unfortunate advice to Dilir only prolonged the tension.

Muazzam complained to the Emperor that Dilir Khan had openly defied his authority and that the Khan's Afghan troops used to rob the people and sack the villages along their line of march; and the latter charge was borne out by the reports of the news-writers. Then Dilir, finding his position in the Deccan intolerable, wanted to go back to the imperial Court without waiting for permission; but the Prince ascribed this course to a wicked desire of creating disorder in Northern India. Imperial orders reached him to force Dilir Khan back to the path of obedience. The Prince set himself to raise an army for a war with Dilir and called in the Mughal detachments from the outlying posts to his banners.

Dilir Khan was pursuing a Maratha band across the Godavari river, when he heard of the arrival of a *farman* from the imperial Court, and divined its purport. His former suspicion and anxiety now deepened into alarm and perplexity. Though it was the height of the rainy season (August), the rivers swollen and the roads miry, he burnt his tents and stores and fled northwards to Malwa with his army.

As soon as he started from the south, Prince Muazzam and Jaswant gave him chase up to the bank of the Tapti, with all the available Mughal troops, calling upon Shivaji to come to their aid! The Deccan was filled with wild rumours of a civil war among the imperialists, which were "so confused that we cannot write them for credible." (*O. C.* 3470, Bombay to Surat, 1 Sep 1670)

A letter, however, came from the Emperor ordering Muazzam back to Aurangabad (September.) The Prince's evil genius, Jaswant Singh, was separated from him and posted at Burhanpur until further orders Muazzam promptly obeyed his father's order and returned to Aurangabad at the end of September, 1670.

These internal troubles paralyzed the Mughal arms. and Shivaji made the most of this golden opportunity. We have seen how he had recovered several of his forts early in the year His cavalry bands roamed over the country, plundering far and wide. In March the English factors at Surat wrote, "Shivaji marches now not [as] before as a thief, but in gross with an army of 30,000 men conquering as he goes, and is not disturbed though the Prince lies near him." (*O. C.* 3415.)

§5. *Second Loot of Surat, 1670.*

In April Bahadur Khan visited Surat with 5,000 horse, to guard the town against an apprehended attack by Shiva In August there were false rumours that Muazzam, then supposed to be in rebellion against his father, was coming to Surat, "to take possession of this town and castle." The Mughals demanded from the Court of Bijapur a contingent of 12,000 horse for service against Shivaji, and some ammunition from the English at Bombay for the fort of Koridru(?) People were expectant as to what the imperialists would do when the rains would cease and campaigning again become possible. (*F. R.* Surat, Vol. 3. Consult. 16 and 18 Aug. 1670. *O. C.* 3457.) But Shivaji, as usual, struck the first blow. On 3rd October he plundered Surat for the second time.

Throughout September he had been assembling a large body of cavalry at Kalian, evidently to invade Gujrat. (*F. R.* Surat, Vol. 3. Consult. 12 Sep. 1670.) The matter was so notorious that on 12th September the English factors at Surat[*] had rightly concluded that "that town would be the first place he would take," and "foreseeing the ensuing danger, [we] had taken a convenient time to empty all our warehouses at Surat of what goods were ready baled and sent them down to Swally;" even their entire Council with the President (Gerald Aungier) were at Swally at the beginning of October. And yet the Mughal governor was so criminally negligent as to keep only 300 men for the defence of the city. On 2nd October came successive reports of Shiva's arrival with 15,000 horse and foot within 20 miles of Surat. All the Indian merchants of the city and even the officers of Government fled in the course of that day and night. On the 3rd, Shivaji attacked the city which had recently been walled round by order of Aurangzib. After a slight resistance the defenders fled to the fort, and the Marathas possessed themselves of the whole town except only the English,

---

*The second loot of Surat Surat Council to Co, 20 Nov 1670 (Hedge's *Diary*, ii, pp ccxxvi—'ix) *F R* Surat Vol 3, (Consult at Swally Marine, October), *Dutch Records*, Trans Vol 29, No 763 *M A* 106 (bare mention) Sabh 63-64

Dutch and French factories, the large *New Serai* of the Persian and Turkish merchants, and the *Tartar Serai* opposite the French factory, which was occupied by Abdullah Khan, ex-king of Kashghar, recently returned from a pilgrimage to Mecca. The French bought off the raiders by means of "valuable presents." The English factory, though it was an open house, was defended by Streynsham Master with 50 sailors, and the Marathas were received with such a hot fire from it that they lost several men, and, leaving the English alone, assaulted the Kashghar king's *serai* from the advantageous position of some avenues next to the French factory, which they were suffered by the French to occupy. The Tartars made a stout resistance all the day, but finding the post untenable they fled with their king to the fort at night, giving up to plunder their house with its valuable property, including a gold *palki* and other costly presents from Aurangzib.

From the safe shelter of the *Tartar Serai* the Marathas prepared to open fire on the English factory the next day, but the resolute attitude of the handful of Englishmen cowed them, and after an angry parley they came to an understanding and agreed not to molest the English. The Dutch warehouse was untouched. As their Surat resident writes, "A messenger came from the invader to assure us that no harm would befall us if we remained quiet ...and we gave him our assurances that we would not interfere for or against him" (*Dutch Records*, Translations, Vol. 29, Surat to Directors, 14 Nov. 1670.) The Turks in the *New Serai* successfully defended themselves, inflicting some loss on the raiders.

The Marathas plundered the larger houses of the city at leisure, taking immense quantities of treasure, cloth, and other valuable goods, and setting fire to several places, so that "nearly half the town" was burnt to the ground. They then approached the fortress of Surat, threatening to storm it; but it was a mere demonstration, as they were not prepared to conduct a siege, and did not venture close to the walls. The third day (5th Oct.) they again appeared before the English factory, threatening to burn it down. Shivaji and his soldiers were greatly enraged at the loss of their men in the first assault on this house, and they clamoured for vengeance. But the wiser among his captains knew that a second attack would result in further loss of life, and at their request two English agents waited on Shivaji in his tent outside the town, with some presents of scarlet cloth, sword blades and knives. The Maratha king "received them in a very kind manner, telling them that the English and he were good friends, and putting his hand into their hands he told them that he would do the English no wrong." (Surat to Co., 20 Nov. 1670, in Hedge's *Diary*.)

On 5th October, about noon Shivaji suddenly retreated from the town, though no Mughal army was near or even reported to be coming. "But he had got plunder enough and thought it prudent to secure himself. When he marched away he sent a letter to the officers and chief merchants, saying that if they did not pay him twelve *lakhs* of Rupees as yearly tribute, he would return the next year and burn down the remaining part of the town. No sooner Shivaji was gone than the poor people of Surat fell to plundering what was left, in so much that there was not a house, great or small, excepting those which stood on their guard, which were not ransacked." Even the English sailors under S Master took to plundering.

During the three days that Surat was undergoing

this fate, the sea-port of Swally marine, ten miles west of it across the Tapti, was not free from alarm. There the English, Dutch and French had built their warehouses and landing-places for ocean-going vessels Here lay during those days all the members of the English factory, their treasure, and most of the goods bought for Europe. Here the *shah-i-bandar* (harbour and custom-master), the *qazi,* and the most eminent merchants (Hindu, Muslim and Armenian) of Surat had taken refuge with the English. Many rich people of the town, too, had fled to the villages north of Surat, across the river and close to Swally. On the 3rd it was reported that Shivaji wanted to send 500 horsemen north of the river to plunder the villages and seize these rich men; and it was feared that he might even come to Swally to demand the surrender of the Surat refugees and blackmail from the European merchants. But the coming of the spring-tide made it impossible for the Marathas to cross the river, and Swally remained safe. So great was the alarm there, however, that on the 3rd the English factors removed their treasure from the shore to one of their ships, and next day loaded all their broadcloth, quicksilver, currall (coral?) &c , on board ship, "to secure them against any attempts of Shivaji." Two other English ships, which were due to sail, were detained at Swally till 10th October, by which time the Marathas were expected to withdraw from the district The English factors with the help of the ships' carpenters even ran up a wooden platform at one end of the marine yard and mounted eight guns on it, "to defend the Company's estate the best we could."

The manly attitude of the English and their success in scaring away the Maratha myriads, greatly impressed the people of the country. These traders had, as a reward of their brave defence of their factory during the loot of 1664, received commercial privileges from the Emperor. And now the son of Haji Said Beg, the richest merchant of Surat, who had found shelter at Swally, publicly swore that he would migrate with his family to Bombay.

The fact that all the three European factories at Surat were untouched while every other shop and house was ransacked by the raiders, naturally excited suspicion. Both at Surat and the imperial Court people "talked of the three Christian nations having made a league with Shivaji when he was here." The foreign merchants therefore received no reward from the ruler of the land *this* time. (Master to Swally Marine, 3 Jan. 1671, in *F. R.* Surat, 105.)

An official inquiry ascertained that Shivaji had carried off 66 *lakhs* of Rupees' worth of booty from Surat, —*viz.*, cash, pearls, and other articles worth 53 *lakhs* from the city itself and 13 *lakhs* worth from Nawal Sahu and Hari Sahu and a village near Surat. (*Akhbarat*, 13-10.)

But the real loss of Surat was not to be estimated by the booty which the Marathas carried off. The trade of this, the richest port of India, was practically destroyed. For several years after Shivaji's withdrawal from it, the town used to throb with panic every now and then, whenever any Maratha force came within a few days' march of it, or even at false alarms of their coming. On every such occasion the merchants would quickly remove their goods to the ships, the citizens would flee to the villages, and the Europeans would hasten to Swally. Business was effectually scared away from Surat, and inland producers hesitated to send their goods to this the greatest emporium of Western India

For one month after the second sack, "the town was in so great a confusion that there was neither governor nor Government," and almost every day was troubled by rumours of Shiva's coming there again. "On the 12th (i e, only a week after his departure) it was again rumoured that he was returning with 6,000 horse and 10,000 foot, and that he had already reached Pent, a place about 25 miles distant At once there was a general exodus and the town was changed from a busy port into the death-like quiet of a desert The Turkish, English and French merchants abandoned their factories" But the Dutch, 52 men in all, with flags flying and drums beating proceeded from their ship to their factory. This was their belated imitation of the English demonstration of January 1664, when "the English President, at the head of some 200 men, had marched through the town, declaring that he meant to withstand Shivaji with this handful of men!" (*Dutch Records*, Trans., Vol 29, letter No 763 and Vol 27, No 719)

At the end of November, and again about 10th December, 1670, the alarm was revived; and the European merchants met together to concert means of guarding their respective interests. The landward defences of Swally were strengthened by adding a breast-work on the north side of the *choultry*, and the entrance to the harbour or "hole" was guarded by stationing a ship there The English used to remove their money and goods from Surat to this place at every such alarm.

In June 1672 the success of the Maratha forces under Moro Pant in the Koli State of Ramnagar, on the way to Surat, kept the city in constant terror for a long time.

The Maratha general openly demanded *chauth* from Surat, threatening a visitation if the governor refused payment. There was the same panic again in February and October 1672, September 1673, October 1674, and December 1679. In short, the destruction of the trade and financial prosperity of Surat was well nigh complete. (*F. R.*)

§6 *Battle of Dindori, 17th Oct. 1670.*

Having concluded the story of the Maratha dealings with Surat, we turn to Shivaji's activities in other quarters.

Prince Muazzam had just returned to Aurangabad after chasing Dilir Khan to the bank of the Tapti, when he heard of the plunder of Surat. He immediately summoned Daud Khan from Burhanpur and sent him off to attack the Maratha raiders. Meantime, Shivaji had left Surat, entered Baglana, and plundered the villages nestling at the foot of the fort of Mulhir. Daud Khan, after sending his baggage from Baizapur back to Aurangabad, marched westwards with light kit to Chandor, a town at which the road from Nasik to Baglana crosses the hill range. Spies brought him news that Shivaji had started from Mulhir, and intended to cross the Chandor range by the pass of Kanchana-Manchana, ten miles west of Chandor. Arriving at the hamlet of Chandor (below the fort) at about 9 P.M., Daud Khan waited to verify the news of the enemy's movements. At midnight his spies reported that Shiva had already issued from the pass and was rapidly following the road to Nasik with half his forces, while the other half of his army was holding the pass to pick up stragglers. Daud Khan at once resumed his march. But the moon set about three o'clock in the morning, and in the darkness the Mughal soldiers were somewhat scattered.

Ikhlas Khan Miana (son of Abdul Qadir *bin* Bahlol Khan, a former Pathan leader of Bijapur), commanded the Mughal vanguard. Ascending a hillock in the early morning, he beheld the enemy standing ready for battle in the plain below. While his men were putting on their armour, which was conveyed on camels, he himself with a handful of followers recklessly charged the enemy. The Maratha rear-guard, which had faced about, was 10,000 strong and commanded by distinguished generals like Pratap Rao Gujar, the Master of the Horse, Vyankoji Datto and Makaji Anand Rao (a natural son of Shahji Bhonsle.) Ikhlas Khan was very soon wounded and unhorsed. After a time Daud arrived on the scene and sent up Rai Makarand and some other officers to reinforce the Van, while he left his elephants, flags and drums at a ruined village on a height, surrounded by *nalas*, with orders to make his camp and rear-guard halt there when they would come up.

For hours together an obstinate and bloody battle raged. Sangram Khan Ghori and his kinsmen were wounded, and many were slain on the Mughal side. The Marathas, "like the *Bargis* of the Deccan, fought hovering round the imperialists." But the Bundela infantry of the Mughal army with their abundant fire-arms kept the enemy back. Daud Khan himself entered the fight, repulsed the enemy with his artillery, and rescued the wounded Ikhlas Khan.

Meantime, in another part of the field, Mir Abdul Mabud, the *darogha* of the divisional artillery, who had been separated from the main army by a fold in the ground, was attacked. He was wounded with one of his sons and some followers, while another son and many soldiers were slain; and his flags and horses were carried off by the enemy There was a lull in the fight at noon.

At that time Daud Khan had less than 2,000 men with him, while the Marathas outnumbered him fivefold. In the evening they charged him again, but were driven back, evidently by the artillery. At night the Mughals bivouacked under the autumn sky, their camp was entrenched, and they engaged in burying the dead and tending the wounded. The Marathas retreated to Konkan without further opposition. This battle was fought near Dindori on the 17th of October, 1670.* About a week later the Peshwa captured the fort of Trimbak (Nasik district.)

As the result of the battle of Dindori, the Mughal power was neutralized for more than a month afterwards. The day after the fight, Daud Khan marched with the broken remnant of his army to Nasik, and halted there for one month, evidently to recoup his strength and also to watch the route from Konkan (by the Tal pass?) The wounded were sent to Aurangabad. Late in November, he removed to Ahmadnagar, but at the end of December he was recalled to the scene of his last battle by the revival of Maratha activity in the Chandor range. (*Dil.* 87, 89, 92.)

§7. *Raid into Berar and Baglana.*

We shall not deal in this chapter with Shivaji's activity at sea and in the western coast-strip in November

---

* Battle of Dindori · entirely based upon *Dilkasha*, i 84-88, (Bhimsen was an eye-witness); with a few points from Sabh 64-65 Date in *Jedhe S.* *Dindori* is 28 m s w of Chandor and 15 m. n of Nasik *Jedhe* states that from Dindori Shivaji went to Kunjargarh and stayed there

and December 1670 after his return from Surat. Early in December a Maratha force under Shivaji himself made a raid into Khandesh, after capturing the forts of Ahivant, Markanda, Ravla, and Javla in Baglana, on the way. Advancing by rapid marches, he plundered Bahadurpura, a village two miles from Burhanpur (the capital of Khandesh), but did not come closer to that city, because of the warning of Jaswant Singh, who had been posted there since September last. Passing into Berar, he fell, when least expected, upon the rich and flourishing city of Karinja, and looted it completely. Four thousand oxen and donkeys were loaded with the booty—consisting of fine cloth, silver and gold, to the value of a *krore* of Rupees, captured here All the rich men of the place were carried off for ransom Only the most eminent one among them escaped in the disguise of a woman. The other towns also yielded vast sums of money. That rich province, with its accumulated wealth of more than half a century of peace and prosperity, afforded a virgin soil to the plunderers in this their first raid. A force, reported to be 20,000 strong, began to loot the country round Ausa and collect the revenue, but they rode away without attacking the fort. In the neighbourhood of Karinja and Nandurbar the Marathas took from the affrighted people written promises to pay them one-fourth of the revenue (*chauth*) in future *

No resistance was made by the Mughals. Khan-i-Zaman, the governor of Berar, moved too slowly to intercept the raiders, and he stopped on reaching Deogarh. Daud Khan, the governor of

---

**Jedhe*, *Dil* 98 *Akhbarat*, year 13—5, 10 F R Surat, 105, Letter of J Trotter, 20 Dec 1670, S Master to President, 19 Dec *Dil* 64 (bare mention of Karinja) Sabh 71 Karinja is 77 30 E 20 32 N

Khandesh, was absent campaigning near Ahmadnagar, while his son Ahmad Khan, who officiated as his deputy at Burhanpur, was at open war with Maharajah Jaswant Sigh, who was trying to raise money for the Prince's expenses and had demanded five *lakhs* from the treasury of Khandesh. Daud Khan's son replied that if the Maharajah could procure Aurangzib's order, he would pay him even 20 *lakhs*, or else not a pice, at which message Jaswant threatened to sack the town. (*F R*. Surat, 105, Bombay to Surat, 5 February, 1671)

Daud Khan from his camp near Ankai Tankai hastened towards Burhanpur. Arriving near the pass of Fardapur he heard that the Marathas returning from Berar had turned aside from Burhanpur and taken the road to Baglana. The situation at the capital of Khandesh was also eased by the arrival there on 1st January 1671 of a new supreme commander, Mahabat Khan, who took Jaswant away with himself when leaving the town.

From Fardapur, Daud Khan swerved to the west and entered Baglana on the heels of the Marathas. While Shivaji had been sacking Karinja in Berar, another Maratha band under Moro Trimbak Pingle had been looting West Khandesh and Baglana, and now these two divisions had united in the neighbourhood of Salhir. They had plundered the village under the hill-fort of Mulhir and laid siege to Salhir. Daud Khan arrived near Mulhir at about 8 P.M., but could advance no further as most of his camp and army were lagging behind

The Khan urged his troops to start next morning in order to raise the siege of Salhir. He himself set out before sunrise. But most of his men had not yet arrived, and the few that had come with him were scattered. They busied themselves in cooking food or taking rest in the camp, instead of resuming the march with their chief. Daud Khan heard on the way that Salhir had already been captured by the Marathas, and so he returned in disappointment to Mulhir, and after a short halt there fell back on his new base near Kanchana-Manchana in the Chandor range.

Shivaji had invested Salhir with a force of 20,000 horse and foot, and one day finding the garrison off their guard he had scaled the wall by means of rope-ladders The *qiladar* Fathullah Khan fell fighting, and his wife's brother then gave up the fort to the enemy. This happened about 5th January 1671. The success of the Marathas continued. They threatened other forts in the province, such as Mulhir, Chauragarh and Talulgarh(?) Their roving bands cut off the grain supply of Neknam Khan, the *faujdar* of Baglana (whose head-quarters were at Mulhir.) They also laid siege to Dhodap, the loftiest hill-fort in the Chandor range.*

In the winter of 1670-71, Shivaji received a visit from Chhatra Sal, the son of Champat Rai Bundela, the late chieftain of Mahewa in eastern Bundelkhand This young man had entered the imperial army at Jai Singh's recommendation, but he was discontented with what he considered the inadequate reward of his services in the Mughal invasion of the Gond country. So, one day he left the Mughal camp on the plea of hunting and made an adventurous journey with his wife to Maharashtra by obscure and roundabout paths. He offered to serve under

---

**Dil* 98-100 *Akhbarat*, year 13—12, 15 *T S* 33*a* K K ii 247-249 (gives another story of the surrender of Salhir)

Shiva against the Emperor. Shivaji received him with honour, praised his manly spirit, but sent him back with the advice to rise against Aurangzib in Bundelkhand, saying, "Illustrious chief ! conquer and subdue your foes. Recover and rule your native land...It is expedient to commence hostilities in your own dominions, where your reputation will gain many adherents. . Whenever the Mughals evince an intention of attacking you, I will distract their attention and subvert their plans, by active co-operation with you." The contemporary historian, Bhimsen, however, tells us that Chhatra Sal returned from Rajgarh in disappointment as he found the provincial spirit of the Deccani Court uncongenial to him and Shivaji never gave his trust or any high office to men from Northern India.*

* *Chhatraprakash*, canto 11, tr in Pogson's *Boondelas*, pp 52-53, *Dil* 132 For history of Chhatra Sal, see *Aurangzib*, v ch 61, and Irvine's *Later Mughals*, ii ch 9

CHAPTER VIII

STRUGGLE WITH THE MUGHALS AND BIJAPUR, 1671-74

§1 *Campaigns of Mahabat and Daud Khan, 1671*

The second sack of Surat and the Maratha ravages in Baglana roused Aurangzib to a sense of the gravity of the situation in the Deccan. As early as 28th November, 1670, he had appointed Mahabat Khan to the supreme command in the Deccan. The events of December only deepened the Emperor's anxiety. On 9th January 1671, he sent orders to Bahadur Khan to leave his province of Gujrat and take the command of one of the imperial army corps in the Deccan, Dilir Khan being directed to accompany him The Emperor also repeatedly talked of going to the Deccan and conducting the war against Shivaji in person, but the idea was ultimately dropped Daud Khan was instructed to attack Shiva wherever he was reported to be Amar Singh Chandawat and many other Rajput officers with their clansmen were posted to the Deccan. Reinforcements, money and provisions were poured into Baglana in January, 1671. (*Akhbarat*, 13-1, 2, 8, 14, 16; *M.A* , 107.)

Mahabat Khan left Burhanpur on 3rd January 1671 with Jaswant Singh, reached Aurangabad on the 10th, paid his respects to the viceroy, Prince Muazzam, and set out to join the army near Chandor. Daud Khan had been appointed his chief lieutenant and the commander of his vanguard; but he despised this office as below his rank, and begged the Emperor to recall him. (*Akh.* 13-12, *Dil* 102)

We shall now trace the history of the war in the Chandor range. Late in December 1670 Shivaji's men had laid siege to Dhodap, and Daud Khan had started on the 28th of that month to relieve the fort. But the *qiladar*, Muhammad Zaman, successfully repelled the attack unaided. Daud Khan had next advanced to the relief of Salhir, but had been too late to save it, as we have already seen. In January 1671, he held a fortified base near the Kanchana pass from which he sallied forth in every direction in which the Marathas were heard of as roving. From the Emperor's letters it appears that Daud Khan was under a general order to right everything that might go wrong in Baglana! Once after a night-march he fell on a body of the enemy near Hatgarh and slew 700 of them. (*Akhbarat*, 13-6 and 15; *Dil.* i 101.)

Late in January 1671, Mahabat Khan joined Daud Khan near Chandor and the two laid siege to Ahivant, which Shiva had recently taken. After more than a month had been wasted in a fruitless exchange of fire, the fort was entered from the trenches of Daud Khan and the garrison capitulated to him. Mahabat Khan became furiously angry at losing the credit of this success. He had been previously treating Daud Khan, a 5-hazari, with discourtesy, and now the relations between them became strained to the utmost. Leaving a garrison to hold Ahivant, Mahabat spent three months at Nasik and then went to Parnir (20 miles west of Ahmadnagar) to pass the rainy season (June to September) there, while Daud Khan was recalled to Court, (about June.)*

---

* *Dil* 102-104, 106, Sabh 73 "Mahabat Khan is come as far as Nasik Trimbak and hath taken 4 castles, Huturnt (=Ahivant) and Salhir are the names of two of them" (*F R* Surat, 105, Bom to Surat, 8 April 1671)

There was excessive rainfall that year and many men and cattle perished of pestilence in the camp at Parnir. But while his troops were dying, Mahabat Khan attended daily entertainments in the houses of the nobles by turns. There were 400 dancing-girls of Afghanistan and the Panjab in his camp, and they were patronized by the officers. (*Dil.* 106.)

§2. *Campaign of Bahadur and Dilir, 1671-72. Battle of Salhir.*

The Emperor was dissatisfied with Mahabat Khan for the poor result of his campaign in the first quarter of 1671 and his long spell of inactivity afterwards, and suspected him of having formed a secret understanding with Shivaji. So, he sent Bahadur Khan and Dilir Khan to the Deccan next winter They marched from Surat into Baglana, laid siege to Salhir (now in Maratha hands), and leaving Ikhlas Khan Miana, Rao Amar Singh Chandawat and some other officers to continue the siege, proceeded towards Ahmadnagar (Oct). (*Dil.* 107, *O C* 3567, *Jedhe.*)

From the environs of Ahmadnagar, Bahadur Khan advanced towards Supa (in the Puna district), while Dilir Khan with a flying column recovered Puna, massacring all the inhabitants above the age of 9 years, (end of December 1671.) Early in January 1672, Shivaji was at Mahad, draining his forts of men to raise a vast army for expelling the invaders from the home of his childhood.* But the pressure on Puna was immediately

---

But the Mughals did not recover Salhir, though Sabh 73 says so They only captured Javla, Markandagarh, Anchalagiri, and Ahivant in Vaishakh (April 1671), acc to *Jedhe*

* *F R* Surat 106, Bombay to Surat, 13 Jan and 20 Jan 1672 The town taken by Dilir Khan is spelt in the English Factory Records as *Puna*

afterwards removed and Bahadur Khan was recalled from this region by a severe disaster to the Mughal arms in Baglana. There, the division left to besiege Salhir was attacked by a large force of Marathas under Pratap Rao, Anand Rao and the Peshwa (Moro Pant). After an obstinate battle, Ikhlas Khan and Muhakam Singh (the son of Rao Amar Singh Chandawat) were wounded and captured with 30 of their principal officers, while Rao Amar Singh and many other commanders as well as several thousand common soldiers were slain, and the entire siege-camp was taken by the enemy.* Shortly afterwards Moro Pant captured Mulhir, and then putting fresh men, munitions and provisions in the two forts, they hurried back to Konkan unmolested. This took place at the end of January and the first week of February, 1672. Shivaji's prestige and confidence in his own power were immensely increased by these successes. Surat was now in constant terror of him, as he entirely dominated Baglana.

From the English records we learn that Shiva now "forced the two generals (*viz.*, Bahadur and Dilir), who with their armies had entered into his country, to retreat

---

Chackne (from the usual practice of tacking two places together in one sub-division) and described as "a place of great concern in a very large plain in the heart of all Shivaji's upper country" This description suggests Puna and not Chakan, but we have no direct evidence that Shivaji got back Puna and Chakan from the Mughals by the treaty of 1665 or that of 1668 The English record a rumour, which we know was baseless, that at the capture of this place Dilir Khan killed Kartoji Gujar, the Maratha Lieutenant-General, (*i e*, Pratap Rao)

* On the Maratha side also many soldiers were slain and only one chief of note, Surya Rao Kankre, a comrade of Shivaji's youth Sabh 74, *Jedhe*, *Dil* 107, Ishwardas, 60*b*, *F R* Surat 87, M Gray to Bombay, 15 Feb Vol 106, Bombay to Surat, 16 Feb, 1672, K K ii 249

with shame and loss."* But the Persian accounts are silent about it. We can, however, be sure that the Satnami rising in March and the rebellion of the Khaibar Afghans in April next, made it impossible for the Emperor to attempt the recovery of his prestige in the Deccan, and Shiva was therefore left the master of the situation throughout the year 1672 (*M.A* 115-116.)

Bahadur Khan returned from Baglana with failure, encamped for some time on the bank of the Bhima, and then went back to Ahmadnagar to canton for the rains. About May 1672 Mahabat left the Deccan for Hindusthan, and a month later Muazzam did the same. Bahadur Khan was appointed commander-in-chief and acting viceroy of the Deccan, in the place of these two, becoming substantive *subahdar* in January 1673 and holding that office till August 1677. (*Dil.* 108-109; *M A* 121.)

§3. *Maratha occupation of the Koli country, 1672.*

So greatly was the spirit of the Marathas roused by their victory over Ikhlas Khan, capture of Mulhir, and expulsion of Bahadur and Dilir from Puna, that their activity continued unabated even during the hot weather and the rainy season of this year. On 5th June, a large Maratha army under Moro Trimbak Pingle captured Jawhar from its Koli Rajah, Vikram Shah, and seized there treasure amounting to 17 *lakhs* of Rupees. The place is only 100 miles from Surat, and adjoins the Nasik district, from which it is separated by the Western Ghats. Advancing further north, he threatened the other Koli

* O C 3633, Surat to Co, 6 April, 1672 Ramaji Pangre's heroic battle with Dilir near fort Kanera (Sabh 73) must be placed here

State of Ramnagar* which is only sixty miles south of Surat. The Rajah, Som Shah, fled with his family (about 19th June, 1672) to Chikli, six miles s. e. of Gandavi and 33 m. s. of Surat. Even Gandavi was deserted by the people in fear of the coming of the Marathas. But the invaders speedily retreated from Ramnagar on hearing that Dilir Khan was assembling his forces for a campaign. Heavy rain stopped the activity of the Marathas for a few days. But soon afterwards Moro Pant, with his army raised to 15,000 men, returned to the attack, and took Ramnagar in the first week of July. Its Rajah took refuge in the Portuguese territory of Daman.

The annexation of Jawhar and Ramnagar gave the Marathas a short, safe and easy route from Kalian up Northern Konkan to Surat, and laid that port helplessly open to invasion from the south. The city became subject to chronic alarm, whenever any Maratha troops were heard of even 60 miles off, at Ramnagar.

§4. *Surat threatened for chauth.*

From the neighbourhood of Ramnagar, Moro Trimbak Pingle sent three successive letters on behalf of his master to the governor and leading traders of Surat demanding four *lakhs* of Rupees as blackmail, and threatening a visit to the city in the case of their refusal. The third of these epistles was very peremptory in tone; in it Shivaji wrote, "I demand for the third time, which I declare shall be the last, the *chauth* or quarter part of the king's revenue under your Government. As your Emperor has forced me to keep an army for the defence

---

* Now called Dharampur The old capital Ramnagar, now known as *Nagar*, stands 24 m s w of Dharampur, the new capital

of my people and country, that army must be paid by his subjects. If you do not send me the money speedily, then make ready a large house for me, for I shall go and sit down there and receive the revenue and custom duties, as there is none now to stop my passage."

At the first news of the arrival of the Maratha army in Ramnagar, the governor of Surat summoned all the leading Hindu and Muhammadan merchants and proposed that they should subscribe Rs. 45,000 for engaging 500 horse and 3,000 foot to guard the town for two months. Officers were immediately sent to make a list of all the Hindu houses in the town for assessing this contribution. But no soldiers were enlisted, and the governor pocketed whatever money was actually raised for the defence.

On the receipt of the third letter from Shiva, the helpless citizens were seized with a panic. The richer men went to the governor that very night and wanted permission to remove their families to Broach and other towns for safety. He kept them waiting till after midnight, gave them the permission, but retracted it next morning, when he held a second conference with the townsmen, asking them to raise the blackmail demanded,—the merchants paying one *lakh* and the *desais* raising two *lakhs* from the cultivators of the villages around. After a discussion lasting a day and a night, in which he reduced his demand to Rs. 60,000, the people finally refused to pay anything, as they knew too well that he would appropriate the money instead of buying the enemy off with it. Thereafter, every time that there was an alarm of the approach of Shivaji's troops, the citizens of Surat hastened to flee from the town, but the governor shut the gates to keep them in !*

We may conclude the history of the Koli Rajahs here. Vikram Shah, the ex-chief of Jawhar, on losing his kingdom in June 1672, fled to the adjoining Mughal district of Nasik. From this place he used to sally forth with roving bands of his own, plunder the peasantry, and cut off communications in the north Thana district, now in Maratha hands. His son joined Dhara Rai Koli (another dispossessed chief) and took to brigandage, causing considerable loss to Maratha territory and military routes. Finally both were captured and executed. (*J. S.; T. S.* 40*a*.)

§5. *Further Maratha successes in 1672, but raid into Khandesh and Berar, Dec. 1672, defeated*

From their base in the Koli country of Jawhar and Ramnagar, a Maratha force under Moro Trimbak easily crossed the Ghats into the Nasik district, in the middle of July 1672, plundered and occupied it. Jadav Rao Deccani, a great-grandson of Lakhji Jadav (the maternal grandfather of Shivaji), with 4,000 men, was the Mughal *thanahdar* of Nasik-Trimbak. He was defeated and captured after losing many of his troops in battle. Siddi Halal, the *thanahdar* of Vani-Dindori (or North Nasik district), was also defeated and his charge looted by the Marathas. For this failure, both the officers were sharply reprimanded by Bahadur Khan, and in anger they

* Conquest of Koli country and its effect on Surat *F R* Surat, Vol 3, Consult Surat 21 June, 1672, Vol 87, Surat to Bombay, 21 and 25 June, Vol 106, Bombay to Surat, 8 July, *O C* 3649, *F R* Surat, Vol 87, Surat to Persia, 1 November 1673, Sabh 72, *Jedhe* The threatening letter is given (in Persian) in the R A S MS Persian 71 (*Khatut-i-Shivaji*), 3, and the reply to it in A S B MS F. 58, p 98

deserted to the Marathas, with two other officers and all the men of their "four great regiments of horse" (October.) Other desertions were apprehended, and Dilir Khan was left in great danger with a weakened army to defend the province of Gujrat against the exultant enemy *

On 25th October, a large Maratha army appeared at Ramnagar again, and Surat trembled in alarm, especially as a party of Shivaji's horse advanced to Chikli. But that city was not Shivaji's objective now. He made a lightning raid into a different corner of the Mughal empire.

He sent his light cavalry to plunder Berar and Telingana † The viceroy Bahadur Khan, on hearing of it, set out from Ahmadnagar due eastwards, left his heavy baggage at Bir (70 miles to the east) and Qandahar, and arrived as fast as he could near the fort of Ramgir (18 35 N. 79 35 E.) in pursuit of the raiders. But they had been two days beforehand with him, looted the village at the foot of the fort, and carried off the families of most of the inhabitants for ransom So the baffled Mughal general returned by way of Indur (modern *Nizamabad*), 95 miles due west of Ramgir. Entering the Qutb-Shahi territory, he ravaged the land at the

---

* *Dil* 116, *F R* Surat 87, Surat to Bombay, 20 July, 1672, Vol 3, Surat, 26 October Bombay to Surat, 18 October, in *F R* Surat 106 *T S* 33*b* for the two deserters

Siddi Halal, formerly an officer of Afzal Khan (of Bijapur), entered the Emperor's service, but used to write secretly to Shivaji news of everything that occurred at the Mughal head-quarters *Akh* 13-18 (MS reads *Shah* for Siddi)

† *Dil* 116, 120-122 (full) The exact month is uncertain The *Shivapur Yadi* merely says that "Shivaji took horse on 29 Dec 1672 and Annaji Pant was sent on 6 Jan 1673"—without giving their destinations

instigation of Dilir Khan. The Marathas in their retreat divided into two bodies; one turned south-west to their own country by crossing the frontier of the Golkonda State, and the other moved northwards by way of Chanda into imperial territory. Dilir Khan was sent off to pursue the first division, while Bahadur Khan tried to bar the advance of the second.

Sending his heavy baggage back to Aurangabad from the neighbourhood of the village of Jamkhed, the viceroy hastened by way of Partur, Shellode and Peedola, and arrived near the pass of Antur (38 miles north of Aurangabad.) Here the Marathas turned at bay, and attacked the Mughal Van under Sujan Singh Bundela. But they were repulsed and pursued till evening, many of the horses of traders and other kinds of booty were recovered from the enemy and restored to their owners. Next day the Mughals crossed the pass and encamped at Durgapur, four miles from the fort of Antur.

The following day, when they were marching to Aurangabad in rather straggling groups, before the time fixed for the starting of the general, one body of 10,000 imperialists was charged by 750 picked Maratha cavalry on the left of the pass of Bakapur, six miles off. After an obstinate battle, in which the Mughals were reinforced by their general, the Marathas retreated, leaving 400 of their number dead on the field. The credit of this victory belongs to the Bundelas under Subh-Karn, whose gallant son Dalpat Rao was wounded in the fight.

The division under Dilir Khan rejoined Bahadur Khan after pursuing the other Maratha band into west Bijapur territory, and capturing much booty. The general cantoned his troops at Pathri, 76 miles s. e. of Aurangabad. This Maratha raid into Khandesh and

Berar, unlike their first incursion in December 1670, was completely foiled, and the Mughal troops showed commendable mobility and enterprise. (Nov.-Dec 1672.)

To guard against a repetition of these two Maratha penetrations into Khandesh from Balaghat, Bahadur Khan set up gates across the tops of the chief passes and posted troops with artillery at each of them. Bajaji Nayak Nimbalkar, "a great Deccani zamindar" and father of Shiva's son-in-law Mahadji, with his family, was now won over by the Mughals. (*Dil.* 122 and 125.)

§6 *Desultory fighting in Desh, 1673*

Maratha activity, thus shut out of Khandesh and Berar, burst forth in another quarter. They next assembled in the Puna district. Bahadur Khan left his baggage at Chamargunda, hastened to meet the invaders, and defeated them after a severe battle.* Then he encamped at Pedgaon, on the north bank of the Bhima, eight miles due south of Chamargunda. This place became the residence of his army for many years afterwards, and here a fort and town grew up from their cantonment, which the Emperor permitted him to name *Bahadur-garh*. (*Dil* 126.)

Pedgaon occupies a position of great strategic importance. It stands on the plain just clear of the long mountain spur running eastwards from Puna. From this place the Mughal general could at will move westwards along the north of the range to protect the valleys of the Mula and the Bhima (the North Puna

---

* It is probably this campaign that is referred to in *M A* 128, among the Court news of 1673, in the following terms "Bahadur Khan had defeated Shiva after a forced march of 120 miles, made large captures of spoils and sent them with Dalpat to the Emperor, who viewed them on 22 Oct."

district), or along the south of it to guard the valleys of the Nira and the Baramati (the southern portion of the district.) Northwards he could communicate with his great depot of arms and provisions at Ahmadnagar, without having to cross any river (except at the foot of that fort); and southwards he could easily invade Bijapur through the Sholapur district In short, the cantonment at Pedgaon served as the Mughal advanced base for some years after this time, exactly as Aurangzib's camp at Brahmapuri, 90 miles s. e. e. of it, did twenty-two years later, when the Mughal empire had extended further south.

It was most probably in this year (1673)* that Shivaji met with a sore disappointment. The fort of Shivner, a mile west of Junnar, was no doubt of strategic importance, as it guarded the Mughal frontier in the north of the Puna district and blocked the shortest route by which he could sally out of North Konkan to overrun Mughal Deccan. But what gave it the greatest value in Shivaji's eyes was that it was his birth-place. The Mughal governor of Shivner was Abdul Aziz Khan, a Brahman convert to Islam and one of the most faithful and valued servants of Aurangzib. Shivaji promised him "mountains of gold" for surrendering the fort into Maratha hands; and he, pretending consent, received the money, appointed a day for the delivery, and asked Shivaji to send 7,000 cavalry to take the fort over. But Abdul Aziz at the same time secretly informed Bahadur Khan of the plot; the Maratha army fell into an ambuscade planned by the Mughals, and retired in disappointment with heavy loss. (Fryer, i. 339-340)

* But *J S* asserts that he once besieged Junnar (i e, Shivner) in Sept 1670

§7. *Gains from Bijapur and raids into Kanara, 1673.*

In another direction, however, a wide door for conquest was now opened to the Marathas Ali Adil Shah II died on 24th Nov , 1672, and was succeeded on the throne of Bijapur by Sikandar, a boy of four years. Khawas Khan (an Abyssinian general) became regent and monopolized all the power in the State, thus breaking his former agreement to share the government of the realm with the other three leading nobles,—by which Abdul Muhammad (ex-wazir) was to hold the eastern province, Bahlol Khan the western (with Panhala fort), Muzaffar Khan the Kanara districts, and the regent the capital He refused to hand over to them the royal forts in their respective districts, and they therefore left him. "Disturbances broke out on all sides," and the Government was weakened by this internal discord

Shivaji was not the man to miss such an opportunity. He broke off friendly relations with the new regent and recalled his ambassador Babaji Nayak Punde, from Bijapur Then he sent a strong force under Annaji Pant on a secret enterprise of great importance. This force assembled at Rajapur. One division of it, equipped for scaling and storming forts, was sent in advance under Kondaji Farzand, with orders to march secretly by night only, while Annaji himself with the rest of the troops remained concealed in the great forest of the Ratnagiri district.

In the pitch dark night of 6th March, 1673, Kondaji arrived at the foot of Panhala, and taking sixty picked Mavles with him, silently scaled the steep hill-side, every man helping his next comrade up by the hand On reaching the summit, they suddenly blew their trumpets from different sides and charged through the fort. The surprise was complete. The wildest confusion and alarm reigned among the garrison, which was heightened by the drums beating to arms and the hastily roused soldiers running hither and thither. A confused hand to hand fighting raged for the rest of the night. Kondaji himself attacked and slew the commandant of the fort. The chief civil officer or Paymaster Nagoji Pandit fled away with his bare life. The other Maratha troops swarmed into the fort, the day dawned, and the whole place was soon occupied by the victors, who seized the local officials and beat them to discover the hidden treasure in their own houses and the Government offices.

On hearing of the victory, Annaji came up from the rear, and Shivaji himself arrived from Raigarh, and spent a month in the newly acquired fort which he planned to turn into an impregnable tower of refuge. The success of the Marathas continued; Parli was captured on 1st April and Satara on 27th July.*

§8. *Battle of Umrani, 1673.*

The loss of Panhala roused the Court of Bijapur from its sleep. Khawas Khan was blamed for his incompetence and neglect in defending the realm. Bahlol Khan was sent to recover the fort, while three other great generals were summoned from the provinces to join him and with Mughal co-operation make a united attack on the Marathas. But, as usual, Shivaji struck the first blow and upset his enemies' plans. He detached Pratap Rao, Anand Rao and several other generals, at the head of

---

* *B S* 436—440, *Jedhe*, the Sanskrit poem *Parnal-parvat-grahan-akhyanam* by Jayaram *Jedhe* says that Panhala was taken by seducing some of the garrison, but Jayaram contradicts him and *Basatin* is silent on the point

15,000 troops to attack Bahlol before his allies could join him. By two night-marches of great speed and secrecy, the Marathas came up with Bahlol at Umrani, 36 miles west of Bijapur city, and completely enveloped his camp at a distance, before he knew of their presence. They quietly cut him off from his water-supply, and next morning charged his camp in successive groups from different quarters. The battle raged all the day with intense ferocity. Many were slain and wounded, though the light and elusive Marathas suffered less than the hard-pressed and densely crowded Bijapuris. But Bahlol's Afghans held their ground with desperate tenacity. Indeed, flight would have meant destruction for them after that day-long fight in April heat without any water to quench the thirst of man or beast and with an exultant light cavalry hanging on their heels.

At nightfall the two forces separated. Bahlol sent a secret message to Pratap Rao saying that he was not really going to fight against Shivaji, but had to make a show of hostility in order to satisfy his Government, and therefore each side should spare the other. Pratap Rao agreed, probably for a bribe, and withdrew his troops from a point in the line of investment, through which Bahlol's wounded army safely fell back on his base Tikota, with the loss of one war-elephant and some baggage only, (about 15th April.)

Shivaji sharply censured his general for letting Bahlol escape when he could have easily crushed him and seized his entire camp.*

From the field of Umrani, Pratap Rao made a dash

---

* Umrani Sabh 78, *Parnal-parvat-grahana*, *B S* 440 Nesari Sabh 79, and *F R* Surat 88 (Narayan Shenvi's letter.)

south-westwards into Kanara, robbing many places, in May (Ch. 10 § 9.) Shortly afterwards, Bahlol with a replenished army, took post near Kolhapur, where he continued for some months, defeating the Marathas in several encounters and forcing all their roving bands to leave Kanara. We hear of his pressing hard upon Shivaji and successfully defending that region throughout June, July and August, 1673. But in September he fell very ill at Miraj, and the Bijapur and Golkonda Governments sought Shivaji's help in defending themselves from a Mughal invasion threatened by Bahadur Khan. As Gerald Aungier, the President of the Bombay Council, wrote on 16th September, "Shivaji bears himself up manfully against all his enemies;. .. and though it is probable that the Mughal's army may fall into his country this year and Bahlol Khan on the other side, yet neither of them can stay long for want of provisions, and his flying army will constantly keep them in alarm; nor is it either their design to destroy Shivaji totally, for the Umaras maintain a politic war to their own profit at the king's charge, and never intend to prosecute it violently so as to end it." (*F. R.* Surat 106.)

At the end of the rainy season, Shivaji opened a grand campaign on 10th October (the *dashahara* day) and raided Kanara, both upland and coast. Here he continued till the middle of December, being finally forced to retire by the pressure of Bahlol, Sharza and other Bijapuri generals. (Ch 10 § 9.)

§ 9. *Battle of Nesari and death of Pratap Rao, 1674.*

It was to restore his prestige after this set back in Kanara that he next month (January 1674) sent Pratap Rao against Bahlol Khan, severely censuring him for his neglect in having let that Bijapuri general off instead of crushing his power once for all, when he was at his mercy at Umrani in April last The Rajah wrote to his general in anger, "Bahlol has come again. Go with your army, destroy him and win a decisive victory Otherwise, never show your face to me again!"

Stung to the quick by this letter, Pratap Rao sought Bahlol out at Nesari, "in a narrow passage between two hills," (24 Feb. 1674.) Smarting under his master's censure, he threw generalship to the winds, and rushed upon the Bijapuri army followed by only six horsemen, the rest of his soldiers hanging back from the mad charge The gallant seven were cut down by the swarm of foes, and much havoc was done among the Marathas who were disheartened by the fall of their leader, "a river of blood flowed" Shivaji greatly mourned the death of Pratap Rao and repented of his angry letter. The dead general's relatives and dependents were well provided for, and his daughter was six years later married to Rajaram, the favourite son of the king.

Anand Rao, a lieutenant of Pratap Rao, rallied the disheartened army of his chief. Shiva appointed him to an independent command and ordered him not to return alive without defeating the enemy.* At this Anand Rao

* The Maratha achievements in this paragraph and the next two are ascribed to Hansaji Mohite by both Sabhasad and Chitnis. But Narayan Shenvi, writing from Raigarh, only a month later, on information supplied by Shiva's ministers, states that it was *Anand* Rao who rallied the Maratha army after the fall of Pratap Rao, and was the leader in all these campaigns *Jedhe* supports him, and I have followed these original authorities

The place of Pratap Rao's death is called *Jesari* (a misreading for *Nesari*) in Sabhasad and *Nivti* in Jedhe, and described as situated in the Panhala district This *Nesari* lies 45 m s of Kolhapur, in the Garh-Hinglaj sub-division of the Kolhapur State, one mile north of the Ghatprabha river, and 11 miles south of Garh-Hinglaj town [Degree sheet 47 L] There is "a narrow passage between two hills" near it There is another Nesari,

went off with the whole body of his cavalry far into Bijapur territory in search of Bahlol. Dilir Khan with the Mughal army advanced promptly to the succour of his brother Afghan, Bahlol Khan. But Anand Rao, not daring to fight two such large forces, retreated towards Kanara, making forced marches of 45 miles a day. The two Khans, unable to overtake the mobile Marathas, gave up the pursuit and turned,—Bahlol to Kolhapur and Dilir to Panhala, whence, after a 5 days' halt with the intention of besieging it, he fell back on his base (Parnir?)

Anand Rao, penetrating further into Kanara, robbed the bazar (*peth*) of Sampgaon, about 20 miles from Bankapur, in Bahlol's jagir, capturing 150,000 *hun* worth of booty (23 March.) Thence he set out on return with 3,000 ox-loads of plunder. Bahlol and Khizr Khan, with 2,000 cavalry and many foot-soldiers, tried to intercept him near Bankapur, but were defeated after a desperate battle and put to flight with the loss of a brother of Khizr Khan. Anand Rao robbed the entire Bijapuri army, captured 500 horses, 2 elephants, and much other prize. (March, 1674.)*

---

but too far from Panhala to be the battle field, *viz*, *Nesargi* of *Ind Atlas*, Sheet 41 N E, 18 miles east of Belgaum, on the Belgaum-Kaladgi road It was the halting place of Little's detachment when co-operating with Parashuram Bhao, (Moor, p 15, *Bom Gaz* xxi 591)

* The Dutchman Van Reade, 15th Dec 1674, (*Dutch Records*, Vol 32, No 824), calls the pillaged bazar "*Honspent*, situated on the borders of Bijapur near Bankapur" Narayan names it "a city called Pench, 8 leagues from Bankapur" Sabhasad refers to this campaign on p 80, but gives other names to the two generals. "Hambir Rao went with his army to Sampgaon [19 m s e of Belgaum] Husain Khan Miana, a great Bijapuri general, with 5,000 Pathans marched against Hambir Rao A severe battle took place between them, from noon till next morning Many men, horses and elephants were slain in Husain's army He was captured with 4,000 horses, 12 elephants, many camels, and property beyond calculation His whole army was destroyed"

But the Bijapuris had their revenge immediately afterwards. Bahlol Khan, "regarding the loss [of the elephants] as a great disgrace to him, became desperate, attacked the robbers again, and being reinforced secured such a victory that the robbers had to abandon 1,000 horses and were pursued for a long distance." It was not the Maratha policy to fight pitched battles during a raid. So, Anand Rao rapidly retreated with his booty to Shiva's dominions, left it there in safety, and then at the beginning of April was ordered to ascend the plateau (*bala-ghat*) for raiding more towns.*

On 8th April, Shivaji held a grand review of his troops at Chiplun, and appointed Hansaji Mohite commander-in-chief with the title of 'Hambir Rao' in succession to Pratap Rao Gujar Bounties were lavishly distributed among the soldiers. [Sabh. 79; *Jedhe S.*] The fort or Kelanja (Mohangarh) fell to him on 24th April

§10 *Defeat of Dilir Khan, January 1674*

Late in January 1674, a Mughal army tried to descend into Konkan and cause a diversion in that quarter simultaneously with the Bijapuri invasion of the Panhala region. But Shiva stopped the paths by breaking the roads and mountain passes and keeping a constant guard at various points where the route was most difficult, and the Mughals had to return baffled. It was probably this expedition to which the English merchants refer in a letter written at the end of January 1674, in the following words, "Dilir Khan hath lately received a rout by Shivaji and

* Sabhasad, 81, says that the raid (under Hambir Rao) extended over Khandesh, Baglana, Gujrat, Ahmadabad, Burhanpur, Berar, and Mahur, to the bank of the Narmada, and that the tired Mughal pursuers always lagged 30 or 40 miles behind, so that the Marathas returned home unmolested and with all their booty.

lost 1,000 of his Pathans, and Shivaji about five or six hundred men." If so, Dilir Khan had either made a rash frontal attack on one of the entrenched passes or fallen into an ambuscade of the Marathas. Throughout these four months, December 1673 to March 1674, Shivaji's wars with Adil Shah and the Siddis were carried on languidly with only occasional outbreaks of vigour. The soldiers on both sides were weary of fighting and their commanders not in earnest to end this paying business The winter rains of this year were very heavy and bred pestilence. Shiva in December and January was compelled to distribute his horses throughout his dominions in order to stable them in comfort.*

Soon afterwards the Mughal power in the Deccan was crippled. The rising of the Khaibar Afghans became so serious that Aurangzib had to leave Delhi (7th April) for Hasan Abdal, in order to direct the war from the rear, and next month Dilir Khan was called to the North-western frontier. Bahadur Khan was left alone in the Deccan with a greatly weakened force. This lull in the war was utilized by Shivaji to crown himself with the greatest pomp and ceremony. (*M. A.* 132; *F. R.* Surat 88, Oxinden's *Letter,* 21 May, 1674.)

The eve of Shivaji's coronation affords a suitable time for making a survey of his territorial position. We have seen in Chapter 3 §5 what his kingdom was in 1648 and in 1659. His gains between November 1659 and February 1660 were shortlived except in S. Konkan. Here he completed the conquest of the Ratnagiri district by taking possession of its western part (including all the

---

* Narayan Shenvi's letter from Raigarh in *F R* Surat, Vol 88, *O C* 3906 and 3939, *Dutch Records,* Vol. 34, No 840

ports except Rajapur and Vingurla) as well as its southern extremity. From this time his power began to impinge on that of the Savants of Vadi (or the *desais* of Kudal, as they were then called), and after a long and confused struggle much of the latter's territory as well as the ports of Rajapur and Vingurla passed into Shivaji's hands, (by the middle of 1663), and all South Konkan owned him as its sole master. He had already wrested the western coast of the Kolaba district from the Siddis.

What he ceded to the Mughals by the Treaty of Purandar (1665) touched only his territories in the Puna and Thana districts, while his acquisitions in middle and south Konkan remained intact Most of these cessions even were recovered in 1670 and 1671

From 1664 the Marathas began to *raid* Kanara,—both the Karwar coast and the uplands of Hubli and Bednur; but their actual *conquest* of the coast was achieved as late as 1675.

Maratha activities in 1671 and 1672 resulted in the annexation of Baglana (north of the Nasik district) and the Koli country (Jawhar and Ramnagar) in North Konkan, between Surat and the Thana district The hill-forts in the Chandor range seem to have repeatedly changed hands between the Mughals and the Marathas. But their importance in Shivaji's eyes was only strategical, as they secured his northward route to Baglana and Khandesh.

Southwards, Shivaji's power was firmly planted by his annexation of Panhala in 1673 and Kolhapur and Phonda in 1675. Thus his boundary in 1675 extended beyond the Kolhapur district well into western Karnatak or Kanara uplands.

The full extent of his kingdom at his death (1680) will be described at the beginning of Ch. 15.

CHAPTER IX

THE CORONATION OF SHIVAJI AND AFTER, 1674—1676

§1. *Why Shivaji wanted to be crowned.*

Shivaji and his ministers had long felt the practical disadvantages of his not being a crowned king. True, he had conquered many lands and gathered much wealth: he had a strong army and navy and exercised powers of life and death over men, like an independent sovereign. But theoretically his position was that of a subject; to the Mughal Emperor he was a mere zamindar; to Adil Shah he was the rebellious son of a vassal jagirdar. He could not claim equality of political status with any king.

Then, again, so long as he was a mere private subject, he could not, with all his real power, claim the loyalty and devotion of the people over whom he ruled. His promises could not have the sanctity and continuity of the public engagements of the head of a State. He could sign no treaty, grant no land with legal validity and an assurance of permanence. The territories conquered by his sword could not become his lawful property,

---

* This chapter is mainly based upon the detailed reports of the English ambassador Henry Oxinden (both *Letters* and *Memorial* or *Narrative*), the English interpreter Narayan Shenvi, and the Dutch merchant Abraham Le Feber (of Vingurla), preserved in *Factory Records,* Surat, Vols 88 and 3, and *Dutch Records,* Vol xxxiv No 841, of the India Office, London These have been supplemented by Sabhasad (82-84) The Persian MS *Tarikh-i-Shivaji, 39a,* confirms the contemporary European records in some particulars in a surprising manner The *Bombay Gazetteer* (xi 369) has pointed out that the Chitnis *bakhar* imputes to Shivaji's coronation in 1674 the ceremonies which marked the Peshwa's coronation of a century later!

however undisturbed his possession over them might be in practice. The people living under his sway or serving under his banners, could not renounce their allegiance to the former sovereign of the land, nor be sure that they were exempt from the charge of treason for their obedience to him The permanence of his political creation required that it should be validated as the act of a sovereign

It is also clear that the rise of the Bhonslés created much jealousy among the other Maratha families which had once been their equals in social status. These men consoled themselves by refusing to adhere to Shivaji as his servants, bragged of their being loyal subjects of Aurangzib or of Adil Shah, and sneered at Shivaji as an upstart rebel and usurper. It was necessary to rectify his position in their eyes A formal coronation alone could show them that he was a king and therefore their superior, and enable him to treat on equal terms with the rulers of Bijapur and Golkonda.

The higher minds of Maharashtra, too, had begun to look up to Shivaji as the champion of Hinduism, and wished to see the Hindu race elevated to full stature of its political growth by the formal assertion of his position as an independent king They longed for the Hindu *swaraj*, and that implied a Hindu *chhatrapati* (Sabh 82.)

§2 *Shivaji recognized by Gaga Bhatta as a Kshatriya*

But there was one curious hindrance to the realization of this ideal. According to the ancient Hindu scriptures, only a member of the Kshatriya caste can be legally crowned as king and claim the homage of Hindu subjects The Bhonslés were popularly known to be neither Kshatriyas nor of any other twice-born caste, but mere tillers of the soil, as Shivaji's great-grandfather was still remembered to have been. How could an upstart sprung from such a *Shudra* (plebeian) stock aspire to the rights and honours due to a Kshatriya? The Brahmans of all parts of India would attend and bless the coronation of Shivaji, only if he could be authoritatively declared a Kshatriya.

It was, therefore, necessary first to secure the support of a pandit, whose reputation for scholarship would silence all opposition to the views he might propound. Such a man was found in Vishweshwar, nicknamed Gaga Bhatta, of Benares, the greatest Sanskrit theologian and controversialist then alive, a master of the four Vedas, the six philosophies, and all the scriptures of the Hindus, and popularly known as the Brahma-deva and Vyas of the age After holding out for some time, he became compliant, accepted the Bhonslé pedigree as fabricated by the clever secretary Balaji Avji and other agents of Shiva, and declared that that Rajah was a Kshatriya of the purest breed, descended in unbroken line from the Maharanas of Udaipur, the sole representatives of the solar line of the mythical hero-god Ramchandra. His audacious but courtierly ethnological theory was rewarded with a huge fee, and he was entreated to visit Maharashtra and officiate as high priest at the coronation of Shiva. He agreed, and on his arrival was welcomed like a crowned head, Shiva and all his officers advancing many miles from Satara to receive him on the way.

§3. *Preparations for coronation.*

The preparations took many months. There was no unbroken tradition about the exact ceremonies and paraphernalia required at the coronation of an independent

Hindu sovereign The Sanskrit epics and political treatises were ransacked by a syndicate of pandits to find out the orthodox ancient precedents on these points, and agents were sent to learn the modern practice of the Rajahs of Udaipur and Jaipur

Invitations had been sent to learned Brahmans of every part of India; the report of the coming ceremony had attracted others Eleven thousand Brahmans, making 50,000 souls with their wives and children, were assembled at Raigarh and fed with sweets for four months at the Rajah's expense. The greatest forethought and organizing power must have been shown by Shiva in providing for the comfort of the numerous guests—Brahmans, nobles, local magnates of the realm, agents of other States, foreign merchants and visitors, and poor cousins, who flocked to the ceremony Nothing went amiss in catering to this crowd of nearly a hundred thousand men, women and children.

The daily religious ceremonies and consultations with the Brahmans left Shiva no time to attend to other business, as the English envoy, Henry Oxinden, found to his chagrin Shiva began by bowing to his *guru* Ramdas Swami and his mother Jija Bai and receiving their blessings. The unhappy discarded first wife of Shahji, now verging on eighty, had forgotten her husband's neglect in the love and devotion of her son, and rejoiced to see, before she closed her eyes, that he had reached the summit of human greatness as the crowned king of the land of his birth, an irresistible conqueror, and a strong defender of the religion which was the solace of her life Like a queen-mother of the same country born 15 centuries earlier, Gautami, the mother of the Andhra king Shri Satakarni, she gloried in the glory of her victorious and orthodox son. A kind Providence seemed to have prolonged her life just long enough to enable her to witness the scene of his coronation, for she died twelve days after it.

§4. *Puja and purification by Shiva.*

Then he set out on a round of worship at the most famous shrines of the land. Chiplun was visited early in May, 1674, and after adoring Parashuram in the great temple there, he returned to Raigarh on the 12th. Four days afterwards he again issued forth to worship the Bhavani goddess he had installed at Pratapgarh, as the ancient Bhavani of Tuljapur was beyond his reach. To this image he presented an umbrella of pure gold, weighing one and a quarter maunds, (worth about Rs. 56,000) and many other costly gifts.

Returning to Raigarh in the afternoon of the 21st, he plunged into devotion there. Under the guidance of his family priest, Balam Bhatta, (the son of Prabhakar Bhatta Upadhyay), he adored Mahadev, Bhavani and other local deities for many days in succession.

But one great defect had to be removed before his coronation could take place. He had to be publicly purified and "made a Kshatriya." On 28th May he performed penance for his ancestors' and his own sin of omission in not having observed the Kshatriya rites so long, and was invested by Gaga Bhatta with the sacred thread, the distinctive badge of the twice-born castes like the "pure" Kshatriyas of Northern India. The next step was to teach him the *mantra* (sacred verses) and initiate him into the rules of the Kshatriya caste. Shivaji very logically demanded that all the Vedic verses appropriate to the initiation and coronation of a true Hindu king should be chanted in his hearing, because the Kshatriyas being one of the holy "twice-born" castes, he as an admitted Kshatriya was entitled to use the Vedic *mantras* equally with the Brahmans. At this there was a mutiny among the assembled Brahmans, who asserted that there was no true Kshatriya in the modern age* and that the Brahmans were the only twice-born caste now surviving! Even Gaga Bhatta was cowed by the general opposition and evidently dropped the Vedic chant and initiated the Rajah only in a modified form of the life of the twice-born, instead of putting him on a par with the Brahmans in this respect. (*T. S.* 39*a*; *Dutch Records.*) This purification and its sequel, the investiture with the sacred thread, were performed with "great ceremony", a vast amount of money was distributed among the Brahmans, Gaga Bhatta alone getting 7,000 *hun* and the crowd of ordinary Brahmans 17,000 *hun*

Next day, Shiva made atonement for the sins, deliberate or accidental, committed in his own life. He was separately weighed against each of the seven metals, —gold, silver, copper, zinc, tin, lead and iron,—as well as very fine linen, camphor, salt, nails (*sic*), nutmegs, and other spices, butter, sugar, fruits and all sorts of eatables (betel-leaves and country wine being among

---

* Exactly the same kind of trouble has been given by the Brahmans of the present generation to Shivaji s descendant, the Maharajah of Kolhapur The following significant passage in *T S* (39*a*) suggests that Shivaji at one time thought of punishing the jealous intolerant Brahmans by removing them from lucrative secular duties like the command of armies and vice-royalties of provinces and confining them to their scriptural functions of fasting and praying 'The Maharajah learning [of the refusal of the Brahmans to teach him the Vedic *mantras*], said, The Brahmans are reverend men It is not proper to appoint them royal servants They ought not to perform any work except worshipping God ' So he removed all the Brahmans from their posts and appointed Prabhu Kayasthas in their places Moro Pant interceded for the Brahmans '

them) All these metals and other articles to the weight of his body, together with a *lakh* of *hun* more, were given away to the assembled Brahmans after the coronation.

But even this failed to satisfy their greed. Two of the learned Brahmans pointed out that Shiva, in the course of his raids, had burnt cities "involving the death of Brahmans, cows, women and children." He could be cleansed of this sin,—for a price. It was not necessary for him to pay compensation to the surviving relatives of the men and women who had perished in his sack of Surat or Karinja. It would be enough if he put money into the pockets of the Brahmans of Konkan and Desh. The price demanded for this 'pardon' was only Rs. 8,000, and Shiva could not have refused to pay this trifle. (*Dutch Records,* Vol. 34, No. 841.)

§5 *Scene of Shivaji's Coronation.*

All his disqualifications having been thus removed with gold, the actual coronation was now begun. The 5th of June was the eve of the grand ceremony. That day had to be spent in self-restraint and mortification of the flesh, like the night of vigil preceding knighthood in the age of chivalry. Shivaji bathed in water brought from the holy Ganges, and gave Gaga Bhatta 5,000 *hun* and the other great Brahmans a hundred gold-pieces each The day was probably spent in fasting.

Next day (6th June, 1674) came the coronation itself. Rising very early in the morning, Shivaji prepared himself by bathing amidst ceremonies intended to avert evil, worshipped his household gods, and adored the feet of his family priest, Gaga Bhatta, and other eminent Brahmans, who all received gifts of ornaments and cloth.

The essential parts of a Hindu king's coronation are

washing him (*abhishek*) and holding the royal umbrella over his head (*chhatra-dharan*) Clad in a pure white robe, wearing garlands of flowers, scented essence, and gold ornaments, Shiva walked to the place appointed for the bath. Here he sat down on a gold-plated stool, two feet square and two feet high. The queen-consort, Soyra Bai, occupied a seat on his left with the hem of her robe knotted up with his, in sign of her being his equal partner in this world and the next (*saha-dharmini*), as the Hindu sacred law lays down The heir-apparent Shambhuji sat down close behind. Then the eight ministers of his cabinet (*ashta-pradhan*), who stood ready at the eight points of the horizon with gold jugs full of the water of the Ganges and other holy rivers, emptied them over the heads of the king queen and crown-prince, amidst the chanting of hymns and the joyous music of the band. Sixteen pure-robed Brahman wives each with five lamps laid on a gold tray, waved the lights round his head to scare away evil influences.

Then Shivaji changed his dress for a robe of royal scarlet, richly embroidered with gold, put on sparkling gems and gold ornaments, a necklace, a garland of flowers, and a turban adorned with strings and tassels of pearls, worshipped his sword shield bow and arrows, and again bowed to his elders and Brahmans Then, at the auspicious moment selected by the astrologers, he entered the throne-room.

The hall of coronation was decorated with the 32 emblematic figures prescribed by Hindu usage and various auspicious plants. Overhead an awning of cloth of gold was spread, with strings of pearls hanging down in festoons. The floor was covered with velvet. In the centre was placed a "magnificent throne," constructed after months of continuous labour in a style worthy of a great king. Even if we reject Sabhasad's statement that it contained 32 maunds of gold (worth 14 *lakhs* of Rupees), we must accept the English observer's report that it was "rich and stately." The base was evidently coated with gold plate, and so also were the eight pillars standing at the eight angles, which were further richly embellished with gems and diamonds. They supported a canopy of the richest gold embroidery from which strings of pearls were suspended in tassels and festoons, interspersed with dazzling gems. The coverings of the royal seat were a grotesque combination of ancient Hindu asceticism and modern Mughal luxury: tiger skin below and velvet on the top!

On the two sides of the throne, various emblems of royalty and government were hung from gilded lance-heads. On the right hand stood two large fish-heads of gold with very big teeth, and on the left several horses' tails (the insignia of royalty among the Turks) and a pair of gold scales, evenly balanced (the emblem of justice), on a very costly lance-head. All these were copied from the Mughal Court At the palace gate were placed on either hand pitchers full of water covered with bunches of fresh green leaves, and also two young elephants and two beautiful horses, with gold bridles and rich trappings. These latter were auspicious tokens according to Hindu ideas.

As Shivaji mounted the throne, small lotuses of gold set with jewels, and various other flowers made of gold and silver were showered among the assembled throng. Sixteen Brahman married women again performed the auspicious waving of lamps round the newly enthroned monarch. The Brahmans lifted up their voices, chanting holy verses and blessing the king, who bowed to them in return The crowd set up deafening shouts of "Victory, victory unto Shiva-raj !" All the instruments began to play and the musicians to sing at once By previous arrangement the artillery of every fort in the kingdom fired salvoes of all their guns exactly at this time The arch-pontiff Gaga Bhatta advanced to the throne, held the royal sun-shade of cloth of gold fringed with pearls over his head, and hailed him as *Shiva Chhatrapati*, or Shiva the paramount sovereign !

The Brahmans stepped forward and poured their blessings on his head The Rajah gave away vast sums of money and gifts of every kind to them and to the assembled beggars and general public "He performed the sixteen varieties of great alms-giving (*maha-dan*) prescribed in the sacred books of the Hindus. Then the ministers advanced to the throne and made their obeisance, and received from his hands robes of honour, letters of appointment, and large gifts of money, horses, elephants, jewels, cloth, and arms Sanskrit titles were ordered to be used in future to designate their offices, and the Persian titles hitherto current were abolished." (Sabh)

The crown-prince Shambhuji, the high-priest Gaga Bhatta, and the prime-minister Moro Trimbak Pingle, were seated on an eminence a little lower than the throne. The other ministers stood in two rows on the right and left of the throne All other courtiers and visitors stood according to their ranks at proper places in a respectful attitude

By this time it was eight o'clock in the morning. The English ambassador, Henry Oxinden, was now presented by Niraji Pant. He bowed from a distance, and his interpreter Narayan Shenvi held up a diamond ring as an offering from the English to the Rajah. Shivaji took notice of the strangers and ordered them to come to the foot of the throne, invested them with robes of honour, and then sent them back.

§6. *Street procession at Raigarh.*

When the presentations were over, the Rajah descended from his throne, mounted his best horse, decked with gorgeous trappings, and rode to the palace-yard. There he mounted the finest elephant in his stable, dressed out most splendidly for the occasion, and then rode through the streets of the capital in full military procession, girt round by his ministers and generals, with the two royal banners, *Jari-pataka* and *Bhagwe-jhanda*, borne aloft on two elephants walking in the Van, while the generals and regiments of troops followed with their respective flags, artillery and band. The citizens had decorated their houses and roads in a manner worthy of the occasion. The housewives waved lighted lamps round him and showered fried rice, flowers, holy grass, &c., on his head. After visiting the various temples on Raigarh hill and offering adoration with presents at each of them, he returned to the palace.

On the 7th began a general distribution of gifts to all the assembled envoys and Brahmans and of alms to the beggars, which lasted twelve days, during which the people were also fed at the king's expense. The more distinguished pandits and sannyasis were not included in this alms-giving, as these men got only 3 to 5 Rupees and the women and children a Rupee or two each.

A day or two after the coronation the monsoon burst, the rains set in with violence, and the weather continued wet for some time, to the intense discomfort of the assembled crowd. On the 8th, Shivaji took a fourth wife without any state or ceremony. Shortly before this he had married* two others. (Letter of Oxinden, 27 May; Oxinden's *Memorial* under date 8 June.)

After the coronation was over, Jija Bai died on 18th June, in the fulness of years and happiness, leaving to her son her personal property worth 25 *lakhs of hun*, "some say more" When the period of mourning for her was over, Shivaji sat on the throne a second time, to celebrate his purification after her funeral (*Dutch Records.*)

§7. *Cost of the Coronation.*

The total cost of the coronation, including the sums distributed in gifts and alms, is put down by Sabhasad at the incredible figure of one *krore* and 42 *lakhs* of *hun*. The Dutch merchant Abraham Le Feber, writing from Vingurla only four months after the event, quotes the popular report that "this ceremony and distribution of largess cost 150,000 pagodas." He evidently means the money spent in the 12 days' general alms-giving from the 7th to the 18th, and not the special gifts to the ministers and other officers, Brahmans and priests But even when all these are taken into account, together with the price of the throne and ornaments made for the occasion and the cost of feeding the assemblage, the total expenditure cannot be put higher than 10 *lakhs* of *hun* or fifty *lakhs* of Rupees.

---

* *Jedhe S* says that the marriage was celebrated with [Vedic] *mantras*, on 30th May, i e, one day after Shivaji was invested with the sacred thread, and we shall not be wrong in supposing that Shivaji made these late marriages in order to assert publicly his right as a 'twice-born' to hear Vedic *mantras* !

§8. *Loot of Bahadur Khan's camp and extensive contest with the Mughals.*

The coronation exhausted Shivaji's treasury and he was in need of money to pay his troops. It was, therefore, necessary for him to be out on raid immediately afterwards. (*F. R.* Surat, 88, Niccolls to Surat, 14 Oct., 1674.)

His first movement was against Bahadur Khan. As early as May 1674 it was the talk of the Maratha Court that Dilir Khan, whom they feared most, having been recalled by the Emperor, the Mughal forces in the Deccan were commanded by Bahadur Khan alone, whom they despised and whose "quarters they intended to beat up after the rains." The blow was struck much sooner, in the very height of the monsoons. Towards the middle of July, a body of 2,000 Maratha light cavalry, made a false demonstration and lured Bahadur Khan some 50 miles away from his cantonments at Pedgaon, while a second force, 7,000 strong, swooped down by another route on his defenceless camp, carried away a *krore* of Rupees in booty and 200 fine horses collected for presentation to the Emperor, and burnt all his tents. (*F. R.* Surat 88, Oxinden to Surat, 21 May; Vol. 87, Surat to Bombay, 1 Aug., 1674.)

The state of war with Bijapur continued, though languidly. A general of that State, probably Rustam-i-Zaman II., lay with his army on the Ghats near Kolhapur (July), ready to descend into Konkan and wrest Rajapur from the Marathas. In August, September and October Maratha bands spread northwards into the Koli country, giving repeated alarms to the port of Surat. But a body of three to four thousand Bhils of Ramnagar held the jungles and passes through that State and opposed the Marathas, who vainly offered them a bribe of one *lakh* of Rupees for a safe passage (middle of October 1674)*. Shortly afterwards the baffled Maratha army, after provisioning their forts in that region, marched away to join Shiva near Aurangabad, and Surat again breathed freely They had found an easier prey in another quarter Late in October, a large army commanded by Shivaji in person advanced into the Deccan plateau, skirted Bahadur Khan's camp, which was "hotly alarmed," looted several towns near Aurangabad, and then burst into Baglana and Khandesh, where they continued for more than a month (Nov. to middle of Dec) Among other places they pillaged and burnt Dharangaon (10 m north of Erandol) and its English factory Qutb-ud-din Khan Kheshgi bravely opposed the raiders, but his small force was routed with the loss of 3 to 4 hundred men, and he fled to Aurangabad for refuge. (*F R* Surat 87, Surat to Bomb 28 Oct., 1664, Vol 107, Bomb. to Surat 2 Nov., 1674, Dungom to Surat, 10 Dec.; O. C. 4062)

It was probably on his return from this raid that Shiva encamped near Junnar, but a shot from a 22 feet narrow-bore gun on the walls of Shivner killed a Rajah of his army and caused the prompt retreat of the Marathas †

At the end of January 1675, a band of 3,000 Maratha cavalry under Dattaji roved in the Kolhapur district The town of Kolhapur saved itself by paying 1,500 *hun*, and Shongaon (near Gargoti, about 30 miles

---

* *F R* Surat, 3 Consult 6 Aug, Vol 87, Surat to Bomb 6 Aug and 22 Oct, 1674, O C 4062

† Fryer (i 338) says that it happened "some four months before" the 22nd of May, 1675, and that the shot was hurled 2 *kos* off!

south of Kolhapur) 500 *hun*. In the middle of February, a Mughal force crossed the Ghats, fell on the town of Kalian, burnt the houses (including those of many Khojas) and then quickly retired, after which the Marathas re-occupied the place. (*F. R.* Surat 88, Rajapur to Surat, 6 Feb.; Vol. 107, Bomb. to Surat, 27 Feb., 1675.)

§9. *Shivaji's false negotiations with Bahadur Khan, 1675.*

Shivaji next opened delusive peace negotiations with Bahadur Khan, who eagerly swallowed the bait, as he was weary of the war and at his wits' end how to guard all parts of his viceroyalty against such a mobile and elusive enemy. For nearly three months (March-May) Shiva kept the Mughals in play, by feeding false hopes of a peace.* His real motives were to gain respite from Mughal attacks in order to provision his forts, to get money out of Adil Shah by the threat of an alliance with the Mughals for the invasion of Bijapur, and to secure his northern frontier during the siege of Phonda.

It was proposed that Shivaji would cede 17 of his forts to Aurangzib and send his son Shambhuji with a contingent to serve under the Mughal subahdar, while the Emperor would create Shambhuji a commander of 6 thousand horse, and grant Shiva all the country on the right bank of the Bhima. The negotiations were deliberately spun out. Shiva "demurred to sending his son to the Mughal general until he had better security

---

* False overtures of peace with the Mughals in 1675 · *F R* Surat 107, Bomb to Surat, 27 Feb 1675; *O C* 4077, Vol 88, Surat to Bomb 15 June and 17 July, also Letter from J Child, 7 August, *Dil* 134—135, *B S.* 401—2, *M A.* 142 (7 July, 1675)

for his safety" Bahadur Khan reported the terms to the Emperor, who sent in reply a *farman* accepting them and pardoning Shiva's past misdeeds Then the viceroy sent messengers to Shivaji to receive the *farman* and deliver the forts But, by this time (July 1675), Phonda had been captured. Shivaji now threw off the mask and dismissed the Mughal envoys with taunts, saying, "What pressure have you succeeded in putting on me that I should seek peace with you? Go hence quickly, or you will be disgraced"

Bahadur Khan, ashamed at being thus outwitted and anxious to cover his foolish credulity and diplomatic defeat by some striking success, hurriedly made an agreement with the Bijapuri wazir Khawas Khan (October) for a joint war on Shiva. (*B. S.* 445) Aurangzib approved of the idea, and is said to have offered to give up one year's tribute from Bijapur if that State heartily co-operated with his viceroy in a concerted attack on Shiva from two sides. But the overthrow of Khawas Khan and the usurpation of the regency by Bahlol Khan (11th Nov.) spoiled this plan, and soon afterwards the Mughals were drawn into the whirlpool of faction-fights at the Adil-Shahi Court.

Meantime, while the Mughal viceroy was being lulled into inactivity by these peace overtures, and Shiva was hastening to the siege of Phonda, he captured Kolhapur (March) but failed to take Raibagh. A little later another division of his army ranged far eastwards, plundering Bijapur and Golkonda territories, especially Yadagiri and two towns near Haidarabad, "bringing away a great deal of riches besides many rich persons" held to ransom At the same time his men robbed

Cuncolim and Veroda* in the Portuguese territory (middle of April.) The other Maratha activities in the latter half of this year will be described in the chapter on South Konkan and Kanara.

§10. *War with the Mughals renewed. Union with Bijapur.*

In November, Bahadur Khan, on being sharply censured by Aurangzib, marched to Kalian, and pressed Shiva hard in North Konkan. In January next (1676), a Maratha band spread near Aurangabad, but Bahadur with light equipment and no tent, made a rapid march from Pedgaon, defeated the rovers near Lasur, 28 miles from the capital, and drove them back towards Junnar. (*O. C.* 4139; *Dil* 140.)

At this time Shiva was taken seriously ill, and passed the next three months on the sick-bed at Satara. His perfect recovery was announced at the end of March. The Marathas looted Athni, 43 m. west of Bijapur, in April. The civil war that had broken out between the Deccani and Afghan parties at Bijapur, was Shivaji's opportunity. Early in May we hear of his having sent out "4,000 horse that ranges up and down, plunders and robs without any hindrance or danger." (*F. R.* Surat, Vol. 89, Rajapur to Surat, 11 Jan. and 9 May 1676; O. C. 4202.)

In May, his prime-minister Moro Trimbak drove the Rajah of Ramnagar out of his country and took Pindol† and Painecah within three days' march of Surat.

---

* F R Surat 88, Rajapur to Surat 1 April, Karwar to Surat 22 April, 1675

† *Pindval*, 11 m s e of Dharampur, in the Dharampur State, south of Surat *Painecah* is probably either *Panva*, 5 m w of Pindval, or *Panaj*, 9 m n of Dharampur (*Ind At*, 24 N E.)

But the monsoons being at hand, he left 4,000 men to garrison the district and retired with the rest of his army to Raigarh at the end of the month (*F R* 89, Surat to Bomb , 27 May and 1 June 1676)

On 31st May Bahadur Khan opened a vigorous and long campaign against Bijapur, where the Afghan faction had seized the Government. The consequence was to drive the new regent Bahlol Khan into the arms of Shiva, and in July we have the report of a peace between the two having been concluded through the mediation of the Golkonda minister Madanna. The terms of this treaty were that the Adil-Shahi Government would pay Shiva 3 lakhs of Rupees down as a contribution and one lakh of *hun* annually as subsidy for protection against the Mughals, and confirm him in the possession of the country bounded on the east by the Krishna, including the Kolhapur district. But the union was shortlived, as no policy could be durable in a State ravaged by civil war and subject to almost daily changes of authority. Shivaji hardly minded the rupture of this subsidiary alliance; his gaze was fixed elsewhere; and in January next (1677), he set out on the greatest expedition of his life, the invasion of the Eastern Karnatak. (*B S.* 450-470, *F. R.* Surat 89, Rajapur to Surat, 24 July 1676)

CHAPTER X

South Konkan and Kanara

§1. *Kanara, its rulers and trade.*

In the seventeenth century, Kanara, the extensive country along our west coast, was held by various Hindu chieftains. North Kanara (now included in the Bombay Presidency) owned the overlordship of Bijapur, which ruled directly over the coast-strip from Karwar (south of Goa) to Mirjan (14 30 N. lat.), leaving the inland districts in the hands of feudatory chiefs, among whom the Nayaks of Sunda were the most important. The portion of Kanara that lay south of Mirjan formed a large and independent principality under the Keladi dynasty, whose capital was then at Bednur.

A Muslim officer with the hereditary title of Rustam-i-Zaman (originally Randaula Khan) was the viceroy of the south-western corner of the Bijapur kingdom. His charge extended on the west coast from Ratnagiri town, going southwards round the Portuguese territory of Goa to Karwar and Mirjan, while landwards it included the southern part of the Ratnagiri district, Kolhapur, Belgaum, a bit of Dharwar and the western corner of the North Kanara district. His seat was at Miraj. The fort of Panhala lay within his province, but it was governed by a commandant directly under the orders of the Sultan. The viceroy administered by means of his agents the flourishing ports of Rajapur in the north and Karwar in the south, through which the trade of the rich inland places flowed to Europe. In both towns the English had factories.

"The best pepper in the world is of the growth of Sunda, known in England by [the name of] Karwar pepper, though five days' journey distant from thence." (Fryer, ii. 42.) Indeed, after the loss of Chaul, Karwar became the greatest port of Bijapur on the west coast. "The finest muslins of western India were exported from here. The weaving country was inland, to the east of the Sahyadris, at Hubli (in the Dharwar district), and at other centres, where the English East India Company had agents and employed as many as 50,000 weavers." (*Bom. Gaz.*, xv., pt. ii. pp. 123-125.)

At Mirjan, a port twenty miles south-east of Karwar, pepper, saltpetre and betel-nut were shipped for Surat. Gersappa, a district annexed by Bednur, was so famous for its pepper that the Portuguese used to call its Rani "the Pepper Queen." (*Ibid*, 333 and 124.)

In 1649 the pepper and cardamon trade of Rajapur was the chief attraction that induced the English Company to open a factory there. Vingurla was spoken of in 1660 as a great place of call for ships from Batavia, Japan and Ceylon on the one side, and the Persian Gulf and the Red Sea on the other. All the ports of the Ratnagiri district did much trade also in calicoes, silks, grain and coarse lac, though pepper was their chief export, "which coming out of Kanara is sent by sea to Persia, Surat and Europe. This country is the store-house for all its neighbours." (*Bom. Gaz.*, x. 175.)

§2. *Shivaji's first raid on Rajapur.*

After the disastrous failure of Afzal Khan, Rustam-i-Zaman had marched against Shivaji (December, 1659) with 3,000 horse, but this show of hostility was made simply to save his credit with his king. The queen, regent, Bari Sahiba, being his enemy, he had made a secret alliance with Shivaji for self-protection This fact was well known to the country around, and the English factors had found proofs of it. But even if Rustam had been in earnest, he could have done little with his small army.

Shivaji had followed up his victory over Afzal's army by pushing on to Panhala and capturing that fort (28 Nov.). Then he entered the Ratnagiri district and began to "take possession of all the port and inland towns." The Bijapuri governors of these places fled to Rajapur, which was at first spared, "because it belonged to Rustam-i-Zaman, who is a friend of Shivaji " (Rajapur to Surat, 10th December 1659, *F. R.* Rajapur)

On the fall of Dabhol, its defeated governor made his escape to Rajapur with three junks of Afzal Khan, of 450, 350 and 300 tons burden respectively. The governor of Rajapur, by order of his master Rustam-i-Zaman, received the junks and landed their cargoes for safe-keeping. Shortly after this Shivaji encountered and routed near Panhala, the combined armies of Rustam and Fazl Khan (the son of Afzal)* The latter, who bore the brunt of the battle, lost many of his followers, while Rustam, who had made a mere show of fighting, retreated to Hukri with slight loss, and there sat still. while the Marathas continued to make their incursions in Adil-Shahi territory. (Rajapur to Bassein, 4 February 1660, *F. R.* Rajapur.)

The news of this battle greatly alarmed Rustam's governor of Rajapur, who took refuge in one of Afzal Khan's junks for escaping to the open sea Before he

---

* *Jedhe S* states that in this battle the Marathas captured 2,000 horses and twelve elephants *Shivapur Yadi* gives the date as 28th Dec 1659

could start, a Maratha force appeared on the bank to seize the junks, but the governor (about 10th January) succeeded in slipping away beyond the range of the Maratha guns, with the help of the English factor Henry Revington, who for his private gain opposed the Marathas, as will be described in Chapter 14.

Shivaji condemned this attack on his ally's town of Rajapur, dismissed Doroji, the general responsible for it, "commanded all things that his soldiers took from the townsmen [at Rajapur] to be restored," and put Rustam-i-Zaman's agents again in possession of the town and port (Rajapur to Surat, 20 February)

The Dutch report states that about this time Shiva with his troops arrived within four hours' march of Vingurla, but was driven off by the *desai* of Kudal (*i e* , Savant-vadi), while another Maratha army which had penetrated to near Bijapur was forced to withdraw after being defeated in a bloody battle by the combined Bijapur and Golkonda troops (early in 1660) (*Dutch Records,* Trans , Vol 24, No 664 and Vol 23, No 651)

The Maratha invasion of the Ratnagiri district in Feb -April 1661 has been described in Ch 4 §5

In March 1663, Rustam-i-Zaman did another friendly turn to Shivaji. Netaji Palkar, Shiva's "lieutenant-general," had raided the imperial territory, but a large Mughal division of 7,000 cavalry pursued him so close as to force him to march 45 or 50 miles a day Rustam met this army near Bijapur and persuaded the Mughal commander to give up the chase as "that country was dangerous for any strange army to march in, likewise promising them to go himself and follow him, by which deceit Netaji got escaped, though not without the loss of 300 horse and himself wounded." (Gyffard to Surat, 30th March and 8th April 1663, *F. R.* Surat 103.) This reverse defeated Shivaji's plan of raiding North Kanara and penetrating to the rich port of Karwar. (*F. R.* Surat, Vol. 2, 9th October.)

On 1st March 1663, Ali Adil Shah II., with all his Court, left his capital for Bankapur.* There they were at first denied entrance by the mother of Abdur Rahim Bahlol Khan, in whose fief it lay. But the gates were soon opened to the king. Adil Shah summoned Bahlol Khan, Shahji and other officers from the Karnatak, who came by forced marches and waited on the king on the bank of the Warda (an affluent of the Tungabhadra.) Bahlol and Shahji were at once arrested and placed in chains (end of June 1663), but Shahji was released in two days, though he continued to be deprived of his command for some time. The Bijapuri invasion of Kanara had already begun. (*F. R.* Surat 103, Gyffard to Surat, 8th April and 20th July 1663.)

§3. *Maratha conquest of South Konkan, 1663.*

Shivappa Nayak,† who governed Bednur for forty-

---

* *F. R.* Surat, Vol. 103, Gyffard to Surat, 20th July 1663. A letter from him to Surat, 30th March, says that the Adil-Shahi Court went there in fear of the Mughals who had come within five leagues of Bijapur in pursuit of Netaji. But *Tarikh-i-Ali II.*, 160-164, (also *B. S.* 391) says that Ali went to Bankapur to direct the operations against the Rajah of Bednur in person.

† In the Persian histories of Bijapur he is styled Rajah of *Malnad*, which is a Kanarese word meaning "hill country." (*Mysore Gazetteer*, ii. 286.) The Portuguese records prove that he died before the close of 1662. Surat, Vol. 104, Karwar to Surat, 18th April 1664 shows that Bhadrappa was "murdered per his Brahmans" very early in 1664,—which agrees with the Portuguese account that he sickened (of small-pox) and died in a few days after making peace with Adil Shah, not without suspicion of having been poisoned. (Pissurlencar, i. 19*n*.)

four years (1618-1662), first as regent and then as king, had extended his kingdom on all sides by his conquests and stretched his sway over the whole of South Kanara, the north-western corner of Mysore, and North Kanara up to the Gangavati river, including the port of Mirjan. At the close of his life his ambition brought him into collision with Bijapur He had conquered Sunda and some other forts belonging to vassals of Adil Shah and had thus come dangerously close to Bankapur, the fortress of asylum of the Bijapuri Sultans in the south-western corner of their kingdom (*Bom Gaz*, xv. pt ii. pp 122-123)

The Sunda Rajah appealed to Bijapur and Adil Shah seized the opportunity of the death of Shivappa and the succession of his weak son Bhadrappa to invade Bednur in person with an overwhelming force.

Ali Adil Shah's campaign was short but vigorous and an unbroken success Bhadrappa Nayak could make no stand against the combined resources of the entire Bijapur kingdom; he lost Sunda, Bednur and many other forts, and was forced to make peace by restoring Sunda to its former chief and promising an indemnity of 7 *lakhs* of *hun* to Adil Shah. On 21st November the victorious Ali II returned to his capital. (*B S* 391-395, *F R*. Surat 103, Karwar to Surat, 28th January and 27th February, also Gyffard to Surat, 24th May and 20th July 1663)

We now turn to the activities of Shivaji in this region While Ali was engaged in the struggle with Bednur, Shivaji had been active in South Konkan and in the north-western part of the Kanara district. By way of Kolhapur and Kudal, he marched to Vingurla (May 1663), "all the way, as he goes along, he gives his *qaul* (assurance), promising them that neither he nor his soldiers shall in the least do any wrong to anybody that takes his *qaul*, which promise he hitherto hath kept" (*F R*. Surat, Vol. 103, Gyffard to Surat, 24th May, 1663.)

His going down the coast caused such alarm that "all the Muhammadan governors as far as Sanquelim and Bicholim were fled," and in consequence the petty robbers on the route became more active than usual In June Shivaji returned from Vingurla after leaving a garrison of 2,000 soldiers there. Shortly before this Shaista Khan had defeated a Maratha army, killing more than 200 men. (*Ibid.*, Gyffard to Surat, 24th May and 22nd June 1663.)

In July the Bijapur Government ordered its governor of Phonda to join forces with the Savant of Vadi and other petty Rajahs and try to drive Shivaji's men out of Rajapur and Kharepatan. But nothing was done, as "there was juggling between them, and he remained possessed of all." (*Ibid*, 20th July 1663, Vol. 86, Surat to Co., 20th November 1663.)

In punishment of Rustam-i-Zaman's secret friendship with Shiva, the Sultan dismissed him from his viceroyalty and gave the province to Muhammad Ikhlas Khan, the eldest son of the late Khan-i-Khanan Ikhlas Khan and a brother of Khawas Khan, while Dabhol and Chiplun were given to Fazl Khan. Shivaji got final possession of Rajapur at this time and kept it permanently in his own hands. (*Ibid.*)

Rustam's agent at Karwar fleeced the English factors there so severely that in July 1663 they were ordered by the Council at Surat to remove themselves and the Company's goods quietly to Hubli. Adil Shah and

Rustam-i-Zaman alike were sensible of the loss of revenue caused by such molestation of traders, and therefore the king sent them a *farman* promising that they would be left in peace at Karwar and would have to pay no other duties than they had formerly done Then the factory was re-established at Karwar. (*F R.* Surat, Vol 2, Consult , 14th August 1663)

§4. *Shivaji in Kanara, 1664*

In 1664 the war with Bednur was renewed. Shivappa Nayak had died in old age, about October 1662 His son and successor, Bhadrappa, was murdered by his Brahmans, (Feb 1664) and an infant grandson named Basava was set up on the throne* under the regency of his mother Chennammaji and her favourite Timmaya Nayak, a toddy-seller, who "by his cunning policy raised himself to be general and protector" of the realm. At this revolution Ali Adil Shah II was so incensed that he sent his generals, Bahlol Khan and Sayyid Iliyas Sharza Khan, to invade Bednur from two sides (April 1664) [*F R.* Surat 104, Karwar to Surat, 18th April 1664 Fryer, i 41-42]

By this time Rustam-i-Zaman seems to have returned to favour at Court Muhammad Ikhlas Khan was transferred from the Government of Karwar and his friends from that of Ankola, Shiveshwar (or Halekot), Kadra and other places in North Kanara and these cities were given to three of Rustam's sons. In August Rustam himself was ordered to go to that region with two other Bijapuri generals and try to expel Shivaji He reached Kudal at the end of August, but did nothing.

* The Portuguese records state that Bhadrappa was succeeded by his brother *Soma Shekar* (Pissurlencar, i 19*n*)

(*F. R.* Surat, 104, Karwar 23rd July and Hubli 28th August, 1664.)

Any serious attack by Adil Shah on Shivaji was now rendered impossible as the Sultan's attention was diverted to Bednur, whither he wanted to march in person with 12,000 horse after the *Dewali* festival (October) and co-operate with Sharza Khan in crushing the Kanara Rajah. Throughout the second half of 1664 the coast region was in an unhappy condition. As the English merchants write, "Deccan and all the south coasts are all embroiled in civil wars, king against king and country against country, and Shivaji reigns victoriously and uncontrolled, that he is a terror to all the kings and princes round about, daily increasing in strength." (*F. R.* Surat, Vol 86, Surat to Co., 26 Nov. 1664.)

Shivaji had planned to march his army down the west coast, get on board his fleet waiting at Bhatkal (14° N, the southern point of the North Kanara district), and raid the coast towns. But Khawas Khan barred his path and turned him back after an obstinate battle (about 25th October), in which six thousand men are said to have fallen. Immediately rumour exaggerated the result as a disaster to Shivaji, who was reported to have been chased and closely invested in a fort by the Bijapuris.*

---

* *Ibid.* But on 2 Jan 1665 the Surat Council declare the above a false report The date of the battle and the fact of Khawas being the victor are taken from the Portuguese records (Pissurlencar, i 12) *Jedhe S* says that in Oct -Nov 1664 Shiva fought Khawas Khan and forced him to flee beyond the Ghats, this was likely, but the other authorities are silent A year *later* (Nov 1665) Shivaji is known to have severely defeated Md. Ikhlas Khan, the *brother* of Khawas Khan, and expelled him from S. Konkan

Details of Khawas Khan's victory in Oct 1664 are supplied by *Basatin-i-Salatin*, 398-402 "Aurangzib sent an envoy to Adil Shah to beg his co-operation with Jai Singh in the war with Shiva. Before Jai Singh arrived, Adil Shah sent an army under Khawas Khan Shiva hearing of it began

Shivaji was anything but crushed He had turned back to settle scores with an old enemy Baji Ghorpare, jagirdar of Mudhol, was a faithful vassal of Bijapur At the siege-camp before Jinji he had carried out his commander-in-chief's orders by arresting the refractory Shahji (1648), without, however, resorting to treachery as alleged in later Maratha stories He used to co-operate loyally with the Adil-Shahi generals sent out to restore the lawful king's authority over the Konkan territory usurped by Shivaji His energy, honesty and devotion to his master made him a dangerous enemy to Shivaji When Khawas Khan was marching to Kudal to expel Shivaji, Ghorpare came from Bijapur with his contingent of 1,500 horse to join him. But Shivaji struck the first blow and prevented the junction of his enemies He suddenly invaded Mudhol Baji Ghorpare, who had hurried to the defence of his jagir, was defeated and slain and 1,200 of his horses were captured Mudhol itself was taken, and so many members of the Ghorpare family were put to death that the incident is known as "the massacre of the Ghorpares "*

---

to close the mountain passes (*ghats*), but Khawas, by making rapid marches, crossed the *ghat* in safety, and descended [into Konkan ?] While the negligent Khawas Khan did not even know of Shiva s position, the latter with his full force surprised him at night and completely hemmed him round in an intricate hilly place, where the Bijapuri army had not space enough to move about or even to marshal the ranks Khawas called his officers together and heartened them in the midst of their despair The Marathas opened fire, the Bijapuris advanced to close quarters and fought a severe battle, losing Siddi Sarwar (the Abyssinian general), Shah Hazrat, Shaikh Miran and some other officers The defeat of the Muslims seemed imminent, when Khawas Khan charged sword in hand, his troops followed him fearlessly in one body, and Shivaji was defeated and put to flight "

* Sabh 39, *Jedhe S* The popular tradition is that Shivaji committed this massacre in obedience to his father's order that if he was his true son he should avenge on Baji Ghorpare the latter's treachery to Shahji in 1648

In their next encounter (Nov 1664), Shivaji is said, in the Marathi accounts, to have defeated Khawas and forced him to retire from Konkan. He then burst into the district now called Savant-vadi, (between Ratnagiri and Goa), the numerous petty chieftains of which were feudatories of Bijapur. The greatest among them was Lakham Savant, the *desai* (chief) of Kudal, who had sided with the Bijapuri generals in these parts against Shivaji and was the first to feel Shivaji's wrath now. After resisting for a short time he escaped with his bare life into the forest, leaving his riches to the victor. Keshava Nayak and Keshava Prabhu of Pernem and Rawal Shenvi of Bicholim* next shared the same fate. All these defeated *desais* took refuge in Goa and lived there in misery, making frequent attempts to recover their own by raising troops and organizing expeditions from

---

The fall of the Ghorpares and Lakham Savant's defeat (which immediately followed it) took place in Nov 1664, nearly a year after Shahji's death, they cannot be placed in 1663

* The geography of this tract in 1664 was as follows.—Leaving out a narrowing coast-strip in the south-west of the Ratnagiri district, from Malvan to Tarikhol, the inland part east of it was divided into the districts of *Kudal* (north), *Vadi* (middle) and *Banda* (south) South-west of Banda lay *Pernem*, and south of the latter lay Bardes and Goa successively, with *Phonda* due east of Goa North-east of Bardes and Goa lay *Bicholim*, with *Sanquelim* further to the east Of these, only Bardes, Goa and Salsette (or the 66 maritime villages of Goa, quite distinct from Salsette near Bombay island) belonged to the Portuguese in the 17th century, while Pernem, Bicholim and Sanquelim were annexed later For Krishna Savant's intrigues against Lakham S. and the latter's faithful assistance to successive Bijapur generals, see Pingulkar, *farmans* 8-12, Sabh 68

Shivaji repeatedly protested to the Goa Government against the conduct of the fugitive *desais* and even invaded the Portuguese territory of Bardes by way of reprisal At last the Viceroy expelled the desais from Goa in May, 1668 [Pissurlencar, i 12-25] Then Lakham Savant submitted to Shivaji, pleading that he was of the same Bhonsle clan Shivaji appointed him as his salaried agent in Kudal, under agreement not to raise forces or build forts but to serve under Shivaji's orders [Sabh 69, Pingulkar, farman 7 date incorrect]

the Portuguese territory against Shivaji's governors Krishna Savant, a kinsman and rival of Lakham for the *desai*-ship, naturally joined Shivaji and was placed by him in charge of Kudal.

Shivaji next plundered Vingurla, "a place of great trade, from whence he carried away vast riches" He had heard that the Dutch had accumulated great wealth by trade in their warehouse in this important port. Another town (probably Malvan) not far from it, suffered the same fate. About this time, *i e*, early in December 1664, his men looted Hubli and many other rich towns of that region, holding several eminent merchants prisoners for ransom. He had sent only three hundred horsemen to Hubli, but these did their work so thoroughly that the town "was little better than spoiled" The merchants who had fled at the attack were too frightened to return there soon, even after the departure of the Marathas. The raiders were said to have been assisted by some of Rustam's soldiers; that noble, as the English remarked, had "begun to taste the sweetness of plunder [so] that in a short time he would get a habit of it." "Shiva and his scouts range all over the country, making havoc wherever he comes, with fire and sword" (*F. R* Surat 104, Karwar to Surat, 6th January 1665, Taylor to Surat, 14th December 1664, Vol 86, Surat to Karwar 23rd March, Surat to Co, 2nd January 1665)

On 12th March 1665, the Surat Council write: "The subjects [of Adil Shah] unanimously cry out against him for suffering Shivaji to forage to and fro, burning and robbing his country without any opposition, wherefore it is certainly concluded by all that he shares with the said rebel in all his rapines, so that the whole country is in a confused condition, merchants flying from one place to another to preserve themselves, so that all trade is lost The rebel Shivaji hath committed many notorious and great robberies since that of Surat, and hath possessed himself of the most considerable ports belonging to Deccan [*i.e.*, Bijapur] to the number of eight or nine, from whence he sets out two or three or more trading vessels yearly from every port to Persia, Basra, Mocha, etc."

§5. *Loot of Basrur and blackmail from Karwar, 1665.*

On 8th February 1665 Shivaji left Malvan with a fleet of 85 frigates and three large ships, sailed past Goa to Basrur,* the chief port of the Bednur kingdom, where he was quite unexpected, so that he took immense plunder in one day. Then setting out on his return, he landed at the holy city of Gokarna, on the coast, 22 miles south of Karwar, and took a purifying bath with all religious ceremonies before the great temple of Mahabaleshwar. From this place he marched to Ankola (nine miles northwards) with 4,000 infantry, sending all his fleet back, with the exception of twelve frigates, which he detained for transporting his army over the rivers on his way back to North Konkan. On the 22nd he reached Karwar. The English factors, having got early news of his coming from the spies they had sent out, put all the Company's ready money and portable goods on board a small hundred-ton ship belonging to the Imam of Maskat, then lying in the river, its captain Emanuel

* Basrur (Sanskrit *Vāsupura*), 12 miles south of Coondapur in the South Kanara District, was "the principal port of the Bednore Rajahs." (*S Canara Gazetteer*, ii 242) Portuguese spelling *Bracolore*, early English *Barcelore*, Hunterian *Barkalur*, Marathi *Basnur*

Donnavado promising to defend it as long as he lived or his vessel kept floating The factors themselves took refuge in the ship Sher Khan,* a son of the late Khan-i-Khanan Ikhlas Khan and a subordinate of Bahlol Khan, arrived in the town that very night, without knowing anything about Shivaji's approach With the help of his escort of 500 men he quickly fortified himself as well as he could to protect the goods he had brought down, and sent a messenger to Shiva in the night, warning him not to enter the town as he would resist him to the utmost Sher Khan was famous throughout the country for his valour and ruling capacity, and his chief, Bahlol Khan, was "one of the potentest men in the kingdom of Bijapur." Shivaji, therefore, shrank from provoking him, and after much discussion "condescended to go a little out of the way, and so came and encamped with his army at the mouth of the river" Kalanadi, sparing the town.

From this place he sent an envoy to Sher Khan, asking him either to deliver the English merchants up to him or, retiring himself, permit him to revenge himself on them, "whom he styled his inveterate enemies" Sher Khan sent this news to the English and desired to know their final answer, which was that they had nothing on board except powder and bullets which Shivaji might come and fetch if he thought they would serve him instead of gold. "This our answer being sent to Shivaji did so exasperate him that he said he would have us before he departed, which the governor of the town hearing, they persuaded all the merchants to agree to send him

* The cause of his coming to Karwar was to charter a ship of Rustam-i-Zaman's to convey Bahlol Khan's mother to Mecca

[Shivaji]a present lest he should recall his fleet, which lay on this side of Salsette." (*F. R* Surat, Vol 104, Karwar to Surat, 14th March, 1665.) To this black-mail the English contributed £112, so as not to endanger the Company's property in Karwar, worth 8,000 *hun*. "With this Shivaji departed on 23rd February, very unwillingly, saying that Sher Khan had spoiled his hunting at the *Holi*, which is a time he generally attempts some such design."*

Thence the disappointed Maratha chief returned to Vingurla (early in March) But soon afterwards Jai Singh's siege of Purandar and vigorous invasion of the neighbouring country called away Shivaji to the defence of his home, and Kanara enjoyed peace for some time

§6. *Bijapuris recover and lose S. Konkan, 1665.*

By the treaty of Purandar (12th June 1665) the Mughals left Shivaji free to annex Adil-Shahi Konkan The affairs of Bijapur also fell into confusion at this time. Bahlol Khan died (June or July.) He had come to Bijapur from the Karnatak war at the king's call, but died of illness only eight days after his arrival. The Sultan being jealous of his large force, 10,000 brave Afghans, tried to sow dissension between his two sons and nephew. Sher Khan, a brave, able and upright man, kept them at peace. But he was soon afterwards poisoned, it was suspected, by Adil Shah, and

* Shivaji's loot of Basrur and visit to Karwar *F R* Surat, Vol 104, Karwar to Surat, 14th March 1665 Sabh 70-71 The Karwar factors wrote on 28 Jan that the great annual bathing festival (*Shivaratri*) would take place only eight days later at Gokarna 4 Feb was *Krishna 14th* Shivaji missed it He took ship for the Basrur expedition (at Malvan) on 8 Feb. [*Shivapur Y*] and bathed at Gokarna on his *return* from Basrur [*F R* Surat, 104]

immediately bitter quarrels broke out between the two sons of Bahlol Khan, which the Sultan fanned and utilized to seize some of their *jagirs*. The affairs of the royal drunkard at Bijapur passed from bad to worse. (*F. R. Ibid.*, Karwar to Surat, 29th August 1665.)

The Bijapuri governor of Hubli fell into disfavour at Court and the governor of Mirjan rebelled. Muhammad Ikhlas Khan, the brother of Khawas Khan, recovered Dabhol and many other places in South Konkan from the Marathas, while the latter were busy fighting Jai Singh. But by November next Shivaji, now an ally of the Mughals, had reconquered all that country after slaying 2,000 soldiers of Muhammad Ikhlas, including several men of note. The Khan fell back on Kudal and waited for Sharza Khan to reinforce him. But no such aid came, as Jai Singh began his invasion of Bijapur that very month and Ikhlas Khan had to hasten from Kudal to the defence of the capital.* But Vingurla and Kudal continued in Bijapuri hands, while Shivaji held Rajapur and Kharepatan. The country about Karwar was at this time subjected to constant pillage by the soldiers of Shivaji's garrisons there, who used to leave their forts in a band of 200 men and raid the small towns. Murtaza Beg, who had lost his fort, also took to plunder with his 200 retainers. (*Ibid.*, 29th August, 21st September and 29th November 1665 and 15th January 1666.)

---

* The Portuguese Viceroy (letter of 7 Dec. 1665, N. S.) ascribes all this to Khawas Khan, saying, "Khawas Khan, with 2,000 horse and many foot, being in our vicinity, Shivaji entered into his territories and easily defeated him and obliged him to retire across the [Western] Ghats, yielding Konkan. And not content with this, he passed those very rough mountains and entered the interior of the [Bijapur] kingdom to a short journey from the capital." [Pissurlencar, i. 14.]

§7. *Shivaji and Rustam, 1666*

In the course of Jai Singh's war with Bijapur. Shivaji had been detached against Panhala. His assault on that fort (16th January 1666) failed and then he went off to Khelna. From this place he sent 2,000 men under a Muhammadan officer to besiege Phonda.* The garrison resisted for two months (February and March) killing 500 Marathas, and finally agreed to surrender in six hours. In the meantime, the Bijapuri Government had sent 5,000 horse and 1,000 foot under Siddi Masaud, Abdul Aziz (the son of Siddi Jauhar), and Rustam-i-Zaman to the Panhala region. They formed a plan for surprising Shivaji, who lay on the top of the hill overlooking Konkan. When their Van, under Rustam, approached, he beat his drums and sounded his trumpets and thus gave his friend Shivaji timely warning to escape. But Masaud chased the Marathas with 600 chosen cavalry and cut off 200 of the enemy. On the way back he intercepted Shivaji's friendly letters to Rustam, which he immediately sent to Bijapur. At this Adil Shah wrote to Rustam that though he reluctantly pardoned this act of disloyalty, he would dismiss him unless he raised the siege of Phonda. Rustam then wrote to his agent Muhammad Khan to save Phonda by all means. This was effected by a stratagem. Muhammad Khan could get together only a small force, with which he went and sat down in a town of his master's about three miles from Phonda, and sent word

---

* First siege of Phonda *F R* Surat 104, "Deccan News," following a letter from Karwar, dated 24th April 1666 *Phonda*, 10 m s s e of Goa city, was the westernmost frontier-fortress of Bijapur nearest to Goa, and a menace to the latter The Portuguese, after some previous failures, annexed it in the 18th century

to the general of Shivaji that he had only come to look after his own country. The general suspected no stratagem, as his master and Rustam were friends. He went with his Muslim soldiery to a hill a mile off in order to say his prayers in public. Muhammad Khan seized this opportunity, he surprised and routed the soldiers left in the siege-camp, and after a long and well contested fight defeated the rest of the Maratha army who had hurried back from the hill Thus the siege of Phonda was raised after the poor men in it had been driven to eat leaves for the last three days "This business, it is generally thought, hath quite broken the long continued friendship between Rustam-i-Zaman and Shivaji. Rustam hath taken now Phonda, Kudal, Banda, Sanquelim and Bicholim, five towns of note, from Shivaji."

§8. *Plot to seize Goa, 1668.*

Soon afterwards, at the end of March 1666, Shivaji went to the Mughal Court For the next four years he gave no trouble to Bijapuri Konkan or Kanara, his opponents during this interval being the Portuguese and the Siddis. The English merchants of Karwar repeatedly speak of Shiva in 1668 and 1669 as being "very quiet" and "keeping still at Rajgarh," and of his credit as decreasing during these years of inactivity, while the "country all about was in great tranquillity." (*F. R.* Surat, 105) In October 1668 Shivaji made an unsuccessful attempt to conquer the territory of Goa by stratagem He smuggled into the towns of this State 400 to 500 of his soldiers in small parties at different times and under various disguises, hoping that when their number was doubled they would suddenly rise one night, seize one of the passes, and admit him before the Portuguese could raise a sufficiently large army for their defence. But either the plot leaked out, or the Portuguese Viceroy's[1] suspicion was roused. He made a narrow search in all his towns, arrested the 400 or 500 men of Shivaji at various places, and evidently extorted the truth from them. Then he sent for Shivaji's ambassador, with his own hand gave him two or three cuffs in the ear, and turned him and the Maratha prisoners out of his territory. On hearing of it Shivaji assembled an army of 10,000 foot and 1,000 horse, threatening to invade the Bardes and Salsette districts of Goa in person. From the north of Rajapur he marched to Vingurla, inspected all his forts in that quarter, "changing their men and putting in (fresh) provisions and ammunition," and then in December returned to Rajgarh as he found "the Portuguese well prepared to give him a hot reception." (Gyffard to Surat, 12th November and 16th December, 1668. *F. R.* Surat 105.)

At the beginning of 1670 came his rupture with the Mughals, which kept him busy in other quarters and prolonged the peace in Kanara till the close of 1672, when, taking advantage of the death of Ali II., he renewed his depredations in Bijapur territory.

Meantime, in September 1671, Rustam-i-Zaman had broken out in rebellion against his master. He had at last been deprived of his viceroyalty and *jagir* for his treacherous intimacy with Shiva, the crowning act of which was the surrender of one of the king's forts to the Marathas. And now he took up arms in the hope of intimidating the Government into reinstating him With

[1] The Viceroy was Conde de S Vicente, who died on 27 Oct 1668, and according to Gyffard's letter he detected the plot "a little before his death"

the underhand help of Shivaji, he occupied Bijapuri territory, yielding three *lakhs* of *hun* a year, and plundered and burnt Raibagh, completing the ruin of that city, which had been previously sacked by the Marathas. But within a month the royal troops crushed the rebellion,—the forts of Mirjan and Ankola alone holding out for several months more. By the middle of 1672 Muzaffar Khan, the new Adil-Shahi viceroy of the Kanara coast, had made peace with the rebel chiefs (*Nayakwaris*) of Shiveshwar and Kadra.*

§9 *Shivaji's failure in Bijapuri Kanara, 1673*

The death of Ali Adil Shah II (on 24th November 1672) was followed by the rebellion of the Rajahs of Sunda and Bednur, who invaded the Bijapur territory across their frontiers. An army under Muzaffar Khan chastised both of them (February, 1673) and wrested Sunda from its Rajah. (*F. R.* Surat, 106, Karwar to Co., 17th February 1673.)

This rebellion had been hardly suppressed when the Marathas made their second incursion into the upland of Bijapuri Kanara, sacking many forts and rich cities in that region. Their general Pratap Rao raided Hubli,† the most important inland mart of the province, causing a loss of 7,894 *hun* to the English Company alone,

* *F R* Surat 106, Karwar to Surat, 20th September, 31st October 1671, 26th June 1672

† The commercial importance of Hubli can be judged from the following remarks of the English merchants —"Hubli, the mart of our Karwar factory, where we sell and buy most of the goods that port affords us" (*F R* Surat 87, 1st November 1673) "Hubli, a great inroad [=inland] town and a mart of very considerable trade" (*O C* 3779) Maratha invasion of Kanara in 1673 *F R* Surat 3, Consult 24th May, 10th and 19th July, Vol 87, Surat to Persia, 1st November *O C* 3779 and 3800 Sabhasad, 70, has only eight lines for the events of 1673-75

besides the private property of the factors (early in May 1673.) The Company's house was the first they entered and dug up, carrying away all the broadcloth in it to their general who sat in the bazar. Muzaffar Khan, however, promptly came to the scene with 4,000 cavalry and saved the town from total destruction. The Marathas fled precipitately with what booty they had already packed up, "leaving several goods out in the streets which they had not time to carry away." When the English at Surat complained to Shiva about the outrage, he denied that it was done by his soldiers.

At Hubli, Muzaffar missed the Maratha raiders by just one day He was probably suspected of having entered into a secret understanding with them, like Rustam-i-Zaman, for immediately afterwards all the nobles under his command and most of his own soldiers forsook him and the Bijapur Government removed him from his viceroyalty. This drove him into rebellion and he tried to retain possession of his fiefs by force. The great fort of Belgaum remained in his hands and also many strong places between Goa and Kanara (June, 1673.) Adil Shah sent a large army to reduce Belgaum in case Muzaffar declined the compromise offered to him.

In June Bahlol Khan with a large Bijapuri army held Kolhapur and defeated the Marathas in several encounters, forcing all their roving bands to leave the Karwar country. He also talked of invading South Konkan and recovering Rajapur and other towns next autumn. In August he is still spoken of as "pressing hard upon Shivaji, who supplicates for peace, being fearful of his own condition." But soon afterwards Bahlol Khan, his irreconcilable enemy, fell ill at Miraj and Shivaji's help was solicited by the Bijapur and

Golkonda Governments to defend them from a threatened Mughal invasion under Bahadur Khan (September)*

At the end of September we find Shivaji at the head of a great army raised for "some notable attempt against the Mughal." He also sewed 20,000 sacks of cotton for conveying the plunder he expected to seize! But on the *dashahara* day (10th October), an auspicious time with the Hindus for setting out on campaigns, he sallied forth on a long expedition into Bijapuri territory, with 25,000 men, robbed many rich towns, including Bankapur, and then penetrated into Kanara, "to get more plunder in those rich towns to bear the expenses of his army." Early in December he reached Kadra (20 miles north-east of Karwar) with a division of 4,000 foot and 2,000 horse, and stayed there for four days. The bulk of his forces occupied a hill near Hubli. But two severe defeats at the hands of Bahlol and Sharza Khan at Bankapur and Chandgarh (a fort midway between the Belgaum and Savant-vadi towns) respectively forced him to evacuate Kanara quickly.†

§10. *Internal troubles in Kanara, 1674.*

Though Kanara had been freed from the Marathas, that province enjoyed no peace Mian Sahib, the *faujdar* of Karwar, (instigated, it was said, by Shiva), rebelled and Adil Shah had to conduct a long war before he could be suppressed. The two sides continued to have skirmishes with varying success In February 1674

---

* *O C* 3800 and 3832, *F R* Surat 106, Bombay to Surat, 16th and 29th September 1673, *B S* 439-443, *Jedhe S*

† *F R* Surat 106, Bombay to Surat, 29th September and 10th October, Vol 88, Karwar to Surat, 17th December 1673 *O C* 3910, Fryer, ii *Dutch Rec*, Vol 31, No 805, *Jedhe S* says that Sharza Khan killed Vithoji Sindhia in Kartik, about Nov

the royal troops captured Sunda, with the rebel's wife in it, but he held out obstinately in his other forts. By 22nd April this "long and tedious rebellion" was at last ended by the arrival of Abu Khan, Rustam-i-Zaman II., as the new viceroy. Mian Sahib's followers deserted him for lack of pay; his forts (Kadra, Karwar, Ankola and Shiveshwar) all surrendered without a blow, and he himself made peace on condition of his wife being released Shivaji was then only a day's march from Karwar, "going to build a castle upon a very high hill, from which he may very much annoy these parts." (*F. R.* Surat 88, Karwar to Surat, 14th February and 22nd April 1674. Orme, *Frag* , 35)

Unlike his father, the new Rustam-i-Zaman did not cultivate the friendship of the Marathas. In August 1674 he seized a rich merchant, subject of Shiva, living at Narsa (16 miles from Phonda) and the Maratha king prepared for retaliation In October Rustam was summoned by Khawas Khan, the new *wazir,* to Bijapur; and, as he feared that his post would be given to another, he extorted forced loans from all the rich men of Karwar and its neighbourhood that he could lay hands on, before he went away. (*F. R.* Surat 88, Karwar to Surat, 2nd September and 27th October, 1674.) In the last week of August, Annaji Datto passed through Kudal with 3,000 soldiers intending to "surprise the fortress Phonda, but Mamet Khan who was there armed himself, so that the aforesaid pandit accomplished nothing." (*Dutch Rec.*, Vol. 34, No. 841)

At Bijapur everything was in confusion, "the great Khans were at difference" The worthless *wazir* Khawas Khan was driven to hard straits by the Afghan faction in the State. Rustam-i-Zaman II. after his visit to the capital evidently lost his viceroyalty This was Shivaji's opportunity and he now conquered Kanara for good First, he befooled the Mughal viceroy Bahadur Khan by sending him a pretended offer of peace, asking for the pardon of the Mughal Government through the Khan's mediation and promising to cede the imperial forts he had recently conquered as well as the twenty-three forts of his own that he had once before yielded in Jai Singh's time. By these insincere negotiations Shivaji for the time being averted the risk of a Mughal attack on his territory and began his invasion of Bijapuri Kanara with composure of mind

§11. *Capture of Phonda and annexation of Kanara coast, 1675.*

In March 1675 he got together an army of 15,000 cavalry, 14,000 infantry and 10,000 pioneers with pick-axes, crow-bars and hatchets, etc.,* Arriving at Rajapur (22nd March), he spent three days there, ordering forty small ships to go to Vingurla with all speed and there wait for fresh commands. Next he marched to his town of Kudal, and on 8th April laid siege to Phonda, the most important Bijapuri fort near Goa. While he was prosecuting the siege, another division of his army plundered Atgiri in Adil-Shahi territory and two other large cities near Haidarabad, carrying away "a great deal of riches, besides many rich persons held to ransom"

---

* Invasion of Kanara and capture of Phonda (1675) *F R* Surat 88, Karwar to Surat 14th and 22nd April, 8th and 25th May, Rajapur to Surat, 1st and 20th April, 3rd, 21st and 31st May, 3rd and 14th June, *B S* 441, Orme *Frag*, 38 40 Sabh 70 (scanty) Delusive peace offer to Mughals, *B S* 445, *O C* 4077

He began the siege of Phonda with 2,000 horse and 7,000 foot, and made arrangements for sitting down before the fort even during the coming rainy season in order to starve the garrison into surrender. Muhammad Khan had only four months' provisions within the walls; there was no hope of relief from Bijapur or even from the Portuguese who now trembled for the safety of Goa and appeased Shivaji by promising neutrality. Rustam-i-Zaman had too little money or men to attempt the raising of the siege. But Muhammad Khan made a heroic defence, unaided and against overwhelming odds.

Shivaji ran four mines under the walls, but they were all countermined, with a heavy loss of men to him. He then threw up an earthen wall only 12 feet from the fort and his soldiers lay sheltered behind it. The Portuguese, fearing that if Shiva took Phonda their own Goa would be as good as lost, secretly sent ten boat-loads of provisions and some men in aid of the besieged (middle of April), but they were intercepted by Shivaji, and the Viceroy of Goa disavowed the act.

The siege was pressed with vigour. By the beginning of May Shivaji had taken possession of two outworks, filled up the ditch, and made 500 ladders and 500 gold bracelets, each bracelet weighing half a *seer*, for presentation to the forlorn hope who would attempt the escalade.

Bahlol Khan, who was at Miraj with 15,000 troops, wanted to come down the Ghats and relieve Phonda, but Shiva had barred the passages with trees cut down and lined the stockades with his men, and Bahlol, being certain of heavy loss and even an utter repulse if he tried to force them, returned to his base His inactivity during the siege was imputed to bribery by Shiva. At length the fort fell about the 6th of May All who were found in it were put to the sword, with the exception of Muhammad Khan, who saved his own life and those of four or five others by promising to put into Shiva's hands all the adjoining parts belonging to Bijapur In fear of death the Khan wrote to the *qiladars* of these forts to yield them to the Marathas, but they at first declined So the Khan was kept in chains. Inayet Khan, the *faujdar* of Ankola, seized the country and forts lately held by Muhammad Khan and placed his own men in them, but he could make no stand against Shivaji whose forces were now set free by the fall of Phonda. He therefore compounded and gave up the forts for money In a few days Ankola, Shiveshwar (which had been besieged by 3,000 Maratha horse and some foot-soldiers since 24th April), Karwar, and Kadra (which alone had made a short stand), all capitulated to Shivaji, and by the 25th of May the country as far south as the Gangavati river had passed out of Bijapuri possession into his hands

§12. *Marathas in Kanara uplands.*

On 26th April, 1675, one of Shiva's generals had visited Karwar and "burnt the town effectually, leaving not a house standing," in punishment of the fort of Karwar still holding out. The English factory was not molested This general, however, went back in a few days. But next month, after the fall of Phonda, the fort of Karwar surrendered to the Marathas.

The rainy season now put an end to the campaign. Bahlol Khan went back to Bijapur, leaving his army at Miraj. Shiva at first thought of cantoning for the rains in a fort on the frontier of Sunda, but soon changed his mind and returned to Raigarh, passing by Rajapur on 12th June.

A Maratha force was detached into the Sunda Rajah's country at the end of May. "They finding no great opposition seized upon Supa and Ulavi belonging to the Rajah." But Khizr Khan Pani (Bahlol's lieutenant) and the *desais* in concert attacked the Maratha garrisons there, killed 300 of the men and recovered both the places. A party of Marathas that was posted at Varhulli, 7 miles south of Ankola, to take custom duty on all goods passing that way, was now forced to withdraw (August 1675.) (*F. R.* Surat 88, Rajapur to Surat, 27th August 1675.)

The dowager Rani of Bednur had quarrelled with her colleague Timmaya, but had been compelled to make peace with him (August), she being a mere cypher, while he held the real power of the State. [*Ibid.*] The Rani then appealed to Shivaji for protection, agreed to pay him an annual tribute, and admitted a Maratha resident at her Court. [Chit. 70, but Malkare 64 puts it earlier and calls the money blackmail.]

The *dalvi,* or general of the *desai* who had been the local Bijapuri governor of North Kanara, had aided Shivaji in the conquest of that district. But now (1675), disgusted with him, the *dalvi* was moving about the country with a force, saying that he would restore his former master. He attacked Shivaji's guards in Karwar town and forced them to retire to the castle. The people were in extreme misery in Shivaji's new conquests: he squeezed the *desais,* who in their turn squeezed the ryots. (*Bom. Gaz.* xv. pt. i. 128.) But Bijapur was now in the grip of a civil war, the Adil-Shahi State was hastening to a dissolution, and Shivaji's possession of South

Konkan and the North Kanara district remained unchallenged till after his death

But Bednur did not really become a Maratha protectorate We learn from an English letter of 29th July, 1679, that the Rajah of Sunda and the Rani of Bednur had sharp wars, "but the former by the assistance of Jamshid Khan has had the advantage of compelling the Rani, on conclusion of the peace, to deliver up to him his castles of Sirsy and Sera, formerly possessed by them, as likewise the port and castle of Mirgy [=Mirjan], a little to the southward of Karwar." (*Orme MSS* 116)

CHAPTER XI

Naval Enterprises

§1. *The Abyssinians of the West Coast.*

The expansion of Shivaji's rule across the Western Ghats into the coast-district of Konkan brought him into contact with the maritime Powers of our western seaboard. Chief among these were the Siddis or Abyssinians of Janjira, a rocky island 45 miles south of Bombay, and guarding the mouth of the Rajpuri creek. Half a mile east of it, on the mainland stands the town of Rajpuri, and two miles south-east of the latter is Danda on the shore of the creek. But these two towns are regarded as one place and formed the head-quarters of the land-possessions of the Siddis, covering much of the modern district of Kolaba. From this tract were drawn the revenue and provisions that nourished the Government of Janjira.

An Abyssinian colony had settled here in the 15th century. One of them secured the governorship of Danda-Rajpuri under the Sultans of Ahmadnagar. But the dissolution of that monarchy and the situation of the district on the extreme frontier of the State beyond the Western Ghats, made it easy for the Siddi to establish himself in practical independence of the central authority, so that, when the partition treaty of 1636 gave the west coast to Bijapur, that Government recognized the Siddi chief as its representative in the district, gave him the title of a *wazir*, and added to his charge the whole seaboard from Nagothna to Bankot, on condition of his protecting Bijapuri trade and Mecca pilgrims at sea.

As the Siddis formed a small military aristocracy dominating a vast alien population, their constitution provided for the rule of the ablest, and on the death of a chief not his son but the first officer of the fleet succeeded to the governorship The Abyssinians were hardy, skilful and daring mariners and the most efficient fighters at sea among the Muslim races, while their courage and energy, joined to coolness and power of command, made them enjoy a high estimation as soldiers and administrators

The Siddi chief of Janjira maintained an efficient fleet, and throughout the 17th century he was officially recognized as the admiral, at first of Bijapur and latterly of the Mughal empire There was no native Power on the west coast that could make a stand against him at sea (*Bom Gaz*. xi. 434, 416)

To the owner of Konkan it was essential that the Siddi should be either made an ally or rendered powerless for mischief. Shivaji found that unless he created a strong navy, his foreign trade would be lost, and his subjects on the sea-coast and for some distance inland would remain liable to constant plunder, enslavement, outrage, and slaughter at the will of a band of pirates alien by race, creed and language The innumerable creeks and navigable rivers of the west coast, while they naturally fostered the growth of rich ports and trade centres, made it imperatively necessary for their protection that their owner should rule the sea On the other hand, the possession of Danda-Rajpuri and its adjacent district was necessary to the owner of Janjira for his very existence The political separation of the two made war against the mainland an economic necessity to him.

§2. *Maratha conquests from the Abyssinians, up to 1661* *

Shivaji had early captured the eastern part of the Kolaba district adjoining the Siddi's territory, but the latter still held Danda-Rajpuri and much of the neighbouring land There were constant skirmishes between the two Powers thus occupying the eastern and western portions of the Kolaba district, but no record of them has come down to us. The Siddi had too small an army to defy the regular Maratha forces on land, and he seems to have confined himself to making raids by surprise and doing petty acts of mischief to Shivaji's villages in that region, as is clear from the Maratha chronicler's description of the Siddi as "an enemy like the mice in a house" (Sabh. 67.)

Very little activity was probably shown by Yusuf Khan who ruled Janjira from 1642 to 1655.

But his successor Fath Khan was a brave active and able leader. In 1659, when Afzal Khan was advancing against Shivaji from the east, Fath Khan seized the opportunity of trying to recover his own. But, on hearing of the destruction of the Bijapur army (November), he retired in haste. Next year, when Ali Adil Shah II. opened a campaign against Shivaji, who was invested in Panhala fort, Fath Khan renewed his invasion of Konkan. The Kay Savant, a loyal vassal of Bijapur,

---

* The dates relating to the struggle with the Siddis given in this section are very doubtful, as Sabhasad is never accurate in his order of events and there is no independent check on his statements here The *Shivapur Daftar Yadi* says that in July 1657, Raghunath was sent to Rajpuri This date cannot be reconciled with the other narratives, and is unsupported by Jedhe The meaning also is not clear An English Factory letter (1659) states, "Those that inhabit Danda-Rajpuri are pirates and rogues, and maintain vessels abroad to rob all that they master" (Foster, 214)

co-operated with the Siddi. After an obstinate battle both the Savant and Baji Rao Pasalkar (Shivaji's general) fell in a single combat, and both parties retreated to their bases. (Sabh. 66.)*

To retrieve the position, Shivaji next sent a larger force, five to seven thousand strong, under Raghunath Ballal Korde, who beat the Siddi forces, captured Tala, Ghonsala, and other forts, and wrested the sea-coast up to Danda. The Marathas continued the campaign even during the rains, and after a long siege captured the fort of Danda, and following up their success opened batteries against Janjira itself But their weakness in artillery defeated their attempt on this sea-girt rock Hopeless of relief from Bijapur, the Siddi came to terms with Shivaji and formally ceded Danda-Rajpuri. Thus, no stronghold was left to the Siddi on the mainland (Sabh 67)

But this peace could not possibly last long To the Siddi the loss of the Kolaba territory meant starvation, and, on the other hand, it was Shiva's "lifelong ambition to capture Janjira" and make his hold on the west coast absolutely secure Hostilities soon broke out again The Siddis resumed their depredations on the coast, while Shiva fired upon Janjira every year during the dry season, without being able to take that island-fortress

The Maratha gains on the Kolaba coast were now organized into a province, and placed under an able viceroy, Vyankoji Datto, with a permanent contingent of 5 to 7 thousand men (Sabh 68) He defeated the Siddis in a great land-battle, totally excluded them from the

* The English merchants of Rajapur write on 10 Dec 1659, of 'Shivaji having already taken the town of Danda-Rajpuri, but not the castle" (F R Rajapur)

mainland, improved the defences of Danda-Rajpuri by fortifying a hill that commanded it, and built a chain of forts (such as Birwadi and Lingana) which effectually prevented Siddi depredations in that quarter. At this the Siddis, in order to "fill their stomachs," had to direct their piracy against the villages and ports further south, in the Ratnagiri district, which had now come under Shiva's sway. The Maratha chief, therefore, realized that he must create a formidable navy and set up fortified bases along the coast, if he was to ensure the protection of his seaside districts and the conquest of Janjira which would continue as a thorn in his side if left in enemy hands. (Sabh. 68.)

§3. *Shivaji's navy described.*

Shivaji's navy had its humble origin in his early conquest of the Thana district. Already in 1659 his first few war-vessels, launched on the creeks near Kalian, Bhivandi and Panvel, are found plying the sea and provoking the alarm and opposition of the Portuguese. With the extension of his power along the entire west coast down to the frontier of Goa, the rapid increase of his navy became not only necessary but also very profitable. With so many naval bases of supply and points of shelter and embarkation in his hands, the entire Malabar coast with its immense riches lay at his mercy. He knew that without naval supremacy his position even as a land power would be precarious. Therefore, as his courtier Sabhasad puts it, "The Rajah put the saddle on the ocean."

The Marathi chronicles speak of Shivaji's fleet as consisting at its best of four hundred vessels of various sizes and classes, such as *ghurabs* (gun-boats), *tarandes,* *tarambes, gallivats, shibars, pagars, manchwas, &c.* But the English factory reports never put their number above 160, and usually as 60 only They were formed into two squadrons (of 200 vessels each, if we accept the Marathi accounts), and commanded by two admirals who bore the titles of *Daria Sarang* (Admiral of the Ocean) and *Mai Nayak* or *Mian Nayak*.*

The numerous creeks on the Bombay coast had developed among many low-caste Hindus of the region (such as the Kolis, Sanghars, Vaghers and the Maratha clan of Angrias) hereditary skill in seafaring and naval fight. The "Malabar pirates" were a terror even to the English From them† Shiva recruited his crew, and he afterwards added to them a body of Muslims, notably a discontented Siddi named Misri and Daulat Khan.

Shivaji's navy immediately took to plundering the coast of Kanara and Goa, and brought to him vast quantities of booty in the same way as his land-forces

---

* Sabh 68 *Ghurabs* are floating batteries or gun-boats carrying two masts and moving slowly *Gallivats* are vessels constructed for swift sailing *Shibars* are trading boats, *manchwas* being a stronger kind of trading vessel than *shibars* (Orme's *Frag* Sec 1) A *tarande* is a large sailing vessel The *machwa* (a round-built two-masted craft of from 3 to 20 tons) and the *shibar* (a large square-sterned, flat-bottomed vessel with 2 masts but no deck) are described in *Bom Gaz* xiii pt ii 717

Sabhasad, 68, speaks of Daria Sarang as a Musalman and of Mai Nayak as a Hindu of the Bhandari caste But a Bombay letter dated 21 Nov 1670 says, 'The admiral of the [Maratha] fleet is one *Ventgee Sarungee*, commonly called *Durrea Sarungee*" Another Bombay letter, 11 Sep 1679, speaks of 'Mia Nayak, a Bhandari of Rajapur' (*Orme MSS* 116) Daulat Khan was an officer distinct from the Daria Sarang (Rajwade, viii 27 and *T S*)

† "The Bhandari [caste of husbandmen] are found in most parts of the Ratnagiri district, but chiefly in the coast villages They supplied the former pirate chiefs with most of their fighting men A strong, healthy and fine-looking set of men they are fond of athletic exercises and do not differ from the Marathas and Kunbis" (*Bom Gaz*, x 124) For the Koli pirates, ix pt i 519-522, and the Angrias, i pt ii 87-88, xi 145.

did. They often fought the Siddi fleet. (Sabh 68) We may here record what little is definitely known about Shivaji's mercantile marine. Soon after getting possession of the ports in North Konkan, he began to engage in foreign trade on his own account. Early in January 1660 he captured at Rajapur one of the junks of Afzal Khan and turned it to his own use. In February 1663 the English at Surat report that he was fitting out two ships of considerable burden for trading with Mocha (in western Arabia) and loading them at Jaitapur, two miles up the Rajapur river, with "goods of considerable value which were by storms or foul weather driven upon his coast." Two years later (12th March 1665), they write that from each of the eight or nine "most considerable ports in the Deccan" that he had seized, he used to "set out 2 or 3 or more trading vessels yearly to Persia, Basra, Mocha, &c." Again, we learn that in April, 1669, a great storm on the Karwar coast destroyed several of his ships and rice-boats, "one of the ships being very richly laden." (*F. R.* Surat, Vols. 2, 86, 105.)

§4. *Doings of the Maratha navy, 1664-1665.*

The rise of the Maratha naval power caused anxiety to the Siddis, the English merchants, and the Mughal Emperor alike. On 26th June, 1664, the Surat factors report that Shiva was fitting out a fleet of 60 frigates for an attack on some unknown quarter, probably "to surprise all junks and vessels belonging to that port and to waylay them on their return from Basra and Persia," or to transport an army up the Cambay creek (Sabarmati) for making a raid on Ahmadabad. At the end of November it was learnt that the fleet had been sent to Bhatkal, to co-operate with his army in the invasion of

Kanara. The English President describes the Maratha vessels as "pitiful things, so that one good English ship would destroy a hundred of them without running herself into great danger." (*F R.* Surat, Vol 86, 26 November 1664.) In addition to the inferior size and build of their ships, the Marathas on land and sea alike were very weak in artillery and, therefore, powerless against European ships of war.

In February 1665, Shivaji's fleet of 85 frigates* and three large ships conveyed his army to Basrur for the plunder of South Kanara. (Ch 10)

He had very early begun to plunder Mughal ships, especially those conveying pilgrims for Mecca from the port of Surat (called *Dar-ul-hajj*, "the City of Pilgrimage.") The Emperor had no fleet of his own in the Indian Ocean able to cope with the Marathas. Early in 1665 when Jai Singh opened his campaign, in accordance with his policy of combining all possible enemies against Shivaji, he wrote to the Siddi to enter into an alliance with the Mughals. (*Haft Anj*, Benares MS, 78*a*) Late in the same year, when Jai Singh was about to begin the invasion of Bijapur, he invited these Abyssinians to join the Mughal force, promising them *mansabs* † By the Treaty of Purandar, the Mughals left the territory of Janjira adjoining Shiva's dominions to him, if he could conquer it (*Ibid*) Shiva also offered

* Duff (i 201n) suggests that by the term *frigates* were probably meant small vessels with one mast, from 30 to 150 tons burden, common on the Malabar coast

† A Siddi Sambal fought on the Mughal side during the invasion of Bijapur in 1666 (*A N* 1012) The informal connection thus established between the Emperor and the Siddis continued, as we find that during Shivaji's siege of Janjira in 1669, Aurangzib wrote to him commanding him to withdraw from the attempt (Bombay to Surat, dated 16 Oct, 1669, *F R* Surat Vol 105)

to attempt the conquest of Janjira for the Emperor. (*Ibid.* 78*b* But *Tarikh-i-Shivaji*, 22*b*, states that Jai Singh definitely refused to make the Siddis give up Janjira to Shiva.)

§5. *Maratha attack on Janjira fails.*

In 1669 Shivaji's attack upon Janjira was renewed with great vigour. In the earlier months of the year the hostile armies made almost daily inroads into each other's country and the warfare closed the roads to all peaceful traffic. In October, the Siddi was so very hard pressed and Janjira was in such danger of being starved into surrender that he wrote to the English merchants of his "resolve to hold out to the last and then deliver it up to the Mughal." (*F R.* Surat 105, Hubli to Surat, 17 July, Bomb. to Surat, 16 Oct.)

The contest came to a crisis next year (1670) Shivaji staked all his resources on the capture of Janjira. Fath Khan, worn out by the incessant struggle, impoverished by the ruin of his subjects, and hopeless of aid from his suzerain at Bijapur, resolved to accept Shiva's offer of a large sum and a rich jagir as the price of giving up Janjira. But his three Abyssinian slaves roused their clansmen on the island against this surrender to an infidel, imprisoned Fath Khan, seized the Government, and applied to Adil Shah and the Mughal viceroy of the Deccan for aid. The Mughals readily agreed, and the Siddi fleet was transferred from the overlordship of Bijapur to that of Delhi, and Siddi Sambal, one of the leaders of the revolution, was created imperial admiral with a *mansab* and a *jagir* yielding 3 *lakhs* of Rupees. His two associates, Siddi Qasim and Siddi Khairiyat, were given the command of Janjira and the land dominions respectively. The Siddi fleet was taken into Mughal service on the same terms as under Bijapur. The general title of Yaqut Khan was conferred on successive Siddi admirals from this time onwards, and the government of Janjira was separated from the admiral's charge and placed under another Siddi, who was regarded as the second leader of the tribe and heir to the admiral's post Yaqut Khan was merely first among his equals "The other Siddi captains preserved the distinct command over their own crews and dependents, and an aristocratical council determined the general welfare of this singular republic." (Orme's *Frag.* 57, K. K ii. 224)

This revolution at Janjira is said by Khafi Khan to have taken place in January or February 1671.* Shortly before it the Maratha fleet had met with a great reverse. In November 1670, Shivaji collected at Nandgaon, 10 miles north of Janjira, 160 small vessels (under Daria Sarang) and an army of 10,000 horse and 20,000 foot, with full provisions for a siege, large numbers of mining tools (pick-axes, shovels and crow-bars), and victuals for 40 days Another body of 3,000 soldiers, with a great number of pioneers, was kept "ready to embark and depart with the fleet at a minute's notice" His secret design was to march to Surat by land, where the fleet would join him, and then the fort would be delivered to him on 29th November, as had been secretly agreed

* But the date is evidently wrong On 4th April 1674, Narayan Shenvi, the English agent, writes from Raigarh to Bombay "I have discoursed with Niraji Pandit concerning the peace you desired might be concluded with the Siddi Fath Khan" (*F R* Surat, Vol 88) This proves (*a*) that Fath Khan was a Siddi and not an Afghan as stated by Khafi Khan, and (*b*) that he was in power in 1674, instead of having been deposed in 1671 Here Khafi Khan is proved by contemporary records to be unreliable But Siddi Sambal was undoubtedly admiral of the fleet from 1671 onwards

upon by its commandant If he succeeded there, he intended to march on and take Broach also.

But the plan failed. The fleet left Nandgaon on 24th November and passed northwards skirting the Bombay island the next day, and Mahim on the 26th. The army under Shivaji marched in the same direction by land. But on the 26th he suddenly turned back and recalled his fleet. He had discovered that the seemingly treacherous *qiladar's* promise to sell the fort to him was only a trap laid for him. Quickly changing his plan, he turned to an easier and surer prey Early in December he suddenly burst into Khandesh and Berar and looted them far and wide. During his absence on this raid, his fleet met with a defeat. In passing by Daman, his admiral had captured a large ship of that place worth Rs. 12,000, bound for Surat. The Portuguese retaliated by capturing 12 of his ships* and leaving the prizes at Bassein went in pursuit of the rest of the Maratha fleet, which, however, succeeded in escaping to Dabhol. (*F. R.* Surat, Vol 105, Bomb. to Surat, 17, 21 and 28 Nov. and 17 Dec., 1670)

§ 6. *Abyssinians recover Danda fort, 1671.*

Siddi Qasim, the new governor of Janjira, "was distinguished among his tribesmen for bravery, care of the peasantry, capacity, and cunning. He busied himself in increasing his fleet and war-material, strengthening the defences of his forts and cruising at sea. He used to remain day and night clad in armour, and repeatedly seized enemy ships, cut off the heads of many Marathas

* Father Navarette says, there were 15 small ships, which the Portuguese drove up to the shore and took without the expense of a grain of powder (Orme's *Frag* 207)

and sent them to Surat" (K K, ii. 225.) His crowning achievement was the recovery of Danda from Shivaji's men. One night in March, 1671, when the Maratha garrison of that fort were absorbed in drinking and celebrating the Spring Carnival (*Holi*), Qasim secretly arrived at the pier with 40 ships, while Siddi Khairiyat with 500 men made a noisy feint on the land-side The full strength of the garrison rushed in the latter direction to repel Khairiyat, and Qasim seized the opportunity to scale the sea-wall Some of his brave followers were hurled into the sea and some slain, but the rest forced their way into the fort Just then the powder-magazine exploded, killing the Maratha commandant and several of his men, with a dozen of the assailants. Qasim promptly raised his battle-cry *Khassu! Khassu!* and shouting "My braves, be composed, I am alive and safe," he advanced slaying and binding to the centre of the fort where he joined hands with Khairiyat's party, and the entire place was conquered

Shiva had been planning the capture of Janjira, and now he had failed to hold even Danda! It is said that during the night of the surprise, at the moment the powder-magazine blew up, Shiva, who was 40 miles away, started from his sleep and exclaimed that some calamity must have befallen Danda! He was, however, unable to make reprisals immediately, as his army was busy elsewhere, in the Nasik and Baglana districts, where the Mughal viceroy was pressing him hard. Qasim, therefore, could easily follow up his success by capturing seven other forts in the neighbourhood Six of them opened their gates in terror of his prowess after his grand victory at Danda The seventh stood a siege for a week and then capitulated on terms, which Qasim faithlessly violated, enslaving and converting the boys and handsome women to Islam, dismissing the old and ugly women, and massacring all the men of the garrison. For some time afterwards the Marathas were forced to stand on the defensive in their own territory. (K. K. ii. 225-228, only authority.)

These disasters fully roused Shiva. The recovery of Danda fort became an absorbing passion as well as a political necessity, with him. To the end of his life and throughout the reign of Shambhuji, hostilities continued between the Marathas and the Siddis, intermittently, indecisively, but with great bitterness and fury Gross cruelty and wanton injury were practised by each side on the captive soldiers and innocent peasantry of the other, and the country became desolate. The economic loss was more keenly felt by the small and poor State of the Abyssinians than by the Marathas, and the Siddis at times begged for peace, but did not succeed, as they were not prepared to accept Shiva's terms of ceding their all to him.

In September 1671, Shivaji sent an ambassador to Bombay to secure the aid of the English in an attack on Danda. But the President and Council of Surat advised the Bombay factors "not to positively promise him the grenadoes, mortar-pieces, and ammunition he desires, nor to absolutely deny him, in regard we do not think it convenient to help him against Danda, which place if it were in his possession would prove a great annoyance to the port of Bombay." (*F. R.* Surat, 87.)

§ 7. *Naval war, 1672-1675.*

Towards the end of 1672, Aurangzib sent a fleet of 36 vessels, great and small, from Surat to assist the Siddi of Danda-Rajpuri by causing a diversion by sea This squadron did Shivaji "great mischief, burning and plundering all his sea-port towns and destroying also above 500 of his vessels" (evidently trading boats)* At this time (21st December) Shiva had six small frigates, which he laid up in Bombay harbour in fear of the Mughal armada, and which the English saved from the latter by pretending that they themselves had attached them as compensation for the plunder of their Rajapur factory in 1661. (O. C 3722) Early in January next, the Mughal fleet visited Bombay after its successful campaign against the Marathas. At this time both Shiva and the Emperor were eagerly courting the naval help of the English in a war with the other side. But the foreign traders very wisely maintained their neutrality, though it was a "ticklish game." (O C. 3734 and 3722) In the following August, however, the ship *Soleil d' Orient* of the new French East India Company founded by Colbert, arrived at Rajapur and secretly sold 80 guns (mostly small pieces) and 2,000 maunds of lead to Shiva's fleet. The French gave similar help in November 1679 when they sold him 40 guns for the defence of Panhala. (*F. R.* Surat 87, Surat to Co., 12 Jan., 1674; Vol. 108, Rajapur to Surat, 30 Dec., 1679.)

The difference between the English and Shivaji was utilized by Reickloff Van Goen, the Dutch commodore, who about March 1673 opened negotiations with the Maratha chief, promising him the help of the entire Dutch fleet (of 22 ships) in retaking Danda-Rajpuri, while Shivaji was to lend 3,000 of his soldiers for a Dutch

* 'Sacked and burnt Dabhol, burnt the fleet of Shivaji at Kelshi (17 55 N, near Bankot) and eight large vessels, robbed all the coast ' [Portuguese records, Pissur, i 35-37]

attempt to conquer Bombay Shivaji, however, durst not trust the Dutch and continued to remain friendly to the English, though he had by this time spent a vast treasure and incurred the loss of nearly 15,000 men in his vain attacks upon the Siddi strongholds. (O. C. 3760.)

The Mughal fleet of 30 frigates, commanded by Siddi Sambal, returned from Surat to Danda-Rajpuri, in May 1673, and after passing the south-west monsoon (June-September) there, sailed down the coast, taking many Maratha trading vessels and some ships of war. On 10th October it entered the Bombay harbour, sent landing parties to the Pen and Nagothna rivers, laid waste the Maratha villages opposite Bombay, and carried off many of the people. These devastations were frequently repeated. But at the end of the month, "some of Shivaji's soldiers [from Raigarh] surprised a parcel of the Siddi's men as they were on shore cutting the standing rice in his country, and destroyed about a hundred of them, carrying away the heads of some of the chiefest unto Shivaji." The great cruelty practised by the Siddis on his subjects and their burning of several small towns in his territory "provoked Shivaji much," and his reprisals were apprehended in the Mughal dominions, especially at Surat. (O. C. 3779 and 3870.)

In February 1674 we learn from an English letter, "The war betwixt the Siddi and Shivaji is carried on but slowly, they being both weary," and the President of Surat was requested by the Siddi "to mediate a peace between them." (O. C. 3939.)

Next month (March 1674), however, Siddi Sambal attacked Shivaji's admiral Daulat Khan in the Satavli river (*i.e.*, the Muchkundi creek in the Ratnagiri district), both the admirals being wounded and the two sides losing 100 and 44 men respectively. The Marathas were left victors, and Siddi Sambal withdrew to Harishwar, a port 21 miles south of Janjira. In May Shivaji, who "was resolved to take that castle (Danda-Rajpuri) let it cost him what it will," was reported to be daily sending down more artillery, ammunition, men and money to strengthen his siege-troops In the course of this year he reduced the whole coast of South Konkan from Rajpuri to Bardes north of Goa, but not the *fort* of Danda-Rajpuri (*F R* Surat 88) By the end of 1672 he had already spent a vast treasure and 15,000 soldiers in his futile attacks on Janjira (*O C* 3760)

§8. *Grand assault on Janjira, 1675-1676*

In September 1675, we read of his making preparations for taking that fort by a land and sea attack. His fleet had by this time increased to 57 sail, of which 15 were *ghurabs* and the rest *gallivats*. The cruise of the Siddi fleet along Shiva's coast in January and February of this year had proved unsuccessful. But it returned in November with reinforcements, and sailed down the coast to Vingurla, plundering and burning that town. Maratha squadrons from Gheria (Vijay-durg) and Rajapur took the sea, seeking a fight, but the Siddi escaped to Janjira. (*F. R.* Surat 107, Bomb to Surat, 7 Sep , Orme, *Frag.*, 49, 53)

That island had been besieged by Shiva with a great force some months earlier The neighbouring coast was dotted with his outposts and redoubts, and he also built some floating batteries and made an attempt to throw a mole across the sea from the mainland to the island of

Janjira.* The siege was raised at the end of 1675, at the arrival of the fleet under Siddi Sambal; but it was renewed next year with greater vigour than before. The Peshwa Moro Pant was sent (August, 1676) with 10,000 men to co-operate with the fleet and the former siege-troops. They felled all the wood around to make floating platforms with breastworks, from which the walls were to be assaulted.

But the attempt failed. Siddi Qasim arrived with the Abyssinian fleet, broke the line of investment, infused life into the defence, made counter-attacks, burnt the floating batteries and forced the Marathas to raise the siege (end of December 1676.)

§ 9. *Naval war, 1676-1680.*

The rest of the struggle with the Siddis is given below in a summary form, on the basis of Orme's narrative (*Frag.*, 55-88) compiled from the English factory records, which I have supplemented by a reference to some additional records in the India Office, London.

In April 1676, Siddi Sambal, who had quarrelled with the other Siddi leaders, was removed by them from the naval command, which was given to Siddi Qasim, with the governorship of Danda-Rajpuri. But Sambal still retained the Mughal fleet. He cruised along Shivaji's coast (in October) burning Jaitapur (at the mouth of the Rajapur river) in December, but was prevented from advancing further up the river and returned to Janjira,

---

* Siege of Janjira: Orme, *Frag.*, 48, 57. A very confused and obscurely written account of this struggle is given in *Shivadigvijay*, 192-196, and *Tarikh-i-Shivaji*. It is evident that these two works have transferred to Shivaji's reign some of the incidents of Shambhuji's sieges of Janjira in 1681 and later.

where Qasim had already raised the Maratha siege under Moro Pant.

Early in 1677 strict orders came from Delhi that the imperial fleet must be delivered to Qasim. But Sambal put off obeying the order for many months, till the two rival Siddi admirals who were living in Bombay came to blows, and finally through the mediation of the English Council the quarrel was settled, and Qasim was installed as admiral, at the end of October Sambal in disgust transferred his services to Shiva, carrying his family and personal retainers with himself, the most notable among them being his gallant nephew Siddi Misri

Qasim left Bombay with the fleet in November; up to March next he cruised off the Konkan coast, making frequent landings and kidnapping the people, all of whom (including the Brahman prisoners) he forced to do menial services of a defiling character. At the end of April 1678 he returned to Bombay to rest during the monsoons. Shivaji, wishing to avenge the degradation of his Brahman subjects, sent his admirals Daulat Khan and Daria Sarang with 4,000 men to Panvel, a town opposite Bombay (July), with orders to cross the creek and burn the Siddi fleet then anchored at Mazagon in Bombay island But insufficiency of boats and the violence of the monsoon prevented the army from crossing, and Daulat Khan, after vainly pressing the Portuguese to allow him a passage through their territory, retired to Raigarh. Siddi Qasim sent his boats and plundered the Alibagh coast.

In October 1678, Daulat Khan was sent with a large army and a mightier train of artillery than before to renew the bombardment of Janjira; but Siddi Qasim could not pay his men for want of remittance from Surat, and had to continue inactive in Bombay harbour.

Shivaji's navy had by this time been increased to 20 two-masted *ghurabs* and 40 gallivats. "None of his harbours admitted ships of a great size, such as were used at Surat, or by the Europeans. The (immense) traffic from port to port of the Malabar and . .. Konkan coasts had from time immemorial been carried on in vessels of shallow burden capable of taking close refuge under every shelter of the land. The vessels for fight (on) these coasts were" also built of the same small size, "and trusted to the superiority of number (and not of gun-power or seaworthiness) against ships of burden in the open sea. Shivaji did not change this system in his own marine." (Orme's *Fragments*, 77-78.)

In February 1680, Qasim sallying from his anchorage in Bombay harbour burnt many villages on the Pen river and brought away a thousand captives Then Shiva and the English made an agreement (March) not to let the Siddi fleet winter in Bombay unless they promised to observe strict neutrality. This brings the narrative down to the death of Shivaji, but the same wearisome story of abortive attacks on Janjira by the Marathas and cruel devastation of the coast district by the Siddis continued under Shambhuji.

§ 10. *War with the English for Khanderi island, 1679.*

The difficulty of capturing Janjira set Shiva thinking of some other island in the neighbourhood which would afford him a naval base. His choice fell on Khanderi ('Kennery') a small rocky island, 1½ miles by ½ mile, situated 11 miles south of Bombay and 30 miles north of

Janjira. As early as April 1672 the people of Surat learnt of his intention to build a fort on the island. The English President at once decided to prevent it, as affecting the interests of Bombay even more than those of Surat, because no ship could enter or issue from Bombay harbour without being seen from Khanderi. (*F R* Surat 87, Surat to Bomb. 22 April; Vol. 106, 1 May 1672)

The progress of the Maratha engineers was very slow, and in September next their fortifications were still incomplete The English and Siddi fleets came there in concert and warned the Marathas to stop their work. Shivaji's admirals, Daulat Khan and Mai Nayak, finding themselves opposed to very superior forces, withdrew from the island (*F R*. Surat, 106, T. Roach to Surat, 26 Sep 1672.)

At the end of August 1679, Shiva again took up the project of fortifying Khanderi, and collected men and materials for the purpose at Chaul He allotted one *lakh* of *hun* from the revenues of Kalian and Chaul to be spent on the work On 15th September we find that 150 men of Shiva with four small guns under command of Mai Nayak are already on the island and have run up breast-works of earth and stone all around it. (*Orme MSS*. 116) A request from the Deputy Governor of Bombay "to quit the place as it belonged to the island of Bombay," was declined by the Marathas in the absence of orders from Shivaji to that effect. The English, therefore, resolved that if the occupation of the island was persisted in and the Maratha fleet under Daulat Khan came there to protect the fortifications, they would "repel them with force as an open and public enemy" (*F R*. Surat 4, Consult., 4 and 15 Sep. 1679.)

The first encounter between the English and the Marathas at sea took place on 19th September and ended in a reverse for the sons of the Ocean Queen. The larger English ships were still outside the bay of Khanderi, because the soundings had not yet been taken and they could not be brought closer to the island. Lieutenant Francis Thorpe, with some *shibars* made a rash attempt to land on the island, "positively against orders." The Englishmen were assailed with great and small shot from the shore works. The impetuous young officer was killed with two other men (John Bradbury and Henry Welch), several others were wounded, and George Cole and many other Englishmen were left prisoners on the island. The lieutenant's *shibar* was captured by the enemy, while two other *shibars* escaped to the fleet in the open sea. Next day the Marathas carried off another English *shibar*, Sergeant Giles timidly offering no resistance. (*Orme MSS.* 116.)

Early in October the Maratha fleet was got ready to go to the succour of Khanderi. The second battle with the English was fought on 18th October, 1679.* At day-break the entire Maratha fleet of more than 60 vessels under Daulat Khan suddenly bore down upon the small English squadron consisting of the *Revenge* frigate, 2 *ghurabs* of two masts each, 3 *shibars* and 2 *manchwas*, —eight vessels in all, with 200 European soldiers on board, in addition to the lascars and white sailors The Marathas advanced from the shore a little north of Chaul, firing from their prows and moving so fast that the English vessels at anchor near Khanderi had scarcely time to get under weigh. In less than half an hour the *Dover*, one,

* A full description is given in *Bombay Gaz.* xiii pt ii p 478 I have followed Orme, 80-81, in addition

of the English *ghurabs*, having Sergeant Mauleverer and some English soldiers* on board, with great cowardice struck its colours and was carried off by the Marathas. The other *ghurab* kept aloof, and the five smaller vessels ran away, leaving the *Revenge* alone in the midst of the enemy. But she fought gallantly and sank five of the Maratha gallivats, at which their whole fleet fled to the bar of Nagothna, pursued by the *Revenge* Two days afterwards the Maratha fleet issued from the creek, but on the English vessels advancing they fled back. Such is the inefficiency of "mosquito craft" in naval battles fought with artillery that even fifty slender and open Indian ships were no match for a single large and strongly built English vessel. At the end of November the Siddi fleet of 34 ships joined the English off Khanderi and kept up a daily battery against the island (Orme, 81-84)

But the cost of these operations was heavily felt by the English merchants, who also realized that they could not recruit white soldiers to replace any lost in fight, and therefore could not "long oppose him (Shiva), lest they should imprudently so weaken themselves as not to be able to defend Bombay itself, if he should be exasperated to draw down his army that way" Moreover, during

* Surat Consultation, 3 December, 1679 "Sergeant Mauleverer etc, English, taken formerly by Shivaji in the Ghurab *Dover*, being in great want of provisions and all other necessaries we having duly considered, and perceiving how cowardly they behaved themselves in the time of engagement, do order them to be stricken out of the muster rolls, but that they may not wholly perish, that some small allowance be made to them for victuals only, if it can be securely conveyed to them [in the Maratha prison] (F R Surat, Vol 4) This was in answer to a letter from Mauleverer, dated 6th November, begging for provisions, clothing and medicines for the wounded, and stating that the prisoners in the Maratha fort (Suragarh?) included 20 English French and Dutch, 28 Portuguese, and 9 lascars (*Orme MSS* 116)

the monsoon storms the English would be forced to withdraw their naval patrol from Khanderi, and then Shiva would "take his opportunity to fortify and store the island, maugre all our designs" So, the Surat Council wisely resolved (25th October), that the English should "honourably withdraw themselves in time," and either settle this difference with Shivaji by means of a friendly mediator, or else throw the burden of opposing him on the Portuguese governor of Bassein or on the Siddi, and thus "ease the Hon'ble Company of this great charge" The Surat factory itself was in danger and could spare no European soldier for succouring Bombay (*F R.* Surat 4, Consult., 25 and 31 Oct, 3, 8 and 12 Dec. 1679.)

§ 11. *Anxieties and devices of the English of Bombay.*

The dreaded reprisal by Shivaji against Bombay almost came to pass "Highly exasperated by the defeat of his fleet before Khanderi," he sent 4,000 men to Kalian-Bhivandi with the intention to land in Bombay by way of Thana. The Portuguese governor of Bassein having refused to allow them to pass through his country, the invaders marched to Panvel (a port in their own territory) opposite Trombay island, intending to embark there on seven *shibars* (end of October 1679.) The inhabitants of Bombay were terribly alarmed. The Deputy Governor breathed fire, but the President and Council of Surat decided to climb down. On receiving a courteous letter from Shivaji sent by way of Rajapur, they wrote "a civil answer, demonstrating our trouble for the occasion his people have given the English at Bombay to quarrel with him about his fortifying so insignificant a rock as Khanderi, which is not in the least becoming a prince of his eminence and qualifications; and though we have a right to that place, yet, to show the candour of our proceedings, we are willing to forget what is past, and therefore have given instructions to the Deputy Governor of Bombay to treat with such persons as he shall appoint about the present differences." The Deputy Governor was "very much dissatisfied" with this pacific tone and held that a vigorous policy of aggression against Shiva's country and fleet would "give a speedy conclusion to this dispute, to the Hon'ble Company's advantage." But the higher authorities at Surat only repeated their former orders that Bombay should avoid a war with Shiva and "frustrate his designs of fortifying Khanderi either by treaty or by the Siddi's fleet assisting us to oppose him thereon." The two English captains consulted took the same view. (*Ibid*.) At the end of December the Marathas dragged several large guns to Thal (on the mainland) and began to fire them at the small English craft lying under Underi for stress of weather. (*Orme MSS*. 116.)

But the hope of hindering the Maratha fortification of the island without fighting proved futile, and the English ships were withdrawn (January, 1680) from Khanderi, which, after "holding out [against the Siddis and the English] to the admiration of all," was freed from enemy vessels by the coming of the monsoons, and remained in Shiva's hands (*F. R.* Surat 108, Bombay to Surat, 1 Jan. 1680.)

But the Siddi occupied Underi ('Henery'), a small island about a mile in circumference, close to Khanderi, with 300 men and 10 large guns, fortified it (9th January, 1680), and tried to silence the Maratha guns on Thal. Daulat Khan with his fleet came out of the Nagothna river and attacked Underi on two nights, hoping to surprise it, "but the Siddi's watchfulness and good intelligence from Chaul frustrated his design." On 26th January, 1680, Daulat Khan assaulted the island at three points, ready to land 2,000 men and conquer it. But after a four hours' engagement he retreated to Chaul, having lost 4 *ghurabs* and 4 small vessels, 200 men killed, 100 wounded, besides prisoners,* and himself severely wounded. The Siddi lost only 4 men killed and 7 wounded, but no vessel, out of a fleet of 2 large ships, five three-masted frigates, one ketch and 26 gallivats, with 700 men on board,"—such was the superiority of the Abyssinian ships to the opener and more slender vessels of the Marathas. Underi continued in Siddi hands throughout Shambhuji's reign, and neutralized the Maratha occupation of Khanderi, the two islands merely bombarding each other. (*Ibid.*, also 31 January.)

* Two letters from Underi to Bombay state that Daulat Khan's flee consisted of above 30 *ghurabs* and *gallivats*, and that he lost 137 men in killed and wounded The letter of 28 Jan adds, "Shivaji had threatened hard Daulat Khan that if he did not take Underi, if ever he came back to Negaom again, he would have his life" On 6th March Daulat Khan came into the town of Rajapur from the fleet, wounded in the foot [*Orme MSS* 116]

CHAPTER XII

INVASION OF THE KARNATAK, 1677-1678

§ 1. *The Madras coast its wealth*

Shivaji's grand coronation in June 1674 had greatly reduced his treasury. Since then he had not been able to seize any very rich prize, though his roving bands had raided many places in Adil-Shahi territory. Added to this, his wars with the Mughals and the Bijapuris in 1674 and 1675 and his siege of Phonda had been costly affairs, and chequered by defeats, while his invasion of the Sunda country or Kanara uplands (May 1675) had failed. In the earlier months of 1676 he had suffered from a protracted illness, which had forced on him a long period of inactivity

He, therefore, looked about for some fresh field of gain. In the Mughal territory, Surat had been sucked dry by his two raids, while his permanent occupation of the Koli country of Ramnagar and Jawhar, close to Surat, had so alarmed that port that its trade and wealth were well-nigh gone. The rich Kanara coast had already been swept clean of booty The disorder and misgovernment of the Bijapur State during the effete rule of the regent Khawas Khan and the civil war between the Afghan and Deccani parties at that Court had so impoverished the central part of the realm as to make it no longer an object of cupidity An attack on the heart of the Adil-Shahi kingdom might also have united all the factions at the capital in a common resistance to the invader

But there was an outlying province of this kingdom

which had enjoyed many years of peace and prosperity and whose wealth was fabulous. The Karnatak plain or the Madras coast was known in that age as the land of gold. It was an extremely fertile tract, rich in agricultural produce, with a population that led a life of primitive simplicity and consumed very little in food and clothing. The many ports on the long sea-board had fostered a brisk foreign trade from remote antiquity, while the rich mines of the hinterland brought wealth into the plains. Thus the annual addition to the national wealth was very large. A part of it was spent on the grand temples for which the land is still famous; but most of it was hoarded underground. (*Dil.* 113*a.*) From very early times the Karnatak has been famous for its buried treasure and attracted foreign plunderers.

From this land Samudra-gupta and the Western Chalukyas, Malik Kafur and Mir Jumla, had brought away vast booties. And at the end of the 17th century, even after the recent raids of Mir Jumla and Muhammad Adil Shah, Shivaji and Nusrat Jang, the land had still enough wealth left in it to tempt the cupidity of Aurangzib. As the Emperor wrote (about 1703) to his general, "Many large treasures of olden times are reported to be buried in the Karnatak. The zamindar of Tanjore, who is of low origin (*be-asal*) and a grandson of Shahji, the father of Shivaji now in hell, is possessed of the country by usurpation. His kingdom is not very strong. Its revenue, according to the late Siddi Masaud Khan, is between 70 and 80 *lakhs* of *hun*. Why should it be left in his possession? Inquire into the state of the country and the means of wresting it from his hands." (*Ruqat*, No. 163.) To this real land of gold Shivaji's eyes were now turned. An attack on this frontier province would scarcely rouse the Government of Bijapur, as the Karnatak formed the fiefs of certain semi-independent nobles who alone were interested in its defence. Moreover, Shiva had a plausible claim to a portion of it.

§2 *Internal discord in Bijapuri Karnatak.*

With the fall of the Vijaynagar empire at the beginning of the 17th century, its various provinces covering the Mysore plateau and the Karnatak plains ceased to obey any common head such as might have held together and protected them. The numberless local chieftains stood up, each for himself, and engaged in incessant fighting with their neighbours out of a vain and ruinous passion for the extension of dominion The defenceless and chaotic condition of these rich countries had drawn more powerful spoilers into the field. As the Jesuit missionary Proenza wrote from Trichinopoly in 1659, "The ancient kings of the country seem to invite the conquest of entire India by the Muslims ...by their jealousies and imprudent acts "

At first the Hindu Nayaks of Jinji, Tanjore and Madura rose against their sovereign Shri Ranga of Vijaynagar (then holding Court at Vellore) The ruler of Madura begged the aid of Golkonda, which came, conquered the Vellore province and expelled Shri Ranga to find a last refuge with his vassal of Mysore Then the same Nayak of Madura invited Adil Shah, who took Jinji fort and annexed that rich province (1649), and advancing further south forced the Nayaks of Tanjore and Madura to pay enormous contributions and promise annual tributes! [*Mission du Madure*, iii 41-47.]

The treaty with the Mughal empire in 1636 having fixed their northern and western boundaries, the States of Bijapur and Golkonda could find an outlet for their territorial ambition in the south and east only, and during the next eighteen years they conquered much of Mysore and the Eastern Karnatak. The acquisitions of Golkonda in this region included the Kadapa and North Arcot districts up to the Palar river, and all the land bordering the sea from Chicacole to Sadras. Bijapur had spread its suzerainty over the district of Karnul, all the Mysore plateau north of Bangalore, and the Madras plain between the Palar and the Kolerun rivers, *i.e.*, the country from Vellore to near Tanjore. The Bijapuri generals continued to make raids into Tanjore and Madura (1650-1665) without annexing any part of these territories. They held only the Jinji province, where we find three such generals (one of them being Vyankoji) in charge of the government in 1673. [*Ibid.*, iii 201.]

The suicidal wars among the Hindus still continued. The new Nayak of Madura at last seized the kingdom of Tanjore and beheaded its perpetually faithless ruler Vishwaray (1674) Adil Shah was appealed to by the son of the murdered king, and he ordered Vyankoji to invade Tanjore and restore it to its old dynasty After a year of patient waiting and plotting, and more by sowing dissension among the enemy than by superior force, Vyankoji took the capital, conquered the country, and usurped the throne of Tanjore with the title and authority of an independent king! He still held his father's jagirs north of the Kolerun, in the province of Jinji Adil Shah sent an army to punish this audacious rebellion of his general, and the Nayak of Madura sent his forces to assist the Bijapuris, and Mysore also assembled its troops, seemingly in order to attack

Madura when its Nayak would be entangled with Vyankoji (1676)

The authority of the central Government vanished from Bijapuri Karnatak In 1672 the boy Sikandar had succeeded to the throne of Bijapur and his guardianship had become an object of contest between rival factions at the capital When his first regent, Khawas Khan, was put to death by Bahlol Khan (18th January 1676), an open civil war broke out in the heart of the kingdom, while the provincial governors ceased to recognize any superior and began to extend their own sway

In the Karnatak plain, the local governors of Bijapur in 1676 were Nasir Muhammad Khan (a son of the former wazir Khan Muhammad, Khan-i-Khanan, and a brother of Khawas Khan) with his seat at Jinji and a jurisdiction extending up to Pondicherry, and south of him Sher Khan Lodi (an Afghan *protege* of Bahlol Khan) with his seat at Wali-ganda-puram Further south were the Hindu Rajahs of Tanjore and Madura

But there was no amity or even peace among these Bijapuri vassals Sher Khan was bent on annexing the territory of Jinji with the armed help of the French traders of Pondicherry Nor was this the limit of his dream. He would, after thus removing his only rival in these parts and doubling his strength, hire more French soldiers, despoil the Hindu Nayaks beyond the Kaveri of their fabulous riches and employ these resources in conquering the kingdom of Golkonda for himself!

And the Hindu rulers of the country were no less divided and senseless Vyankoji was "the mortal enemy of the Nayak of Madura" and in June 1676 solicited French troops and ships for conquering the petty princes (*poligars*) in his neighbourhood The ruler of

Madura similarly applied for armed help from the French for a war further south (January 1675.)

Sher Khan Lodi opened the attack. He conquered Porto Novo and several other places belonging to Jinji and finally, on 14th Sep. 1676, a French force under Francois Martin by a night-attack stormed the fort of Valdaur (12 miles west of Pondicherry) on his behalf. By the end of that month he had completely defeated Nasir Muhammad and driven him into Jinji. Tindavanam was next besieged. At last, about 4th November, Nasir Muhammad made peace by ceding Valdaur, Porto Novo and most of his territory to Sher Khan. But he knew it for certain that Sher Khan would not be content to leave him even the fort of Jinji, and that he could not hope for protection from his sovereign who was now entirely in the hands of Bahlol Khan, the clansman and patron of Sher Khan.

In this state of despair, Nasir Muhammad was invited by the Golkonda Court to come over to its side and join it for conquering Sher Khan's lands. The paralysis of the Government of Bijapur and this civil war between its local agents tempted the Qutb Shah to seize this opportunity of easily conquering Bijapuri Karnatak. Earth-hunger is the ever-present passion of absolute rulers. But there was a special reason which led the Golkonda Sultan to embark on a policy of conquest in the Karnatak. His all-powerful *wazir* Madanna Pandit was a devout Hindu and Madanna's nephew Gopanna was a Vaishnav saint, for whose benefit the gods were believed to work miracles. It was the heart's desire of the minister to conquer Bijapuri Karnatak nominally for Golkonda, but really to place the whole of it under Hindu rule as had been the case before 1648.

For accomplishing this pious design, no better agent could be found than Shivaji, the ever-victorious captain and the sword-arm of the Hindu revival of that age. Madanna induced his master to agree to a joint enterprise with Shivaji, in which Qutb Shah, as the sleeping partner, would supply all the expenses and munitions of war, while the Maratha king, as the active partner, would do all the fighting with his own troops Bijapuri Karnatak was to be conquered "in the name and for the benefit of the king of Golkonda," while Shivaji for his pains would get all the spoils of war and collections of black-mail as well as the territory in the uplands of Mysore

An incursion into the Eastern Karnatak had been discussed in Shivaji's inner council for some time past. As far back as July 1675, the French director Monsieur Baron, while on a visit to Rajapur, had learnt about the Maratha king's ambitions about the Karnatak from his chief minister.*

§3. *Shivaji's claims in the Eastern Karnatak.*

According to the usual good luck of Shivaji, a most valuable source of local knowledge in the scene of his projected invasion was secured by him before he started. Raghunath Narayan Hanumanté had been left by Shahji as the guardian and regent of his younger son Vyankoji and had ruled the province with absolute authority. When Vyankoji grew up, he naturally wished to be master in his own dominions and could not brook the supremacy of his minister any longer. During his long years of power, Raghunath had dishonestly enriched

* Kaeppelin, 155 Martin (tr by me in *Mod Rev*), Bertrand's *Mission du Madure*, 1st ed, tome 3

himself from the public revenue* and he was now called upon to render accounts.

At this he resigned his post, took leave of his master on the pretext of making a pious pilgrimage to Benares, and left Tanjore with his younger brother Janardan and all their family and property. But power and wealth were still the gods adored by the aged ex-minister. His pilgrimage was made to the holy shrine of Adil Shah, where his reputation and personal cleverness so impressed the Government that he was pressed to enter its service as a high minister. But he could not have failed to see that the Adil-Shahi monarchy was tottering to its fall, and he was therefore glad to accept Shivaji's invitation to come to his Court instead of joining a Muslim master. Raghunath went to the Maratha capital and was received with the highest honours.

But his revenge had yet to be gratified against his late master. In his private audiences with Shivaji, Raghunath constantly described the vast extent and riches of the Karnatak kingdom left by his father to Vyankoji, and the ease with which it could be conquered, and urged the king to claim his lawful share of this patrimony from his half-brother. The great local knowledge and influence of the Hanumante family he promised to place at Shivaji's service in effecting its conquest. It is very doubtful whether Shivaji would, of himself, have cared to assert his right to his father's Karnatak territory. He certainly did not need it. As he rightly said on his death-bed, "I received [from my father] the Puna territory

* Martin says that on Shambhuji's accession the governor of the Karnatak was disgraced suddenly for his "malversations scandaleuses," but was afterwards re-established in his service. [Kaep. 167.] The officer meant was evidently Raghunath, the *diwan*, as Shantaji was not reinstated.

worth only 40,000 *hun*, but I have won a kingdom yielding one *krore* of hun." (Sabh. 104.)*

§4. *Diplomatic preparations for the Karnatak expedition.*

The political situation in the neighbouring countries was eminently favourable to the design. The Mughal Emperor had, no doubt, returned to Delhi on 27th March, after a two years' absence in the Panjab, but his best troops were still engaged in controlling the revolted hillmen of the N. W. frontier. At Bijapur the Afghan leader Bahlol Khan had seized the guardianship of the boy-king Sikandar (11th Nov., 1675) and murdered the deposed regent Khawas Khan (18th Jan., 1676.) But his favouritism to his clansmen turned the Government into "Afghan rule" and roused the antagonism of the Deccani party and its allies, the Abyssinians. The Deccanis murdered Khizr Khan, the right-hand man and ablest servant of the new regent, and civil war broke out between the Afghans and the Deccanis throughout the State (Feb.) To make matters worse, Bahlol Khan alienated Bahadur Khan, the Mughal viceroy, who openly took the side of the Deccani party and on 31st May began a campaign against Bijapur which was to continue for more than a year. The rotten and tottering Adil-Shahi Government was in no condition to trouble Shivaji at such a time.

---

* Tanjore was conquered by Vyankoji in 1675 and not by Shahji. Though the Bijapuris captured Tanjore fort (March 1659) and occupied the territory of this kingdom for two years afterwards, they were forced to vacate the country by famine pestilence and mutual dissensions (1662.) Shahji was one of the two Bijapuri generals who commanded this army, the other being Mulla. Next year he attacked Trichinopoly (with the Tanjore Nayak's help), but was driven back to Jinji by the ruler of Madura. [*Mission*, iii. 51, 119-123.]

Over the Mughal viceroy of the Deccan, Shivaji's clever diplomacy won a complete triumph. Bahadur Khan had now grown weary of his more than two years' war with Shivaji, which had been chequered by as many defeats as successes and which seemed to promise no decisive end as far as he could look into the future. He had already coquetted with Shiva for a friendly understanding and offered to make peace between him and the Emperor and get a command of 6,000 horse for his son Shambhuji, (June, 1675.) And now, on the eve of opening the Mughal campaign against Bijapur, (May, 1676), it was as much his interest to make friends with the Marathas on his right flank as it was Shiva's to secure Mughal neutrality in his rear during his invasion of the Karnatak. When two parties find a mutual advantage in being at peace, the terms are quickly settled.

Shiva sent his Chief Justice, Niraji Raoji, "a clever logician," to Bahadur Khan, with costly presents to induce him to promise neutrality during his projected absence in the Karnatak, the conquest of which was expected to take one year. Bahadur received a large bribe for himself in secret, and a certain sum in public as tribute for his master, and made a formal peace with the Marathas. (Sabh. 85.)

Having thus secured his flank and rear, Shiva made preparations for starting on this his longest campaign. In June, 1676, Netaji Palkar had returned to Maharashtra, after ten years' service under the Delhi Government as a Muhammadan, and he had "now been remade a Hindu" by means of religious purification, and some important command was probably given to him, though the Maratha chroniclers are silent about the unhappy renegade. (*F. R.* Surat 89, Rajapur to Surat, 24 July,

1676) The premier (*Peshwa*) Moro Trimbak Pingle was left as regent, assisted by Annaji Datto the superintendent of correspondence (*surnis*), with a portion of the army to guard the kingdom. The Konkan districts were entrusted to Annaji Datto with strong garrisons and a large body of disposable infantry. (Sabh. 85-87.)

With Golkonda close friendship and co-operation were secured Madanna Pandit, the all-powerful wazir of Abul Hasan Qutb Shah, had already made a subsidiary alliance with Shiva, promising him an annual tribute of one *lakh* of *hun* for the defence of the realm. Prahlad Niraji, a shrewd diplomatist, had been posted at Haidarabad as Maratha envoy. Shivaji decided to get from Golkonda the expenses of the campaign and the assistance of an auxiliary force, by promising a share of the conquest. But he was careful to avoid the least show of force, and trusted to his personal magnetism and power of persuasion in winning Qutb Shah's alliance.

§5. *March to Haidarabad.*

He wrote to his envoy at Haidarabad to arrange for a friendly interview between him and Qutb Shah. The indolent and gay king of Haidarabad was at first afraid of meeting the man who had slain Afzal, wounded Shaista, and defied Aurangzib in the very midst of his Court. But Prahlad Niraji took the most solemn oaths in support of Shiva's honesty of purpose. Madanna Pandit also told the king that he was satisfied on that point, and most probably he also urged the importance of a personal interview in strengthening the alliance between the two kings. (Sabh 85-86.)

Qutb Shah having agreed to receive him, Shivaji started from Raigarh at the beginning of January, 1677, and advanced due east by regular marches. On entering Haidarabad territory he issued strict orders to his men not to rob or molest any inhabitant of the country, but to buy all necessary things with the owners' consent. The hanging or mutilation of the first few offenders struck such terror among the Maratha troops and camp-followers that they strictly obeyed his order and behaved with exemplary propriety ever after, and the most perfect discipline was maintained among that horde of 50,000 armed men.*

Haidarabad was reached early in February, 1677. Qutb Shah had proposed to advance from his capital and welcome Shivaji on the way. But the Maratha chief very gracefully declined the offered honour, saying, "You are my elder brother. You should not come forward to receive a junior like me." So, the Sultan remained at Haidarabad, but his ministers Madanna and Akanna with many of the highest citizens met Shivaji several miles before the capital and conducted him into it.

§6. *Shivaji's grand entry into Haidarabad.*

The city of Haidarabad had been gaily decorated to welcome the great friend and protector of her king. "The streets and lanes on all sides were coloured with a thin layer of *kunkum* powder and saffron. Maypoles and triumphal arches were erected and flags hung at intervals throughout the city. The citizens in their hundreds of

---

* Sabh 86 The army that followed Shivaji into the Karnatak is estimated by H Gary in a letter dated 16th Jan 1678, as 20,000 horse and 40,000 foot (O C 4314) Sabhasad mentions only "a select force of 25,000 horsemen" (p 85) The Madras Council estimates the force at "16 to 20 thousand horse and several thousand of foot, raised and raising among the woods" (19 June, 1677, O C. 4266)

thousands lined the roads" to gaze on the scene, while the ladies crowded on the balconies to bless the visitor.

The guests responded to the city's civility. The Maratha army, for once, abandoned its rude simplicity and magnificently attired itself. Shiva had distributed among his captains and select soldiers strings of pearls (*torah*) for their helmets, gold bracelets, bright new armour, and rich accoutrements embroidered with gold, "and made the whole army look splendid." His generals in their equipment and trappings rivalled the grandeur of hereditary nobles.

At the auspicious hour chosen for the interview,* the Maratha army 50,000 strong entered the city The citizens gazed with admiration not unmixed with awe at the men who had vanquished the greatest kings of North India and South India alike, and caused wailing at the Court of Bijapur and consternation among the peerage of Delhi. Here rode the fleet hardy horsemen who had poured like a swift resistless flood to the farthest districts of Mughal Deccan and carried their raids to the very gates of Bijapur and Golkonda There tramped the Mavle infantry, whose feats were the theme of many a ballad and legend throughout the Southern land, whose assault no fort had been able to withstand, and whose swords were dreaded by every foe they had met in battle The leaders were men whose names had become household words. Hambir Rao Mohite, the dashing but far-sighted commander-in-chief; Anand Rao and Manaji More, two generals second only to Hambir Rao; Suryaji Malusare and Yesaji Kank, the gigantic captains of the

---

* Shivaji at Haidarabad Sabh 86-88, Malkaré 77, *T S* 36*a*-37*b*; *Dil* 112-113

Mavles, each able to subdue an elephant in single combat; Sonaji Nayak, the royal door-keeper; and Babaji Dhandhere, (probably the captain of the body-guard.)

Nor even among such heroic figures did the citizens fail to notice the high brows, the bright but sunken eyes, and the painted foreheads of the Maratha Brahmans, whose administrative capacity and diplomatic skill had facilitated and confirmed the conquests achieved by the swords of these men: Raghunath and Janardan Narayan Hanumante, until recently the uncrowned kings of Tanjore; Prahlad Niraji, the resident ambassador at Haidarabad; Dattaji Trimbak the chronicler (*waqnis*), Kesho Pant, and Nilo Moreshwar and Gangadhar Pant the auditors (*majmuadars*.) With them were mingled the more retiring and studiously unostentatious figures of the Kayastha writers: Nila Prabhu, the accomplished Persian draftsman (*munshi*), Balaji Avji, that jewel of a secretary (*chitnis*) whom Shivaji loved to keep close to his person; and also, but of another caste, Shamji Nayak, the Keeper of the Seal.

But none of them attracted so much attention as the moving spirit of all this host. In the centre of a brilliant throng of ministers and generals, rode a short spare figure, rendered still thinner by his recent illness and the fatigue of an unbroken march of 300 miles. His quick beaming eyes were glancing right and left, and a natural smile played on his long light brown face distinguished by a Roman nose. The assembled citizens gave cheers for "Shiva Chhatrapati"; flowers made of gold and silver were showered on him from the balconies crowded with ladies and the road-side alike. Every now and then the women came forward and waved lighted lamps round his person with verses of welcome and blessing. Nor was Shiva less liberal In his turn he kept showering handfuls of gold and silver among the crowd on the two sides and presented costly robes of honour to the chief citizens of every ward.

§7. *Interview between Shivaji and Qutb Shah.*

In this way the procession arrived at the *Dad Mahal* or Palace of Justice There all stopped before the gate, keeping perfect order, while Shivaji attended by five of his officers ascended the stairs and entered the palace-hall where Qutb Shah was waiting for him. The Sultan came forward, embraced Shivaji, and seated him by his side on the royal carpet. The wazir Madanna was also permitted to sit down; all others remained standing. The ladies of the harem looked on the scene with wonder through the latticed windows around.

For three hours did the two monarchs hold a friendly conversation. After the usual exchange of compliments and conventional inquiries about health, Abul Hasan Qutb Shah listened with rapt attention to the stories of Shivaji's heroic feats. To the slothful voluptuary of Golkonda, who had never drawn a sword in anger nor ridden to a tented field in his life, it sounded like the most fascinating of romances when Shivaji recounted how he had slain the gigantic Afzal Khan single-handed and hacked at Shaista Khan in the bosom of his harem, how he had challenged Aurangzib in full Court, what hair-breadth escapes he had made in his flight from Agra, how he had sacked Surat and stormed so many hill-forts. At last he gave his royal guest and the chief Maratha officers ornaments, jewels, horses, elephants, and robes of honour, and dismissed them for the day, after graciously anointing Shivaji with scent and giving him betel-leaf with his own hand, and accompanying him to the foot of the staircase.

Then Qutb Shah heaved a sigh of relief; he now felt convinced of Shiva's honesty of purpose and determination to befriend him. The Maratha ambassador at his Court was praised and rewarded for the truth of his assertions. Shivaji returned with his army to the residence selected for him, scattering alms all the way.

Next day, the wazir Madanna Pandit gave a grand dinner to Shivaji and his chief men. The Rajah's meal was cooked by the prime-minister's venerable mother, and Madanna and Akanna sat with due respect and attention before Shivaji as he fed. The guests were conducted back to their quarters with presents of elephants, horses, and clothes.

§8. *Alliance with Golkonda.*

They then proceeded to business. Abul Hasan, being very favourably impressed by Shivaji's personal charm, character and ability, and the strength and discipline of his army, bade his wazir grant him whatever he wanted. After some discussion a secret compact was made regarding the coming campaign. The Sultan was to pay Shivaji a subsidy of 3,000 *hun* a day, or four and a half *lakhs* of Rupees a month, and send 5,000 men (consisting of 1,000 horse and 4,000 foot) in charge of one of his generals (*sar-i-lashkar*), Mirza Muhammad Amin, to co-operate in the conquest of the Karnatak. A train of artillery with material was also supplied by Qutb Shah, and probably a large sum of money as advance payment of the promised subsidy. In return for this aid, Shivaji promised his ally such parts of his conquests in the Karnatak as had not belonged to his father Shahji.

The defensive alliance against the Mughals was strengthened anew with solemn oaths taken by Shivaji in the presence of Qutb Shah, while the latter promised to pay his annual tribute of one *lakh* of *hun* regularly and to keep a Maratha ambassador at his Court.

While these secret negotiations were going on, social functions and ceremonies were also being held in public. Shivaji paid a second formal visit to Abul Hasan and was presented with "an immense quantity of jewels and ornaments and innumerable horses and elephants." (Sabh 88) The two kings sat down together on the terrace of the palace and received the salute of all the Maratha officers, who were rewarded by Qutb Shah with gifts according to their ranks and achievements Even Shivaji's charger did not go unrewarded; a string of precious stones* was placed round its neck, as the worthy companion of his glorious deeds!

Another day, the leading nobles of Haidarabad gave a dinner to Shivaji Then a combat was got up between Yesaji Kank, the Mavle captain, and a *mast* elephant of Qutb Shah, for the diversion of that king and also as a demonstration of the valour of Shivaji's men Yesaji, after keeping the huge brute at bay with his sword for some time, cut off its trunk and put it to flight.†

A month was spent at Haidarabad, ostensibly in going through these ceremonies, but really in concluding

* A necklace, reputed to be this historical one, passed from Satara into the possession of Mr Purushottam Vishram Mawji of Bombay and was shown to me by that gentleman

† *T S* 37*a* But Chitnis, 136, says that to Qutb Shah's question, "How many famous elephants have you?" Shivaji answered by parading several thousands of his well-built Mavle infantrymen and saying, "*These are my elephants*"

the alliance, getting delivery of the promised arms money and material, and equipping the local auxiliary force that was to assist in the campaign.

§9. *Visit to Shri Shaila.*

At last, all his objects having been gained, Shivaji left Haidarabad, early in March 1677, and marched due south towards the Krishna. From the city of Karnul he levied a contribution of five lakhs of *hun*. (Malkaré, 79) Then he proceeded to the Nivritti Sangam where the Bhavanashi flows into the Krishna, 24 miles north-east of Karnul. This spot "is considered by the Hindus a most holy place of pilgrimage." Here and also in the whirlpool of Chakratirtha, a short distance below the junction, the Rajah bathed, performed the religious ceremonies of a pilgrim, and then made a rapid journey 37 miles due east to Shri Shaila, lightly attended, while his army waited for him at Anantpur (44 m. east of Karnul)

As the Krishna winds its way eastwards to the sea, it forms some 70 miles below Karnul a sharp loop northwards, flowing through a wide and steep-sided trench of nearly a thousand feet in depth. Here, in the heart of the uninhabited Nallamala forest, surrounded by rugged hills and a desolate fever-haunted belt of land, rises a plateau 1563 feet high, overlooking the river, on which stands the famous Shiva-temple of Shri Shaila, "the most ancient and sacred in Southern India."* Entering the plateau by a large archway (now no more) called the *Kailash-dwara* (or Gateway of Shiva's Heaven),

---

* Shri Shaila *Kurnool Dist Manual,* 14, 144, 181-183 Shivaji's visit: Sabh 88, Malkaré, 79, says that he spent the first nine days of Chaitra Shukla (24 March—1 April, 1677) there.

the pilgrim sighted the temple enclosure, an oblong space, 660 feet by 510, surrounded by thick walls varying from 20 to 26 feet in height, built of large hewn blocks of greyish stone exactly squared and laid together, and elaborately sculptured with a profusion of accurately designed figures of elephants, horses, tigers, hunters, warriors, and *yogis*, as well as numerous scenes from the Hindu epics and religious books. In the centre of this enclosure is the square temple of Mallikarjuna (*linga*), the chief deity worshipped here, the walls and roof being entirely covered with gilded brass plates presented by Krishna Dev, the victorious Rajah of Vijaynagar (1513.) There is a smaller temple dedicated to Shiva's consort. A flight of stone steps, built by a Vijaynagar queen, leads down from the plateau to the bed of the Krishna, called Patal-Ganga, and a ford called Nila-Ganga, a little below, both of which are considered as sacred bathing-places.

Shivaji ascended this difficult plateau, bathed in the Krishna and spent some ten days at Shri Shaila doing religious rites. The quiet and secluded beauty of the scenery and the spiritual atmosphere of the place penetrated his soul, and he believed that he would find no purer spot to die in. So, he attempted to cut off his own head before the goddess, but his ministers restrained his religious frenzy and recalled him to a sense of his duty to his subjects and the Hindu world at large. Here he built a *ghat*, named Shri-Gangesha, a monastery, and a *dharmashala*, fed a lakh of Brahmans, and gave away large sums to them.

§10. *Capture of Jinji and siege of Vellore.*

Leaving the sacred hill in the first week of April, Shivaji overtook his army at Anantpur and hastened southwards, evidently by way of Nandiyal and Kadapa, to Tirupati. From the last-named place he descended into the plains of the east coast, and passed through Kalahastri to Peddapolam (about seven miles west of Madras), in the first week of May. After some days' halt at Peddapolam, he turned to the south-west, sending an advanced detachment of 5,000 cavalry through Conjeveram (9th May) to Jinji. The commander of this force paid a visit to Nasir Muhammad Khan within the fort and persuaded him to give up Jinji in return for a cash sum on account and a jagir yielding half a lakh of Rupees a year,* (about 13th May) On hearing of this success, Shivaji himself hastened to the fort and took possession of it for himself, instead of handing it over to the Golkonda agents as he had promised.

Shivaji placed the fort of Jinji in charge of a Mavle captain named Rayaji Nalgé, and the surrounding district under Vital Pildev Atré Garadkar as governor, assisted by a *sabnis* and a caretaker of buildings. The military and revenue administration of Maharashtra was transferred here without any change. [Malkaré, 80.] He "constructed new ramparts round Jinji, dug ditches, raised towers and bastions, and carried out all these works with a perfection of which European skill would not have been ashamed." [Andre Freire, S. J., in *Mission du Madure*, iii. 271.]

From Jinji, Shivaji turned back northwards to

---

* Madras *F R*, Martin By this treaty Nasir Muhammad was granted a jagir in the dependencies of Golkonda But when Shivaji kept hold of Jinji, the Golkonda officers naturally refused to put Nasir Muhammad in possession of the promised lands "Poor Nasir was tossed about and received not more than a fraction of what had been promised him Beggared of his former grandeur, he felt so disappointed that he died shortly afterwards "

Vellore, where he arrived about 23rd May. This fort was held for Bijapur by a brave Abyssinian officer named Abdullah Khan, who put up an obstinate defence. Vellore is one of the strongest fortresses in Southern India. A deep wet ditch, swarming with crocodiles, surrounds it The outer ramparts are wide enough for two carts to be driven abreast. Four concentric lines of circumvallation protect it. [Sabh. 91.] Shivaji had, therefore, to begin a regular siege, for which he was not properly equipped. Occupying two neighbouring hillocks, which he named Sajira and Gojira, he mounted batteries there and opened the attack. The fort defied the Marathas for fourteen months * Leaving Narahari Rudra (*sabnis*), with 2,000 horse and 5,000 Mavle infantry, to conduct the protracted siege, Shivaji himself marched southwards (about 20th June) to fight Sher Khan Lodi

§11. *Condition of the invaded country.*

The flood of Maratha invasion swept over the Karnatak plains. Only a few fortified places offered resistance and stood like islands above the waste of waters, for some time. The vanguard of a thousand horsemen rode a day or two's march ahead of the main body which Shivaji accompanied The report of his exactions and the fury of his soldiery had preceded him, and at the news of his coming, all who had anything to lose made haste to remove their property to the safe refuge of the neighbouring woods or the fortified sea-ports of the

* *Jedhe Shakavali* says that Vellore fell on Shravan Shukla 14 (=22 July' 1678) But Madras Diary, 21 Aug, records the fall of Vellore that day, after a siege of 14 months If we read *Bhadra* instead of *Shravan* in *Jedhe S*, the date would be 21 August

Europeans. The rich men were the first to flee, lest he should seize and torture them for ransom.

Shivaji was in need of money. On his refusal to deliver the fort of Jinji and his other conquests in this region to Golkonda as required by the treaty, the Qutb-Shahi Government rightly stopped the payment of the promised subsidy of 3,000 *hun* a day. Therefore, he sent letters to the chief places in the coast districts, in advance of his march, demanding loans to the amount of two *lakhs* of *hun*, out of which Madras and Pulicat were asked to contribute half a lakh each. The loan, which was only another name for a forced contribution, was naturally refused, and this fact, the Madras President feared, "would serve him for a pretence to play his old pranks."

Nor was this fear unfounded. As Shivaji passed by Madras southwards, he took minute account of all the rich men in the country around him with a view to estimating each man's ransom correctly. A net-work of his collectors of blackmail spread throughout the invaded province.

This was the authorized or regular exaction. But the sufferings of the people of the unhappy land, whose only crime was their wealth, did not end with paying it. Behind Shivaji's army came a vast crowd of some 20,000 unattached persons, mostly hungry Brahmans in search of official employment in the province to be conquered. Nothing could exceed their shameless greed and dishonesty. The newly appointed administrators of Shivaji and even their soldiers plundered the wayfarers and the town-dwellers without fear or mercy.

The disorder was further aggravated by local robbers. Most of the petty chiefs (the poligars or 'woodmen' as they are called in the old English and French records) of that region made peace with Shivaji by sending him tribute, and some even joined his army with their followers to share in the plunder. Nay more, the shock of the Maratha invasion dissolved the civil government and tempted every private robber to come out of his den with his band and hang in the rear of the Maratha army in the hope of picking up what the lion would leave undevoured [Martin's *Memoires*]

§12. *Struggle with Sher Khan Lodi*

The southern half of the Bijapuri Karnatak plains was ruled over by Sher Khan Lodi, a Pathan noble, with his seat of government at Wali-ganda-puram * By nature he was more fitted for civil government than for war. He was entirely guided by his Brahman advisers, who had foolishly taught him to underrate Shivaji's strength, and this delusion was also shared by his son Ibrahim Khan, in disregard of the warnings of Francois Martin.

With a force of 4,000 cavalry and three or four thousand second-rate infantry (of the militia type), "whom the mere name of Shivaji caused to tremble," Sher Khan arrived at Tiruvadi, 13 miles west of Cuddalore, on 10th June, to wait for the Marathas. Shivaji reached the neighbourhood with 6,000 cavalry,

* Now an obscure village in the Perambalur taluq of the Trichinopoly district, but in the 17th and 18th centuries one of the most important posts on the main road from Madras to Trichinopoly (Orme's *Indostan*, 4th ed , i 172) The fort is at Ranjangudi, 3 m n of the village W

My account of this contest is based upon Martin's *Memoire* (see my trans in *Modern Review*, Feb 1924) and Madras *Factory Records*, vol 27, "Letters from our Brahmans Wardapa from Shivaji Raja's camp, 27 June, and Nellor Ramana 16th July, 1677" *Jedhe S* has misread *Bairagi* for *Lodi*

on 26th June At the sight of him Sher Khan immediately put his men in battle order and advanced to the attack. The Marathas calmly waited for the onset. Their attitude made Sher Khan realize that he had taken a false step and he ordered a retreat! Then Shivaji charged the confused and wavering ranks of the enemy and turned the retreat into a rout.

Sher Khan flung himself with the remnant of his army into the fort of Tiruvadi in his rear. At night he tried to escape from it to Tevenapatam, a suburb of Cuddalore. The Maratha horse, noticing the movement, gave chase and drove him into Akala Nayak's wood, which lay in the way. Five hundred of the Khan's horsemen offered battle and held up the pursuers for two hours. Then the moon set and Sher Khan ran away with some of his cavalry and elephants southwards out of the wood. Shivaji's men continued the chase. Sher Khan fled before them at full gallop and had just time to throw himself the next day (27th June) with a hundred horsemen, into the poor fort of Bonagir-patam, (or Bowanigiri) on the Vellar river, 22 miles south of Tiruvadi, where he was immediately blockaded by the Marathas. In this encounter Shivaji's men captured 500 horses, two elephants, twenty camels and many oxen tents and war drums from the Khan.

The fort of Tiruvadi held out for some time under Sher Khan's father-in-law. Leaving Babo Sahib with some horse to invest the place, and quartering his main army three miles south of Tevenapatam, Shivaji himself appeared before Bonagir-patam. On 30th June, Valdaur, Tevenapatam and several other forts of the Khan fell to the Marathas, their garrisons having vacated them in terror. Soon afterwards, Sher Khan gave up the struggle On 5th July he made terms with Shivaji, giving up all his territories and promising a ransom of 20,000 *hun* in cash, for which he left his eldest son as a hostage, while Shivaji agreed to give him a free exit from the fort and the delivery of his property in Gondelur.

We may conveniently bring the story of Sher Khan to its close here After leaving Bonagir-patam and visiting Shivaji, he sought asylum in the forest of Ariyalur, a village 15 m. s. e of Wali-ganda-puram. The chieftain of this place (a Kallar by caste) received him most hospitably and gave him two villages yielding Rs. 1,500 a year for his support The Khan professed to be too poor to pay his promised ransom, and in consequence his hostage Ibrahim Khan was harassed by the Marathas for the money At last in February 1678, the Hindu princes of those parts, among whom the Khan was popular and highly respected, subscribed the amount and secured his son's release. In April Sher Khan retired to the Court of the Nayak of Madura [Kaep.]

§13 *Shivaji on the Kolerun river.*

His victory over Sher Khan being now complete, Shivaji at the end of the first week of July left the vicinity of Cuddalore, marched south across the Vellar river, and cantoned his army for the rainy season at Tirumalavadi, on the north bank of the Kolerun river, 10 miles due north of Tanjore, (arriving there about 12th July) Here an envoy from Chokka-nath ('Socca Linga' in Jesuit letter), the ruler of Madura, waited upon Shivaji, who demanded from him one *krore* of Rupees "for the present, for his expenses," arguing that the Nayak bore the sign of being worth nine *krores*. The envoy "answered that part of his master's country the Nayak of Mysore had taken and part Vyankoji, and that if he (Shiva) would restore him the said country, the Nayak of Madura would give him seven *lakhs*. The Nayak sent all his family away from Chartanapalli (Trichinopoly), where they were before, to Madura [for safety], and while the river Kolerun remained full he feared nothing [from the Marathas.]" But shortly afterwards Raghunath Pant came from Maharashtra and was cordially welcomed by Shivaji, who then sent him to Madura with the Nayak's envoy to settle the amount of the blackmail by negotiation. The Nayak agreed to pay six *lakhs* of *hun*, out of which 1½ *lakhs* were delivered immediately, and Shivaji promised to retire with his army. (Nellor Ramana's letter to Governor of Madras, 16 July, 1677.)

§14. *Interview between Shivaji and Vyankoji.*

In the meantime, messages had been passing between Shivaji and his half-brother Vyankoji for a meeting At Shivaji's request, the Rajah of Tanjore had sent his ministers for a preliminary discussion. They returned to their master with three of Shivaji's ministers carrying a letter of invitation from him. Reassured by their report and Shiva's solemn promises of safety, Vyankoji arrived at Tirumala-vadi about the middle of July, with an escort of 2,000 horse. Shiva advanced to Tirumanur (6 m n. e.) to welcome him on the way. The brothers spent some days together exchanging gifts and feasting each other. Then Shivaji opened his business. He demanded three-fourths of whatever Shahji had left at his death,—money,

* Meeting between Shivaji and Vyankoji *F R* Fort St George. Vol 27, Letter from Nellor Ramana, 27 July, 1677, Martin, f 285, *Mission du Madure*, iii 269, *Dil* i 113 The Marathi accounts are later and much less reliable

horses, jewels, and territory,—offering to let Vyankoji enjoy the remaining quarter. The latter declined, at which Shivaji burst into anger and rebuked him. Vyankoji was watched and feared that he would not be allowed to return to freedom, unless he yielded to his brother's demand. So, one night soon afterwards, he approached the bank of the Kolerun under the pretext of necessity, jumped on a raft which had been kept ready for him, and crossed over to his own territory, on the opposite bank, with only five attendants, (about 23rd July)

Shivaji learnt of his brother's flight next morning and, ascribing it to the advice of the Tanjore ministers,—Jagannath Pant (the *diwan*), Konher Mahadev and Shivaji Shankar (two *majmuadars*) and Niloji Nayak (a merchant), he placed them under arrest and threatened to send Janardan Narayan Hanumante to take possession of the kingdom of Tanjore. He was highly indignant at his brother's conduct, as implying a distrust of his solemn pledge of safety, and cried out in open Court, "Was I going to imprison him? My fame has spread over the sea-girt earth I asked for my father's property, only because one should keep his heritage. If he does not wish to part with it, he is under no compulsion to give it. Why did he flee for nothing? He is very young and has acted like a child." (Sabhasad, 90.) Shivaji sent some of his officers to Tanjore to recall Vyankoji, but they returned unsuccessful

After a time the captive ministers of Vyankoji were set free, and sent back to Tanjore with presents and robes of honour. Thus Shivaji cleared himself in the eyes of the public. But though he gave up the idea of invading the Tanjore territory south of the Kolerun, he seized the whole Karnatak north of that river, both the jagirs of Vyankoji and those of Sher Khan, Vellore and Arni alone still holding out.*

The French envoy M. Germain, who spent three days in Shivaji's camp on the Kolerun, gives a graphic account of the Maratha king's Spartan simplicity and efficient arrangements:—"His camp is without any pomp and unembarrassed by baggage or women. There are only two tents in it, but of a thick simple stuff and very small,—one for himself and the other for his minister. The horsemen of Shivaji ordinarily receive two pagodas per month as pay. All the horses belong to him and he entertains grooms for them...... Ordinarily there are three horses for every two men, which contributes to the speed which he usually makes. This chief pays his spies liberally, which has greatly helped his conquests by the correct information which they give."

§15. *Shivaji's return northwards.*

His hope of recalling Vyankoji being futile, Shivaji broke up his camp on the Kolerun about 27th July. Thence after a short halt at Wali-ganda-puram (28 m. north), he crossed the Vellar river (10 m. n) and stopped at Tundumgurti for a day or two. Here he received a visit from the Dutch Chief of Tevenapatam bearing many presents (about 31st July), and from this place sent his army on to Elavanasur (22 miles further north) to take

---

* *F R* Fort St George, Vol 18, Madras to James and Chamberlaine, 24 Aug, 1677 Letter of Nellor Ramana, 2 Aug, (Vol 27), says that Shivaji kept the three Tanjore ministers with him for some time after leaving Tirumalvadi, and that Jagannath induced the garrison of Elavanasur to give it up to him *Jedhe S* records that Shivaji next captured Chidambaram, Vriddhachalam and Jagdevgad (=Kaveripatan) and laid siege to Kolhar

that fort from Vyankoji's men, while he himself, with Simaji Nayak and others of his great men, turned 16 miles north-east to worship at the great Shiva temple of Vriddhachalam, (1-3 August.)

On 22nd September Shivaji was at Vanikamvadi, (40 miles s w. of Vellore) and wrote to the English governor of Madras . "In the Karnat country. . I intend to build new works in several forts and castles You may likely have with you such men as know how to make great carriages for guns and how to contrive mines. We have need of such men at present, especially those that know how to make mines and to blow up stone-walls. If there be any such men with you that know how to make mines, you would be pleased to send some 20 or 25, or at least 10 or 5 such men, for I shall pay them very well and shall entertain them in several of my forts." (*F* R. Fort St. George, Vol. 27) The English politely declined the request, saying that, being merchants, it was their duty to maintain strict neutrality. On 3rd October, Shivaji was within two days' march of Madras. (Love, i. 371) Shortly before, he had pillaged Porto Novo, and made himself master of the South Arcot district. (Love, i 357) In October Arni surrendered to him, and so also did some other forts in the North Arcot district.

§16. *Shivaji's return through Mysore and conquests.*

Shivaji had been now absent from his own realm for ten months and the administration there was suffering from the lack of the master's control. At a grand council of his officers which he held in September it was decided to return to Maharashtra. [Martin] This resolution was strengthened by the news that Aurangzib had ordered his governor of the Deccan to punish Qutb Shah for having joined and assisted the arch-rebel Shivaji, and a combined Bijapuri and Mughal army had invaded Golkonda territory near Malkhed.* (September 1677.) Therefore at the beginning of November 1677, Shivaji himself with 4,000 cavalry marched away from the Karnatak plains, leaving the bulk of his army in occupation of his new conquest and "promising to return quickly." (*F. R.* Surat, Vol. 107, Madras letter of 20 Nov. 1677.) Ascending the Eastern Ghats into the tableland, he took easy possession of his father's jagir districts,—Kolar, Uskota, Bangalore, Balapur and Sera, in the eastern and central parts of the present kingdom of Mysore, repressed the turbulent poligars of that No Man's Land, and then returned home through the Bellary and Dharwar districts, reaching Panhala early in April, 1678. (Sabh. 91.)

About 21st August 1678, the fort of Vellore surrendered to Shivaji's forces after a siege of 14 months, "Abdullah Khan, the Captain, that held it out all this time, having behaved himself very resolutely therein. But his men from 1,800 foot and 500 horse, being by the extremity of the siege and sickness reduced to 200 foot and 100 horse, and no supplies sent from Bijapur,......... he could not hold it longer, and therefore delivered it upon condition to have 30,000 pagodas in money, a small fort and country worth 30,000 pagodas per annum." (Madras *Diary and Consult.* 1678-79, p. 105; *B. S.* 476.)

The territory annexed by Shivaji in the Karnatak was estimated to yield 20 *lakhs* of *hun* a year and included a hundred forts, taken or built by him. (Sabh. 90.) In August 1678, the Madras factors write, "Shivaji by his

---

* *History of Aurangzib,* iv ch. 42, §7-8

deputies has a full and quiet possession of all these countries about those two strong castles of Jinji and Vellore, which are worth 22 lakh of pardoes or 550 thousand pounds sterling per annum, at five shillings the pardoe, in which he has a considerable force of men and horse, 72 strong hills and 14 forts [in the plain],—being 60 leagues long and 40 broad." (*Diary and Consult.* 1678-79, pp. 105-106) But gold, and not land, was his chief object. The whole of the Karnatak was "peeled to the bones" by his system of "organized plunder" and exaction, which is graphically described by the Madras President as well as by Francois Martin The booty carried off in this expedition* was so vast as to stagger the imagination of the Maratha chroniclers, and they made no attempt to compute its value

Over the Karnatak plains thus conquered, he at first placed Shantaji, a natural son of Shahji, as viceroy with Jinji for his head-quarters, assisted by Raghunath Narayan Hanumanté as diplomatic adviser and auditor (*majmuadar*), and Hambir Rao as commander of the army of occupation The tableland of Mysore was placed under Rango Narayan as viceroy, but subject to the higher jurisdiction of Jinji [Sabh. 91; Madras to Surat, 20 Nov. 1677, *Mission*, iii. 269.]

§17 *Struggle with Vyankoji renewed; final settlement.*

But the new conquest was not to enjoy peace in the absence of the master's eye. Vyankoji set on foot

* 'With a success as happy as Cæsar's in Spain, he came, saw and overcame, and reported so vast a treasure in gold, diamonds, emeralds, rubies and wrought coral that have strengthened his arms with very able sinews to prosecute his further victorious designs" (H Gary to Co, dated Bombay, 16 Jan, 1678, *O C* 4314) "Peeled to the bones" in Madras records of Oct 1677 "Organized pillage" in Martin, Kaep 164

intrigues with the Nayaks of Madura and Mysore and the poligars, and even appealed to the Court of Bijapur and the Muslim nobles in his neighbourhood to organize "a confederacy for regaining their own." But no help came to him except from some petty chiefs.

In November 1677, Shivaji's troops showed a disposition to cross the Kolerun river and enter the territory of Tanjore. Vyankoji opposed them. The two armies stood facing each other across the Kolerun for some days, without any action. Envoys from the two parties tried to effect a compromise, but without success. Vyankoji delayed giving battle, because for some days in succession vultures had been flying into his camp, which was a bad omen.

At last, on 16th November, Vyankoji crossed the Kolerun at the head of 4,000 cavalry and 10,000 infantry, and attacked Shivaji's army of 12,000 men, led by Shantaji Bhonsle.* Shantaji boldly resisted from morning to nightfall, though his cavalry was of inferior quality. The contest was very severe, and many were slain or wounded, including several persons of note In the end, Shantaji was worsted and fled for two miles. The Tanjore horsemen, after pursuing him for a mile, returned to their tents to rest from the day's fatigue. But Shantaji, on reaching his camp, "consulting with his captains what the importance and shame [of the defeat] would be, resolved to dress and saddle their horses again, and so immediately rode away by other ways, and in the dead of night surprised them fast at rest after so hard

* The Maratha accounts say that Hambir Rao commanded Shivaji's troops in this battle, the Madras Factory Records and the Jesuit missionary say it was Shantaji There is no real conflict, both were present, the viceroy and the c-in-c

labour, their horses unsaddled, and made a great slaughter of them, taking nigh 1,000 horse, the three chief commanders, the tents and all their baggage, and 100 horses more taken by woodmen who fell to share the plunder The rest fled over the river Kolerun for Tanjore."*

Skirmishes continued between detachments of the two armies throughout December, and they pillaged and ruined the country with equal violence Shivaji soon afterwards found it necessary to recall much of his army from the Karnatak as he was threatened with an attack in his homeland. So, peace was made between the two brothers, Shivaji retaining the Jinji territory, some other forts, and for a time the Mysore tableland (Kolar &c) which had once belonged to his father, while Vyankoji was left in undisturbed possession of his dominions south of the Kolerun and some portion of the country north of it, in return for a payment of 3 lakhs of *pardoes* (Rs 6 lakhs) in cash. The army of occupation under Hambir Rao was recalled to Maharashtra, and

---

* *F R* Surat, Vol 107, Madras letters of 20 and 29 Nov 1677 Father Andre Freire wrote from a town of Jinji district in 1678, 'The soldiers of Vyankoji, transported by fury, fell on the enemy's army like lions, broke the ranks, &c Shantaji, obliged to flee, preserved enough coolness to place a large detachment in ambush, the victors, carried away by the ardour of success, fell into the trap, taken in the rear by the detachment, they saw in an instant the fugitives returning against them with irresistible impetuosity After some hours of fierce combat, they were crushed and left the field of battle Shantaji's losses were, nevertheless, very much more considerable than those of the vanquished " [*Mission*, iii 270]

Sabhasad, 91, describes the battle thus "Vyankoji's army was four times as large as that of Hambir Rao, but the latter defeated the former, capturing 4,000 of his horses, besides elephants, jewels, ordinary officers, and Vikaji and Pratapji (two natural sons of Shahji) and other officers of high rank " *Jedhe S* says that the battle took place near Ahiri, and that Hambir Rao captured 3,000 horses and several elephants and *sardars* of Vyankoji

Raghunath organized a local force of 10,000 horse (both *paga* and *silahdar*) for the defence of the new province.[*]

§18. *The European traders during Shivaji's invasion.*

As soon as Shivaji descended into the Karnatak plains (early in May 1677), the European traders on that coast hastened with presents to keep him amicably disposed towards them from the outset. On 14th May the English Governor of Madras received a letter from him, brought by his Brahman agent, Mahadji Pant, asking for some cordial stones (bezoar) and other counter-poisons. The English supplied these, together with Maldiv cocoanuts and presents worth 60 *hun*. These were acknowledged with thanks on the 25th, in Shivaji's letter from Vellore in which he asked for a fresh supply of "good counter-poisons," entreating the Governor "not to be bashful in asking for the cost," and sending a robe of honour for the Governor. But, again, the English supplied him with presents, worth 52 *hun*, (18th June.) Two Brahmans in the service of the English attended Shivaji's camp and sent news of his doings and intentions to Madras. On 22nd September, Shivaji again wrote to the Governor asking him to send 20 or 25 men who knew how to make gun-carriages and dig mines and blow up stone-walls, and promising to pay them very well. The Governor maintained his neutrality.

---

[*] *F R* Surat 107, Madras to Surat, 27 May 1678, Martin, Sabh 93, Malkaré, 82 Malkaré adds that Arni and Venidurg were left to the son of Vedaji Bhaskar, out of respect for Shahji's grant to him Shivaji does not seem to have retained any of his conquests in eastern Mysore such as Kolar and Bangalore, after 1678 A late tradition runs that by a polite fiction, the Bangalore, Ooskota and Shilagutta parganas (*i e*, the modern Mysore and Kolar districts) were handed back by him as a present to Vyankoji's wife for her wardrobe expenses!

[Madras *Diary*, 1677, pp. 112-115, *O.C.* 4266; *F.R.* Madras, 27.]

At the near approach of the Marathas and the consternation and flight among the people all around, Francois Martin, the Governor of Pondicherry, sent (22nd May) a Brahman to Shivaji at Vellore, with a letter appealing to him to protect the French factories in the Karnatak as he had hitherto protected them at Rajapur in his own dominions This agent had three interviews with Shivaji who demanded French help in his war with Sher Khan, and finally asked what they would give him for leaving them in peace The French pleaded poverty in consequence of their recent war with the Dutch and stoppage of trade. On 2nd July, Martin sent his Brahman agent again with a fresh appeal for protection written as from M. Baron, the director. Shivaji wished for European envoy to be sent to him. Sieur Germain (with A Cattel as interpreter) was accordingly sent to Shivaji's camp on the Kolerun, where they were introduced by Janardan Pant, and returned after three days with a *farman* of reassurance for Pondicherry. (August.) But the local Maratha officials of Shivaji who visited that city continued to extort money from the people As Martin wrote, "It was nothing but a continual search for the men whom they believed to be capable of yielding money The intendants are in concert with the governor (*subahdar*) of this province. All the ways of extracting money are permitted The letters that were written to Shivaji had no effect at all." [Martin, tr by me in *Mod. Rev* Feb. 1924]

On 31st July the Chief of the Dutch factory at Tevenapatam (Cuddalore) waited on Shivaji at Tundumgurti with presents (scarlet silk stuffs, sandal wood, rose water, Maldiv cocoanuts, cloves, and sword blades) Shivaji was pleased and gave the party robes of honour. But some goods of their factory had been robbed and they asked for their restitution Evidently they had no relief. As Martin writes, "The Dutch were as prisoners in their house at Tevenapatam and forced to give presents in order to have free entry and exit." [*F. R.* Madras 27, Martin]

§19. *Vyankoji's true character.*

A striking illustration of the deliberate falsification of history by later Maratha writers is furnished by the attempt of Chitnis and others to paint Vyankoji as a dull incompetent sluggard, without any noble ambition or martial spirit, or even the power to appreciate an able and useful minister like Raghunath N. Hanumante. Contemporary records enable us to correct these misrepresentations and put Vyankoji's character in a true light, as no unworthy brother of Shivaji. The Persian histories mention his gallant fight against the Mughals during Jai Singh's invasion of Bijapur (1665.) He himself, and not his father, annexed Tanjore (to which, therefore, Shivaji had no legal claim.) The Jesuit missionary Andre Freire thus praises his civil administration of the newly conquered kingdom of Tanjore: "He sought to make himself beloved by the inhabitants. The justice and wisdom of his government began to close the wounds of the preceding reign and to develop the natural resources of the country. By repairing the canals and tanks, he has given fertility to the vast fields which had been left untilled for many years, and the last crop has surpassed all that was seen before" [Letter of 1676 in *Mission*, iii. 249]

Raghunath Hanumante was no saint in money matters. I have found no evidence for Parasnis's story that Raghunath administered Vyankoji's own kingdom as his wazir for a year after Shivaji's return No authentic historian records such an arrangement, and it is improbable from the known facts. Therefore, *Tanjavar-chen Rajgharané*, 36-38 and 42-43, should be rejected as apocryphal.

CHAPTER XIII

HIS LAST YEARS

§1. *Adventures during return from the Karnatak.*

After his marvellous success in the invasion of the Karnatak, Shivaji left the Madras plains (early in November, 1677) and ascended the Mysore plateau, conquering its eastern and central parts.*

Leaving Mysore (January, 1678) he crossed the Tungabhadra, and by way of Kopal and Gadag, reached Lakshmishwar in the Dharwar district. The desai, named Khangauda, had evacuated his fort in terror, and it was occupied by the Marathas. Bankapur, 20 miles s. w. of Lakshmishwar, was next threatened, in the middle of January, 1678. (O. C. 4314.) From this place Shivaji turned his steps northwards, and arrived near Sampgaon in the Belgaum district. At Belvadi, a small village 12 miles s. e. of Sampgaon and 30 miles s. e. of Belgaum, Savitri Bai, the widowed lady proprietor, plundered some transport bullocks of Shiva's army when passing by. Her fort was at once besieged, but she defended it most heroically for 27 days, after which it was carried by assault and she herself was captured.†

---

* His route is thus given in Sabhasad, 91 Kolhar—Balapur—Kopal—Lakshmishwar—*Khangauda* desai chastised—Sampgaon district—Balvada *desain* invested, captured, and "taught a lesson"—Panhala *Kopal* is north of the Tungabhadra, 22 m west of the ruins of Vijaynagar, and 105 miles due south of Bijapur Gadag is 35 m west of Kopal, and Lakshmishwar, 24 m south of Gadag

† *T S*, 38*a*, thus describes her fate · "A woman named Savitri was the *patelni* (village headman's wife) of Belvadi From the shelter of her fort she fought Shiva for one month On her provisions and n.

This long check by a woman, before a petty mud-fort, greatly lowered Shivaji's prestige. As the English merchants of Rajapur wrote on 28th February, 1678: "He is at present besieging a fort where, by relation of their own people come from him, he has suffered more disgrace than ever he did from all power of the Mughal or the Deccans (=Bijapuris), and he who hath conquered so many kingdoms is not able to reduce this woman *desai*!" (*F R.* Surat, 107)

Soon afterwards Shivaji had another and very great disappointment,—probably the greatest in his life, which we describe in the words of the Rajapur factors in their letter of 3rd April. "Jamshid Khan, since the death of his master the Nawab [Bahlol Khan, on 23rd Dec., 1677] found himself incapable of longer holding out, agrees with Shivaji to deliver up [the fort of Bijapur and the person of Sikandar Adil Shah] to him for 600,000 pagodas. Siddi Masaud, having intelligence of this, feigns a sickness, at last death, and causes a *handol* publicly to be sent away with part of the army to Adoni, the residue (of his troops) about 4,000 sent to Jamshid, pretending that since the leader was dead, if he would entertain them they would serve him He presently accepts their service and receives them into the Fort, who within two days seized his person, caused the gates to be opened and received the Siddi in alive, (21st Feb., 1678.) Shivaji upon his march hearing this news returns, and

---

running short, she made a sortie, demolished all the siege trenches, and dispersed and slew many of the besiegers For one day she kept the field heroically, but at last fled vanquished, was captured and greatly dishonoured Sakhuji Gaikwar was the doer of this evil deed Shivaji, on hearing of his act, put out both his eyes and thus gave him his deserts He was imprisoned in the village of Manauli"

is expected at Panhala in a short time." (*F. R.* Surat, Vol. 107.)

In an age when almost every man had his price, Shivaji cannot be blamed for trying to make gains by bribery. The fort of Bijapur was for sale, and he only made a bid for it, and took his chance with other competitors for the position of keeper of the puppet Adil Shah, even as Shahji had been the keeper of a puppet Nizam Shah. Masaud and Bahlol were not more disinterested, but certainly less efficient than he would have been as regent of Bijapur.

The news of the delivery of the Adil-Shahi capital to Siddi Masaud (21st February) reached Shivaji on his way from Belvadi through Turgal to Bijapur, and he swerved aside to the west and returned to his own stronghold of Panhala in the first week of April, 1678.

§2. *Maratha activity in 1677.*

At this stage we may conveniently inquire into what happened in Maharashtra during Shivaji's absence from home in the Karnatak expedition (January 1677—March 1678.) An army was sent under Shambhuji to annex some Portuguese territory near Goa. He demanded 60 villages from the Portuguese on the ground that they belonged to the fort of Phonda, which was now in Shivaji's possession; but on meeting with a refusal, he made a rash assault on the Portuguese, who beat him off. Then the Marathas left the district for Daman, hoping to find less opposition there (Nov. 1677.) But no permanent gain resulted from this campaign. (*Dutch Rec.*, Vol. 34, No. 844.) The Maratha embassy to Goa in December 1677, will be described in Chapter 14.

During this period the armies left at home under Moro

Trimbak in the Desh and under Annaji Datto in Konkan, naturally confined themselves to minor raids, without venturing on any distant expedition. The Surat district was, as usual, subjected to contribution by the Maratha forces now quartered close by at Navsari, Gandavi, and Pindval, with Trimbakji in actual command, in the absence of the Peshwa. Their officers used boldly to enter even the city of Surat, with 40 or 50 troopers at a time and publicly demand provisions and money from the governor. In November, 1677, Dattaji taking advantage of the crushing repulse of Dilir and Bahlol by the Golkonda troops (two months earlier), roved the inland parts of Kanara and looted Hubli. Early in January, 1678, Moro Pant "plundered Trimbak, Nasik and other considerable places in the Mughal territory." Dilir Khan hastened there with the remnant of his broken army, (middle of February.)*

§3. *Conquest of the north bank of the Tungabhadra.*

Shivaji's return home (March, 1678), revived Maratha activity. The districts that he retained in Central and Eastern Mysore as the result of his Karnatak expedition, had to be connected with his old dominions by the conquest of the southern corner of the kingdom of Bijapur, which consisted of the Kopal region north of the Tungabhadra opposite the Bellary district, as well as part of the Dharwar and Belgaum districts intervening between Kopal and Panhala. The Kopal district was held by two Afghans, Husain Khan Miana of Kukanur and his brother Qasim Khan of Kopal. They were fellow-

* *F. R.* Surat 89, Surat to Bomb., 26 May; Vol. 107, Rajapur to Surat 8 Dec. 1677; Bomb. to Surat, 21 Feb. 1678.

clansmen of Bahlol Khan, and on the death of that chief and the ruin of his family, the defence of this frontier was entrusted to them.

Husain Khan is spoken of by Sabhasad as a high and powerful noble of the rank of Bahlol Khan, a brave general renowned for his martial spirit, and the leader of 5,000 Pathan archers, lancers, musketeers, and artillerymen. In January 1677, Bahir Rao invaded the Gadag district. Husain Khan Miana opposed him near Yelburga. After a long and bloody fight, the Pathans were defeated. Husain Khan, on account of his corpulence, could not ride on horseback. The elephant on which he was trying to escape was wounded in the trunk by Nagoji Jedhe and forced to turn back. Nagoji was shot dead, but the Khan was captured with 2,000 of his horses and some elephants. Shivaji offered to set him free if he gave up the fort of Kopal, but he declined and was kept a prisoner. Early in 1678, Shivaji conquered the Gadag district. At last after two years the Peshwa Moro Pant negotiated with Qasim Khan (the commandant of Kopal) through Husain's son and induced him to give up the fort for money (3rd March 1679.) Husain was now released and entered the Maratha service for a living.*

* I have here followed *Jedhe* with a few points from *T S*, 33*a* These two works call the victor Bahir Rao, while Sabhasad and Malkaré call him Hambir Rao (In bad MSS *Hambir* may be read as *Bahir*, but in January 1677 Hambir Rao was on the march to Haidarabad with Shivaji) The place of battle is put by Jedhe 'near *Yelgedla*', which I emend into *Yelburga* (30 m n e of Gadag, now in the Lingasagar district), and not into *Yelagi* (20 m south of Belgaum) *T S* says that Husain Khan was the "sardar of *Kakanur*",—a city 15 m north of Kopal, and that Bahir Rao fell in the battle and Husain, out of wounded honour, took poison on being set free by Shivaji (which is, not historically true) Sabhasad, 80—81, places the battle in Sampgaon *B. S* 451 merely says that Shiva imprisoned Husain Khan by deception

Kopal is rightly called by Sabhasad "the gate of the south," and its possession enabled the Maratha dominion to be extended to the bank of the Tungabhadra river and even across it into the Bellary and Chittaldurg districts. Many of the local chieftains, who had long defied the Bijapur Government and withheld taxes in this ill-subdued border country, were now chastised by the Marathas and reduced to obedience,—among them being the poligars of Kanakgiri (25 miles n. e. of Kopal), Harpan-halli (40 miles s. of Kopal), Raydurg, Chittaldurg, Vidyanagar (? old Vijaynagar), and Bundikot (? Gudicota, 45 miles e. of Harpan-halli) This country was now formed into a regular province of Shivaji's kingdom and placed under Janardan Narayan Hanumante as viceroy. (Sabh.)

Late in April 1678, Shivaji's troops plundered Mungi-Pattan, on the Godavari, 30 miles south of Aurangabad. (*M. A.* 166.) It was probably next month that they made a second attempt to get possession of Shivner They invested the village (of Junnar) at its foot, and at night tried to scale the fort. "Three hundred Marathas climbed the fort-walls at night by means of nooses and rope-ladders But Abdul Aziz Khan was an expert *qiladar.* Though he had sent away his sons and followers to reinforce the *faujdar* Yahiya Khan in the village, he personally with a few men slew all the infantry of Shiva who had entered the fort. Next morning he hunted out the few who had concealed themselves in the hill [side] below the fort and among rocks and holes, and released them with presents, sending a message to Shivaji to the effect, 'So long as I am *qiladar,* you will never take this fort.' " (*Dil* 157)

§4. *The Mughals, Bijapur, and Shivaji, 1678.*

A rupture now took place between Shiva and Qutb Shah, and the diplomatic system so patiently built up by Madanna Pandit fell to the ground. Qutb Shah's indignation had been rising as he found himself made a mere cat's paw by Shiva in the Karnatak adventure. He had borne all the expenses of the expedition and supplied artillery and an auxiliary force for it. But not one of the conquered forts was given to him, not one pice of his contribution was repaid out of the fabulous booty carried away by Shiva from that land of gold. And now the Maratha plot to capture Bijapur by treachery destroyed the last trace of patience in the Golkonda king, especially as he had been playing for some years past the flattering role of a chivalrous friend and protector of the boy Adil Shah. So, Abul Hasan arranged for a peace between the new Bijapuri regent, Siddi Masaud, and his rivals (especially Sharza Khan), promised him money to pacify the unpaid mutinous soldiery, and bound him to wage war against Shiva and "confine him to Konkan." The Adil-Shahi nobles prepared to open the campaign in October next, with about 25,000 cavalry and numerous infantry. But Dilir Khan spoiled the whole plan. (O. C. 4266; *F. R.* Surat 107, Rajapur to Surat, 3 April, 1678; G. Robinson to Surat, 31 Aug.)

Dilir Khan had exacted heavy and humiliating concessions from Siddi Masaud when he made peace with him at Kulbarga (Nov. 1677.) The odium of that treaty fell on the new regent, and all the disorders in the State and all the sufferings of the people were laid at his door. Distracted by domestic factions, daily insulted and threatened by the Afghan soldiers, and hopeless of preventing Shiva's boundless violence and encroachments with the resources of the ruined, divided and bankrupt State, Siddi Masaud wanted to come to terms with Shivaji, but Dilir Khan forbade it, assuring him that the imperial army was ready to help him in fighting the Marathas Masaud was, however, too bewildered by the disturbances in all parts of the country to listen to this advice. He wrote to Shiva, "We are neighbours We eat the same salt. You are as deeply concerned in [the welfare of] this State as I am The enemy [*i e*, Mughals] are day and night trying to ruin it We two ought to unite and expel the foreigner." [*B. S.* 452-470]

§5 *Shambhuji deserts to the Mughals.*

At the news of these negotiations, Dilir Khan grew angry and set himself to conquer Bijapur. Only respect for treaties had kept him from doing so before; but Masaud's breach of faith absolved him from the obligation to spare Adil Shah And he now received a most unexpected accession of strength Shivaji's eldest son Shambhuji was the curse of his old age. This youth of twenty-one was violent, capricious, unsteady, thoughtless and notoriously depraved in his morals. For his outrage on a married Brahman woman he had been confined in Panhala fort, but escaped with his wife Yesu Bai and a few comrades to join Dilir Khan (13th Dec, 1678.) Shivaji sent a force in pursuit, but was too late. Dilir Khan, on getting Shambhuji's letter, had detached from his camp at Bahadurgarh 4,000 men under Ikhlas Khan (the commander of his vanguard) and Ghairat Khan (his nephew) to advance and escort the fugitive They met him 8 miles south of Supa, and Dilir himself joined them at Karkamb, 12 miles further north-east. Dilir Khan was thrown into transports of joy by the desertion of Shivaji's heir to his side. "He felt as happy as if he had conquered the whole Deccan!" (*B. S.* 471.) "He beat his drums in ecstasy and sent a report to the Emperor. Shambhu was created a 7-hazari and a Rajah and presented with an elephant." The Khan with his valuable new ally halted at Akluj (50 miles south of Bahadurgarh) for some time to prepare for the invasion of Bijapur. [*Dil.* 159.]

§6. *Maratha plot to seize Bijapur.*

In this danger Siddi Masaud immediately asked for help from Shiva, as agreed upon. The Rajah sent six to seven thousand heavy cavalry to guard Bijapur. Masaud could not fully trust his ally, he asked the Maratha contingent to halt beside the stream of the village Itangihal (5 m. n. w. of the city), but they came nearer, encamped at Khanapura and Khusraupura, and demanded that one of the gates and one of the towers of the fort should be entrusted to them. Masaud wisely declined. Then they moved to Zuhrapura and encamped on the plain just outside the walls, thus increasing Masaud's suspicion. Soon the allies began to quarrel openly.* The Marathas were detected in trying to smuggle arms and men into the fort, by concealing the arms in sacks of grain and disguising the soldiers as drivers of the pack-oxen! Then Shiva threw off the mask. He began to plunder and devastate Adil-Shahi territory again. His men looted the suburbs of Bijapur,—Daulatpura (=Khawaspura), Khusraupura and Zuhrapura, and carried off the rich *banias* for ransom. Near the tomb of Shaikh Ahmad Khawas-Khani, they

* "It is reported that Shivaji has in person plundered Shahpur, the suburbs of Bijapur, and had liked to have got into the royal city, the conquest whereof is his sole aim, lest it should fall into the Mughal's hands, and then he knows he could not long subsist" (Bombay to Surat, 4 April 1679, in *Orme MSS* 116)

slew Ali Raza and wounded Siddi Yaqut. But when they reached the tomb of Ibrahim Adil Shah, west of the city, a shot from the fort-guns killed the Maratha commander and the men fled away. Masaud now made peace with Dilir Khan

A Mughal force was invited to Bijapur, royally welcomed, and sent off with a Bijapuri army under Venkatadri Murari (the confidant of the regent) and other officers, against the Marathas. They reached Tikota (13 miles w. of Bijapur), when spies brought the report that Shiva himself had arrived at Selgur (55 miles w. of Bijapur and the same distance east of Panhala) with 7 to 8 thousand men and wanted to make a night-attack on the Mughal or the Bijapuri army, whichever would advance first But a new quarrel between Masaud and Sharza Khan now paralyzed the power of Bijapur. (*B. S.* 471—477)

§7. *Dilir captures Bhupalgarh.*

Dilir Khan next marched to the fort of Bhupalgarh,* which Shivaji had built as a store-house of his property and a refuge for the families of his subjects in that neighbourhood during his wars with the Mughals. By great labour the imperialists dragged some guns to the top of a neighbouring height during the night, and next morning began to batter the walls and towers. The assault was launched about 9 A M. and the Mughals fought with

* Shambhuji's desertion to the Mughals and capture of Bhupalgarh *Jedhe S* , *B S* 471, 477-478, 500-501 (best) *Dil* 159-163 (reliable) *F R* Surat, Vol 108, Rajapur to Surat, 16 Dec , 1679, Bombay to Surat, 1 Jan , 1680 (return) Sabh 93-94 Bhupalgarh, 20 m n w of Jath 45 m s w. of Pandharpur, and 10 m s e of Khanapur in the Satara district, the modern name of the village is *Banur* (*Atlas,* 40 N E), described in *Bom. Gaz* xix 455-456

vigour till noon, when they captured the fort after heavy slaughter on both sides. Vast quantities of grain and other property and large numbers of people (who had sought refuge there from the neighbouring districts) were captured by the victors. Seven hundred survivors of the garrison were deprived of one hand and then set free; the other captives were evidently sold into slavery.

Before this Shivaji had sent 16,000 horse to relieve the fort. They arrived too late, but hovered on the four sides of the Mughals. Suddenly they learnt that Iraj Khan and Bajaji Rao [Nimbalkar] were bringing provisions from Parenda to the besieging army, and then they immediately hastened to intercept the convoy. But Dilir Khan detached Ikhlas Khan with 1,500 cavalry to the aid of Iraj Khan. Twelve miles from Bhupalgarh he overtook the Marathas. Ikhlas Khan's small force was enveloped and he took refuge in a walled village and repelled the Maratha assault with his back to the wall, doing great havoc among the enemy with his artillery, and slaying nearly one thousand of Shiva's men. Then large reinforcements arrived from Dilir Khan, at whose approach the Marathas fled. Dilir then went back to Bhupalgarh, burnt everything that he could not carry off, dismantled its fortifications, and returned to Dhulkhed. (*B. S.* 477—478; *Dil.* 160.)

The fugitive Marathas, however, scored a success. Near Karkamb (30 miles south of Parenda), they fell in with Iraj Khan, looted all his grain and the property of his troops, and forced him to flee with a few men into a small fort hard by, where he was afterwards relieved by his kinsman, Mir Muhammad Khan, the *qiladar* of Parenda. (*Dil.* 161.)

The fall of Bhupalgarh took place on 2nd April, 1679. Then followed a period of puzzling intrigue and counter-intrigue between the Mughal viceroy and the Bijapur nobility, and also quarrels between Masaud and Sharza Khan, Masaud and Dilir, and Masaud and his favourite Venkatadri About the middle of this year Shivaji sent to Aurangzib a well-reasoned and spirited letter of protest against the *jaziya*, which was drafted by Nila Prabhu in eloquent Persian

§8. *Shivaji's letter on religious toleration.*

To the Emperor Alamgir—

"This firm and constant well-wisher Shivaji, after rendering thanks for the grace of God and the favours of the Emperor,—which are clearer than the Sun,—begs to inform your Majesty that, although this well-wisher was led by his adverse Fate to come away from your august Presence without taking leave, yet he is ever ready to perform, to the fullest extent possible and proper, everything that duty as a servant and gratitude demand of him ..

"It has recently come to my ears that, on the ground of the war with me having exhausted your wealth and emptied your treasury, your Majesty has ordered that money under the name of *jaziya* should be collected from the Hindus and the imperial needs supplied with it. May it please your Majesty! That architect of the fabric of empire, [Jalal-ud-din] Akbar Padishah, reigned with full power for 52 [lunar] years. He adopted the admirable policy of universal harmony (*sulh-i-kul*) in relation to all the various sects, such as Christians, Jews, Muslims, Dadu's followers, sky-worshippers (*falakia*), *malakia*, materialists (*ansaria*), atheists (*daharia*),

Brahmans and Jain priests. The aim of his liberal heart was to cherish and protect all the people. So, he became famous under the title of *Jagat Guru,* 'the World's spiritual guide.'

"Next, the Emperor Nur-ud-din Jahangir for 22 years spread his gracious shade on the head of the world and its dwellers, gave his heart to his friends and his hand to his work, and gained his desires. The Emperor Shah Jahan for 32 years cast his blessed shade on the head of the world and gathered the fruit of eternal life,—which is only a synonym for goodness and fair fame,—as the result of his happy time on earth. (*Verses*)

> He who lives with a good name gains ever-lasting weath,
> Because after his death, the recital of his good deeds keeps his name alive.

"Through the auspicious effect of this sublime disposition, wherever he [Akbar] bent the glance of his august wish, Victory and Success advanced to welcome him on the way. In his reign many kingdoms and forts were conquered [by him.] The state and power of these Emperors can be easily understood from the fact that Alamgir Padishah has failed and become distracted in the attempt to merely follow their political system. They, too, had the power of levying the *jazıya;* but they did not give place to bigotry in their hearts, as they considered all men, high and low, created by God to be [living] examples of the nature of diverse creeds and temperaments Their kindness and benevolence endure on the pages of Time as their memorial, and so prayer and praise for these [three] pure souls will dwell for ever in the hearts and tongues of mankind, among both great and small. Prosperity is the fruit of one's intentions. Therefore, their wealth and good fortune continued to increase, as God's creatures reposed in the cradle of peace and safety [under their rule], and their undertakings succeeded

"But in *your* Majesty's reign, many of the forts and provinces have gone out of your possession, and the rest will soon do so too, because there will be no slackness on my part in ruining and devastating them. Your peasants are down-trodden; the yield of every village has declined,—in the place of one lakh [of Rupees] only one thousand, and in the place of a thousand only ten are collected, and that too with difficulty. When Poverty and Beggary have made their homes in the palaces of the Emperor and the Princes, the condition of the grandees and officers can be easily imagined. It is a reign in which the army is in a ferment, the merchants complain, the Muslims cry, the Hindus are grilled, most men lack bread at night and in the day inflame their own cheeks by slapping them [in anguish.] How can the royal spirit permit you to add the hardship of the *jaziya* to this grievous state of things? The infamy will quickly spread from west to east and become recorded in books of history that the Emperor of Hindusthan, coveting the beggars' bowls, takes *jaziya* from Brahmans and Jain monks, *yogis, sannyasis, bairagis,* paupers, mendicants, ruined wretches, and the famine-stricken,—that his valour is shown by attacks on the wallets of beggars,—that he dashes down to the ground the name and honour of the Timurids!

"May it please your Majesty! If you believe in the true Divine Book and Word of God (*i e.,* the *Quran*), you will find there [that God is styled] *Rabb-ul-alamin,* the Lord of all men, and not *Rabb-ul-musalmin,* the Lord of the Muhammadans only. Verily, Islam and Hinduism are terms of contrast. They are [diverse pigments] used by the true Divine Painter for blending the colours and filling in the outlines [of His picture of the entire human species.] If it be a mosque, the call to prayer is chanted in remembrance of Him. If it be a temple, the bell is rung in yearning for Him only. To show bigotry for any man's own creed and practices is equivalent to altering the words of the Holy Book. To draw new lines on a picture is equivalent to finding fault with the painter.........

"In strict justice the *jaziya* is not at all lawful. From the political point of view it can be allowable only if a beautiful woman wearing gold ornaments can pass from one province to another without fear or molestation. [But] in these days even the cities are being plundered, what shall I say of the open country? Apart from its injustice, this imposition of the *jaziya* is an innovation in India and inexpedient.

"If you imagine piety to consist in oppressing the people and terrorizing the Hindus, you ought first to levy the *jaziya* from Rana Raj Singh, who is the head of the Hindus. Then it will not be so very difficult to collect it from me, as I am at your service. But to oppress ants and flies is far from displaying valour and spirit.

"I wonder at the strange fidelity of your officers that they neglect to tell you of the true state of things, but cover a blazing fire with straw! May the Sun of your royalty continue to shine above the horizon of greatness!" [*History of Aurangzib,* iii. Ch. 34 App.]

§9. *Dilir invades Bijapur. Shivaji aids Adil Shah*

On 18th August, 1679, Dilir crossed the Bhima at Dhulkhed, 40 m due north of Bijapur, and opened a new campaign against Masaud. That helpless regent begged aid from Shivaji, sending to him an envoy named Hindu Rao charged with this piteous appeal. "The condition of this royalty is not hidden from you. There is no army, money, or ally for defending the fort and no provision at all. The enemy is strong and ever bent on war. You are a hereditary servant, elevated by this Court And, therefore, you will feel for this house more than others can. We cannot defend the kingdom and its forts without your aid Be true to your salt, turn towards us. Command what you consider proper, and it shall be done by us" (*B S*. 493)

Shiva undertook the defence of Bijapur,* ordered 10,000 of his cavalry to reinforce Masaud, sent from his forts 2,000 ox-loads of provisions to the city, and bade his subjects send grain and other necessaries to Bijapur for sale, so that the citizens and soldiers there might not suffer from scarcity. His envoy Visaji Nilkanth brought to Masaud his cheering message, "You hold the fort. I shall go out and punish Dilir Khan as he deserves." Visaji reported to the regent that 5,000 Maratha troopers had reached Ainapur (20 m. s. e. of Miraj) and 5,000 others Bhupalgarh, waiting for his call to come, when needed

The Mughal general Sujan Singh took Mangalvide from Shiva's men about September (*M.A.* 182), and came

* Shivaji as the ally of Bijapur in 1679 *B S* 493-497, 504, Sabh (silent) *F R* Fort St George, Vol 28, p 34, Vira Raghav from Golkonda to Madras, 14 January, 1680, (Qutb Shah deterred by Mughal envoy from sending an army to aid Bijapur, but sends money secretly to Shivaji to enlist troops for the defence)

nearer to Bijapur. Masaud conciliated Sabaji Ghatge and sent him with the army of Turgal to Indi (28 m. n. of Bijapur.) This detachment had a skirmish with Shambhuji who was out foraging, about fifteen men were slain on each side; Sabaji was wounded, but he captured 50 horses, 50 oxen, and 4 camels from the enemy. Shivaji's envoy now reached Bijapur with Anand Rao at the head of 2,500 horse. They were welcomed by Masaud and stationed in the Nauraspura suburb. Bajaji [Nimbalkar], now in Mughal service, laid siege to the fort of Akluj, but a Bijapuri general named Bahadur marched up from Sangula (32 m. s.) and drove him away.

But on 15th September, Dilir Khan left his camp at Dhulkhed and came very close to Bijapur, reaching Baratgi, 6 m. n. e. of the city, on 7th October. Here he halted and held palavers with Masaud's envoys. On 30th October Shivaji arrived at Selgur, midway between Panhala and Bijapur, with 10,000 cavalry. His first detachment left Nauraspura next day to welcome him there. Shiva wanted to visit Adil Shah; Masaud permitted him to come with an escort of 500 men only. But the Peshwa Moro Trimbak dissuaded Shivaji from falling into the power of Masaud by entering the fort.

So, on 4th November, 1679, the Maratha king divided his army into two bodies: he himself with 8 or 9 thousand troopers started by the road of Muslah and Almala, and Anand Rao with 10,000 cavalry by way of Man[a] and Sangula, to raid the Mughal dominions and divert Dilir from the environs of Bijapur But Dilir Khan, to whom the capture of Bijapur seemed easy, paid

[a] The river Man flows a little to the south of Sangula (20 m s of Pandharpur) Is *Mān* a copyist's error for Jât (town)?

no heed to the Maratha plunder and devastation of those provinces, which was a familiar annual evil, and hoped for the highest rewards from the expected conquest of the Adil-Shahi capital. So, he pressed his attack on it, without retreating. [*B S.* 493—'95.]

§10 *Dilir's ravages. Return of Shambhuji.*

But his siege of Bijapur was a failure. After vainly trying to make peace with Masaud, he left the environs of the city on 14th November and marched westwards, intending to invade the Miraj-Panhala region and create a diversion there, which would quickly recall Shiva home The scheme seemed promising, as Shambhuji bragged of his ability to capture forts quickly with his Maratha followers and thus make the progress of the imperialists easy, while the petty chiefs (*nayak-wars*) of Miraj had been already won over by a Mughal agent.

But his first work was to ravage the Bijapuri territory with insane cruelty. By way of Bahmanhali, Maknapur, and Jalgeri, he reached Tikota (13 m. w. of Bijapur), a rich and populous village, where the wealthy men of the neighbourhood had taken refuge with their families. "The Mughals were utterly unexpected When Ikhlas Khan with [Dilir's] vanguard arrived there and began to plunder it, the wives of the Hindus and Muslims with their children jumped into the wells near their houses and committed suicide. The village was utterly sacked. Nearly 3,000 men, both Hindus and Muslims, were taken prisoner [for being sold into slavery] .. Leaving Tikota on 18th November, by way of Honvad and Telsang, ravaging the country and carrying off the people as slaves, the imperialists reached Athni (43 m w. of Bijapur.)" Here, according to the English factory records, a breach took place between the Mughal general and his Maratha ally. Athni, "a considerable mart," was burnt down and Dilir proposed to sell the inhabitants who were all Hindus. Shambhuji objected to it, but was overruled, and began to grow sick of his associates. (*F. R.* Surat 108, Bomb. to Surat, 1 Jan., 1680.) On 21st November, Dilir left Athni for Ainapur, 12 miles westwards, but learnt on the way that Shambhuji had fled away to Bijapur.

Since his coming over to the Mughals in December 1678, Shambhuji had been constantly approached by Shivaji's agents with all sorts of persuasions and promises to return to his father Even Mahadji Nimbalkar, his brother-in-law, though now a Mughal servant, censured him for his act of desertion. (Shambhu reported the matter to Dilir, who put Mahadji in confinement for some days. *Dil.* 160.) But by this time Shambhuji had made up his mind to leave the Mughals.* In the night of 20th November he slipped out of the camp with his wife Yesu Bai disguised in male attire and only 10 troopers for escort, rode hard to Bijapur in the course of the next day and was warmly received by Masaud. Dilir, on learning of Shambhu's flight on the 21st, promptly returned towards Bijapur and sent an agent, Khwajah Abdur Razzaq, to that city to bribe the regent to capture the Maratha prince (28th.) In the night of the 30th, Shambhuji, getting scent of the matter, issued in secret from Bijapur, met a body of cavalry sent by his father to escort him, and galloped away to Panhala,

* According to Sabhasad, 93, Aurangzib wrote to Dilir to arrest Shambhu and send him a prisoner to Delhi, but the Mughal general, to keep his word to his guest, informed the Maratha prince of the letter and connived at his flight Unlikely story *B S* 501 says that Aurangzib summoned Shambhu to his Court.

which he reached about the 4th of December (B S. 501) '

§11. *Last campaign of Shivaji*

We shall now trace the history of Shivaji's movements from 4th November, 1679, when he marched out of Selgur (55 m w of Bijapur) The Maratha cavalry, 18,000 strong, rapidly moved northwards in two parallel divisions under Shivaji and Anand Rao, and poured like a flood through the districts of Mughal Deccan, plundering and burning all the places in their track and taking an immense booty in cash and kind In the middle of the month, Jalna, a populous trading town, 40 miles east of Aurangabad, was captured and plundered.

Here the godly saint, Sayyid Jan Muhammad, had his hermitage in a garden in the suburbs As Shivaji in his raids always spared the holy men and holy places of all religions, most of the wealthy men of Jalna had taken refuge in this hermitage with their money and jewels. The raiders, finding very little booty in the town and learning of the concealment of the wealth in the saint's abode, entered it and robbed the refugees, wounding many of them The holy man appealed to them to desist, but they only abused and threatened him for his pains (K K ii 271 ; *Dil* 165 ; *T. S.* 39*a*) Then the man of God, "who had marvellous efficacy of prayer," cursed Shiva, and popular belief ascribed the Rajah's death five months afterwards to these curses.

Retribution visited the Maratha army very much sooner. Jalna, both town and suburb, was thoroughly plundered and devastated for four days Then as the Marathas, loaded with booty consisting of "countless gold, silver, jewels, cloths, horses, elephants and camels," were retreating, an enterprising Mughal officer, Ranmast Khan,* attacked their rear-guard. Shidhoji Nimbalkar with 5,000 men held him in check for three days, but was at last slain with many of his men. In the meantime, very large reinforcements were hastening up to the Mughals from Aurangabad, close at hand, under Kesari Singh and Sardar Khan. When these came to a halt six miles from the fighters, Kesari Singh sent a secret message to Shiva as a brother Hindu, to run away at once before the Mughals could complete their circle and cut him off. Shivaji trusted to his chief spy, Bahirji, under whose skilful guidance the Maratha army escaped by an obscure path after three days and nights of anxious and ceaseless marching. But they had to sacrifice much of their booty, besides losing 4,000 horsemen killed and Anand Rao wounded.

From this disastrous expedition, Shivaji returned to Patta-garh† (about 22nd November) and rested his

* Ranmast Khan, brother of Khizr Khan Pani, received a robe of honour from the Emperor on 18th September, 1682, and was created Bahadur Khan in August next (*M. A.* 222, 235.) *T. S.* speaks of him as thanahdar or qiladar of Jalna at this time. We afterwards meet him as thanahdar of Akluj (*Dil.*)

† Patta, 20 m. s. of Nasik and the same distance east of Thal Ghat (*Ind. Atlas*, Old sheet 38), 19 42 N. 73 54 E. The fort was renamed Vishram-garh or the Castle of Rest. Bombay writes (29 Nov.) that he "fled here with 500 horse, having lost the greatest part of his army near Bijapur, where Dilir Khan wholly routed him, and took 2000 horses besides prisoners." [*F. R.* Surat 108.) Here the place of battle and the Mughal general are incorrectly named. Rajapur (30 Dec.) puts the loss at "above 4,000 horse," and the commander *Hummedbough* [=Anand Rao, rather than Hambir Rao] himself very much wounded. The above Bombay letter adds: 'The Peshwa was intended for Surat, but the overthrow he received by one Ranmast Khan, who killed him 2000 men and took 400 horse, which diverted him." But the rumour that reached Bombay evidently confounded the campaigns of Shivaji and his Peshwa together, and Surat wrote on 13 Dec., "The advice you (*i. e.*, Bombay) gave us of Shivaji and his Peshwa being routed by the king's army in two several encounters is here quite contrary reported." Sabh. 92-93, *J. S.*, *T. S.* 39*b*, Malkaré 87, all ascribe

exhausted and stricken army for some days, and then, at the beginning of December, went to Raigarh, where he seems to have passed the whole of that month.

As Dilir Khan was advancing westwards from Bijapur (middle of November) and seemed intent on laying siege to Panhala, and the presence of Shambhuji in the enemy's camp threatened a civil war in the Maratha State, Shivaji tried to convert Panhala into an impregnable refuge by removing to it the guns of many of his other forts, besides 40 pieces bought from the French. As early as 24th November he had sent Somaji, the brother of Annaji Datto, to remove about 30 pieces of cannon from the forts of Ankola, Karwar, Someshwar, and Phonda, and drag them to Panhala "by the strength of men and buffaloes." (*F. R.* Surat 108, Rajapur to Surat, 30 Dec., Karwar to Surat, 24 Nov., 1679.)

Towards the close of November, a fresh Maratha army of 12,000 men assembled near Rajapur in South Konkan. They fired the town (26th) and set out (on the 28th) for Burhanpur, but abandoned the idea and turned off towards Malkapur, where Shivaji himself was reported to have arranged to meet them with 20,000 more cavalry. Evidently, he did not do so, and the Maratha division that raided Khandesh, in the last week of November, "burning and plundering Dharangaon, Chopra, and many other considerable towns adjacent", was led by one of his generals. [*F. R.* Surat 108, Rajapur to Surat, 6 Dec., Vol. 4, Surat Consult. 8 Dec. 1679.]

---

the victory over Shivaji to Ranmast Khan. No encounter took place between Dilir and the Marathas near Bijapur from Nov. 1679 to Shiva's death, as *B. S.* clearly shows.

§12. *Domestic troubles of Shivaji.*

Early in December, Shivaji was greatly relieved by the news that his rebel son Shambhuji had left the Mughals and come back to Panhala (about 4th Dec.) Here Shivaji arrived at the end of the month, to meet the returned prodigal and try to reform him by persuasion.

The recent rebellion of Shambhuji had revealed the serious danger that threatened the newly founded Maratha kingdom. The character of his eldest son filled Shiva with the gloomiest anticipations of the future. A profligate, capricious and cruel youth, devoid of every spark of honour, patriotism or religious fervour, could not be left sole master of Maharashtra. And yet, the only alternative to Shambhu was Rajaram, a boy of 10, whose accession would have meant a regency. But there was such mutual jealousy and discord among the old ministers of the State, especially between Moro Trimbak, the premier, and Annaji Datto, the viceroy of the West, that a council of regency would have broken up in civil war and the ruin of the State as surely as the Puna council of ministers did a century later. A division of the kingdom between the two princes was proposed, Shambhuji taking Maharashtra and Rajaram the Karnat country beyond the Tungabhadra; but the plan was not given effect to. (Sabh. 94, 102.)

Shivaji tried hard to conciliate and reason with Shambhu. He appealed to all the nobler instincts of the prince as well as to his self-interest, read him many a lecture, showed him his treasury, revenue returns, list of forts and muster-rolls of troops and horses, and urged him to be worthy of such a splendid heritage and to be true to all the high hopes which his own reign had raised in the Hindu world. (Sabh. 94.) But a born judge of character like Shivaji must have soon perceived that his sermons were falling on deaf ears, and hence his last days were clouded by despair. (Sabh. 102-103.)

After December, 1679, Shivaji's health seems to have declined, and he seems to have had a premonition of the approach of death. (Sabh. 101) This fact made the choice of an heir a live issue, and the plots and counter-plots in his harem and cabinet thickened in consequence.

§13. *Death of Shivaji.*

On 23rd March, 1680, the Rajah was seized with fever and blood dysentery. The illness continued for twelve days. Gradually all hopes of recovery faded away, and then, after giving solemn charges and wise counsels to his nobles and officers, and consoling the weeping assemblage with assurances of the spirit's immortality in spite of the perishableness of the body, the maker of the Maratha nation performed the last rites of his religion and then fell into a trance, which imperceptibly passed into death. It was the noon of Sunday, 4th April, 1680, the full moon of the month of Chaitra.*

He had not yet completed the 53rd year of his age. The Muslim world ascribed his premature death to the curse of the saint Sayyid Jan Muhammad of Jalna. In

* Last illness and death of Shivaji Sabh 101-104, *F R* Surat 108, Bombay to Surat, 28 April, 1680 (followed by me), *M A* 194, *Dil* 165 (one sentence only), K K ii 271 (one sentence), *Storia,* ii 231 *T S* 40b (one sentence), and *Dig* 462-467 are "loose, traditional works" and charge Soyra Bai with murder Orme's story (*Frag* 89) has been rejected by me, (*Ind Hist Quarterly,* iv 605) In 1680 the Chaitra full moon extended over both 3rd and 4th April (Sat and Sunday) I follow Sabhasad who gives Sunday, which agrees with the English *F R*

Maharashtra there were some whispers of his wife Soyra Bai, the mother of Rajaram, having administered poison to him to prevent his giving the throne to Shambhuji.

The oldest Marathi *bakhar*, that of Sabhasad, is silent on the point, and with good reason. A servant of Rajaram, in a book written by order of that king and for his eyes, could not possibly have mentioned his mother's murder of her husband even if it had been true. Shambhuji on his accession put Soyra Bai to death on the charge of her having poisoned her husband, but it was in all probability a false pretext for wreaking vengeance on his step-mother for her late attempt to crown her own son. Readers of Macaulay's account of the death of Charles II. will remember how at that very time in Europe hardly a sovereign died without the event being ascribed to poison.

It is true that throughout life Shivaji (like all other Eastern sovereigns) was on his guard against being poisoned. We find him, during the Karnatak expedition, repeatedly writing to the English to send him Maldive cocoanuts, bezoar stone and other "good counter-poisons" (*i.e.*, antidotes), offering even to pay for them. But it merely indicated common precaution. (For the use of the bezoar stone as an antidote to poisons, see Irvine's *Storia do Mogor.*)

APPENDIX

SHIVAJI'S WIVES AND CHILDREN.

Wives —1 Sai Bai (*nee* Nimbalkar), died 5 Sep 1659 [*Jedhe S*], mother of Shambhuji (born 14 May 1657)

2 Soyrā Bai (*nee* Shirké), put to death by Shambhuji in 1680, mother of Rajaram (born 24 Feb 1670)

3 Putlā Bai (*nee* Mohité), burnt herself with Shivaji's corpse, 1680

4 Sākwār Bai (*nee* Gaikwad), married January 1656 [*Jedhe S*], remained a captive in the hands of the Mughals for many years after the fall of Raigarh in 1689

5 One wife who died about 1st March 1674, [according to the letter of Narayan Shenvi from Raigarh, dated 4th April]

6 & 7 Two wives, married just before the coronation, [according to Oxinden's *Letter* from Rairi, dated 27 May],—"married on 30th May 1674 with Vedic *mantras*" [acc to *Jedhe S*, which does not mention how many ladies were married on that day]

8 One wife, married on 8th June 1674 [Acc to Oxinden's *Narrative* at Rairi, under date 8th June, "The Rajah was married to a fourth wife without any state or ceremony"]

The first four wives are mentioned by nearly all the sources *Jedhe S* records that (*a*) Jadav Rao's daughter and (*b*) Ingle's daughter were married on 8th April and 15th April 1657 respectively, without naming the bridegroom! Sabhasad, p 72, says that Shivaji had seven wives For other views, Rajwade *Sankirna Lekh Sangraha*

Children —1 Shambhuji 2 Rajaram 3 Sakhu Bai, mar to Bajaji Nimbalkar (son of Mahadji) 4 Ambika Bai, mar to Harji Mahadik 5 Raj Kumari Bai, mar to Ganoji Raj Shirké

CHAPTER XIV

SHIVAJI'S RELATIONS WITH THE ENGLISH AND THE PORTUGUESE

§1. *Shivaji's first encounter with the English, 1660.*

Early in January 1660, Shivaji's general Doroji seized the port of Rajapur, in pursuit of three junks of Afzal Khan in which Afzal's agent at Dabhol had fled there with his own and his master's property, on the capture of the latter place by the Marathas (Ch. 10.) From this incident sprang the first collision between the English and the Marathas, but its real cause was not any hindrance offered by Shivaji to the legitimate trade of the East India Company or its servants. It was solely due to the greed and crooked dealing of Mr. Henry Revington, the Chief of the Company's Rajapur factory. An Indian broker employed by him had lent some money to Rustam-i-Zaman and taken a bill for it, falsely in the Company's name as creditor. When Rustam's governor of Rajapur was trying to run away from the invaders in one of the Dabhol junks, the broker influenced Mr. Revington to assist him in getting his money back. Mr. Revington sent an English ship, the *Diamond,* to stop the junk occupied by the governor and make him pay what he falsely represented as "monies due to the Company." A part of the amount was immediately paid in goods. But just then Shivaji's horsemen appeared on the bank to seize the junks of Afzal Khan and called upon the English to give up the one in which the governor was. The English declined, and the governor gladly seized this device for escaping capture by the Marathas and urged the English "to take possession of two of these junks and own them." Mr. Revington took one of the vessels over, renamed it the *Rajapur Merchant*, and placed it under an English captain

In a parley with Doroji, the Maratha general, the English refused to give up the goods in the junk unless he gave them an order on the revenue of the town for the money claimed by them. The largest junk, which had not been taken over by the English, weighed anchor and fell down the creek to beyond the range of the Maratha guns, after firing on Shiva's men on both banks. At this disappointment, the Marathas seized the English broker Balji at Jaitapur (at the mouth of the creek, 11 miles west of Rajapur), on the ground that "the English would not take the junk for them, but let her go" (*Ibid;* also Surat Council to Company, 6 April 1660, *F. R.* Surat, Vol. 85.)

Mr. Philip Gyffard was sent to the Maratha camp to demand the release of the broker, but they seized him too, and carried away the two prisoners to Kharepatan fort that night, threatening to detain them unless the English captured the junks for the Marathas and delivered to them the goods they had taken on the governor's junk (18th January 1660)

On 13th February, Revington wrote a letter to Shivaji promising him the friendly help of the English in an attack on Danda-Rajpuri, and soliciting an order for the release of the two captives as they had been seized only because the English "would not take the junks lying in Rajapur river and be enemies to those who are our friends" But before this the broker had already appealed to Shivaji and Rustam-i-Zaman, and orders had come from them for the release of the two. Balji was immediately set free, "but Mr. Gyffard was kept by a rogue Brahman in Kharepatan castle, out of the lucre and expectation of a bribe." Mr. Revington protested against it to Shiva and Rustam. (Rajapur to Surat, 15 February 1660)

Before any reply could come from Shivaji, Mr Revington, learning that the Maratha governor of Kharepatan was sending Mr. Gyffard away to Satavli (9 miles north-west of Rajapur) or to Khelna fort, despatched a party of 30 soldiers, who waylaid the Maratha escort in a town 10 miles from Rajapur and rescued Mr. Gyffard by force. (*Ibid*, 23 February.)

§2. *English factors of Rajapur prisoners of Shivaji, 1661-1663.*

The second Maratha attack on the English took place at the beginning of March next, and here again the Englishmen were clearly in the wrong, though the Company's official attitude was correct and neutral.

In 1660, while Siddi Jauhar, acting on behalf of the Bijapur Government, was investing Shivaji in Panhala fort, the English factors of Rajapur supplied him with some grenades "which (the vendors promised) undoubtedly will be the chiefest disturbers of the besieged." Some Englishmen of Rajapur were also bribed to go to the Bijapuri camp outside Panhala and help in the bombardment of the fort, by 'tossing balls with a flag that was known to be the English's." (Ch. 4.)

Shivaji punished this act of hostility about 3rd March 1661, when he surprised Rajapur, plundered the English factory, and carried off four of the factors,—Henry Revington, Richard Taylor, Randolph Taylor, and Philip Gyffard,—as prisoners.

A graphic account of this second sack of Rajapur is given by the Dutch Chief at Vingurla: "Shivaji sent 1,000 horse and about 3,000 foot soldiers to take possession of Rajapur. This force, on reaching the town, invited the principal inhabitants to come out and escort it in, according to custom, promising to do no harm. These simple men, suspecting no evil, went to the place of meeting, accompanied by the English President Revington, with two or three other Englishmen, who thought it well to pay this mark of respect. They were all immediately seized and their property confiscated, after tortures had been inflicted. Revington and those who accompanied him were placed in one of Shivaji's fortresses . . The factory was entirely stripped, even the floor being dug up in search of hidden treasure. The robbers also plundered many foreign merchants, who yearly bring goods to Rajapur from Persia and Muskat."*

While the English prisoners were still at Rajapur, the Brahman agent of Shivaji told them that his master would give them a fine salt port (*mit bandar*) on the coast, if they helped him in taking Danda-Rajpuri, but they declined to "discourse about it" unless he set them free. Then Shivaji laid a ransom on the captives, and sent them to Waisati fort. Many other persons—Hindu merchants (*banians*), Indian Muslims, Persians and Arabs—were

---

* *Batavia Dagh Register*, 1661, p. 215, quoted in Foster, xi 4-5. The date given is "about the middle of March" [New style], which was equivalent to "about the 5th of March" in the Old style followed in this book. The English report has been lost.

The Dutch statement, that "the Englishmen who had remained behind in Rajapur were likewise imprisoned and one died under torture," was based on false rumour, as only three factors besides Revington were carried off into captivity, and the factor who died at Rajapur, evidently Richard Napier, had been reported on the 16th February before as "dangerously ill and not expected to live" (*F. R.*, Rajapur to Company.)

kept there in his prison in a miserable plight and beaten to extort ransom.

The Englishmen steadily refused to pay any ransom and tried to secure their liberty by feigned negotiations for helping the Marathas with English ships in capturing Danda-Rajpuri, but taking care to impose such terms as always left the English "a hole to creep out of their obligation" after recovering liberty. Then they tried the effect of threat by saying that if they were not released their countrymen at Surat would grant Aurangzib's desire by transporting a Mughal army into the Deccan [*i.e.*, the Konkan district] by sea. (*Orme MSS.*, Vol. 155, pp. 1-21, letter from the English prisoners at Songarh, 10th June 1661.)

Raoji Pandit had been sent by Shivaji to take charge of all the prisoners in Songarh and "do with them as he thought fit." The four Englishmen were well-treated. But their captivity was prolonged past endurance. To the demand for ransom they replied that they could pay nothing, having lost their all in the sack of Rajapur. Shivaji's absence on a projected expedition for recovering Kalian (June, 1661) also delayed the progress of the negotiations about an alliance with the English against the Siddis. The "disconsolate prisoners in Raigarh," after a year's confinement, lost their temper and wrote in disrespectful and abusive terms to the President and Council at Surat, charging the latter with making no exertion for their release. The reply of the Surat Council (on 10th March, 1662) was a stern but well-merited rebuke: "How you came in prison you know very well. 'Twas not for defending the Company's goods, 'twas for going to the siege of Panhala and tossing balls with a flag that was known to be the English's None but what [is] rehearsed is the cause of your imprisonment.*

It seems that the four Englishmen made an attempt to escape from Songarh, but were caught and sent off to Raigarh to be kept in "closer confinement" Towards the middle of 1662, when their captivity had lasted a year and a half, the Council at Surat, finding all appeals to Shivaji and his suzerain fruitless, commissioned some of the English ships to make reprisals by capturing on the high seas Deccani vessels, whether belonging to the king of Bijapur or Shivaji or any merchant of the country, especially the one bringing the Dowager Queen Bari Sahiba back from Mecca. They hoped that such a success would compel the Bijapur Government to put pressure on Shivaji to release the Englishmen. But no good prize offered itself to the English privateers. The Surat Council also influenced the Mughal governor of Surat to write to Shaista Khan, who was then reported to be pressing Shivaji hard (about November 1662), to importune him to move for their release.†

On 3rd February, 1663, the Council commissioned the captain of H M S *Convertite* to capture two vessels of considerable burden which Shivaji was fitting out at Jaitapur for Mocha and loading with "such goods as were driven by storms upon his coast, which was of considerable value." (*F. R.* Surat, Vol. 2.) But such a step became unnecessary, as Raoji Pandit, the Maratha governor of Rajapur, sent for the four captives from

---

* *Ibid*, also Surat to the Prisoners in Rairi castle, 10 March, 1662, *F R* Surat, Vol 85

† Surat to R Taylor, 17 May, 1662, 1662, *F R* Surat, Vol 85, Surat Consult, 21 July, *F R* Surat, Vol 2, also under 21st July, 19th August and 14th November in Vol 85

Raigarh and set them free (about 5th February) with a solemn assurance from Shivaji that the English would enjoy his protection in future. The Council at Surat say that they "had desisted from calling that perfidious rebel Shivaji to an account, because they had not either conveniency of force or time." They were still resolved to avenge the wrong done to their masters' property and the sufferings of their "loving brethren," but sadly realized that "as yet we are altogether uncapable for want of shipping and men necessary for such an enterprise, wherefore patience."*

Therefore, instead of resorting to force, they began negotiations with Shivaji for compensation for the loss done to their factory at Rajapur. These were protracted for many years till the hearts of the Englishmen grew sick. Even when Shivaji agreed as to the amount of the damages and admitted his liability for it, the actual payment was repeatedly put off and never fully carried out. With the help of the Factory Records preserved in the India Office, London, we can clearly trace the history of these negotiations through their successive stages,—the alternate hopes and disappointments of the English, their diverse tactics, their series of embassies, and their final conviction, at the close of Shivaji's life, that they would get nothing at all from him. The records of this long-drawn diplomatic intercourse afford striking examples of the perseverance and patience of the English traders, though one is apt to smile when he reads how they held diametrically opposite views of Shivaji's character and feelings at different stages of the

* F R Surat 103, Rajapur to Surat, 6 Feb , Vol 2, Surat to R Taylor, 9 Oct 1663

negotiations, as they hoped for or despaired of a settlement of their claims. Our psychology is naturally coloured by our emotions.

Shivaji's encounter with the English during his two raids on Surat (in 1664 and 1670) and the dispute between them in connection with his fortification of the Khanderi island have been dealt with in earlier chapters.

§3. *Negotiations for Rajapur factory damages*

The policy of the English traders is thus clearly set forth in a letter from the Deputy Governor and Council of Bombay to the President and Council of Surat, dated 25th November, 1668 ·

"According to your commands, we shall at convenient time enorder such as we employ to treat Shivaji's servants civilly wherever they meet them, but not to enter into any contract with them, letting them know the great damage the Hon'ble Company hath suffered and the abuses offered to our people on several occasions, for which we expect satisfaction and reparation before we enter into any league with their master,—all of which, we suppose, will come to his ears by one or more of his servants, though we are not of opinion that ever he will be brought to a peaceable treaty till he be forced to it" (*F. R.* Surat, Vol 105.)

In another letter, dated 17th March, 1669, the Bombay Council write, "Shivaji Rajah having by his servants requested a favour of no great import, not exceeding Rs. 300 we having much occasion for a good correspondence with his people on the main [-land] from whence most of provisions come hither, and wood [*i.e.*, fuel] in special, (which is not to be had other where), we were the more ready to gratify Shivaji Rajah." (*Ibid.*)

On 5th March, 1670, the Surat Council instruct Bombay thus. "The war broke out between Shivaji and the Mughal hath put a check to some overtures which were made to the President of an accommodation with Shivaji touching the Company's demands on him, but we hope they will yet go forward,.. but we would not have you appear too forward lest you undervalue our pretence [=lawful claim] and make him cool." (*F. R.* Surat, Vol. 3.)

In October Shivaji tried to put the English of Bombay in distress, evidently because they refused to sell him war-material (esp. lead) for his contest with the Siddi of Danda-Rajpuri. Bombay writes to Surat on 14th October, 1670: "A few days since we, as usually, sent our boats to the main [-land] for wood to burn our *chunam* with; but..... our boats returned empty, being forbid by Shivaji's people to cut any more wood in those parts." (*F. R.* Surat, 105.) On 12th August 1671 Bombay writes to Surat, "The Deputy Governor [of Bombay] received an answer from Shivaji,.. . by which your Honour, etc., will see how he slights our friendship." (*Ibid.*)

But in September 1671 Shivaji sent an ambassador to Bombay to treat with the English His chief motive was to secure English aid against Danda-Rajpuri, especially a supply of "grenadoes, mortar-pieces and ammunition." The Bombay Council immediately realized that unless he obtained these war-materials he "would not pay a penny" of compensation for the loot of their factory at Rajapur. The President of Surat sent the following instructions to the factors at Bombay: "Let him know that if he gives us such encouragement that we settle in his port, he may obtain from us those advantages that other nations do in whose ports we trade. But we would not positively have them [the English representatives in these negotiations] promise him those grenadoes, mortar-pieces and ammunition he desires, nor absolutely deny him, in regard we do not think it convenient to help him against Danda-Rajpuri, which place, if it were in his possession, would prove a great annoyance to the port of Bombay; and on the other side, our denial is not consistent at present with our interest, in respect we believe the keeping in suspense will bring him to a speedier conclusion of the treaty, hoping thereby to be furnished with those things he desires." (*F R.* Surat, 87.)

The negotiations, as might have been expected from the diverse aims of the two parties, could not possibly end in an agreement. They were protracted till December, when Shivaji was out on his forays and "now not easily to be found or treated with" The English proposed to send Lieut. Stephen Ustick to treat directly with him, (*F. R* Surat, 106, Bomb. to Surat, 8 Nov. and 15 Dec , 1671) This envoy was directed to "set out in a handsome equipage befitting the Company's honour," with Ram Shenvi, the Company's interpreter. (*F. R.* Surat, 87, Surat to Bombay, 30 Sep., 1671.)

As early as the end of November, the Council of Surat gave up all hope of a settlement. They wrote to Bombay (30th November, 1671), "Ram Shenvi hath private[-ly] discoursed with us [as to] what Shivaji proposes to us by way of accommodation and what he demands from us in order to the supply of his wars against Danda-Rajpuri, in both which we find so much subtility, self-policy and unsecure inconstancy on his part, and so great difficulties and apparent hazard on the Company's to deal with him on these terms, that we begin to despair of bringing the business to any issue in the way it is now carried . We do confirm our former resolution that till the matter of satisfaction for the Company's and nation's former losses be first determined, we cannot with honour or safety concede to any thing which he proposeth."

The instructions to Lieut. Ustick were "that he endeavour to end the dispute touching satisfaction of past damages. , as also to procure his [i.e., Shivaji's] general *qaul* or *farman* for us to trade with freedom and security in all the ports of his country and inland cities whatsoever, paying 2 per cent. custom." (*F. R.* Surat, 87)

The Maratha envoy had brought with himself to Bombay Rs 6,000 worth of the cloth looted at Surat in October 1670, consisting of *katanis, rumals,* etc., and asked the English to buy them; but "they being not commodities proper for the Hon'ble Company to deal in" the factors refused to buy them. (*F. R.* Surat, 87, Surat to Bombay, 1 January, 1672.) But as Shivaji had presumably no ready money to spare, the English were prepared to accept these goods in part payment of "what shall be agreed on to be due for satisfaction of our former losses, provided that the commodities were not over-rated, but cheap and good in their kind." (*Ibid,* 30 November, 1671.) A compromise was, however, made with the Maratha ambassador; the English lent him Rs. 1,500 upon his goods payable at two months' time. Lieut. Ustick was to have set out on his embassy on 15th January, 1672, but was detained at Bombay by a message from Shivaji saying that he was then too busy opposing the Mughal generals in Puna and Baglana to receive the envoy (*F. R.* Surat, 106, Bombay to Surat, 13 and 20 January, 1672.)

§4 *Mission of Lt Ustick to Shiva fails, 1672.*

At last Lieut. Ustick was sent on his mission on 10th March, 1672, and came back on 13th May, with failure "He, after a long and tedious attendance, had half an hour's discourse with him (Shivaji) and his Brahmans to little effect, but at last [Shivaji] proffered 5,000 pagodas towards our losses, and promiseth, if your Honour will please to settle a factory at Rajapur, to show all kindness and civility imaginable to the said factory." (*Ibid,* 13 March and 14 May, 1672.)

The negotiations broke down on the question of the amount of the indemnity A Bombay letter to the Company, dated 21st December, 1672, (O. C. 3722) states, "We demanded one hundred thousand Rupees, they offered 20,000, declaring that Shivaji never made more advantage by what was robbed of the English; that what was taken in the chests, trunks and warehouses of particular men (*i.e.*, European private traders), it may be was plundered by his soldiers, but he never had anything thereof, and therefore would not satisfy for it; but what (booty) was received and entered into his books he was willing to restore and make satisfaction for .. While these things were transacting, Shivaji was engaged in a great design against the Koli country, whereupon the (Brahman) minister appointed to treat (with Mr. Ustick) being called away, Mr Ustick also returned to Bombay." But the English factors deliberately held back from pressing the negotiations to a close. As they write, "We have a hard and ticklish game to play, for the King (Aurangzib) being highly enraged against

Shivaji, should he understand that we. hold any correspondence with him, it might probably cause him to order some disturbance to be given to your general affairs, not only in these parts but in Bengal also. On the other hand, we are forced to keep fair with Shivaji also, because from his countries we are supplied with provisions, timber and firewood, and likewise your inhabitants of Bombay drive a good trade into the main [-land], which would be a great prejudice to your island if it were obstructed. On these considerations we judge it your interest to suspend the treaty at present...We shall have great difficulty to recover anything for those gentlemen (*i e.*, private traders) who suffered particularly in that loss at Rajapur, for Shivaji. . by the merchants of Rajapur hath understood what did belong to the Company and what to particular men; the latter he disowns totally. Had it not been for our standing on some satisfaction for them, we had ended the dispute before now." (*Ibid.*)

§5. *Embassay of Thomas Niccolls, 1673.*

Between May and December 1672 two envoys were sent by Shivaji to the English factors at Bombay. In February 1673, a third envoy, Pilaji, came from Shivaji, but was dismissed without effecting anything. In May the Bombay Council resolved "to send Mr. Thomas Niccolls with a Banian broker to make a final demand of the damage done us at Rajapur, and now lately by his forces in Hubli."*

On 19th May, Niccolls left Bombay with 37 persons in all for Rairi castle, which he was permitted to ascend on the 23rd. He interviewed Shambhuji on the 24th as

* The latter amounted to 7,894 pagodas, or £3,500 (*F R* Surat, Vol 3, Surat Consult., 24 May, 1673)

Shivaji was absent on a pilgrimage. On 2nd June Shivaji returned to the castle, and next day Niccolls was received in audience. The Rajah took the English envoy by the hand and showed him where he should sit, which was on the left hand near one of his side-pillows, and then asked him his business But in spite of the kindness of his manners, Shivaji did nothing to settle the dispute and on the 6th dismissed Niccolls, saying, "He would send on an answer to the President by one of his own people named Bhimaji Pandit, a day or two after me." So Niccolls returned to Bombay (17th June) without achieving anything. (Niccolls' diary in *O. C.* 3787.)

Soon afterwards Bhimaji arrived at Bombay (21st) and after some discussions left with Narayan Shenvi (the interpreter of the English) to represent matters to his master. Late in September the two returned to Bombay with the following letter (O. C. 3952):—

From Shivaji Rajah to the Hon'ble Gerald Aungier, Governor of Bombay · "I received your Honour's letter by Bhimaji Pandit and Narayan Shenvi, who manifested the good correspondence that your Honour doth use with me; likewise they treated with me about the business of Rajapur which I have answered and do send them again to treat with your Honour, my desire being only to keep the same correspondence which your Honour doth with me. I shall not say more but desire you that there may be no difference in our friendship, for I am very well acquainted of your Honour's prudence. I sent your Honour a present, which I desire you to accept of."

A Committee of the Bombay Council was appointed to meet on 1st October and receive Shivaji's objections to the Company's demands On 3rd October the Maratha envoy offered 7,000 pagodas, which was refused. Later he increased it to 10,025 pagodas, to be allowed in custom duties, etc. (*O. C.* 3758; *F. R.* Surat, Vol. 106 Bombay to Surat, 29 September, 1673.)

The Surat Council agreed with Bombay (10 July, 1673) "to accept so small a sum as eight to ten thousand pagodas, which is not the quarter part the damage the nation sustained in Rajapur;" of this amount 8,000 pagodas were to be paid in money or goods, and the balance in the form of exemption from all custom duties at the port of Rajapur for five or at least three years. (*F. R.* Surat, Vol. 3.)

The repeated evasions of Shivaji at last thoroughly disgusted the English merchants. As the Surat Council records (*F. R.* Surat, Vol. 3, 19 July, 1673), "Seeing there is no probability of security from such a heathen, who, while we are in treaty with him for satisfaction for our losses at Rajapur, gives orders for the robbing our factory at Hubli, we can think of no better way to recover the Hon'ble Company and nation's right than by taking what vessels belong to his ports." A little earlier, on 24th May, they had concluded, "It is absolutely necessary to break with him, but not at this time when we have war with the Dutch." But by 1st October an amicable settlement was in sight, "Shivaji holds a fair understanding with us and we with him, the old difference of Rajapur being in a manner concluded upon honourable terms, to our advantage and reputation." (*O. C.* 3779.) The hopes of the English ran high; on 23rd October Bombay writes to Surat (*O. C.* 3870), "We are near a conclusion with our neighbour Shivaji for the old wrongs of Rajapur ....The new controversy touching Hubli we have reserved for another time,... .....so that if Shivaji attempts Surat you may be somewhat the safer, though we advise you not to trust him, yet we daresay if he hath a kindness for any nation it is for the English, and we believe he will not disturb any house where the English flag is."

But the treaty though fully agreed on between Shivaji's envoy and the English in the third week of October was not signed and confirmed by Shivaji himself for more than two months afterwards, as he was absent on a long campaign (O C. 3910, Bombay to Co., 13 December, 1673.)

§6 *Embassy of Henry Oxinden, 1674.*

The English, therefore, decided to send a formal embassy to Shivaji to conclude the business, especially as his grand coronation was to take place in June 1674. Mr Henry Oxinden was chosen for the mission, and Narayan Shenvi was sent to Raigarh (arriving there on 24th March), "to prepare business against Mr Henry Oxinden's arrival to him." (*F. R.* Surat, Vol. 3, Surat Consult , 16 April, 1674.)

The story of Oxinden's mission to Shivaji, from 13th May to 16th June, is graphically told at great length in his *Letters* and *Memorial or Narrative* which also give valuable details about Shivaji's coronation, the course of the negotiations, and the final agreement.

Shivaji held out for some time on the question of restoring to their owners the ships of the English or of the inhabitants of Bombay wrecked on his coast, but on 11th June Niraji Pandit (a minister of Shivaji whom the English had engaged to act as their intermediary with his master) sent word to Oxinden that "the Rajah had granted all our demands and articles, except our money passing current in his country." On the 12th all the ministers (*ashta pradhan*) signed the treaty, which was formally delivered to Oxinden at Niraji Pandit's house. (*F. R.* Surat, Vol. 88.)

In November Shivaji's request to buy 50 great ordnance from 40 to 60 cwt. weight and 2 great brass guns, was politely declined by the English as "so public an action as that must needs provoke this king" [Aurangzib.] (Surat to Bombay, 13 November 1674.)

§7. *English traders of Rajapur interview Shivaji, 1675.*

In the terms of the above agreement, the English factory at Rajapur was re-opened in 1675, with some difficulty, as the following letter from the Rajapur factors to Surat, dated 6th February 1675, shows:—

"It was thought fit to send the broker with the President's letter to Annaji Pandit and the Subahdar, giving them notice of our arrival. Mr. Ward being earnest for our old house, Annaji told him that he should not have it, and that he did not care whether we stayed here or no; if we did not, his master would save 1,000 pagodas by it; and further will have it [that] the house was allowed for in that sum granted us by his master towards satisfaction for our losses. He is not only one of Shivaji's great favourites but Governor-in-Chief of all Konkan, so that we cannot settle in any place but it is under his jurisdiction." (*F. R.* Surat, 88)

In March next the factors of Rajapur had an audience with Shivaji of which a detailed and very interesting report has been preserved (Rajapur letter, 20 April 1675. *F. R.* Surat, 88):—

"The Rajah came on the 22nd [March] about

midday, accompanied with abundance of horse and foot and about 150 *palankins*. So soon as we heard of his near approach, we went out of our tent and very near met him He ordered his *palankin* to stand still, called us very near him, seemed very glad to see us and much pleased [that] we came to meet him, and said the sun being hot he would not keep us now, but in the evening he would send for us.

"[23rd March?] The Rajah came. He stopped his *palankin* and called us to him. When we were pretty near him we made a stop, but he beckoned with his hand till I was up close with him. He diverted himself a little by taking in his hand the locks of my periwig and asked us several questions, at length asked us how we liked Rajapur and said he was informed we were not well pleased there, but bid us not be in the least dissatisfied for what [had] passed. He would order things for the future to our full satisfaction, and that we might be sure that no reasonable request we should make to him would he deny us .. ..

"The next morning [25th March] we were sent for again in the Rajah's name. We were admitted into his presence. I was placed so near him on his right hand that I could touch him. With him we continued about two hours, which was most part spent in answering many of his questions At length we presented him our paper of desires [previously "translated into the country language"], which after had been read to him with a little pause, seriously looking on us, [he] said that it was all granted us. He would give us a *farman* for all" But the siege of Phonda, which Shivaji began immediately afterwards, delayed the granting of such a *farman*

§8. *History of the Rajapur indemnity.*

In September 1675 Mr. Samuel Austen went to Raigarh on an embassy from Bombay to demand satisfaction for the damage done to the Company's factory at Dharangaon in Khandesh. This Shivaji refused to pay, saying that the factory was looted by "vagabonds and scouts without order or the knowledge of his general." He, however, "after a strict debate" gave his *qau* (assurance of safety) to all the English factories "to prevent like injuries." (O. C. 4106.)

But the Rajapur damages long continued unpaid On 19th July 1676 Surat wrote to Bombay suggestin that a "discreet and sober" Englishman with Girdharda should be sent to dun the Rajah for the money, as Narayan Shenvi was dilatory.

On 11th October news was received from Narayan Shenvi at the Maratha Court, that Shivaji was willing to satisfy his debt to the Company in "*vairats* or *batty,*" and the Council agreed to accept them if no better terms could be secured. Six days later the Surat Council in disgust order the Rajapur factory to be withdrawn, since, "so long as that pirate and universal robber [Shivaji] lives, that hath no regard to friend nor foe, God nor man, there can be no security in any trade in his country." This was only a threat to Shivaji's ministers, and the factory was dissolved only in 1681.

Early in 1677 the patience of the English seemed to have been exhausted. Surat wrote to Bombay on 26th January 1677, "If Shivaji still continues to baffle you, we desire you to seize and make prize of some of his vessels belonging to Dabhol, Chaul or Kalian or any other of his ports, letting the men have their liberty and taking care that none of the goods be embezzled or made away, for this will be the only way to make him rightly understand himself." (*F. R.* Surat, 89) The threat, however, was not carried out. The people of Bombay were entirely dependent on Shivaji's territory on the mainland for their fuel, timber, fresh provisions, and cattle, and he could also have effectually stopped the passage of their export merchandise across the Konkan and Kanara coast-strip, the whole of which was now in his hands. He, on his part, depended on Bombay for salt and European manufactures.*

In January 1678, as we learn from a Surat letter, "for Shivaji's former debt, they [*i e.*, the Rajapur factors] are forced to take betel-nuts as Shivaji's ministers will rate it at." (*F R.* Surat, 89.) But even thus the indemnity was not paid. The Surat Council, in April, May and July, express their indignation at the deceitful fair promises of Shivaji's ministers and that Rajah's evasion of the demands made upon him, and decide to withdraw the factories at Karwar, Hubli and Rajapur, if matters did not improve. (*Ibid.*) On 18th March 1680 Bombay writes to Surat, "We are very glad the management of the business with Shivaji is to your liking. He hath confirmed all .A hundred *khandi* of betel-nut is sent us on account of our demand for satisfaction of the two vessels lost." (*F R.* Surat, 108) On the 4th April following, the Rajah died.

Shivaji never paid the promised indemnity in full as long as he lived, and the Rajapur factory was closed in Shambhuji's reign (December 1682 or January 1683.) (*F R* Surat, 91.)

* At the marriage of Rajaram (15 March, 1680) he ordered 2,000 wax-candles from Bombay (Peshwas' Daftar)

In 1684, after Richard Keigwin, the usurping Governor of Bombay, had made a treaty with Shambhuji. the latter wrote to his subahdar of Rajapur: "Captain Henry Gary and Thomas Wilkins, ambassadors, and Ram Shenvi, interpreter, on behalf of the English, came to me earnestly desiring peace with me, intimating that my father Shivaji Rajah did contract to pay them 10,000 pagodas Padshahi on account of goods taken from them, of which account 3367 being paid, there remains 6633, requesting me to pay the same . I have promised them to satisfy what remains unpaid of the said 10,000 pagodas." (To be paid in kind by rebuilding the English factory-house at Rajapur, and in cocoa-nuts betel-nuts, &c., by degrees.) (*F. R.* Surat, 109.)

§9. *Shivaji and the Portuguese.*

Portuguese India touched only a fringe of Shivaji's activities and did not influence his policy or history to any appreciable extent. The smallness of the population of Portugal for maintaining a colonial empire, the suppression of the national energy during the sixty years of Spanish domination (1580—1640), the ruinous naval war with Holland (1650—1663), and the rapid moral decline of their settlers in Asia,—all made the Portuguese in India in Shivaji's time a decadent Power, anxious only to hold their own, and timidly averting an armed encounter with every other State by employing friendly appeal, patient endurance, and diplomatic evasion. Their territory of Goa was then much smaller than now, as it did not include Phonda, Bicholim, Pernem or Sanquelim. But their Konkan possessions, called the Province of the North, practically stretched from Chaul to Daman along the coast and for a short distance inland.

Out of these, Bombay island was given up to the English in 1668 Immediately east of these lay the dominions of the Mughal and Adil Shah, and the conquest of them by Shivaji made the Maratha power impinge upon the Portuguese territory on the coast. But though there were occasional plunderings and skirmishes between the two, these never led to a regular war, before Shambhuji's time.

The points of conflict between Shivaji and the Portuguese arose out of four things, namely,—

(*a*) The Portuguese claim to dominate the Indian seas and insistence that all Asiatic vessels plying there should take passports from them for a fee. But though they helped the Siddi of Janjira in his earlier wars with Shivaji, they had no naval war with the Maratha king.

(*b*) The *desais* of the south Ratnagiri district on being dispossessed by Shivaji, took refuge in Goa and made it a base of their operations against him, thus violating the neutrality of Portuguese territory.

(*c*) The interruption of trade from the upland parts to Goa (especially in rice, livestock, &c) by Shivaji's officers.

(*d*) Shivaji's claim to *chauth* from the Daman villages which had once been subject to the Koli Rajahs.

But the Portuguese vicercys very wisely avoided war with him and remained strictly neutral during his wars with the Mughals and Bijapur, though solicited by both.

When, in 1659, Shivaji's first few vessels, built at Kalian and Panvel, began to ply the sea, the Portuguese viceroy ordered his deputy at Bassein to hinder their voyage. But with the growth of Shivaji's power, the Government of Goa found it politic to assume a more friendly attitude towards him. The occasional petty conflicts between the two fleets have been described in Chapter 11.

Lakham Savant and other *desais* of the country immediately north of Goa, had opposed Shivaji's advance at the end of 1664, but they had been signally defeated, deprived of their lands and forced to flee to the Portuguese district of Bardes, from which they fitted out expeditions for recovering their former possessions. (Ch. 10 §4.) The viceroy's repeated warnings to them to maintain peace had no effect, and at last on 19th November 1667, Shivaji's forces made a dash into Bardes in order to punish these desais, and carried off a number of Portuguese subjects and cattle. The viceroy complained to Shivaji against this act of war while he was maintaining amity. He sent (24th Nov.) Ramoji Shenvi Kotari as his envoy to the Maratha king, who replied in friendly terms. Next, Shivaji's agent Sakho Pant came to Goa and a treaty of peace was arranged, (signed by the viceroy on 5th December and sealed by Shivaji on the 11th.) Father Gonsalo Martins, S.J., was sent by the viceroy to Shivaji's Court to get the treaty ratified and take delivery of the released captives. It was also promised in this treaty that trade between Portuguese India and Shivaji's territory above the Ghats would no longer be obstructed by his officers.

But the desais continued to violate the neutrality of Goa by sallying out to attack Shivaji's men, and the viceroy had to expel them from the Portuguese dominions at the beginning of June 1668.

The treaty of amity and peace with Shivaji was

renewed on 10th Feb. 1670, each side agreeing to a restitution of the shipping of the other side detained by it during their recent quarrel. In addition,

(*a*) the viceroy removed a constant source of friction by extending to Shivaji's ships equality of treatment with Mughal vessels in the matter of granting Portuguese passes on the payment of the customary fee. The small Maratha coastal traders (especially provision-boats) were not required to take out passes

(*b*) The viceroy, who had helped the Siddi during Shivaji's grand attack on Janjira in 1669, now offered as a mutual friend to mediate between these two Powers and compose their quarrel. Shivaji's envoy Vittal Pandit had come to Goa to try to win Portuguese support for his master's war

(*c*) Shivaji repeated his promise to forbid his officers to harass or overtax the trade between Goa and the country above the Ghats.

(*d*) Shivaji agreed not to build any fort or stone-house at any place in his dominions on the Portuguese frontier unless a river separated the two.

The Rajahs of Ramnagar (of the predatory Koli tribe) had been accustomed from early times to levy an annual blackmail from the Daman district in their neighbourhood. This money was popularly called *chauth* or one-fourth of the revenue, but in practice the proportion varied from 10 to 25 p c. in the different villages, and the Rajah was known as the *Chauthia Rajah*

(*Storia do Mogor*, ii. 132.) Shivaji after his annexation of Ramnagar (1676) demanded this payment from the Portuguese as his lawful right in succession to the Koli Rajah. The viceroy of Goa delayed giving a direct answer as long as possible, by every diplomatic device, such as calling for reports from his local officers, examining the old revenue accounts, settling the details about particular villages, &c., while at the same time he professed unbroken friendship with Shivaji and eagerness to give him every satisfaction. The negotiations were thus spun out for over two years. Shivaji's envoy Pitambar Shenvi, who had reached Goa in December 1677 on this mission, died next August, and was succeeded by his grandson Jivaji and later by Ganesh Sethi. At last Shivaji's patience was worn out and he threatened war, but his premature death gave the Portuguese a short respite.*

*I pass over the abortive negotiations of the Portuguese with the Mughals and with Shivaji from which nothing of consequence resulted. The details are given in P S Pissurlencar's careful and fully documented work, *Portugueses e Maratas, i. Shivaji*, on which I have based this section. Several treaties and letters are given in Biker, iv

CHAPTER XV

Government, Institutions and Policy

§ 1 *Extent of his kingdom and dependencies.*

At the time of his death Shivaji's kingdom included all the country (except the Portuguese possessions) stretching from Ramnagar (modern Dharampur State in the Surat Agency) in the north, to Karwar or the Gangavati river in the Bombay district of Kanara, in the south. The eastern boundary embraced Baglana in the north, then ran southwards along an irregular shifting line through the middle of the Nasik and Puna districts, and encircled the whole of the Satara and much of the Kolhapur districts. This tract formed what the Marathi documents describe as his *swaraj* or 'own kingdom' and the Persian accounts as his 'old dominions.' Here his ownership was recognized as legally established and beyond question. A recent but permanent acquisition was the Western Karnatak or the Kanarese-speaking country extending from Belgaum to the bank of the Tungabhadra opposite the Bellary district of the Madras Presidency.

This, the consolidated portion of his kingdom, was divided into three provinces, each under a viceroy. The northern division, including the *Dang* and Baglana, the Koli country south of Surat, Konkan north of Bombay, and the Deccan plateau or *Desh* southwards to Puna, was governed by Moro Trimbak Pingle. The southern division, which was made up of Konkan south of Bombay, Savant-vadi and the North Kanara coast,—formed the viceroyalty of Annaji Datto. The south-eastern division, ruled by Dattaji Pant, covered the Satara and Kolhapur districts of *Desh* and the Karnatak districts of Belgaum and Dharwar to Kopal west of the Tunga-bhadra. (Sabh. 77; Parasnis MS.; a Persian MS. roll of Mr. Rajwade; English summary in Mawjee, *J. Bo. B. R. A. S.*)

Shivaji's latest annexation was the country extending from the Tungabhadra opposite Kopal to Vellore and Jinji, *i.e.*, the northern, central and eastern parts of the present kingdom of Mysore and portions of the Madras districts of Bellary, Chittur and Arcot. His two years' possession of them before his death was too short to enable him to consolidate his gains here, and this province was really held by an army of occupation and remained unsettled in 1680; only the forts garrisoned by him and as much of the surrounding lands as they could command, acknowledged Maratha rule.

Besides these places there was one region where the contest for mastery was still undecided at the time of his death. This was the Kanara highlands, including the South Dharwar district and the principalities of Sunda and Bednur. Shivaji had inflicted some defeats upon the local Nawab, a vassal of Bijapur; but Bankapur, the provincial capital, was still unconquered by him when he breathed his last. So also was Bednur, which merely paid him tribute.

Outside these settled or half-settled parts of his kingdom, there was a wide and very fluctuating belt of land subject to his power but not owning his sovereignty. They were the adjacent parts of the Mughal empire (*Mughlai* in Marathi), which formed the happy hunting-ground of his horsemen. In these he levied blackmail (*khandani, i.e.*, ransom, in Marathi), as regularly as his army could repeat its annual visit to them The money paid was popularly called *chauth*, because it amounted to *one-fourth* of the standard assessment of the land revenue of a place. But as this paper assessment was always larger than the actual collection, the real incidence of the *chauth* was considerably more than one-fourth of what the peasants paid to their legitimate sovereign The payment of the *chauth* merely saved a place from the unwelcome presence of the Maratha soldiers and civil underlings, but did not impose on Shivaji any corresponding obligation to guard the district from foreign invasion or internal disorder. The Marathas looked only to their own gain and not to the fate of their prey after they had left. The *chauth* was only a means of buying off one robber, and not a subsidiary system for the maintenance of peace and order against all enemies. The lands subject to the *chauth* cannot, therefore, be rightly called spheres of influence.

The territory, old and new, under Shivaji contained 240 forts, out of which 111 were built by him and 79 were situated in Madras. [Sabh. 98-101, a helpful list by D. V. Kale in *Shivaji Souvenir*, 1927.]

§2. *His revenue and hoarded treasure.*

His revenue is put by his courtier Sabhasad (p. 102) at the round figure of one *krore of hun*, while the *chauth* when collected in full brought in another 80 *lakhs*. (*T. S. 35a.*) If these statements are correct, Shivaji's theoretical income at its highest was seven *krores* of Rupees. The sum actually realized was considerably less than this paper-estimate,—probably sometimes falling as low as one-tenth of it

The treasure and other valuable things left behind

by Shivaji are enumerated in great detail by Sabhasad (95-96) and the *Tarikh-i-Shivaji* (42-44.) But we cannot be sure that all the figures have been correctly copied in the MSS. of these two works that have come down to us. Moreover, the gold and silver coins were of such an immense variety of denominations countries and ages,—a faithful index to the wide range and thorough character of Shivaji's looting campaigns,—that it is impossible to reduce the total value of his hoard to any modern currency with even tolerable accuracy. The curious English reader is referred to my translation of *T. S* in the *Modern Review* of January 1910 and to Manker's translation of Sabhasad.

§3. *Strength of his army.*

The growth of his army is thus recorded: at the outset of his career he had 1,200 household cavalry (*paga*) and 2,000 *silahdars* or mercenary horsemen who provided their own arms and mounts. (Sabh. 8.) After the conquest of Javli (1656) their number was increased to 7,000 *paga*, 3,000 *silahdars* and 10,000 Mavle infantry. (Sabh 11.) He also enlisted 700 Pathans from the disbanded soldiery of Bijapur (*T. S.* 15*b*.) After the destruction of Afzal Khan (1659) he raised his forces to 7,000 *paga*, 8,000 *silahdars*, and 12,000 infantry (Sabh. 27.) At the time of his death (1680), his army consisted of 45,000 *paga* (under 29 colonels), 60,000 *silahdars* (under 31 colonels) and one *lakh* of Mavle infantry (under 36 colonels.) (Sabh. 96-97.) But *T. S.* states that he left 32,000 horses in his stables, besides 5,000 given to the *bargirs*.

The core of his army was, therefore, formed by 30 to 40 thousand regular and permanently enlisted cavalry in his own service, and about twice that number of infantry militia (*hasham*), whom he used to withdraw from the cultivation of their fields during the campaigning season only, as in England under King Alfred The infantry garrisoning his forts were permanently recruited, though they were given fields in their neighbourhood. The number of the *silahdars* who hired themselves and their horses out to him varied greatly from year to year, according to his need, their expectation of plunder in the impending campaign, and the demand for their services in the neighbouring States at a particular time. In the earlier stages of his career, local chieftains with their retainers used to join him in his raids (*e g* , Surat, 1664) and swell his army by the adhesion of a body of irregulars The same thing happened in his invasion of Madras (1677.)

His elephants are numbered 1,260 by Sabhasad (p 97), but *T S* gives 125 and Chit 300, which are more likely figures. The camels were 3,000 (*T. S*) or 1,500 (Chit.) The number of his artillery-pieces is not mentioned Chitnis (a doubtful authority) tells us that 200 guns were kept ready for field service and the rest were placed in the forts. Each field gun had some elephants and a battalion of infantry attached to it.

§4 *Council of Eight Ministers.*

His earliest administrative Council, in the days of Dadaji Kond-dev, was composed of four officers only, *viz.*, the *Peshwa,* the *Majmuadar,* the *Dabir,* and the *Sabnis* (Sabh. 7.) When, in 1647, Shiva became his own master, he added a Master of the Horse (*Sar-i-naubat*) and a second *Dabir* to the above four (Sabh. 8) In 1656, after the conquest of Javli (which practically doubled his territory) the Council was further expanded by creating a *Surnis* and a *Waqnis* and two distinct commanders for the infantry and cavalry arms (Sabh. 11.) After his return from Agra he appointed (1667) a Lord Justice to try all suits in the kingdom according to the Sanskrit law-books (Sabh. 57.) By 1674 the number of ministers had risen to eight (*Ibid.* 83), which continued till his death.

This Council of eight ministers, *ashta pradhan,* was in no sense a Cabinet. Like Louis XIV and Frederick the Great, Shivaji was his own prime-minister and kept all the strings of the administration in his own hands. The eight *pradhans* merely acted as his secretaries: they had no initiative, no power to dictate his policy; their function was purely advisory when he was in a mood to listen to advice, and at other times to carry out his general instructions and supervise the details in their respective departments. It is very likely that Shivaji never interfered with the Ecclesiastical and Accounts departments, but that was due entirely to his low caste and illiteracy. The Peshwa's position at Court was, no doubt, higher than that of the other *pradhans,* because he was closer to the king and naturally enjoyed more of his confidence; but they were in no sense his subordinates. The solidarity of the British Cabinet, as well as its power, was wanting in the Maratha Council of Eight.

The eight ministers were the following:—

1. The prime-minister, (Persian *Peshwa,* Sanskrit *Mukhya Pradhan.*) His duties were to look after the welfare of the State in general terms, to represent the king in his absence, and to keep peace among the other officers, so as to promote harmony in the administration.

All royal letters and charters had to bear his seal below the king's.

2 The auditor, (Persian *Majmuadar*, Sanskrit *Amatya*) He had to check all the accounts of public income and expenditure and report them to the king, and to countersign all statements of accounts both of the kingdom in general and of the particular districts.

3 The chronicler, (Persian *Waqia-navis*, Sanskrit *Mantri*.) His duties were to compile a daily record of the king's doings and Court incidents, and to watch over the king's invitation-lists, meals, companions, &c., so as to guard against murderous plots.

4. The superintendent, (Persian *Shuru-navis*, Sanskrit *Sachiv*) He had to see that all royal letters were drafted in the proper style, to revise them, and to write at the head of charters the words *Shuru shud*, or 'here begins.' He had also to check the accounts of the *mahals and parganas*.

5. The foreign secretary, (Persian *Dabir*, Sanskrit *Sumant*.) He was the king's adviser on relations with foreign States, war and peace It was also his duty to keep intelligence about other countries, to receive and dismiss foreign envoys, and maintain the dignity of the State abroad.

6. The commander-in-chief, (Persian *Sar-i-naubat*, Sanskrit *Senapati*)

7. The ecclesiastical head, (Persian *Sadr* and *Muhtasib* joined together, Marathi *Pandit Rao* and *Danadhyaksha*) It was his function to honour and reward learned Brahmans on behalf of the king, to decide theological questions and caste disputes, to fix dates for religious ceremonies, to punish impiety and heresy, and

order penances, &c He was Judge of Canon Law, Royal Almoner, and Censor of Public Morals combined.

8. The chief justice (Persian *Qazi-ul-quzat*, Sanskrit *Nyayadhish*) He tried civil and criminal cases according to Hindu law and endorsed all judicial decisions, especially about rights to land, village headmanship, &c.

All these ministers with the exception of the commander-in-chief, were of the Brahman caste, and all of them, with the exception of the last two, had also to take the command of armies and go out on expeditions when necessary. All royal letters, charters and treaties had to bear the seals of the king and the Peshwa and the endorsement of the next four ministers, *i.e.*, other than the Commander-in-chief, the Ecclesiastical Head, and the Chief Justice.*

The actual work of State correspondence was conducted by Kayasthas, of whom two were famous, *viz.*, Balaji Avji the *chitnis* and Niloji (Nilkanth Yesaji) the *munshi* or Persian secretary. The muster-rolls of the army were written and the pay-bills drawn up by a class of officers called *sabnises*, who corresponded to the *bakhshis* or paymasters of the Mughal army, but occupied a much lower rank.†

§5. *Army organization.*

We now turn to Shivaji's civil and military regulans.

Every fort and outpost (*thanah*) was placed under the officers of equal status, *viz.*, the *havladar*, the *sabnis*

---

says Chitnis But Oxinden's letters imply that *all* the ministers endorsed Shivaji's treaty with the English

†Sa. 83, Chitnis, 167-168, *Sanads and Letters*, 123-130, *Bhonsalyanche Bakhar* (1823), printed in *Itihas Sangraha*

and the *sar-i-naubat,* who were to act jointly "No fort was to be left solely under a *havladar,* lest a single traitor should be able to deliver it to the enemy. The *havladar* and the *sar-i-naubat* were selected from the Maratha caste and the *sabnis* from the Brahmans,"—so that one caste served as a check upon another. The stores and provisions in the forts were in charge of a Kayastha officer called the *karkhanah-navis,* who wrote the accounts of their incoming and expenditure. In the larger forts, where the bounds were extensive, the walls were divided into five or six sections, and each of these was guarded by a special *tat-sar-i-naubat.* The environs of a fort were watched by men of the *Parwari* and *Ramushi* castes.

The *havladar* of a fort was empowered to change the lower officers and to write official letters and seal them with his own seal All letters from Government were to be addressed to him. He was to lock the fort-gates at sunset and open them at sunrise, carry the keys with himself and sleep with them under his pillow. He had to make frequent tours of inspection in and outside the fort, pay surprise visits to the sentinels, while the *sar-i-naubat* had to inspect the work of the patrolling parties and the night-watch. Minute written instructions were given by Shivaji for keeping in each fort munition, provisions, building-materials, and other necessary stores adequate to its size, and for keeping proper watch, and these regulations were rigidly enforced.

All soldiers, whether musketeers, spearmen, archers or swordsmen, were recruited only after a careful personal inspection by Shivaji himself and taking security for every new soldier from the men already in his service.

In the State cavalry (*paga*), the unit was formed by 25 troopers (*bargirs*); over 25 men was placed one *havladar*, over 5 *havladars* one *jumladar*,* and over 10 *jumlas* or 1,250 men one *hazari*. Still higher ranks were the 5-*hazaris* and the supreme commander or *sar-i-naubat* of cavalry. For every twenty-five troopers there were a water-carrier and a farrier.

The *silahdars*, or troopers who supplied their own horses and arms, were organized on a different plan, but were under the orders of the same *sar-i-naubat* of cavalry, and ranked lower than the *paga* horsemen.

In the infantry, whether fort-garrisons or Mavle militiamen, there was one corporal (*nayak*) to every nine privates (*paiks*); over 5 *nayaks* one *havladar*, over two (or three) *havladars* one *jumladar*, and over 10 *jumladars* one *hazari*† There seems to have been no 5-*hazari* among the infantry, but only 7-*hazaris*, over whom was the *sar-i-naubat* of infantry. Shivaji's Guard brigade of 2,000 select Mavle infantry was splendidly equipped dressed and armed at great expense to the State. (Sabh. 58)

The *paga jumladar* had a salary of 500 *hun* a year and the right to use a *palki*. Attached to him was a *majmuadar* on 100 to 125 *hun*. A *hazari* drew 1,000 *hun* a year; under him were a *majmuadar*, a Maratha *karbhari* (manager or steward), and a revenue-writer (*jama-navis*) of the Kayastha caste, for whom 500 *hun* was assigned. The accounts of military income and disbursement had to be made up with the signature of all the four. A commander of 5,000 drew 2,000 *hun* and had the same three civil officers attached to his office.

---

* Chit., 81, says that there was an intermediate officer called *subahdar* in command of 5 *jumlas*, below the *hazari*

†Chit., 83, gives one jumladar over *five* havladars and one hazari over *five* jumladars

Karkuns (collectors), reporters, couriers and spies were posted to every higher command down to a *hazari*, under the orders of the *sar-i-naubat*.

An infantry *jumladar* drew 100 *hun* a year, and had a *sabnis* (muster-writer) on 40 *hun* A *hazari* drew 500 *hun* and his *sabnis* 100 to 125 *hun*.

It was Shivaji's settled policy* to use his army to draw supplies from foreign dominions every year. "The troops were to go into cantonments in the home territory during the rainy season (June—September) Grain, fodder and medicines were kept in stock for the horses, and the huts of the troopers were kept thatched with grass. On the day of *Dashahara* (early in October) the army should set out from the camp for the country selected by the Rajah. At the time of their departure a list was made of all the property that every man, high or low, of the army carried with himself. The troops were to subsist in foreign parts for eight months and also levy contributions No woman, female slave or dancing-

* The method followed by the Pindharis in 1810-16, as described by a contemporary English officer, may be taken to illustrate the conduct of the Maratha troops in Shivaji s time, though not of the more developed forces of the Peshwas "Until the close of the rains and the fall of the rivers, their horses were carefully trained, to prepare them for long marches and hard work The rivers generally became fordable by the close of the *Dassera* The horses were then shod and all that were so inclined set forth on a foray All were mounted, though not equally well, . the favourite weapon was a bamboo spear, from 12 to 18 feet long . It is not surprising that a body so constituted, and moving without camp-equipage of any kind, should traverse the whole of India in defiance of the most active pursuit by regular troops along the same line of march

As it was impossible for them to remain more than a few hours on the same spot, the utmost despatch was necessary in rifling any towns or villages into which they could force an entrance, every one whose appearance indicated the probability of his possessing money, was immediately put to the most horrid torture It was their common practice to burn and destroy what could not be carried away" [Prinsep s *History of Marquess of Hastings*, i 38-39]

girl was to be allowed to accompany the army. A soldier keeping any of these was to be beheaded. No woman or child was to be taken captive, but only men. Cows were exempt from seizure, but bullocks might be taken for transport only. Brahmans were not to be molested, nor taken as hostages for ransom. No soldier should misconduct himself [during a campaign.]

Eight months were to be passed in such expeditions abroad. On their return to their own frontier in Baishakh (April) the whole army was to be searched, the property found was to be compared with the old list, and the excess was to be deducted from their salary. Any one secreting any booty was liable to punishment on detection by the general.

The generals on their return should see the Rajah, deliver their booty in gold silver jewels and costly cloth to him, present their accounts, and take their dues from the Treasury. The officers and men were to be promoted or punished according to their conduct during the late campaign. Then they would again remain for four months in camp." [Sabh. 27-30.]

§6. *Revenue system and administration.*

"The land in every province was to be measured and the area calculated in *chavars*. The measuring-rod was 5 cubits and 5 *muthis* (closed fists) in length. A cubit was equal to 14 *tansus*, and the measuring-rod was [therefore] 80 *tansus* long. Twenty *kathis* (rods) square made a *bigha* and 120 *bighas* one *chavar*. The area of each village was thus ascertained in detail. An estimate was made of the expected produce of each *bigha*, three parts of which were left to the peasant and two parts taken by the State.*

"New *ryots* who came to settle were to be given money for seeds, and cattle, the amount being recovered in two or four annual instalments. The revenue should be taken in kind at harvest time."

Shivaji wanted to sweep away the middle-class of revenue farmers and come into direct relations with the cultivators. "The ryots were not subject to the authority of the *zamindars*, *deshmukhs*, and *desais*, who had no right to exercise the powers of a political superior (over-lord) or harass the *ryots*"

"In the Nizam-Shahi, Adil-Shahi and Mughal territories annexed, the ryots had formerly been subject to *patils*, *kulkarnis* and *deshmukhs*, who used to do the collection work and pay what they pleased to the State, sometimes only 200 or 300 *hun* for a village yielding 2,000 *hun* as revenue. These *mirasdars* (hereditary landlords), thus growing wealthy, built forts, enlisted troops, and grew powerful They never waited upon the revenue officer of Government and used to show fight if he urged that the village could pay more to the State. This class had become unruly and seized the country. But Shivaji dismantled their castles, garrisoned the strong places with his own troops, and took away all power from the *mirasdars* Formerly they used to take whatever

---

* Captain Robertson in 1820 and 1825 gave a different and more complicated account of Shivaji's revenue system (*Bom Gaz*, xviii Pt ii pp 321-322) It is quite probable that the system was not so simple and uniform as Sabhasad represents it, but we do not know the Captain's authorities and have no means of testing his statement about a system founded nearly two centuries ago by a dynasty which had long passed away, and the continuity of whose tradition had been broken A *tansu* was the breadth of the second and third fingers (or, in Mughal India, the breadth of 8 barley corn)

they liked from the *ryots*. This was now stopped. Their dues were fixed after calculating the (exact) revenue of the village, and they were forbidden to build castles." (Sabh. 32-33.)

Similarly, military fief-holders were given no political power over their tenants. "The *sar-i-naubats, majmuadars, karkuns* and the officers in the Rajah's personal service were given assignments on the revenue (*tankha barat*) for their salary. The lands cultivated by them were subject to assessment like the fields of the *ryots*, and the amount of the revenue due was deducted from their pay. For the balance they got orders on the Treasury of the capital or the districts. Men serving in the army, the militia or the forts were not to be given proprietory (*mokasa*) rights over any village in entirety. Their dues were to be paid either by assignment of revenue or by cash from the Treasury. None but the *karkuns* had any jurisdiction over the land. All payments to the army were to be made by the *karkuns*. The grant of *mokasa* rights would have created disorder among the peasants; they would have grown in strength and disobeyed the Government collectors; and the growing power of the *ryots* would have ended in rebellion at various places. The *mokasa*-holders and the *zamindars* if united would become uncontrollable. No *mokasa* was to be granted to any one." (Sabh. 30-31.)

Over two *mahals*, yielding a revenue of from 75,000 to 1,25,000 *hun* in the aggregate, a *subahdar* on 400 *hun* and a *majmuadar* on 100 to 125 *hun* a year were appointed. The *subahdar* was to have a *palki* allowance of 400 *hun* All civil and military officers with a salary of 125 *hun* or more were given the right to hold parasols (*aftab-gir*) over their heads, with an allowance from the

State for bearers (Sabh 31.) Where necessary, a *subahdar* was posted over a tract yielding only one *lakh* of Rupees To the disturbed provinces across the frontier, a military force was sent with the collectors of blackmail. (Sabh. 32.) The *subahdars* were all Brahmans, under the Peshwa's supervision (Sabh 77)

§7. *Religious policy.*

Shivaji's religious policy was very liberal. He respected the holy places of all creeds in his raids and made endowments for Hindu temples and Muslim saints' tombs and mosques alike. He not only granted pensions to Brahman scholars versed in the Vedas, astronomers and anchorites, but also built hermitages and provided subsistence at his own cost for the holy men of Islam, notably Baba Yaqut of Keloshi (4 m. s of Bankot on the Ratnagiri coast) (Sabh 33) "The lost Vedic studies were revived by him One maund of rice was (annually) presented to a Brahman who had mastered one of the books of the Vedas, two maunds to a master of two books, and so on. Every year the Pandit Rao used to examine the scholars in the month of Shravan (August) and increase or decrease their stipends according to their progress in study. Foreign pandits received presents in goods, local scholars in food. Famous scholars were assembled, honoured and given money rewards No Brahman had occasion to go to other kingdoms to beg." (Chit 85, 43.)

Shivaji's spiritual guide (*guru*) was Ramdas Swami, one of the greatest saints of Maharashtra, (born 1608, died 1681.) An attempt has been made in the present generation to prove that the Maratha national hero's political ideal of an independent Hindu monarchy was inspired by Ramdas; but the evidence produced is neither adequate nor free from suspicion.* The holy man's influence on Shivaji was spiritual, and not political. After the capture of Satara, (1673) Shivaji installed his *guru* in the neighbouring hill-fort of Parli or Sajjangarh, and guides still point to the credulous tourist the seat on the top of Satara hill from which Shivaji used to hold converse with the saint, across four miles of space! A charming anecdote is told, that Shivaji could not understand why Ramdas used to go out daily on his begging tour, though his royal disciple had made him rich beyond the dreams of avarice, and that he next day placed at his feet a deed making a gift of all his kingdom to the saint Ramdas accepted the gift, appointed Shivaji as his vicar, and bade him rule the realm thenceforth not as an autocratic owner, but as a servant responsible for all his acts to a higher authority. Shivaji then made the tawny robe of a Hindu *sannyasi* his flag, *bhagwe jhanda,* in order to signify that he fought and ruled in the livery of his ascetic lord paramount, and conducted himself "As ever in his great Taskmaster's eyes."

§8. *Effect of Shivaji's reign.*

So much for Shivaji's regulations in theory. But in practice they were often violated except where he was personally present. Thus, the assertion of Sabhasad and Chitnis that his soldiers had to deliver to the State every item of the booty taken by them, is contradicted by the sack of Dharangaon (1679), where the English factors were robbed of many things without these being

*Shivaji and Ramdas Chit 44-53, also his *Shambhuji Bakhar,* 5-6; Prof Bhate's *Shivaji ani Ramdas*, the publications and now-defunct monthly magazine of the Ramdasi coterie of Dhulia (notably Mr Rajwade)

entered in the official papers of the Maratha army or credited to Shivaji's Treasury (Ch. 14.) Shivaji could not be everywhere and at all times; hence it was impossible for him to prevent private looting by his troops and camp-followers. In the wake of the Maratha army, gangs of private robbers took to the road. The Pindharis were the logical corollary of the Maratha soldier, to whom rapine was a normal duty.

Shivaji justified his spoliation of his neighbours by saying, as he did to the Mughal governor of Surat (1672), "Your Emperor has forced me to keep an army for the defence of my people and country. That army must be paid by his subjects" (Ch 8 §4.) Such a plea might have been true at the beginning of his career and in relation to Mughal territory only, but cannot explain his raids into Bijapur and Golkonda, Kanara and Tanjore. It fails altogether as a defence of the foreign policy of the Peshwas

But whatever might be the moral quality of the means he employed, his success was a dazzling reality. This petty jagirdar's son proved himself the irrepressible opponent of the Mughal empire and all its resources. This fact deeply impressed the minds of his contemporaries in India and abroad Aurangzib was in despair as to how he could subdue Shiva A significant statement is made in a news-letter of his Court in 1670 that the Emperor read a despatch from the Deccan, recounting some raids of Shiva and then "remained silent" In the inner council of the Court he often anxiously asked whom he should next send against Shivaji, seeing that nearly all his great generals had failed in the Deccan, and Mahabat Khan irreverently replied with a sneer at Qazi Abdul Wahab's influence over the Emperor, "No general is necessary. A decree from the Chief Qazi will be sufficient to extinguish Shiva!" The young Persian king, Shah Abbas II., sent a letter taunting Aurangzib, "You call yourself a Padishah, but cannot subdue a mere zamindar like Shiva. I am going to India with an army to teach you your business."

To the Hindu world in that age of renewed persecution, Shivaji appeared as the star of a new hope, the protector of the ritualistic paint-mark (*tilak*) on the forehead of Hindus, and the saviour of Brahmans. [Bhushan's poems.] His Court, as later his son's, became the rallying-point of the opposition to Aurangzib. The two rivals were both supermen, but contrasts in character.

APPENDIX

Portraits of Shivaji.

We have reliable information about Shivaji's personal appearance in 1664, when he was seen by some Englishmen at Surat The chaplain Escaliot writes, "His person is described by them who have seen him to be of mean [=medium] stature, lower somewhat than I am erect, and of an excellent proportion Actual [=active] in exercise, [he] seems to smile, a quick and piercing eye, and whiter than any of his people" The cultured Frenchman Thevenot, who travelled in the Deccan from November 1665 to February 1667, says of him, 'The Rajah is small [in size] and tawny [in complexion], with quick eyes which indicate abundance of spirit" It is a pity that neither the English factor of Rajapur whose wig Shivaji examined with his fingers in curiosity (March, 1675), nor Henry Oxinden, the English envoy present at Shivaji s coronation (1674), has left any description of his personal appearance The latter only says that he weighed about 16,000 pagodas (according to Le Feber, 17,000 pagodas or about 160 pounds) The four old portraits of Shivaji reproduced in this book are described below

A There is a contemporary and authentic portrait of Shivaji preserved in the British Museum, *viz*, MS Add 22,282 (Picture No 12) It bears a Dutch inscription, Shivaji the late Maratha prince' This volume of Indian portraits evidently belonged to some Dutch owner who had written the name of each person in Dutch on the portrait *before 1707*, as Aurangzib's portrait is inscribed, 'the *present* Great Mughal' Mr Irvine holds that the portraits were true to life so far as the artist could make them They are well executed, in the usual style The following description of this Shivaji portrait is supplied by Mr Irvine —

"Three-quarter length, looking to right,—same face as in Orme's *Fragments* Black beard and moustache—long hair at sides—gold *pagri* —jewelled aigrette—black plume—white *jigha* (pearls)—flowered coat with white ground—purple silk scarf thrown across shoulder—worked sash—*peshqabz* (dagger) sticking out from waist on left side—right hand hidden in hilt of a *pattah* or rapier—left hand holding a *dhup* or straight sword"

B The fine steel engraving given in Orme's *Fragments* (1782) is the British Museum portrait as retouched by a European artist

C The Italian traveller Manucci in 1706 presented to the Venetian Senate a volume of 56 portraits drawn for him by Mir Muhammad, an artist in the household of Shah Alam, *before 1688* This volume (now in Paris) contains a portrait of Shivaji (No 39 in Blochet's list,) which Mr Irvine has reproduced by photography in his edition of the *Storia do Mogor*, Vol III, picture No XXXV Earlier and less faithful woodcuts of it are to be found in Langles' *Monuments Anciens et Modernes* (Paris 1821) and De Jacigny and Raymond s *Inde* (Paris, 1845)

D The portrait of Shivaji given in Constable's edition of Bernier's *Travels* (p 187) follows an engraving in F Valentyn's *Oud-en Nieuw Oost-Indien* (1724-26), the pictures in which were most probably acquired by the Dutch E I Co's mission to the Mughal Court in 1712

CHAPTER XVI

SHIVAJI'S ACHIEVEMENT, CHARACTER AND PLACE IN HISTORY

§1. *Shivaji's policy how far traditional.*

Shivaji's State policy, like his administrative system,* was not very new. From time immemorial it had been the aim of the typical Hindu king to set out early every autumn to "extend his kingdom" at the expense of his neighbours. Indeed, the Sanskrit law-books lay down such a course as the necessary accomplishment of a true Kshatriya chief. (Manu. vii. 99-103, 182.) In more recent times it had also been the practice of the Muhammadan sovereigns in North India and the Deccan alike. But these conquerors justified their territorial aggrandizement by religious motives. According to the Quranic law, there cannot be peace between a Muhammadan king and his neighbouring "infidel" States. The latter are *dar-ul-harb* or legitimate seats of war, and it is the Muslim king's duty to slay and plunder in them till they accept the true faith and become *dar-ul-islam*, after which they will become entitled to his protection.†

The coincidence between Shivaji's foreign policy and that of a Quranic sovereign is so complete that both the history of Shivaji by his courtier Krishnaji Anant and the Persian official history of Bijapur use exactly the same

---

* For an earlier parallel and possible model, see the Adil-Shahi rules given in *B. S* 348-352

† For a detailed account and authorities, see *History of Aurangzib*, iii ch 34 §1

word, *mulk-giri*, to describe such raids into neighbouring countries as a regular political ideal. The only difference was that in theory at least, an orthodox Muslim king was bound to spare the other Muslim States in his path and not to spoil or shed the blood of true believers, while Shivaji (as well as the Peshwas after him) carried on his *mulk-giri* into all neighbouring States, Hindu no less than Islamic, and squeezed rich Hindus as mercilessly as he did Muhammadans. Then, again, the orthodox Islamic king, in theory at least, aimed at the annexation and conversion of the other States, so that after the short sharp agony of conquest was over the latter enjoyed peace like the regular parts of his dominion But the object of Shivaji's military enterprises, unless his Court-historian Sabhasad has misrepresented it, was not annexation but mere plunder, or to quote his very words, "The Maratha forces should feed themselves at the expense of foreign countries for eight months every year, and levy black-mail." (Sabh., 29.)*

Thus, Shivaji's power was exactly similar in origin and theory to the power of the Muslim States in India and elsewhere, and he only differed from them in the use of that power. Universal toleration and equal justice and protection were the distinctive features of the permanently occupied portion of his realm, as we have shown elsewhere.

* "Instead of commencing with the removal of the existing government, and the general assumption of the whole authority to himself, a Maratha chieftain begins, by appearing at the season of harvest, and demanding a consideration for his forbearance in withholding the mischief he has it in his power to inflict The visit is annually repeated, and the demand proportionally enhanced Whatever is thus exacted is called the *chauth*, and the process of exaction a *mulk-giri* expedition" [Prinsep's *History of the Marquess of Hastings*, i 22]

§2. *Causes of Shivaji's failure to build an enduring State.*

Why did Shivaji fail to create an enduring State? Why did the Maratha people stop short of the final accomplishment of their union and dissolve before they had consolidated into an absolutely compact political body?

An obvious cause was, no doubt, the shortness of his reign, barely ten years after the final rupture with the Mughals in 1670. But this does not furnish the true explanation of his failure. It is doubtful if with a very much longer time at his disposal he could have averted the ruin which befell the Maratha State under the Peshwas, for the same moral canker was at work among his people in the 17th century as in the 18th. The first danger of the new Hindu kingdom established by him in the Deccan lay in the fact that the national glory and prosperity resulting from the victories of Shivaji and Baji Rao I. created a reaction in favour of Hindu orthodoxy; it accentuated caste distinction and ceremonial purity of daily rites which ran counter to the homogeneity and simplicity of the poor and politically depressed early Maratha society. Thus, his political success sapped the main foundation of that success.

In the security, power and wealth engendered by their independence, the Marathas of the 18th century forgot the past record of Muslim persecution; the social grades turned against each other. The Brahmans living east of the Sahyadri range despised those living west, the men of the hills despised their brethren of the plains, because they could now do so with impunity. The head of the State, though a Brahman, was despised by his Brahman servants belonging to other branches of the caste,—because the first Peshwa's great-grandfather's great-grandfather had once been lower in society than the Desh Brahmans' great-grandfathers' great-grandfathers! While the Chitpavan Brahmans were waging social war with the Deshastha Brahmans, a bitter jealousy raged between the Brahman ministers and governors and the Kayastha secretaries We have unmistakable traces of it as early as the reign of Shivaji. "Caste grows by fission" It is antagonistic to national union. In proportion as Shivaji's ideal of a Hindu *swaraj* was based on orthodoxy, it contained within itself the seed of its own death As Rabindranath Tagore remarks:

"A temporary enthusiasm sweeps over the country and we imagine that it has been united; but the rents and holes in our body-social do their work secretly; we cannot retain any noble idea long.

"Shivaji aimed at preserving the rents; he wished to save from Mughal attack a Hindu society to which ceremonial distinctions and isolation of castes are the very breath of life. He wanted to make this heterogeneous society triumphant over *all* India! He wove ropes of sand; he attempted the impossible. It is beyond the power of any man, it is opposed to the divine law of the universe, to establish the *swaraj* of such a caste-ridden, isolated, internally-torn sect over a vast continent like India."*

Shivaji and his father-in-law Gaikwar were *Marathas*, *i e.*, members of a despised caste. Before the rise of the national movement in the Deccan in the closing years of the 19th century, a Brahman of Maharashtra used to

---

* From his *Rise and Fall of the Sikh Power*, as translated by me in *Modern Review*, April 1911

feel insulted if he was called a Maratha. "No," he would reply with warmth, "I am a *Dakshina* Brahman." Shivaji keenly felt his humiliation at the hands of the Brahmans to whose defence and prosperity he had devoted his life. Their insistence on treating him as a Shudra drove him into the arms of Balaji Avji, the leader of the Kayasthas, and another victim of Brahmanic pride. The Brahmans felt a professional jealousy for the intelligence and literary powers of the Kayasthas, who were their only rivals in education and Government service, and consoled themselves by declaring the Kayasthas a low-caste not entitled to the Vedic rites and by proclaiming a social boycott of Balaji Avji who had ventured to invest his son with the sacred thread. Balaji naturally sympathized with his master and tried to raise him in social estimation by engaging Gaga Bhatta who "made Shivaji a pure Kshatriya." The high-priest showed his gratitude to Balaji for his heavy retainer by writing a tract [or rather two] in which the Kayastha caste was glorified, but without convincing his contemporary Brahmans.*

There was no attempt at well-thought-out organized communal improvement, spread of education or

*Nor has he succeeded in convincing posterity In 1916 Mr Rajwade, a Brahman writer, published a denial of the Kayastha claims (*Chaturtha Sam Britta*), on the occasion of editing this tract He has provoked replies, one of which, *Rajwade's Gaga Bhatti* by K T Gupte, makes some attempt at reasoning and the use of evidence, while another, *The Twanging of the Bow* by K S Thakre, has the same tone as Milton's *Tetrachordon* or *Against Salmasius*! This is happening in the 20th century, and yet Mr Rajwade and Prof Bijapurkar (who persistently treated Shivaji's descendants as Shudras) are nationalists, even Chauvinists

It was with a house so divided against itself that the Puna Brahmans of the 18th century hoped to found an all-Indian Maratha empire, and there are Puna Brahmans in the 20th century who believe that the hope failed only through the superior luck and cunning of the English!

unification of the people, either under Shivaji or under the Peshwas. The cohesion of the peoples in the Maratha State was not organic but artificial, accidental, and therefore precarious. It was solely dependent on the ruler's extraordinary personality and disappeared when the country ceased to produce supermen among its rulers.

A Government of personal discretion is, by its very nature, uncertain. This uncertainty reacted fatally on the administration. However well-planned the machinery and rules might be, the actual conduct of the administration was marred by inefficiency, sudden changes, and official corruption, because nobody felt secure of his post or of the due appreciation of his merit. This has been the bane of all autocratic States in the East and the West alike, except where the autocrat has been a "hero as king" or where a high level of education, civilization and national spirit among the people has reduced the evil.

§3 *Hindrances to true nationality in Shivaji's age.*

The society of Shivaji's age and country was so different from our own that some straining of the historical imagination is necessary before we can understand the difficulties that he had to combat.

Land was the only stable thing in an ever-changing world, subject to the appalling outbursts of Nature's forces, which swept away man and his handiwork, and the even more violent transformations of political revolution. But the new conquerors always left the land to the old peasant because he alone could till it in that age of sparse population, and the revenue collection to the old hereditary middlemen, because they alone knew the details of the locality and could ensure some payment from the land to a distant sovereign who would have found it impossible to collect his dues from each petty tiller of the soil directly. The offices in connection with land, therefore, tended to become hereditary and the contractor of revenue blossomed in time into a landowner with a permanent family claim to a portion of the yield of his village or district. Attachment to one's ancestral land was the strongest passion in that age of little trade and no large-scale industry. I know of a Brahman family which migrated from the Ratnagiri district to Ahmadabad six generations ago, and no longer own an inch of land of their own in their ancient home nor keep any business connection with it, and yet they have carefully preserved for two centuries the old title-deeds of their long-abandoned lands.

And, in that age land-rights were unsettled and perplexing in the variety and complication of the personal claims to one and the same tract. Illustrations of this state of things can be found almost everywhere in the Deccan; I give the case of Savant-vadi as readily available in print. In this small region there was in the sixteenth century a *desai* (or zamindar) of the Prabhu caste at Kudal for collecting the revenue on behalf of the Bijapur Sultan, with a *dalvi* or captain of the Rajput caste under him to lead his troops. The *dalvi* rebelled against his master the *desai* and sought the help of a neighbouring *savant* or chief of the Maratha caste. At first the desai suppressed the rebel with the support of his sovereign. But in the third generation an able *savant* rose to power, secured the desai-ship of Banda from Adil Shah, and after extirpating most of the Prabhu desais annexed the Kudal pargana. But some members of the dispossessed family escaped and revived their claim to the land. Next, Shivaji stepped in to oust the *savant*[1] Further complication was introduced by two branches of the same family (even two brothers) fighting for the same estate and transmitting their disputes to their sons and grandsons.

Into this world of bewildering confusion of land-rights and revenue offices,—where nothing was generally known for certain or acknowledged as a clear final settlement,—Shivaji (like all other conquerors) burst as a new dissolving force. He had to give his own decision on these claims. All who lost their suits before him, all who were displaced in office by his nominees, immediately turned against him and tried to make their claims good by joining his enemies and opposing his Government There was no national feeling, no acceptance of the law of the land however honestly administered.

To every one in that age his own fief (*watan*) was the only reality, the only object of a man's lifelong endeavour, his highest reward on earth, while Fatherland (*patria*), if thought of at all, was felt to be an abstract idea, a nonentity *Watan* could yield honour power and the pleasures of life, while *patria* was a mere word, a fancy of the imagination.

A further hindrance to the growth of patriotism was the infinitely minute sub-division of society, which made the formation of one nation, or a compact body of men moved by community of life thought and interests, impossible, and even inconceivable. Apart from the impassable chasm between the Hindus and the Muslims living on the same soil and under the same rulers, the Hindus themselves were split up into innumerable mutually warring (or, at best, contemptuously detached and indifferent) fragments Not only did caste despise and persecute caste, but even among the members of the same caste there were ditsinctions as sharp as those marking off the Muhammadan from the Hindu or the Shudra from the Brahman. Certain families claimed to be of nobler blood (*kulin*) than all others of the same caste and locality, and depressed and insulted the latter in society. The highest aim of a Hindu in that age—as even in our own times,—was to elevate his own family (and often also his own sub-division of a caste) in the social scale by lavish bounty to the Brahmans and the caste elders, by hypergamy, or by a nearer approach to the practices of the highest or "twice-born" castes. But the dominant families (or castes) tried to keep the newer or lower ones down at their former level of degradation by turning all the engines of social persecution against them They took away from such daring aspirants and disturbers of the primeval stereotyped usage and custom, not only the benefit of the clergy but also all the amenities of social life and the services of the public servants of the village. This boycott or outcasting (*grāmanya*) was a more terrifying penalty than death itself.

It was only human nature if the noblest members of the despised families (or castes) resented this injustice and tyranny of soceity and, in the bitterness of public humiliation, sought to be avenged on the persecuting church and State by going over to the enemies of their country and faith. Such action, on the part of the oppressors and the oppressed alike, is impossible where a true sense of nationality has taken root. Patriotism could not grow on the Indian soil (except among compact clans of blood-kindred like the Rajputs.) The State, as an impersonal continuous being,—higher and more durable than our individual selves, could not be conceived of by the rulers of Hindu India whose sole care was for the benefit of self and not for the good of the community as a whole.

As an acute English observer wrote in 1803. "Every Maratha prince, and every jagirdar or military chief in the [Maratha] empire, has a *khazana* or collection of treasure, consisting of specie and jewels, which is lodged in a secret depository within the walls of a strong fortress, often erected for the purpose, on one of the most inaccessible mountains in his dominions This private treasure is the first and never-ceasing object of his ambition to increase. No want of money for supporting a war, *even in defence of his own territory*, ever induces a Maratha chief to supply the deficiency from his private treasury; the loss of which would be to him a much more grievous calamity than the subjugation of his country "*

Such were the men among whom Shivaji tried to build up his edifice of an independent national State, the men whom he had to employ as his instruments, the men to whom he had to leave his uncompleted task. The leaders were actuated by an insane pride of birth, an all-devouring jealousy about precedence, an ambition that blinded them to all consequences an incapacity for self-subordination to law and corporate loyalty that marks lesser breads, a lack of political vision and of practical realism. As for the masses, they were human sheep, worthy to be led by such shepherds, their horizon was

* *Asiatic Annual Register* for 1803, p 4 A recent example was that of Daulat Rao Sindhia in 1809, as described by Capt Broughton 'While Sindhia is daily submitting to these and similar insults [from his unpaid soldiery], he possesses a privy purse of 50 lakhs, which no distress either of himself or his troops is sufficiently powerful to induce him to violate" (*Letters from a Mahratta Camp*, Const ed, p 106)

bounded by the hard conditions of their daily toil, with a simple emotional faith as their only solace.

In such conditions no superman even can create a nation and leave an enduring State behind him. Shivaji with his transcendent genius could have barely laid their true foundations if a long reign of internal peace had been granted to him and he had been followed by a line of worthy successors. But he lived for less than six years after his coronation, and his kingdom perished with his sons.

§4. *Neglect of the economic factor by the Marathas.*

The Maratha rulers neglected the economic development of the State. Some of them did, no doubt, try to save the peasantry from illegal exactions, and to this extent they promoted agriculture. But commerce was subjected to frequent harassment by local officers, and the traders could never be certain of freedom of movement and security of their rights on mere payment of the legal rate of duty. The internal resources of a small province with no industry, little trade, a sterile soil, and an agriculture dependent upon scanty and precarious rainfall,—could not possibly support the large army that Shivaji kept or the imperial position and world-dominion to which the Peshwas aspired.

The necessary expenses of the State could be met, and all the parts of the body-politic could be held together only by a constant flow of money from outside its own borders, *i.e.*, by a regular succession of raids. As the late Mr. G. K. Gokhale laughingly told me when describing the hardships of the present rigid land assessment in the Bombay Presidency, "You see, the rate of the land revenue did not matter much under Maratha rule.

In those old days, when the crop failed our people used to sally forth with their horses and spears and bring back enough booty to feed them for the next two or three years Now they have to starve on their own lands."

Thus, by the character of his State, the Maratha's hands were turned against everybody and everybody's hands were turned against him. It is the Nemesis of a *Krieg-staat* to move in a vicious circle It must wage war periodically if it is to get its food, but war, when waged as a normal method of supply, destroys industry and wealth in the invading and invaded countries alike, and ultimately defeats the very end of such wars Peace is death to a *Krieg-staat;* but peace is the very life-breath of wealth. The *Krieg-staat,* therefore, kills the goose that lays the golden eggs To take an illustration, Shivaji's repeated plunder of Surat scared away trade and wealth from that city, and his second raid (in 1670) brought him much less booty than his first, and a few years later the constant dread of Maratha incursion entirely impoverished Surat and effectually dried up this source of supply. Thus, from the economic point of view, the Maratha State had no *stable* basis, no normal means of growth *within itself.*

§5. *Excess of finesse and intrigue*

Lastly, the Maratha leaders trusted too much to finesse. They did not realize that without a certain amount of manly openness and fidelity to promises no society can hold together. Stratagem and falsehood may have been necessary at the birth of their State, but it was continued during the maturity of their power. No one could rely on the promise of a Maratha minister or the assurance of a Maratha general. Witness the long and finally fruitless negotiations of the English merchants with Shivaji for compensation for the looting of their Rajapur factory. The Maratha Government could not always be relied on to abide by their treaty obligations.

Shivaji, and to a lesser extent Baji Rao I., preserved an admirable balance between war and diplomacy. But the latter-day Marathas lost this practical ability. They trusted too much to diplomatic trickery, as if empire were a pacific game of chess. Military efficiency was neglected, war at the right moment and in the right fashion was avoided, or, worse still, their forces were frittered away in unseasonable campaigns and raids conducted as a matter of routine, and the highest political wisdom was believed to consist in *raj-karan* or diplomatic intrigue. Thus, while the Maratha spider was weaving his endless cobweb of hollow alliances and diplomatic counter-plots, the mailed fist of Wellesley was thrust into his laboured but flimsy tissue of statecraft, and by a few swift and judicious strokes his defence and screen was torn away and his power left naked and helpless. In rapid succession the Nizam was disarmed, Tipu was crushed, and the Peshwa was enslaved. While Sindhia and Holkar were dreaming the dream of the overlordship of all India, they suddenly awoke to find that even their local independence was gone. The man of action, the soldier-statesman, always triumphs over the mere scheming Machiavel. Punic perfidy never succeeds in the long run.

§6. *Character of Shivaji.*

Shivaji's private life was marked by a high standard of morality. He was a devoted son, a loving father and an attentive husband, though he did not rise above the ideas and usage of his age, which allowed a plurality of wives and the keeping of concubines even among the priestly caste, not to speak of warriors and kings. Intensely religious from his very boyhood, by instinct and training alike, he remained throughout life abstemious, free from vice, respectful to holy men, and passionately fond of hearing scripture readings and sacred stories and songs. But religion remained with him an ever fresh fountain of right conduct and generosity; it did not obsess his mind nor harden him into a bigot. The sincerity of his faith is proved by his impartial respect for the holy men of all sects (Muslim as much as Hindu) and toleration of all creeds. His chivalry to women and strict enforcement of morality in his camp was a wonder in that age and has extorted the admiration of hostile critics like Khafi Khan.

He had the born leader's personal magnetism and threw a spell over all who knew him, drawing the best elements of the country to his side and winning the most devoted service from his officers, while his dazzling victories and ever ready smile made him the idol of his soldiery. His royal gift of judging character was one of the main causes of his success, as his selection of generals and governors, diplomatists and secretaries was never at fault, and his administration was a great improvement on the past.

His army organization was a model of efficiency; everything was provided for beforehand and kept in its proper place under a proper caretaker; an excellent spy system supplied him in advance with the most minute information about the theatre of his intended campaign; divisions of his army were combined or dispersed at will over long distances without failure; the enemy's pursuit or obstruction was successfully met and yet the booty was rapidly and safely conveyed home without any loss. His inborn military genius is proved by his instinctively adopting that system of warfare which was most suited to the racial character of his soldiers, the nature of the country, the weapons of the age, and the internal condition of his enemies. His light cavalry, stiffened with swift-footed infantry, was irresistible in the age of Aurangzib. More than a century after his death, his blind imitator Daulat Rao Sindhia continued the same tactics when the English had galloper guns for field action and most of the Deccan towns were walled round* and provided with defensive artillery, and he therefore failed ignominiously.

§7. *Shivaji's genius analyzed.*

The greatness of Shivaji's genius can be fully realized not from the extent of the kingdom he won for himself nor from the value of the hoarded treasure he left behind him, but from a survey of the conditions amidst which he rose to sovereignty.

He was truly an original explorer, the maker of a new road in mediæval Indian history, with no example or guide before him. When he chose to declare his independence, the Mughal empire seemed to be at the height of its glory. Every local chief who had, anywhere in India, revolted against it had been crushed. For a small jagirdar's son to defy its power, appeared as an act of madness, a courting of sure ruin. Shivaji, however, chose this path, and he succeeded.

---

* Owen's *Selections from Wellington's Desp*, 284, 289

His success can be explained only by an analysis of his political genius. First and foremost he possessed that unfailing sense of reality in politics, that recognition of the exact possibilities of his time (*tact des choses possibles*) which Cavour defined as the essence of statesmanship. His daring was tempered and guided by an instinctive perception of how far his actual resources could carry him, how long a certain line of action or policy was to be followed, and where he must stop. For the lack of this political insight his rash son Shambhuji came to a miserable end and undid the work of Shivaji's life

Shivaji possessed the true master's gift of judging character at sight and choosing the fittest instruments for his work. This is proved by the successful execution of his orders by his agents in his absence Many of the distant expeditions of his reign were conducted not by himself in person but by his generals, who almost always carried out his orders according to plan. This was a novel feat in an Asiatic monarchy, where everything depends on the master's presence. It was the training gained in Shivaji's service, aided by the Maratha national character for personal independence and initiative, that enabled the disorganized Maratha people to stand up against all the resources of the mighty Aurangzib for eighteen years and ultimately to defeat him, even though they had no king or capital to form the centre of the national defence.

His reign brought peace and order to his country, assured the protection of women's honour and of all sects without distinction, extended the royal patronage to the truly pious men of all creeds (Muslims no less than Hindus), and presented equal opportunities to all his subjects by opening the public service to talent irrespective of religion or caste.* This was the ideal policy for a State with a composite population like India.

His gifts were peace and a wise internal administration. The stability of these good conditions was the only thing necessary for giving permanence to Shivaji's work and ensuring national consolidation and growth. But that stability was denied to his political creation. Only his example and name remained to inspire the best minds of succeeding generations with ideals of life and government, not unmixed with vain regrets.

§8. *Shivaji's political ideal and difficulties.*

Did Shivaji merely found a *Krieg-staat, i.e.,* a Government that lives and grows only by war? Was he merely an *entrepreneur* of rapine, a Hindu edition of Alauddin Khilji or Timur?

I think it would not be fair to take this view. For one thing, he never had peace to work out his political ideas. The whole of his short life was one struggle with enemies, a period of preparation and not of fruition. All his attention was necessarily devoted to meeting daily dangers with daily expedients and he had not the chance of peacefully building up a well-planned political edifice.

In the vast Gangetic valley and the wide *Desh* country rolling eastwards through the Deccan, Nature has fixed no boundary to States. Their size changes with daily changes in their strength as compared with their

---

* He was himself a Hindu, sincere in belief and orthodox in practice, and yet he employed a number of Muhammadan officers in the highest positions, such as Munshi Haidar (who became Chief Justice of the Mughal empire on entering Aurangzib's service), Siddi Sambal, Siddi Misri, and Daulat Khan (admirals), besides commanders like Siddi Halal and Nur Khan (*Dil* i 100) He gave legal recognition to the Muslim *qazis* in his dominions

neighbours'. There can be no stable equilibrium among them for more than a generation. Each has to push the others as much for self-defence as for aggression. Each must be armed and ready to invade the others, if it does not wish to be invaded and absorbed by them. Where friction with neighbours is the normal state of things, a huge armed force, sleepless vigilance, and readiness to strike the first blow are the necessary conditions of the very existence of a kingdom The evil could be remedied only by the establishment of a universal empire throughout the country from sea to sea.

Shivaji could not for a moment be sure of the Delhi Government's pacific disposition or fidelity to treaty. The past history of the Mughal expansion into the Deccan since the days of Akbar, was a warning to him. The imperial policy of annexing the whole of South India was unmistakable to Shiva as to Adil Shah or Qutb Shah. Its completion was only a question of time, and every Deccani Power was bound to wage eternal warfare with the Mughals if it wished to exist. Hence Shivaji lost no chance of robbing Mughal territory in the Deccan.

With Bijapur his relations were somewhat different. He could raise his head or expand his dominion only at the expense of Bijapur Rebellion against his liege lord was the necessary condition of his being. But when, about 1662, an understanding was effected between him and the Adil-Shahi ministers, he gave up molesting the heart of the Bijapur kingdom With the Bijapuri barons whose fiefs lay close to his dominions, he had, however, to wage war till he had wrested Kolhapur, North Kanara and South Konkan from their hands In the Karnatak division, *viz* , the Dharwar and Belgaum districts, this contest was still undecided when he died. With the provinces that lay across the path of his natural expansion he could not be at peace, though he did not wish to challenge the central Government of Bijapur. This attitude was changed by the death of Ali II. in 1672, the accession of the boy Sikandar Adil Shah, the faction-fights between rival nobles at the capital, and the visible dissolution of the Government. But Shivaji helped Bijapur greatly during the Mughal invasion of 1679.

§9. *His influence on the spirit.*

Shivaji's real greatness lay in his character and practical ability, rather than in originality of conception or length of political vision. Unfailing insight into the character of others, efficiency of arrangements, and instinctive perception of what was practicable and most profitable under the circumstances,—these were the causes of his success in life. To these must be added his personal morality and loftiness of aim, which drew to his side the best minds of his community, while his universal toleration and insistence on equal justice gave contentment to all classes subject to his rule, He strenuously maintained order and enforced moral laws throughout his own dominions, and the people were happier under his sway than elsewhere.

His splendid success fired the imagination of his contemporaries, and his name became a spell calling the Maratha race to a new life. His kingdom was lost within nine years of his death. But the imperishable achievement of his life was the raising of the Marathas into an independent self-reliant people, conscious of their oneness and high destiny, and his most precious legacy was the spirit that he breathed into his race.

The mutual conflict and internal weakness of the

three Muslim Powers of the Deccan were, no doubt, contributory causes of the rise of Shivaji. But his success sprang from a higher source than the incompetence of his enemies. I regard him as the last great constructive genius and nation-builder that the Hindu race has produced. His system was his own creation and, unlike Ranjit Singh, he took no foreign aid in his administration. His army was drilled and commanded by his own people and not by Frenchmen. What he built lasted long; his institutions were looked up to with admiration and emulation even a century later in the palmy days of the Peshwas' rule.

Shivaji was illiterate; he learnt nothing by reading. He built up his kingdom and Government before visiting any royal Court, civilized city, or organized camp. He received no help or counsel from any experienced minister or general.* But his native genius, alone and unaided, enabled him to found a compact kingdom, an invincible army, and a grand and beneficent system of administration.

Before his rise, the Maratha race was scattered like atoms through many Deccani kingdoms. He welded them into a mighty nation. And he achieved this in the teeth of the opposition of four great Powers like the Mughal empire, Bijapur, Portuguese India, and the Abyssinians of Janjira. No other Hindu has shown such capacity in modern times.

Before he came, the Marathas were mere hirelings, mere servants of aliens. They served the State, but had

---

* His early tutor, Dadaji Kond-dev, was a Brahman well versed in the Shastras and estate management. He could only teach Shivaji how to be a good revenue collector or accountant. Shivaji's institutions, civil and military, could not have been inspired by Dadaji.

no lot or part in its management; they shed their life-blood in the army, but were denied any share in the conduct of war or peace. They were always subordinates, never leaders.

Shivaji was the first to challenge Bijapur and Delhi and thus teach his countrymen that it was possible for them to be independent leaders in war. Then, he founded a State and taught his people that they were capable of administering a kingdom in all its departments. He has proved by his example that the Hindu race can build a nation, found a State, defeat enemies; they can conduct their own defence; they can protect and promote literature and art, commerce and industry; they can maintain navies and ocean-trading fleets of their own, and conduct naval battles on equal terms with foreigners. He taught the modern Hindus to rise to the full stature of their growth.

He has proved that the Hindu race can still produce not only *jamadars* (non-commissioned officers) and *chitnises* (clerks), but also rulers of men, and even a king of kings (*Chhatrapati.*) The Emperor Jahangir cut the *Akshay Bat* tree of Allahabad down to its roots and hammered a red-hot iron cauldron on to its stump. He flattered himself that he had killed it. But lo! within a year the tree began to grow again and pushed the heavy obstruction to its growth aside!

Shivaji has shown that the tree of Hinduism is not really dead, that it can rise from beneath the seemingly crushing load of centuries of political bondage, exclusion from the administration, and legal repression; it can put forth new leaves and branches; it can again lift up its head to the skies.

BIBLIOGRAPHY OF AUTHORITIES FOR THE HISTORY OF SHIVAJI

Character of Shivaji records

The royal period (1660-1700) of Maratha history differs fundamentally from the Peshwa period (18th century) not only in the extent but also in the nature of its historical records. Not only is there a striking contrast between the wealth of contemporary documents in Persian and English that illuminate the history of the Peshwas and the comparative poverty of the same for Shivaji's reign and those of his two sons. But even when we come to Marathi sources, we find that not a single *State-paper* or official despatch of Shivaji's time in this language has been unearthed after a devoted search for half a century. But thousands of *private* legal documents, deeds of grant, decisions of lawsuits, orders on petitions and similar papers have been collected, and for the sufficient reason that they did not belong to the State archives (which perished long ago with their contents) but were the property of private families by whom they have been carefully preserved as title-deeds.

The Marathas in the 17th century were a poor and rude people, dispersed through many States, and with no literature of their own except folk-songs and religious poetry. Shivaji for the first time gave them peace wealth and an independent national Court, without which it is not possible to produce literature or store official records. But this happy state of things lasted barely 18 years, from his last rupture with the Mughals in 1670 to the death of Shambhuji in 1689. Thereafter every Maratha fort and city was occupied by the Mughals and the Maratha State records were burnt or dispersed. Even during these 18 years of their power and prosperity, the Marathas were more busy with the sword than with the pen, no literature proper, no long history or biography was produced then.

Hence, the Maratha kingdom before the Peshwa period utterly lacks the State papers, detailed official histories, personal memoirs and letter-books of which Mughal history is so full.

Early Marathi accounts

The only *contemporary* records of Shivaji's and even Shambhuji's times that now survive are in English and Persian and none at all in Marathi. The earliest Marathi history of his reign,—if we may apply this dignified title to Sabhasad's brief and confused recollections,—was written in 1694, and the skeleton *Jedhe Shakavali* later still. Laudatory poems by bards hankering for rewards from patrons who are flattered to the top of their bent, cannot claim to be histories. On the other hand, the Persian and English sources were absolutely contemporary, promptly set down in writing, often detailed and dated, and carefully preserved since then. Their writers belonged to a higher intellectual type than the Marathi chroniclers, as is clearly seen from a comparative study of the materials in the three languages

Even the *Sabhasad Bakhar*, though written by a contemporary of Shivaji, is not based on State-papers and written notes, because it was composed while Rajaram was closely besieged in Jinji fort, to which he had escaped from Maharashtra by the skin of his teeth, leaving everything behind him, and after roving hither and thither in constant risk of capture Such a master and his servants, running with their lives in their hands, before relentless pursuers, could not have burdened themselves with papers during their perilous flight across the entire Deccan peninsula Sabhasad's work, therefore, is entirely derived from his memory—the half-obliterated memory of an old man who had passed through many privations and hardships But he was a contemporary and servant of Shivaji, while Malhar Ram Rao Chitnis wrote 130 years after that king's death, and had no State-papers of Shivaji's or Shambhuji's times, because he does not cite a single document, and all his true facts are derived from Sabhasad, thereby proving that he had no independent source of information Therefore, I have totally rejected Chitnis

The Dattaji-Malkare type of bakhars

Next after Sabhasad's work (1694) both in point of time and reliability, is a group of shorter histories, all derived from the same original and all forming one type In Marathi they are known as the *91 qalmi* (or *96 qalmi*) *Bakhar* (printed in the *Prabhat* by Rajwade and in the *Bharatvarsha* by Parasnis), and to readers of Grant Duff as the *Raigarh life*, Frissell's English version of which has been printed by Forrest The *Tarikh-i-Shivaji* represents an amplified Persian translation of the same work, evidently made from an earlier and longer Marathi original than the *91 qalmi Bakhar*. Warren Hastings presented a MS of it to the India Office, London, and some other copies exist in the British Museum and elsewhere

The I. O L. MS ends with the death of Shivaji, but contains at the end a supplement in the form of a bare list of Shivaji's descendants at Satara down to Ramraja, the adopted son and (then reigning) successor of Shahu This translation fixes the lower limit of the date of the Marathi original as 1770 The earliest limit might well go up to 1720, the time of the restoration of Shivaji's kingdom in a settled form under Shahu on the final abandonment of the Mughal claims to it

The nucleus of this group or type of works was some very short sketch of Shivaji's history in the possession of Dattaji (Shivaji's *Waqnis* or chronicler), from which Anaji Ranganath Malkare's son Khandoji took a copy [The colophon calls the original a detailed history, *tafsil-war*, which I consider very unlikely] Khandoji, though he nowhere says so, padded out the original by interpolating in it every movement and posting of his father in Shivaji's reign, as Dattaji could not have cared for such small fry as Anaji Ranganath Malkare and considered him worthy of mention almost as often as the Prime Minister himself I have designated it as the Malkare Bakhar and not Dattaji's work, because the latter has not come down to us

This recension has been printed, but the Marathi text, in both the editions, is full of copyists' errors or wrong readings, and the English translation (in Forrest) is horribly incorrect in the proper names and dates (But their correction would be very easy for one who knows all the sources for Shivaji) The Persian version clearly goes back to Malkare's source but also derived a portion of its information from some other work than Dattaji's After the necessary corrections of names and dates have been made and the loose traditions weeded out, the substratum that remains is of high historical value and is in several points corroborated by unimpeachable records of Shivaji's time When judiciously used it is a very helpful supplement to Sabhasad

The Marathi Shakavalis criticized

The *Jedhe Shakavali* or skeleton chronology in its surviving fragment runs from 1618 to 1697, without any formal preface or conclusion Its correctness depends upon three conditions, *viz*, (*a*) the Jedhes' personal knowledge of what they wrote down, (*b*) their promptness in recording every event after its happening, instead of trusting to a dim and distant memory, and (*c*) the accuracy of the transcriber of the only manuscript of it (copied in the middle of the 18th century) that has come down to us This family did not record the successive occurrences in a bound volume (or in a big family Bible as in old English houses), but on loose sheets of paper, which were afterwards compiled together, we know not with what accuracy nor with what gaps between For the period before 1660,—in which year Shivaji first clearly demonstrated his power of standing on his own legs and former vassals of Bijapur like the Jedhe chieftains found that it was safer to join him than to keep aloof or play a double game (which is Bhave's charge against Kanhoji Jedhe),—the dates in the Jedhe Chronology are often demonstrably wrong (*e g*, the death of Ibrahim Adil Shah, the fall of Daulatabad, etc) Even for later times, some months and years have been wrongly given or at least copied (*e g*, the fall of Vellore) Several of the entries, particularly those relating to the Muslim States, were merely borrowed by Jedhe's clerks from other sources, because we know that short Persian manuals of historical dates were in circulation in polished society in the 18th and early 19th centuries Hence, it is not always safe to rely on Jedhe's testimony for any doubtful date when not supported by some other authority

On the other hand, a hereditary writer-servant of Shivaji's family like Dattaji or Malhar Ram Rao, is a better authority for the date of Shivaji's birth, as the *tithi* (lunar day) of his birth was annually celebrated at his Court and was entered in the memorandum kept by the secretariat officers

Such skeleton chronologies (*Shakavalis*) were in use among various noble families in Maharashtra in the 18th century, and have been recovered in parts only There was a short kernel of the leading events common to them all, but each family added entries about what happened to its own ancestors or about events in its neighbourhood, and therefore they cannot serve as independent checks on one another Many mistakes were also made in reading the old Modi script of the original MSS

For a detailed discussion of the sources the reader is referred to my paper on "the Sources of the History of Shivaji critically examined" published in the *Journal* of the Bihar and Orissa Research Society, March, 1924

Four new sources of error produced in the 19th century

While our knowledge of Shivaji's history has grown during the last hundred years by the discovery and publication of contemporary Persian, French, Portuguese, and Marathi records unknown to Grant Duff, certain new sources of error have also come into the field, and tend to deceive the unsuspecting historian by their cross-lights and false lights They are —

(i) The extinction of the Peshwa's rule in 1817,—and even earlier, his virtual deposition from sovereignty in 1803,—naturally led to a revolution in the mental attitude of the Marathas The fallen house of usurping Brahman ministers was felt to be a wrong horse to back and the old dynasty of Bhonslé kings came into vogue in public estimation and was exalted by the paramount British Power One may even say that patriotism could now find a free vent and Shivaji could be professed as a national idol without any fear of exciting the jealous suspicion of the Chitpavan dynasty on the throne of Puna It became a social and political disadvantage for a noble family in Maharashtra to describe its founder as a creation of the Peshwa period, rather than as a follower of Shivaji Then began a mad struggle among them to rewrite their family history and represent their first famous ancestors as patriotic supporters of that great king in weal and woe Witness the longing of every Greek State to get its name enrolled in the second Book of the *Iliad* While some of these claims are true, all cannot be so

Forgery of grants and royal letters

(ii) The evil was aggravated by the formation of the Inam Commission (1824) which called upon every holder of land or State-pension to prove his rights by producing old documents and giving his family history The result was a vast crop of reports submitted to the English Government and designated variously as *Kaifiyat, Yadi, Haqiqat* and *Karina* Composed between 1820 and 1830 they profess to give the family history (often with copies of alleged charters) from Shahji's time, (c 1637) and in the cases of the prouder families from an even earlier date, such as the first Muslim invasion of the Deccan (1294) Their only foundation was family tradition, dim with distance of time, or the daring imagination of the hereditary family priest and astrologer

The holder of even the smallest plot of land or right to village-office now produced title-deeds in the form of grants and confirmations by the Hindu and Muslim kings before the British conquest Some of these professed to be original, others copies of long-decayed originals certified by former *qazis* or kings as true Of this class thousands of documents in the Marathi language have been printed But their value is exceedingly small Ninety-eight per cent of these papers is of no historical significance at all, as they relate to the petty local rights of petty private individuals Several are palpable forgeries It is not possible to give detailed examples in this book

The forger in each case had some genuine documents of the post-Shiva period before him and has transferred their exact language to his own fabrication which professes to belong to an earlier age! It is, therefore, very unsafe to rely for any date or event, on the sole testimony of these papers unless their authenticity has been placed beyond doubt by other and more unimpeachable sources, but such corroboration is mostly impossible

The forgery of documents for establishing rights to property is a very ancient practice, from which the priestly and ruling classes have been no more free than others (Cf Harsha s copper plate grant)

Worthless laudatory poems

(iii) Some Sanskrit poems of Shivaji s time have survived and have been recently printed Bardic flattery and exaggeration have been found in all countries to be the greatest perverters of historical truth In India the art of literary beggary was carried to nauseating lengths by the Brahman Court flatterers of the Hindu kings and even of some of the Mughal Emperors The very training, mode of life and literary models of these Brahman poets made them unfit to be sober recorders of fact Even for the events that they personally witnessed, one has to largely discount their narrative, while for the events of earlier times or elsewhere, they are absolutely untrustworthy It is not the business of priests and poets to keep public records or copies of State-papers, at best they reproduce the traditions current among their class

The absurd flights of exaggeration which a venal poet can take in flattering his patron may be exemplified from the poem of Lal Kavi who alleges that during the invasion of Deogarh (1669) the entire Mughal army was defeated and put to flight, but the defeat was turned into a victory by the boy Chhatra Sal charging the enemy host single-handed and routing it without anybody s aid! A parallel to this is afforded by Paramanand s allegation that Malik Ambar's crushing defeat of the Mughal and Adil-Shahi armies at Bhatvadi (1624) was mainly due to Shahji and his Bhonsle contingent (*Shiva Bharat*, canto 4)

(*iv*) Maratha history has been muddled also by the silly but very bitter quarrel between the Brahman and Prabhu castes, which began (with growing wealth and public safety) under Shivaji burst into a flame in Shambhuji s reign (at the outcasting of Balaji Avji), and has been revived and widely extended in modern times by the help of a cheap printing press, the multiplication of newspapers as sectional organs, and the easy means of distributing writings Each caste interprets the past history of the country and "discovers" old documents so as to heighten its own glory and depress its rival caste A historical statement or argument is valued differently according as it comes from a Chitpavan or a Karhare, a Brahman or a Prabhu!

Materials rejected

I have not found it safe to make any but a very cautious and sparing use of these three classes of materials in my book Tested in those points where genuine contemporary evidence of other kinds is available, the whole class of Kaifiyat literature and the Tanjore inscription (carved in 1803) are often proved to have recorded opium-eaters' tales as history Many of their dates are ludicrously incorrect and persons are made to tread the earth and figure in action before their birth or after their death as known beyond doubt !

No higher credence can be claimed by the *bakhar* literature of the 19th or very late 18th century They do not make the least pretence of being based upon old written records, but contain loose traditions (often palpably false) in their latest and most perverted form, a maximum of legends, supernatural marvels and bazar gossip, with a minimum of facts and dates Nearly all of them are of unknown date and authorship They are no more history than the Sanskrit *Puranas,* and they bear the signs of being the production of some ignorant credulous dull-brained persons and not the work of any intelligent minister of State or scholarly author

Value of European Factory Records.

The records of the English factories on the Bombay coast and inland are of the highest value for dates and facts Sometimes the factors frankly confess that the reports they have heard and are writing down immediately after are so contradictory that they know not what to believe But, on the other hand, the English at Rajapur and Karwar employed paid spies who travelled in Shivaji's dominions and brought back news of his doings and plans, the information from the different factories helped to check and correct one another, and a false rumour is usually followed by its contradiction Above all, these factory records have the supreme merit of having been preserved in the original manuscript without any later garbling or interpolation

The value of the *Memoire* of Francois Martin (of Pondicherry) is the highest imaginable for Shivaji's Karnatak expedition His agents were frequently in attendance in the camp of Shivaji and the reports they brought back were immediately entered in his diary. The English of Madras also sent a clever Brahman to Shivaji on two or three occasions The reports of such witnesses entirely displace the later gossip about the Karnatak expedition given in the Marathi books The Jesuit letter for 1677 is mostly wrong and based on distant rumour, it cannot stand against Martin's testimony for this episode in Shivaji's life

SOURCES

A. Marathi

101 *Shiva-chhatrapati-chen Charitra* by Krishnaji Anant Sabhasad, written in 1694 at Jinji, by order of Rajaram, ed. by K. N Sane, 3rd ed 1912 A small book of barely 100 pages, composed from memory without the help of written memoranda or documents The events are not arranged in the order of time Some of the statements are incorrect Weak in topography, no dates Language very condensed and sometimes obscure

But the most valuable Marathi account of Shivaji and our main source of information from the Maratha side Later biographies in the same language have mostly copied this Sabhasad Bakhar and padded out their source (Sabhasad) by means of Sanskrit quotations, miracles, rhetorical flourishes, emotional gush, and commonplace remarks and details added from the probabilities of the case or from pure imagination [In Sane's 4th ed the text has been very unwisely mixed up]

Translated into English by J L Manker as *Life and Exploits of Shivaji* (Bombay, 1st ed 1884, 2nd ed 1886)

102 *Chitra-gupta Bakhar*, composed about 1760, contains merely Sabhasad's facts (and even language), interspersed with copious extracts from the Sanskrit Scriptures Useless

103 *Shiva chhatrapati-chen Sapta-prakaran-atmak Charitra*, written by Malhar Ram Rao Chitnis in 1810, and ed by N J Kirtane 2nd ed 1894 Incorrect, rambling or pure guess-work in many places No State-paper used, no idea of correct chronology Muhammadan names grossly incorrect and anachronistic Moro Pant is perpetually conquering and having to conquer again "twenty-seven forts in Baglana &c" (pp 41, 71, 124 and 176) ! Worthless modern fabrication

104 *Shivadigvijay*, ed or published by P R Nandurbarkar and L K Dandekar, (Baroda, 1895) Falsely described as written by Khando Ballal (the son of Shivaji's secretary Balaji Avji) in 1718 Fabricated by a writer familiar with the style of modern vernacular novels written by imitators of Bankim Chandra Chatterji Too much gush (esp pp 453, 208, 444), rhetorical padding and digression The author speaks of an English *general* being present at Shivaji's coronation (p 435) and of goods from *Calcutta* being used in decorating his hall in 1674 (p 417) !!! Shiva bows to his mother two years after her death (p 296) ! Tanaji Malusare visits Haidarabad seven years after his death ! (p 301)

105 *Shivapratap* (Baroda), an utterly worthless modern fabrication, does not even claim to be old

106 *Shrimant Maharaj Bhonsle-yanchi Bakhar* [of Shedgaon], pub by V L Bhave (Thana, 1917) Utterly worthless expansion of Sabhasad with forged letters and imaginary details

107-8 Two alleged old *bakhars* (called *More-yanchi Chooti Bakhar* and *Mahabaleshwar-chi Juni Mahiti*) pub in Parasnis's *Itihas Sangraha, Sfuta lekh*, i 21-29 and ii 9-12 Full of palpable historical errors and deliberate fabrication (probably of the same factory and date as No 106)

109 *Jedhe-yanchi Shakavali*, ed by B G Tilak in *Chaturtha Sammelan Britta* (Puna) A bare record of events with dates, kept by the Jedhe family of Bhor (Puna district)

The Shivapur deshpandes have preserved two *Shakavalis*, one in their *Yadi* (very short) and the other in their *Bahi* I have secured a transcript of the very large *Shivapur Deshpande Shakavali* preserved in the library of the Bombay Royal Asiatic Society (Forbes collection) The above three Shakavalis as well as three others are printed in the *Shiva-Charitra Pradip* (a very useful book) which also gives the *Jedhe Karina* (an amplification of the *Shakavali* from the purely family point of view) An uncorrected English translation of the Jedhe Shakavali and Karina is given in the *Shivaji Souvenir*

110 *Sanads and Letters*, ed by P V Mawjee and D B Parasnis (1913) and

111. *Marathyan-chya-Itihasachin-Sadhanen*, ed by V K Rajwade and others, Vols viii and xv-xxiv contain a few political letters and a vast mass of private legal documents and charters of Shivaji and his times Some of them are clearly forgeries made to deceive the Inam Commission and other judicial bodies Some others seem to have been faked to support "popular" history or family prestige

Many documents of this class have been also printed in the Annual Proceedings (*Varshik Itibritta*), Conference Reports (*Sammelan Britta*) and Quarterly (*Traimasik*) of the Bharat Itihas Samshodhak Mandal of Puna, in the *Shiva-Charitra-Pradip*, (1925), *Shiva-Charitra-Sahitya* (ed by K V Purandare, 1926), *Itihas Ani Aitihasik*, Vol 5 (ed by Rajwade), *Marathi Daftar*, Vol 3 (ed by V L Bhave, 1928), *Shiva Samsmriti* and *Shivaji Souvenir* (English tr), ed by G S Sardesai (1927)

112 *Powadas*, or Marathi ballads, collected by H A Acworth and S T Shaligram, 2nd (really 3rd) ed , 1911 All legendary and of a much later date than Shivaji's lifetime The Afzal Khan ballad is the oldest, and probably belonged to Shambhuji's reign Only two of the ballads deal with Shivaji, but are unhistorical A new and critical edition by Y N Kelkar (1927)

English tr of ten of the ballads (with an excellent introduction), by Acworth (Longmans, 1894)

113 *Savant-vadi-Samsthanchā Itihas*, by V P Pingulkar (1911) Useful, but the dates of some of the Persian *farmans* have been wrongly transcribed, and the seal has been incorrectly ascribed to the Emperor (whose name stands on the top of it) instead of to the owner of the seal (whose name is modestly put below that of the Emperor)

114 *Ajnā-patra* of Ramchandra *Amātya*, 2nd ed 1923 A book of "good counsels," but not a genuine document by a contemporary of Shivaji. Throws no real light

115 V L Bhave published a number of pamphlets on incidents of Shivaji's life, which, in spite of their minute and lawyer-like argument, are vitiated by the fact that he lumped together all the dates and incidents given by every known work, without critically sifting their evidence

116 *Tanjāvarchā Shilālekh*, a prodigiously long (2652 lines in print) inscription in Marathi carved in December, 1803, on stone in the Vrihadishwar temple of Tanjore Printed by Rajwade in the *Prabhat* and included in his *Sadhanen*, vol ix (1906), another ed by T Sambamurti Row in Tanjore (1907) Utterly worthless modern concoction of the history of Shahji and Shivaji, evidently for exalting the junior Bhonsle branch, (the House of Tanjore)

117 *91 qalmi Bakhar*, also called *96 qalmi Bakhar*, containing that number of paragraphs (mostly very short) The manuscript from which Rajwade printed his text (in vol ix of his *Sadhanen*) is described in the colophon as in the handwriting of Khando Anaji Malkaré, the son of Anaji Ranganath Malkare, who was appointed accountant (*majmuadar*) of the army of Hambir Rao by Shivaji An incorrect text (with many variants) is printed in Parasnis's *Bharat-varsha* It is the same work as the "Raigarh Life of Shivaji," (Eng trans in Forrest's *Selections from the Letters &c , in the Bombay Secretariat*, Maratha Series, vol i, pp 1-22, 1885) The

expanded Persian translation is known as the *Tarikh-i-Shivaji* (For its nature and value, see the introductory discussion to this Bibliography)

B Sanskrit

118 *Radha-madhava-vilasa-Champuh,* by Jayaram Pindyé ed by Rajwade (1922) Fulsome adulation of Shahji and the boy Shivaji by a Court poet Gives no useful information

119 *Shiva Bharat,* by Paramānand ed with a Marathi trans copious notes and portentously long disquisitions (*à la Rajwade*) in a sumptuous edition by S M Divekar (1927) An epic poem on Maloji, Shahji and Shivaji (ending abruptly with Shiva's conquest of the Ratnagiri district in April 1661, canto 32, v 9) Narrated in the form of a dialogue between the poet and the Brahmans of Benares where Paramanand had come on a pilgrimage (between 1664 and 1673) A Hindu priest-pilgrim to far off Benares could not, in those days of difficulty of transport and unsafe travelling, have burdened himself with history books, and yet our poet, writing about 1670 professes to give minute details and long lists of generals (sometimes on *three* sides) for battles that were fought in 1624 and even earlier! This holy Brahman must have had a prodigious memory for non Scriptural matters! His nauseating flattery of his patron and absurd exaggerations have been already noted in my preliminary paragraphs Such a work cannot be taken literally as history

120 *Parnāl-parvat-grahan-ākhyānam,* by Jayaram, ed by S M Divekar (1923) Matter-of-fact straightforward narrative, singularly free from the usual hyperbole and verbosity The five cantos cover only a small portion of Shivaji s career (1673) Very reliable and useful

121 *Shiva-raj-Rājyābhishek-Kalpataru,* a short poem in 234 verses, describing Shivaji's coronation (1674) in the form of a dialogue between Govinda and Nishchala, two Brahmans on a pilgrimage to the holy places in South Konkan, (Asiatic Society of Bengal, MS 3088) Merely descriptive

C. Hindi

122 Bhushan s *Granthavali,* ed by Shyam Bihari Mishra and Shukdev Bihari Mishra (Nagri Pracharini Sabha, Benares, 1907)

Fulsome adulation of Shiva, by means of an infinite variety of similes and parallels from Hindu Scriptures and epics! No history, no date But shows us the atmosphere and the Hindu mind of the time Its authenticity has been denied and its composition ascribed to the Court of Chhatra Sal (about 1725), by a critic in the *Nagri Pracharini Patrika*

123 *Chhatra-prakash* by Lal Kavi (Nagri Pracharini Sabha, Benares) Canto xi deals with Chhatra Sal s visit to Shiva English trans, in Pogson's *History of the Boondelas,* (Calcutta, (1826)

D Persian

Most of the Persian sources have been described and discussed in my *History of Aurangzib,* Bibliographies at the end of Vols ii and iii (1st ed), and for convenience of reference I here give them the numbers which they bear in that work.

2. *Padishahnamah*, by Abdul Hamid Lahori.
4 *Amal-i-Salih* by Kambu
5 *Alamgir-namah* by Mirza Md Kazim
6 *Masir-i-Alamgiri* by Saqi Mustaid Khan
9 *Muntakhab-ul-Lubab*, by Khafi Khan
10 *Nuskha-i-Dilkasha* by Bhimsen Burhanpuri.
11 *Fatuhat-i-Alamgiri* by Ishwardas Nagar
29 *Akhbarat-i-Darbar-i-muala*
116 *Muhammad-namah* (or History of Muhammad Adil Shah) by Md. Zahur, the son of Zahuri, (my own copy made from the Kapurthala MS)
27. *Tarikh-i-Ali Adil Shah II* (only the 1st ten years of his reign), by Sayyid Nurullah, (copy made for me from the India Office MS)
25 *Basatin-i-Salatin*, by Md Ibrahim Al Zubairi The lithographed ed (Haidarabad) cited in this 3rd ed (while a MS was cited in the first two editions of my *Shivaji*)
19 *Tarikh-i-Shivaji*, India Office Persian MS 1957, (Ethe No 485), same as Rieu i p 327 Trans. by me in *Modern Review*, 1907 and Jan. 1910
16 *Adab-i-Alamgiri* by Qabil Khan
44 *Haft Anjuman* by Udiraj Tala-yar, Paris MS and Benares MS.
45 *Faiyyaz-ul-qawanin*
39 *Khatut-i-Shivaji*, R A S MS
21 *Ahkam-i-Alamgiri* by Hamid-ud-din Khan, tr. by me as *Anecdotes of Aurangzib*
33 *Ruqat-i-Alamgiri*, lithographed bazar ed
117 *Parasnis MS* —A volume in which some Persian letters from the Mughal Government to Shivaji and his descendants have been copied (evidently for the use of Grant Duff) by order of the Rajah of Satara. Some of the dates are wrong There is a MS English translation in another volume

E English

[When I began my study of Shivaji's history, Foster's *English Factories in India* had not reached the period of his activities I had, therefore, to get transcripts of the old records in the India Office, London, at great cost and some risk of error in the copying (Two serious ones were discovered too late for the second edition) Now that Foster's series has been continued to 1670, I have retained my references to the documents themselves as more convenient to inquirers than citations of the pages of Foster's book.]

124 *Original Correspondence* (O C), India Office MS. records. This series includes letters from Surat and Bombay to the E I Co , (London) and letters between Surat and Bombay and the subordinate factories There is a catalogue of these, giving writer, place and date, but very little indication of the contents In most cases there is a volume for every year *O C* volumes deal indiscriminately with all parts of India where the Company

had factories From 1682 to 1689 they contain little beyond duplicates of what is given in the *F R*

125 *Factory Records* (*F R*) India Office MS records There is a distinct series for each principal factory, such as Rajapur, Surat, Bombay, Fort St George, &c They include (*a*) Consultations at these factories and (*b*) copies of letters received and dispatched by them (some being repeated in O C) There are several gaps in the period 1660-1689 and the existing volumes are unindexed

Surat Consultations—none extant for 1636 '60, 64, 67 68, 71, 73, 75, 76, 78, 80, 81, and 84-96, but the gaps are partially filled by the *Letters received and dispatched* and the *O C* Only four volumes have survived for 1660-1683

Surat *Letters*—about 20 volumes for the period in question

Records of Fort St George Diary and Consultation Book, for 1672-78 and 1678-79, printed at Madras (1910 and 1911) A few other papers are given in Love s *Vestiges of Old Madras*, 3 vols

Orme MSS in the India Office Library (catalogued by S C Hill) contain copies of several factory records the originals of which have perished

After 1683 the English factory records are very scanty

Diary of W Hedges, ed by Yule, (Hakluyt Soc) Vol II p ccxxvi gives Surat to Co, 20 Nov 1670

126 *Dutch Factory Records* preserved in the India Office, London Vols 23-29, covering 1659-70, are in English translations, while Vols 30-42, covering 1670 89, are in Dutch They are very disappointing to the historian of Shivaji and contain very few references to the Marathas The volumes from 1671 onwards contain scarcely any remarks on the affairs of Western India "Up to 1664 or so, the compiler copied the letters from India into the *Dagh Register*, verbatim or almost so From about 1665 to the end of the series, the Indian letters were copied into a different Register *viz*, 'Incoming letters', the *Dagh Register* refers to this for details, and gives at most an occasional scrap of news It is conceivable, but I fear very improbable that the Registers of Incoming Letters, or some of them, may be in existence at Batavia" (Moreland)

127 *Storia do Mogor* or travels of Manucci, tr by W Irvine, 4 vols

128 Bernier s *Travels*, ed by Constable

129 Tavernier's *Travels*, ed by Ball, 2 vols

130 J Fryer's *New Account of East India*, ed by W Crooke, 2 vols (1909)

131 Orme s *Historical Fragments of the Mogul Empire &c*, London (1805)

132 J Grant Duff s *History of the Mahrattas*, (1826)

The Madras District *Manuals* are the old ed, while the *Gazetteers* are the new ed

English translations are mentioned under their Marathi Persian or Hindi originals

F. Portuguese

133 *Vida e accoens do famoso e felicissimo Sevagy* escrita por Cosme de Guarda, natural de Murmugao (Lisbon, 1730) Composed in 1695 (p 40) Contains 168 pages Full of gross inaccuracies, mistakes of persons, useless digressions, bazar gossip and things known to us from other sources It may more properly be styled 'The marvellous *romance* of Shivaji,' as it contains a minimum of facts dates and proper names and a maximum of words and general descriptions It tells us nothing new that is historically true C da Guarda was not the real author's name.

Dr D G Dalgado of the Academy of Sciences, Lisbon, informed me (on 15 Feb 1919) that he could find no Portuguese State-paper relating to Shivaji in the Lisbon Archives he had consulted

134 *Colleccao de Tratados* by J F J Biker, tomo iv (Lisbon, 1884) Contains treaties and diplomatic correspondence They were first printed in the *Government Bulletin* of Goa, which I inspected during my visit to Goa in October 1924

135 *Portugueses e Maratas, i Shivaji*, by Panduranga Pissurlencar, (reprinted from the *Boletim do Instituto Vasco da Gama* The fullest and most scholarly work on the Portuguese relations with Shivaji Supersedes all other works on the subject

G French

136 *Voyage des Indes Orientales*, par M Carre, 2 vols (Paris, 1699) Contains an account of Shivaji in 1671-72 Hearsay

137 *La Mission du Maduré*, par J Bertrand, tome 3 (Paris, 1850) Contains the annual Jesuit letters from the Madura mission

138 *Memoires* of Francois Martin, 1664-1696 (MS T 1169 of the Archives Nationales of Paris) I secured a transcript of the portion relating to Shivaji and published a condensed English translation of it in the *Modern Review*, Feb 1924

The *Journal* of B Deslandes (from the Paris MS) has been translated by me into English and published in the Puna Mandal's periodical

139 *La Compagnie Indes Orientales et Francois Martin*, par Paul Kaeppelin (Paris, 1908) Extremely valuable narrative with exact citations of original documents (and even extracts from them)

140 The *Histoire de Sevagi et de son successeur*, par J D'Orleans, S J, appended to his *Histoire des Deux conquerans Tartares*, (Paris, 1688), though the earliest life to be printed, is worthless I have published an English translation of it in the *Modern Review*, May, 1924

The other French and Dutch works that treat of Shivaji—of very little value,—are described in Orme's *Fragments* (ed of 1805), pp 171-179

CHRONOLOGY

[All the dates in this book are given in the Old Style or unreformed Calendar which continued in England down to 1752, and the New Style dates (usually *ten days ahead* for Shivaji's lifetime), which occur in the French, Portuguese and Dutch writings, have been reduced by me to the Old Style In some cases a discrepancy of one day may be noticed, but it is due to the difference between different astronomical works in converting Hindu lunar or Hijera dates into the Christian era I have followed the conversion-tables in Swami-Kannu Pillai's *Indian Ephemeris*

Sh =Shivaji Kh =Khan

c =*circa*, about

1626 14 May Malik Ambar dies, Fath Khan succeeds as Nizam Shahi *wazir*

1627. 10 April Birth of Shivaji
12 Sep Ibrahim Adil Shah dies, Muhamad Adil Shah succeeds
29 Oct Jahangir dies

1628 4 Feb Shah Jahan crowned Emperor
c Feb Shahji raids Mughal Khandesh, is expelled

1630 c Dec Shahji comes over to the Mughals, deserts them about June 1632

1633 17 June Mughals capture Daulatabad (with Husain Nizam Shah in it)
August Shahji crowns a puppet Nizam Shah

1635 Jan-Feb Khan-i Dauran pursues Shahji
c Oct Khawas Kh murdered at Bijapur

1636 July-Oct Khan-i-Zaman, with Bijapuri aid, pursues Shahji to Mahuli and utterly defeats him Shahji gives up puppet Nizam Shah and enters Bijapur service

1637 Shivaji and his mother are brought to Puna from Shivner

1639 Shivaji visits his father at Bangalore, but is soon sent back to Puna

1646 Muhammad Adil Shah falls seriously ill and continues helpless till his death (1656)
? Shivaji secures Torna fort

1647 May or June Dadaji Kond dev dies
? Shivaji gains Kondana

1648 25 July Shahji arrested by the Adil-Shahi c-in-c before Jinji
15 July Murad Bakhsh appointed viceroy of Mughal Deccan

1649 Sep Shaista Khan appointed viceroy of Mughal Deccan *vice* Murad (who reaches Delhi on return in December)
c Dec Shahji released [*Jedhe* gives 16 May]

1656 15 Jan Shivaji captures Javli
6 April Sh comes to Raigarh and takes it
28 Aug Baji Chandra Rao More escapes from Shivaji's hands
24 Sep Sh arrests Mohite and gains Supa
4 Nov Muhammad Adil Shah dies, Ali II succeeds

1657. 28 Feb Aurangzib arrives near Bidar, begins siege of it on 2 March, takes it on 29 March

27 April Aurangzib starts for Kaliani, which surrenders on 1 Aug.

c 27-29 April. Sh's attempt to loot Ahmadnagar fails

30 April Sh loots Junnar

14 May Birth of Shambhuji

4 June Nasiri Kh defeats Sh near Ahmadnagar

24 Oct Sh takes Kalian-Bhivandi

11 Nov Kh Muhammad, wazir, murdered at Bijapur

1658. 8 Jan Sh takes Mahuli

14 Jan Sh goes to Rajgarh

25 Jan Aurangzib starts from Aurangabad to contest the throne, leaves Burhanpur on 20 March

21 July First enthronement of Aurangzib

30 Aug Sh sends Sonaji to Delhi

1659. 10 March Sh goes from Rajgarh to Shivapatan

c April Adil Shah orders Maval deshmukhs to join Afzal Kh

11 July Sh goes to Javli

5 Sep Sai Bai (w of Sh) dies

11 Nov Afzal Kh killed, his army defeated

28 Nov Sh gains Panhala, which he enters on 2 Dec

? Sh takes Danda town

28 Dec Sh defeats Rustam and Fazl Kh near Kolhapur

1660. c 5 Jan Sh raids Dabhol

c 10 Jan Sh raids Rajapur (first time)

14 Jan Sh raids Bijapuri territory (towards Gadag)

25 Feb. Shaista Kh marches out of Ahmadnagar

2 March Sh enters Panhala, is besieged by Jauhar

9 May Shaista Kh enters Puna

6 June Sh takes Wasota

21 June Shaista Kh arrives before Chakan, lays siege, and takes it on 15 Aug

13 July Sh escapes from Panhala

c 26 Aug Shaista returns from Chakan to Puna

22 Sep Panhala yielded to Jauhar

20 Nov Parenda sold to Mughals by Bijapuri qiladar Ghalib

1661. 3 Feb Shiva defeats Kar Talb Kh at Umbarkhind

Feb Sh loots Nizampur, captures Dabhol-Prabhavali

c 3 March Sh seizes Rajapur and takes English factors prisoner They are released c 5 Feb 1663

29 April Sh enters Shringarpur

c May Mughals take Kalian from Shiva

c 3 June Sh at Mahad for two days Sh passes the summer in Wardhangarh

21 Aug Kavji Kodhalkar raises the siege of Deiri by Bulaki

1662. Jan-Mar ? Sh defeats Namdar Kh at Miryan Dongar and raids Pen

1663. March Long chase of Netaji by Mughals

30 Mar Sh in Raigarh (more probably Rajgarh)

5 April Sh surprises Shaista Kh in Puna
May Sh goes by way of Kudal to Vingurla (c 18 May), returns soon
Nov Jaswant lays siege to Kondana

1664 6-10 Jan Shivaji s first loot of Surat
c 15 Jan Shaista Kh leaves Aurangabad, Muazzam succeeds as viceroy
23 Jan Death of Shahji
5 Feb Sh returns to Rajgarh
c Feb Bhadrappa, Rajah of Bednur, murdered
28 May Jaswant raises siege of Kondana, Sh visits it on 30th
July Sh raids Ahmadnagar
Oct Sh massacres Ghorpares of Mudhol
c 25 Oct Khawas defeats Sh, who retrieves his position soon afterwards
Nov Sh conquers Savant-wadi
c 5 Dec Sh plunders Vingurla
c 10 Dec Marathas loot Hubli (1st)

1665 8 Feb Shiva sails from Malwan, plunders Basrur, and on return bathes at Gokarna reaches Karwar (22 Feb) and leaves for Bingur (23 Feb)
14 Mar Sh at Bingur 25 m n of Karwar
3 Mar Jai Singh reaches Puna
30 Mar Dilir Kh alights near Purandar and begins siege
14 April Rudramal capitulates
11 June Sh meets Jai Singh before Purandar, visits Dilir (12th)
12-13 June Treaty of Purandar
14 June Sh leaves Jai Singh's camp for Rajgarh
18 June Shambhuji reaches Jai Singh
June-July Bahlol I (minister of Bijapur) dies
27 Sep Sh returns to Jai Singh s camp (Purandar) to receive a *farman* (on 30th)
Oct-Nov Sh reconquers S Konkan from Bijapuris (except Kudal and Vingurla)
20 Nov Jai Singh and Shiva start on invasion of Bijapur
25 Dec First battle with Bijapuris, 2nd battle on 28th

1666 5 Jan Jai Singh begins his retreat from environs of Bijapur
11 Jan J S sends Shiva away to attack Panhala
16 Jan Shiva's attack on Panhala fails
5 March Sh starts for Agra
20 March Netaji comes back from Bijapuri side to Jai S
Feb-March Shiva's first attempt on Phonda fails
9 Mar Sh reaches outskirts of Agra
12 May Sh has audience of Aurangzib
19 Aug Sh escapes from Agra
20 Aug Raghunath Korde arrested at Agra
20 Nov Sh returns to Rajgarh [11 Dec acc to *Shivapur Yadi*]
Dec Pir Mian and Taj Kh slain at Devrukh

1667. 23 Mar Jai S recalled from Deccan, Muazzam sent as viceroy.
April Sh writes to Aurangzib offering submission
3 Apr Trimbak and Raghunath escape from Agra
c 1-8 May. Bahlol and Vyankoji lay siege to Rangna, Sh raises it
2 July Jai Singh dies at Burhanpur
Aug Sh makes peace with Adil Shah
27 Oct Shambhuji reaches Aurangabad, sees Jaswant (28th) and Muazzam (4th Nov), leaves Aurangabad on return, 5th Nov

1668 9 March Muazzam writes to Sh reporting Emperor's recognition of his title of Rajah
5 Aug Pratap Rao goes with a contingent to serve at Aurangabad
Oct Sh's plot to surprise Goa detected
c 20 Oct Sh at Ashtami (near Chaul)
Nov Sh inspects his forts in Ratnagiri district, returns to Raigarh early in Dec

1669. c 1 March Sh at Raigarh and very quiet
April Siddi besieges some of Sh's forts
9 April Aurangzib issues general order for temple destruction throughout Mughal empire, Benares Vishweshwar demolished in Aug 1669, Mathura Keshav Rai in Jan. 1670
May-Oct Sh continues vigorous attack on Siddi of Janjira
Oct Ludi Kh holds Kalian
c 1 Nov Sh seizes Portuguese vessels, they make reprisals

1670. c 1 Jan Sh breaks with Mughals Pratap Rao returns from Aurangabad
4 Feb. Tanaji captures Kondana (Singhgarh)
24 Feb Rajaram born
Sh. recovers Purandar (8 Mar), Kalian (c 15 Mar), Lohgarh (13 May), Mahuli (16 June), Karnala (22 June), Rohira (24 June)
Aug Sh invades Mughal territory, siege of Shivner fails
Grand attack on Janjira
3-5 Oct. Sh loots Surat (second time)
17 Oct Battle of Dindori
c 25 Oct Moro Pant captures Trimbak
c 24 Nov Sh marches north of Bombay, turns back on 26th
Dec. Sh captures Ahivant &c, raids Khandesh and Berar, sacks Karinja

1671. c 5 Jan Shiva captures Salhir
c 10 Feb Siddi Qasim recovers Danda
Early Feb Mahabat and Dilir besiege Ahivant
May Mahabat captures Ahivant &c
June? Bahadur and Dilir lay siege to Salhir, raise the siege in Oct
Sep Sh's ambassador visits Bombay
Oct Sh in Raigarh
Dec. Dilir sacks Puna, massacre

1672 c 10 Jan Shiva at Mahad, assembling an army against Dilir
c 1-7 Feb Moro Pant raises siege of the *machi* of Salhir after defeating Ikhlas Kh, Muhakam S and other Mughal generals, then takes Mulhir
c 15 Feb Sh at Raigarh
c 15 Mar—8 May Lt Ustick visits Raigarh on embassy to Sh, fails.
21 April Abdullah Qutb Shah dies, Abul Hasan succeeds
June Muazzam leaves Deccan, Bahadur Kh acts as viceroy till Aug 1677
5 June Moro Pant captures Jawhar town, and Ramnagar (c 19th)
July Moro Pant raids Nasik district
24 Nov Ali II dies, Sikandar Adil Shah succeeds, Khawas Kh becomes wazir (for 3 years)
Nov-Dec Maratha raid into Berar and Telingana foiled by Mughals
29 Dec Shiva breaks with Bijapur and sets out on campaign

1673 6 March Anaji gains Panhala for Shiva
9 March Sh starts from Raigarh, reaches Panhala c 16th
1 April Sh gains Parli
c 15 April Battle of Umrani
Early May Pratap Rao sacks Hubli (2nd) Bahlol expels Maratha raiders from Kanara uplands, then takes post at Kolhapur and presses the Marathas hard from June to Aug
2 June Sh returns to Raigarh from pilgrimage
27 July Sh gains Satara
10 Oct (*Dashahara*) Sh starts on Kanara expedition, reaches Satara 13th, takes Pandavgarh on 13th [7th, acc to *Shivapur Yadi*], loots Bankapur
c 15 Oct-12 Dec Sh absent campaigning in Kanara
Nov Sharza Kh kills Vitoji Shinde in battle
4-8 Dec Sh at Kadra, his troops twice defeated by Adil-Shahis
16 Dec Sh returns from Kanara

1674 c 20 Jan Dilir repulsed in attempt to descend into Konkan
24 Feb Pratap Rao slain at Nesari
c 1 March One wife of Sh dies
23 March Anand Rao loots bazar of Sampgaon, then fights Khizr Kh
March Daulat Kh defeats Siddi fleet in Muchakundi creek
3 April Narayan Shenvi meets Sh at Raigarh
8 April Sh reviews his troops at Chiplun, arrives near Karwar 22nd, takes Kelanja 24th
7 April Aurangzib leaves Delhi for Hasan Abdal to suppress Khaibar Pass rebellion, returns 27th March 1676
12 May Sh returns to Raigarh after pilgrimage to Chiplun
16 May Sh goes on pilgrimage to Pratapgarh, returns to Raigarh on 21st
26 May Sh invested with sacred thread, marries with Vedic *mantras* on 30th

6 June Shivaji's coronation, *Rajyabhishek* era founded
8 June Sh marries again, "without ceremony"
18 June Jija Bai dies
c 15 July Sh plunders Bahadur Kh 's camp at Pedgaon
c 26 Aug Anaji arrives at Kudal, is foiled by Muhammad Kh.
24 Sep Second enthronement of Shiva
Nov—15 Dec Sh raids Baglana and Khandesh

1675 End of Jan Dattaji raids Kolhapur district
4 Feb Shambhuji invested with sacred thread
c 15 Feb Mughals sack Kalian
6 Mar Shiva starts on campaign, takes Kolhapur, reaches Rajapur (22nd) and halts four days, English merchants meet him, then he marches to Kudal
8 April Sh lays siege to Phonda, captures it c 6 May, his general burns Karwar town 26th April
May Sh captures Shiveshwar, Ankola, Karwar fort, &c
March—May Shiva befools Bahadur Kh by false peace proposals.
12 June Shiva passes by Rajapur, on return to Raigarh
June-Aug Marathas invade Sunda country.
July-Dec Grand attack on Janjira fails
7 Sep Shiva at Raigarh, embassy of Austen
Nov Bahadur Kh invades N Konkan
11 Nov Bahlol arrests Khawas and becomes wazir of Bijapur (for 2 years)

1676. 18 Jan Bahlol murders Khawas Civil war in Bijapur
Jan -Mar Shiva very ill, his perfect recovery reported in Surat letter of 7th April.
May Moro Pant occupies Ramnagar, returns to Raigarh at end of the month
31 May Bahadur Kh crosses the Bhima near Halsangi for attacking Bahlol
1 June Bahlol defeats Bahadur at Halsangi, Islam Kh slain. [*M A* gives 13 June as date]
19 June Netaji Palkar made a Hindu again by purifying rites
June-Dec Attack on Janjira renewed
Early Oct Narayan Shenvi present at Raigarh
1 Nov Shambhuji goes to Shringarpur
Dec Siddi Sambal burns Jaitapur.

1677 Jan Hambir Rao defeats Husain Kh Miana near Yelburga
Feb Shiva reaches Haidarabad, halts for one month, leaves in March
c 24 Mar—1 April Sh at Shri Shaila
4 May Date of Sh's grant to a Brahman for *puja* at Tirupati
c 5 May. Sh reaches Peddapolam (near Madras); his cavalry advances through Conjeveram (9 May) to Jinji
c 13 May Jinji sold to Shivaji, he arrives there c 15th
c 23 May Sh arrives at Vellore, begins siege
26 June Sh arrives at Tiruvadi, routs Sher Kh. Lodi, who flees to Bonagirpatam (27th), which Shiva invests

5 July Sher Kh gives up his territories to Shiva by treaty
c 12 July Sh arrives at Tirumala-vadi (on the Kolerun)
c 23 July Vyankoji flees away from Sh s camp
c 27 July Sh begins return from Tirumala-vadi, at Tundumgurti (31 July,) Vriddhachalam (1-3 Aug,) Vanil am vadi (22 Sep), two days march of Madras (3 Oct)
c 2 Sep Skirmish between Marathas and Portuguese of Daman
Oct Arni falls to Sh
c 5 Nov Sh ascends Mysore plateau on return home
16 Nov Vyankoji attacks Shantaji near Ahiri
Nov Dattaji loots Hubli (3rd)
Dec Shivaji s envoy Pitambar Shenvi reaches Goa
23 Dec Bahlol Kh dies after long illness
7 July Bahadur Kh captures Kulbarga, and Naldurg on 2 Aug [acc to *M A* 14 May]
Aug Bahadur is recalled from Deccan, Dilir left in charge
Sep Dilir invades Golkonda, is defeated at Malkhed and driven back to Naldurg
Nov Masaud on behalf of Bijapur makes humiliating peace with Dilir

1678 Jan Moro Pant plunders Trimbak, Nasik, &c
c 16 Jan Sh at Lakshmishwar
c 26 Jan—23 Feb Sh besieges Belvadi
21 Feb Siddi Masaud becomes wazir of Bijapur
2 April Aurangzib reimposes *jaziya* on Hindus
c 4 April Sh reaches Panhala
c 25 April Marathas plunder Mungi-Pattan
May ? Sh's second attempt on Shivner fails
May Sh returns to Raigarh
21 July Vellore capitulates to Sh
c 1 Sep Pitambar Shenvi dies at Goa
18 Sep Muazzam (Shah Alam) reappointed viceroy of Deccan
Oct Daulat Kh bombards Janjira
Dec Raghunath Shenvi Kotari sent from Goa as envoy to Shiva
13 Dec Shambhuji escapes to Dilir Kh

1679 25 Feb Shah Alam reaches Aurangabad
3 Mar Moro Pant secures Kopal fort
2 April Dilir captures Bhupalgarh
9 April Anand Rao captures Balapur
18 Aug Dilir crosses the Bhima to invade Bijapur, halts up to 16 Sep
Sep Mughals capture Mangalbirah
c 10 Sep Sh seizes and fortifies Khanderi island
19 Sep First naval battle between English and Shiva, second battle 18 Oct
7 Oct Dilir arrives near Bijapur fort, leaves on 14 Nov
30 Oct Shiva arrives at Selgur to aid Adil Sh
4 Nov Sh starts from Selgur to raid Mughal provinces
c 15-18 Nov Sh raids Jalna, fights Ranmast Kh for 3 days

c 21 Nov Sh reaches Patta, halts for about a fortnight
20 Nov Dilir sacks Athni Shambhu escapes from his camp or 21st
30 Nov Shambhuji flees from Bijapur, reaches Panhala c 4 Dec
c 24-30 Nov Marathas raid Khandesh, sack Dharangaon
c 4-25 Dec Sh resides in Raigarh ?

1680. c. 1 Jan Shiva reaches Panhala
13 Jan Shiva meets Shambhuji in Panhala
26 Jan Daulat Kh's attack on Underi fails
Feb ? Sh returns from Panhala to Raigarh
7 March Rajaram invested with sacred thread.
15 March Rajaram married
22 March Shiva's last illness begins.
4 April Death of Shivaji

INDEX

ERRATA AND ADDENDA

P 44, l 2, *for* eight *read* eighth
,, 83 ,, 15 ,, 1657 ,, 1658
,, 142 ,, 4 ,, about the third week of *read* on 5th
,, 219 *n* ,, one day *read* two days
,, 240 l 10 ,, returned to &c *read* marched home northwards, being at Bıngur (25 m, n of Karwar) on 14th March
,, 265 ,, 3 ,, March *read* February
,, 301 *n*, 412 l 27 for *Memoire* read *Memoires*
,, 413 l 32 for *Chooti* read *Chhoti*
,, 30, 291, 295 *add note* A gentleman suggests that the family-name *Kank* is a misreading for *Nikam*